T0265574

BEFORE IT WENT
ROTTEN

Simon Matthews

BEFORE IT WENT ROTTEN

THE MUSIC THAT ROCKED LONDON'S PUBS 1972-1976

Oldcastle Books

First published in 2023 by
Oldcastle Books Ltd,
Harpenden,
Herts, UK

oldcastlebooks.co.uk
@OldcastleBooks

Editor: Steven Mair
© Simon Matthews, 2023

ISBN
978-0-85730-574-9 (Paperback)
978-0-85730-575-6 (eBook)

2 4 6 8 10 9 7 5 3 1

Typeset in 11.75 on 14.4pt Goudy Old Style
by Avocet Typeset, Bideford, Devon, EX39 2BP
Printed and bound in Great Britain by
CPI Group (UK) Ltd, Croydon CR0 4YY

MIX
Paper | Supporting
responsible forestry
FSC® C171272

CONTENTS

INTRODUCTION

This book was commissioned by Ion Mills, publisher and owner of Oldcastle Books, after the publication of *Looking For a New England* in early 2021. Thanks, therefore, are due to him for initiating the project, and to his team in assisting in its production. He suggested something that looked at the music that emerged from the London pub-rock scene of the mid-70s. Traditionally seen as the poor relation to the glamorous era of the 60s, and the punk rebelliousness that came a few years later, the pub-rock period is actually the thread that connects them, a time when ideas (and careers) germinated.

So, this is a book about that. What it is not is a book about guitar solos, amplifiers, drum kits and well-honed anecdotes. There are plenty of other accounts that deal with these. Instead, it tries to tell the story of the musicians, as they worked within the day-to-day circumstances of that time.

Some disclaimers are needed.

Firstly, throughout the book reference is made to whether or not records sold, and if they did, their chart placings are given. We need to be clear that at that time many of the independent record shops that stocked singles and albums by 'pub-rock' and related bands were not 'chart return shops'. However many copies they sold of a release by, say, Ducks Deluxe, they counted for nothing in assessing whether that record should be placed in the UK Top 30, or Top 50. The majority of 'chart return shops' were long-established High Street businesses, branches of Woolworths or the record-selling sections of department stores, and it was data compiled every week from these staid outlets that produced the Top 30 listings of that time. It is possible, therefore, that some 'pub-rock' records outsold material that was listed in the charts, without ever featuring in their own right. Trying to reassess this now, though, would be an immense task and like music industry insiders then I opted to go with what would have been relied on at that time.

Secondly, however one defines it, 'pub-rock' was very much a minority interest. This was a time when the music papers reviewed 25-30 singles each week, up to 150 a month; and this was just their selection of what was available. As can be seen in the discography at the back of the book, 'pub-rock' and related releases ran at 5-10 a month at best, and in some months none at all. Even towards the end of this period, in 1975-76, they accounted for no more than 5% of what was being written about. There can't have been more than 20,000 young people in the UK actively interested in this scene, out of a total population, in the 15-25 age bracket, of around 7 million. It's important to remember, therefore, that the artistes described in this book were pioneers, operating mainly without reward and drawing their inspiration from sources that the majority of those interested in music either rejected or found baffling. And yet... this is the motherlode that people keep returning to, the dynamo that powered the cultural and musical changes that occurred post-1976.

Thirdly, I am aware that this is a white male perspective. The pub-rock scene featured only a few black musicians, and fewer women. The passage of time has depleted their numbers further and despite making every effort to contact those who survive, I drew a blank. This is a matter of regret as their perspectives would have been welcome, particularly for the insights that they provided on the social mores of the time. Given these circumstances I have had to rely on comments and accounts from them that are already published, rather than fresh primary material.

Finally, wherever possible all the sources quoted are referenced in the text. Occasionally a lack of sources (or individuals who can corroborate events) has meant that some assumptions have had to be made. I should add that historian Alwyn Turner made available his personal archive of *ZigZag* magazines, from which much was gleaned, and for which I am grateful.

My thanks are due to the following who helped piece this account together, by telephone, email and one-to-one interviews or just by facilitating contact with others: Michael Harty, Chris Birkin, Frank McAweaney, Sean MacBride, Peter Buck, Pete Lockwood, Carl Matthews, Bobby Valentino, Mark Howarth, Billy Jenkins, Patrick Hickey, Glen Matlock, Kevin Burke, Des Henly, Horace Trubridge, Nick Hogarth, Charlie Hart, Dave Kelly, Gerald Moore, Mo Witham, Danny Adler, Paul Gray, Tony O'Malley, Deke O'Brien, Colin Bass, Rod Demick, Chris Money, Billy Rankin, John Greene, Ian Gomm, Martin Belmont, Lyndon Needs, Alan Hooper, Tim Hickey, Ed Lukasiewicz and Duncan McKenzie.

Simon Matthews
Sligo, 2022

ONE NIGHT IN 1974

It was a Friday afternoon in October. The clock said 2.38pm. He sat at his small battered desk on the second floor of the GLC Regional Housing Office, King's Cross Road, London WC1. A few other people worked away, barely talking, telephones occasionally ringing, amidst a haze of cigarette smoke. He was preparing a mail out, targeted at waiting list applicants. In a fortnight they were letting 50 spare flats across Hornsey and Archway, some brand new but a bit odd, including a dozen bedsits in a new tower block; others were 'hard', unmodernised and old in tenements; some above shops or peculiar multi-floor arrangements within a house. His job as a Lettings Officer was to get armfuls of housing applications out of the banks of filing cabinets where they were kept, check the date of last contact, and send whoever it was a pro-forma letter asking them to confirm attendance on a specific date, at a specific time, so they could be offered one of the properties. He'd worked on it for two days, gradually piling up the documents on a small table next to the franking machine and photocopier, clearing a space on his desk between the chipped grey telephone and the well-thumbed A-Z. Like many of his colleagues a street map of Islington and Camden was fixed on the wall behind his desk, next to an old, badly torn, Tube map, and yellowing plans of key estates. His job was to reach a hundred. He was nearly there. Once that was done it was simple; you wrote the name and address of the applicant in pen on the letter, put the signature of the Area Housing Manager on the bottom, (using a rubber stamp that had to be constantly replenished via an inking pad), sealed it in an envelope and ran it through the franking machine.

Just after 3pm one of the Housing Assistants came around, handing out pay slips. His went straight to the bank but a few of the others still wanted cash in an envelope. He glanced at his monthly statement; no surprises. It amounted, as it always did, to £34 a week reducing to £22 after tax, pension, Trade Union and National Insurance deductions. It wasn't fantastic, but it was enough to live on and even save a little. By 4pm he had finished addressing, signing and enveloping the hundred letters, and had also left a copy of each on every file. He made himself a mug of tea in the airless, windowless cubicle where they had a kettle, sink, fridge and permanently untidy larder. Then, one by one, he pushed the envelopes through the franking machine, collected them into an oozing, brown mass and strapped a thick rubber band around them. He sat, drank the tea, and then carried the package past the manager's office and left it with the elderly porter on the ground floor who dealt with the post collection every evening.

He left at 5pm. It was raining, windy, overcast and noisy. He waited for the 239 bus at the crowded stop outside King's Cross Station. It was cheaper than getting the Tube. None came for 20 minutes, then three together. It was easy to pick them out; they were single-deck, one-person operated unlike the stream of double-deckers that slowly circulated and dispersed. The first ignored the crowd and sped past, empty. He chose the second, running quickly to catch it and sitting at the back, surrounded by steamed-up windows, next to an old man with an immense bronchial cough. The bus moved slowly in heavy traffic along York Way and paused by the railway goods yards where an engine was being marshalled onto a long line of parcels vans, the guard walking slowly back, swinging a paraffin tail lamp. They passed scrapyards, garages and gloomy industrial buildings, and then stopped for almost five minutes by the new estate being built at Maiden Lane. At Camden Road the cafés were closing and the kebab shops getting ready for an evening's business. The stuccoed Georgian and early Victorian properties were coming back to life, as they always did, however battered they were, lights clicking on in selected windows, and the bus slowly emptied. He got off just before Tufnell Park and walked down Corinne Road to the house where he lived.

It was on the corner where the road bent north, and his room was upstairs, at the front with a fine bay window. He unlocked the door, turned on the light, closed the window and pulled the curtains across. He had a decent amount of space. A low-slung double bed (a mattress on an improvised wooden frame) in one corner. A tall chest of drawers diagonally opposite. A 50s Bush radio next to the bed. A record player opposite, on a tiny table next to the chest of drawers, with his album collection leaning in a neat parade against the table legs. There was a small electric fire in the fireplace, next to which, positioned at a homely angle, was an old armchair he had bought at a jumble sale for 50p. The floor was covered with grey-green carpet squares with a faux oriental rug in the centre. Improvised bookshelves ran up the main wall, crammed with an immense number of paperback books. He hung his jacket behind the door, collected a frying pan from the wooden cutlery and crockery box beneath the chest of drawers, opened the lower drawer (his larder), took out a packet of sausages, some bread and butter and went downstairs to the kitchen.

Adelaide, the young black woman who collected the rent for the co-op, was cooking a pot of vegetables. She was in her dressing gown with her hair piled up in a turban. They exchanged greetings and he waited while she finished preparing her meal. She manoeuvred past him and went back to her room, taking her pot with her. He made a cup of tea and a sausage sandwich. Then, he sat in the corner by the sink, opened that week's copy of *Sounds* and began reading, drinking and eating.

Finished, he knocked on the door of the downstairs front room where his friend Kevin lived. A young Irishman with unruly black hair and blue eyes, Kevin worked during the day for two older Irishmen who owned a removal van. He started and finished early. They spoke, agreed to go out at 7pm. He went back upstairs and had a wash in the bathroom on the landing. He hardly ever used the bath. They had an Ascot, but the water it trickled out was never sufficient or warm enough, except on the hottest of summer evenings. In his room he changed into jeans, t-shirt, bomber jacket, Dr Martens and a scarf. He put a £5 note in his wallet and met Kevin in the hallway. Outside it was still windy, scraps of rubbish had been blown up and about, far into the night, accelerated by the passing traffic. They walked to the Boston Arms.

Kevin rolled a cigarette and they drank Guinness. Where's Amanda he asked, referring to Kevin's girlfriend, who worked as a temp at the BBC. She's away, said Kevin, vaguely. At the end of the long wooden saloon, covered in brown panelling and heavily embossed scarlet wallpaper, a trio of men played pool beneath a huge colour picture of the triumphant Kilkenny hurling team. Tammy Wynette played on the jukebox. What's up tonight, asked Kevin. Scarecrow are on at The Lord Nelson he said. Should be decent. They drank up and outside saw the 4 bus, ran alongside it and jumped on the platform as it slowed by the lights. They sat in the deserted upper saloon all the way to Holloway Road without being asked for their fares. Here they changed again, stepping off outside The Lord Nelson. Seems quiet, said Kevin. He went to the bar and asked. No, they're tomorrow night now, said the barman, it's a party with donations instead. Kevin and he took a look inside the main stage area. There were posters up advertising a benefit gig for Chilean refugees, organised by the DHSS Archway branch of NALGO, with folk singers, leaflets, papers and two speakers. It doesn't appeal and they discuss their options. We could try Charlie and The Wide Boys at the Carousel, he says. Kevin shakes his head. No, it'd be expensive and start late. I need to be up early in the morning.

They catch another bus on Holloway Road and arrive at the Brecknock. It is 9pm. In the stage area to the side there are about 200 people, mostly young men, watching a band. The walls around the stage are encrusted with posters, stickers, photographs... some care of record companies and agencies, some self-produced. Many are torn and the effect is as if a huge brightly coloured selection of litter and waste paper had been swept up and splattered there by a storm. The band are finishing their first set. The area partially clears. Kevin and he find a table set to one side; they get beer and bags of nuts. They are opposite two young women. He asks what they think of the band. Really good, says one, but a bit loud. The other, with cropped ginger hair, looks superciliously at them and smokes. You don't like it then? Kevin asks aggressively. They talk disjointedly above the sound of the jukebox.

The band start another set. They're a six-piece with vocals, saxophone, keyboards, guitar, bass and drums. Kevin and he get up and watch, standing in a closely packed throng just in front of the slightly raised stage. They're not bad, he says. A couple of numbers in there is an altercation behind them. Some pushing and shoving. Somebody shouts play something proper. What, like you, says the singer. Another couple of numbers pass, then a glass flies through the air splintering against the rear wall. The band duck, the crowd parts and the doorman, a wrestler employed on music nights by the landlord, gets the offender, a thin, unshaven man in his late 30s in a headlock, dragging him out and propelling him into the street. Woah, everybody ok, asks the singer. The drummer pushes the remains of the glass away with his boot. They launch quickly into *Route 66* followed by *I'm A Believer* and then one of their own, a country-rock singalong about hitchhiking home from college. The frisson passes.

He goes to the bar to get two more beers. The woman with cropped red hair is there. They talk again, noise permitting. She seems friendly and writes down her sister's phone number on his hand with a biro borrowed from the barman. I live up in Muswell Hill, she says. He finds Kevin. The band finish their set with *Waiting For My Man*. The crowd disperses. They drink up and leave. The two women are just ahead of them. The one he spoke with waves faintly to him and they walk on into the night. Couple of sixth formers, I reckon, says Kevin dismissively. Probably, he says. They cross the road to a crowded kebab shop. Outside the pub the excluded man has come back. He accosts the doorman, who pushes him away again. He stumbles back against a low boundary wall, picks up a discarded half-brick and throws it in the direction of the doorman. It misses, and hits the ex-GPO van that the band are loading their gear into. A fight starts. The guitarist in the group kicks the man who reels back with a massive nosebleed. A passing police car stops and four policemen emerge, walking towards the pub. Come on, let's go, says Kevin. They leave the kebab shop and walk back, past the darkened houses, the flats above shops and the council blocks.

At the house he fetches a jar of brown rice and a small tin of Chinese fish curry from his larder, cooking them in the kitchen. Adelaide comes in to make some tea. I'll pay my rent in the morning, he says. You should come to the next co-op meeting, she says. We're discussing whether to put it up to £7.50; you'd be good at it, working for the GLC. None of the others knows what they're talking about. I might, he says, and eats his curry. She goes back to her room and he drinks more tea.

Upstairs, he locks the door and lets in cold air through the window. He tries to find Radio Caroline, but settles instead for the BBC World Service. Whilst the midnight news is narrated like a sacred prayer, he transfers the phone number from his hand to a scrap of paper, putting it in his wallet. In bed, he thinks about Saturday. He has options. Record shops. Clothes shops. Maybe Swanky Modes. Or a jumble sale. He falls asleep as faintly, in the hall below, Kevin talks quietly into the payphone. In the night an ambulance passes, on its way to the Whittington Hospital.

THE PUBS

Our fictional narrator lived in a different world, and one that has now largely gone. Like anyone, then and now, he would have taken his immediate surroundings as being part of a reasonably fixed continuum. An environment that was, perhaps, a bit different from the recent past, but still recognisable to people who had been around a decade or two earlier. This was certainly true with regards to watching live music in pubs.

If he and his Irish friend had ventured forth the week that they sat their O Levels in May 1971 they could have seen Alex Harvey, doing a vigorous jazz-rock set with Rock Workshop at The Green Man, Great Portland Street, or folk guitarist Martin Carthy at The Roebuck, Tottenham Court Road. Elsewhere, central London was replete with colleges, universities and cinemas providing live music alongside more established venues like the Marquee, the Lyceum or the Roundhouse. (The latter admittedly a recent interloper.) Pubs in Camden, Islington and Hackney were conspicuous by their absence, being deemed, for the most part, either too small or too rough to function as effective venues.

But there were outliers. The Greyhound, 175-177 Fulham Palace Road, London W6, offered rock bands five or six nights a week with the likes of Brewers Droop, Amazing Blondel and Gnidrolog all performing there in May 1971. Admission was free. In the 60s The Greyhound had been a respected Irish music venue, featuring the likes of fiddle player Jimmy Power, whose contributions to the 1967 LP *Paddy in the Smoke: Irish Dance Music from a London Pub* were *'recorded during the ordinary Sunday morning sessions at one of the many London pubs embellished by Irish musicians'.*[1] From there it transitioned to being a folk club, showcasing artists like The Young Tradition, Shirley Collins and Dave and Toni Arthur. By 1970, under landlord (and former boxer) Duncan Ferguson, it was a rock venue, and would remain so throughout this period. But not one without dangers to the visiting music enthusiast. As one punter remembers, it was *'run by a hard as nails Glaswegian called Duncan. When I was going there, the crowd would be a mix of Punks, Mod Revivalists, Skinheads and there was still a few "Teddy Boys" knocking around. It would often kick off between the rival factions, and Duncan would instruct his two sons, that worked behind the bar, to "Sort it oot"; they had long hair and wore flared trousers, and would leap over the bar, roll up their sleeves and have a punch up, they never ever called the police!'* [2]

The mention of flared trousers and long hair seems to date this account to no later than 1976-77. Possibly the earlier years were a bit less combustible? It's hard to imagine anyone brawling at a Gnidrolog gig. On the other hand, other punters recall The Greyhound as being *'a well-known venue with bands playing most nights, owned by a Scottish guy called Duncan Ferguson who was a bit of a ruffian, and hung out with the West London footballers'*. It also had lunchtime striptease and was where rock singer Frankie Miller lived on occasion, despite having a combatative relationship with Ferguson's dog. It was a rough place. [3]

Otherwise, inner London boasted little by way of music in pubs, unless you count Tooting as 'inner', though in truth many would still have regarded it as respectable and vaguely suburban in 1971. That week saw Savoy Brown at The Castle, 38 Tooting High Street SW17, the back room of which functioned as the Tooting Blues Club. Involved in continual touring to promote their breakthrough Decca LP *Looking In*, this was home territory for a band that hailed from Battersea.

Some distance across the city, at The Green Man, 190 Plashet Grove E6 you could have watched Egg, an earnest, 'progressive' trio, performing material from their second LP *The Polite Force*, to an audience that sat cross-legged on the floor. A few miles north, at The Red Lion, 640 High Road E11, 50p got you admission to a show by East of Eden, about to hit No 7 in the UK charts with their single *Jig-a-Jig*. Both venues had a long history of dances and live music, with The Red Lion well known for its large ballroom area.

And finally, spread out across South London, May 1971 offered John Peel favourites The Edgar Broughton Band at the Winning Post, Twickenham, promoting their LP *The Edgar Broughton Band*; Hawkwind at The Harrow Inn, Abbey Wood (admission 40p); Duffy Power at The Three Tuns, Beckenham; and, incredibly, Funkadelic at The Greyhound, Croydon, on a UK tour with a set culled from their US album *Free Your Mind... And Your Ass Will Follow*. The Three Tuns, a large mock-Elizabethan pub on Beckenham High Street, was well known as the site of the Beckenham Arts Lab, much associated with David Bowie circa *Space Oddity*. One imagines that Duffy Power, formerly a coffee bar rocker of some repute, did a similarly introspective turn there. But Hawkwind? In Abbey Wood? This was the band en route for Glastonbury Fayre and gearing up for *In Search of Space*, featuring new recruit, and dancer, Stacia, a light-show and heavy biker presence. All jammed into The Harrow Inn, about which little survives, other than online comments noting that it was '*moderately rough*' with one local stating after its closure, '*I got offered a sawn-off shotgun in there one night.*' Interestingly, it was just down the road from Thamesmead where Stanley Kubrick had only a few weeks earlier completed filming some of the memorably violent scenes in *A Clockwork Orange*.[4]

Which brings us to The Greyhound, Croydon, the least typical of all these venues. On Park Lane, opposite the Fairfield Halls, it was a modern ground-floor pub built into an office building; a lot of new office blocks appeared in Croydon around this time. The music happened in a set of function rooms immediately above the bar area and went by the name, initially at least, of the Croydon Blues Club. Sundays were a particularly favoured night. With the surrounding premises empty at the weekend and not too many houses in the area, volume wasn't an issue in the way it could be elsewhere. The music room itself was a good size, with a decent stage, and no furniture, but in a major early 70s design failure it was carpeted, and in the years that followed approximately a million cigarettes would be stubbed out on it, joined by immense amounts of spilt alcohol mingling with other ominous and unpleasant-looking stains. It must have seemed odd to Funkadelic, coming to Earth in such surroundings. And lively too; the bar had shutters that could be pulled down when fighting began.

This was what was on offer in London's pubs one week in May 1971. A selection of hopeful names, perennial troupers and major acts. Some of the venues were established within a wider, larger circuit, and had been so for many years. In fact, depending on how far you want to go back, performing music in pubs, either on its own or as part of an evening's entertainment, was definitely an English tradition. As any student of Victorian music hall will know, many music halls started as pubs, and many pubs, even if they didn't develop into full-scale variety theatres, offered music hall type ensemble billings, staged in the saloons, ballrooms and back rooms attached to them.

Most of these were clustered around inner London, with a concentration in Camberwell, but few if any survived into the 60s in their original incarnation.[5] Importantly they set a template for how typical pubs should be built: with a room, hall or saloon that could be used for general entertainment purposes. Many examples, hundreds even, of such venues existed across London and most put on dances, comedians and occasional live music, one or more nights a week, through the 50s, 60s and 70s without ever becoming regular 'music venues' or advertising in the music press. They formed a kind of secondary or even tertiary layer beneath the variety theatres for many years. A particularly strong locale for this type of entertainment was London's East End, where there was even a mini-revival of the genre in the early 60s, at places like The Rising Sun, Bow, the Deuragon Arms, Hackney and the Iron Bridge Tavern, Poplar.

Of these the Deuragon needed to be approached with some care.[6] Run by the Kray brothers, it hosted music, satire and drag artistes. The music was normally the type of light jazz singalong standards on offer everywhere, though an early version of the Bonzo Dog Doo-Dah Band had a residency at one point. Satire came via comedian Ray Martine, a considerable TV figure in the 60s and

70s, whose live album *East End West End* was recorded there on New Year's Eve 1962.[7] Drag was usually by Gaye Travers, whose shows attracted the likes of Noel Coward and Kenneth Williams. the Iron Bridge Tavern was run by actress-singer Queenie Watts, whose film, TV and stage work stretched from Ken Loach's *Poor Cow* to *Come Together*, the latter an extended 1970 Royal Court Theatre revue that included The Alberts and The Ken Campbell Roadshow. Like Martine she released an LP, *Queen High*, with backing from Stan Tracey on a couple of tracks. Her reputation was such that she also appeared in Joan Littlewood's *Sparrows Can't Sing*, the finale of which takes place in a typical East End pub similar to the one Watts herself ran.

The success of this milieu appealed to Daniel Farson, a broadcaster, writer and Soho habitué of some standing. He purchased The Waterman's Arms on the Isle of Dogs, converting it, quite extravagantly, into a miniature music hall, hosting performers like Shirley Bassey and drawing an audience that included at various times Francis Bacon, Clint Eastwood, Brian Epstein and Judy Garland. By May 1963 there was an ITV series, *Stars and Garters*, cashing in on this localised renaissance. Filmed on a stage set modelled on the kind of pub run by Farson or Watts, it was scripted by Marty Feldman and Barry Cryer, presented by Ray Martine and featured Kathy Kirby, a platinum blonde singer who looked an absolute dead-ringer for Marilyn Monroe. None of this was rock and roll, or anything like it. But it did overlap slightly and both Joe Cocker and Dusty Springfield appeared on *Stars and Garters* during its three-year run. And it was hugely popular.[8]

Anyone who was in a band during the 70s will confirm that venues of this kind still existed then, occasionally putting on a group or singer and reliant on word of mouth, coverage in the local paper or just posters put up outside the venue itself to attract an audience. Considering that, and looking through *Melody Maker*, *New Musical Express*, *Sounds* and *Time Out* for the period 1972-76, there seems to have been about five different types of music venue: folk clubs, jazz clubs, established pop and rock venues, *Stars and Garters*-type places (for want of a better description) and traditional Irish clubs and pubs. The latter didn't advertise much in the music press either, and location-wise were heavily grouped around west and north London. In size they ranged from huge ballrooms like the Gresham, Archway Road, featuring the major show bands, (GLC) to niche places like the Sugawn Kitchen, Balls Pond Road which doubled as a theatre. An awful lot of country and western was performed in them, and some were listed, rather confusingly, under the 'Folk' heading in *Melody Maker*.[9]

Out of this mass of pubs, clubs, bars, ballrooms, backrooms, function rooms, shebeens and saloons, folk venues seem to have been the most common, with roughly as many of them as there were jazz and pop/rock put together. What is clear is that, looking at everything as a whole, there weren't that many established pop/rock pub venues circa 1971 in the first place and the scene tended to be pretty fluid anyway with some opening as others closed. It clearly stretched some way beyond London too. The East End diaspora into Essex, Hertfordshire, Canvey Island and Southend-on-Sea remained a traditional bastion for music in pubs, albeit the media, then as now, was resolutely London-centric, carrying few advertisements of what was on offer in such locations.

The transient nature of this scene reflected the practicalities landlords faced in running such a venue. The key issues here were obtaining a music licence from either the local council or the Greater London Council (GLC) (which is why so many of these places came and went; licences either expired or were revoked following objections by residents or the police), the length and conditions of the tenancy offered to the landlord by the brewery (which again might not be renewed, or might even be terminated if there were complaints) and, of course, how feasible it was to stage music there on a regular basis. Did it have a music area that could be separated from, and managed separately 'on the night' from the main drinking area?

Having jumped through these hoops there was then the question of what kind of crowd you might attract. In folk clubs this wasn't a problem. Audiences listened in silence and were well behaved. Jazz was a bit noisier, but the punters were usually not too much trouble, tending to be late 20s and older. The days of duffle-coated trad enthusiasts trading blows over the use of a saxophone were long gone. The problem lay with rock venues. Attracting an audience somewhere between 16 and 25 years old, 'doormen' were needed to keep order in most places, given the considerable capacity for fighting, brawling and out of control (and underage) drinking, as well as the distribution and consumption of various substances. The bands played at a fair volume too, even if most of them deployed a smaller PA system than would usually be required at the Hammersmith Odeon.

In practice, most landlords either handled the bookings themselves or used some type of agency to do so. The breweries weren't involved. From their point of view, they granted the tenancy for a fixed period, either by advertising it in *The Morning Advertiser* or by renewing a lease that had been with a family for generations. Landlords were obliged to buy their beer from the brewery at rates far higher than the open market, so not unnaturally, with rent and staff, including in some cases a manager, to pay they looked to maximise their sales and draw in a crowd. And they had to, given the rapidly changing environment within which they operated. The urban depopulation, and associated redevelopment, that affected London for 40 years after 1945 swept away many pubs, added to which the growth of TV ownership and access to better housing meant that sitting in a saloon bar all evening drinking a pint was no longer the kind of cheap entertainment it had once been. Whether it was staging ersatz music hall like Watts and Farson, or bingo, or comedians, or strippers, every effort had to be made to keep decline at bay and increasingly pubs tried live music as part of their sales pitch to their neighbourhood. They might put on bands one night a week, or every night a week. They might offer residencies or have a constantly changing roster. They might pay a small fee, or split the beer money. But, whichever way they cut it, they had to keep bringing in the customers.[10]

If they didn't, they would close as music venues, which might happen anyway even if they were successful due to licences being revoked or particular landlords moving on. Such was the fate of Bluesville, 376 Seven Sisters Road N4, the Bag o' Nails, Kingly Street W1 and Klooks Kleek, The Railway Hotel, West Hampstead in 1970.[11] The Oldfield Tavern, Greenford, the Northcote Arms,

Southall, The Toby Jug, Tolworth and The Pied Bull, Liverpool Road N1 all went in 1972 and an attempt by Rank to convert three redundant cinemas, in Brixton, Mile End and Edmonton, into night-time concert halls, appending the name Sundown to their location, failed after only a few months shortly afterwards.

Even after bands and booking agents began venturing into pubs in larger numbers, closures continued at a steady rate. The Tally Ho, Kentish Town and Cooks Ferry Inn, Angel Road, Edmonton, didn't have live music after 1973, with the latter closing and being demolished a year later when the North Circular Road was widened. The Nightingale, High Road N22 put on nothing after 1974, the same year that the Wake Arms, Epping, aka Groovesville, closed. Both the Tithe Farm House, Harrow and The Village Roundhouse, Dagenham shut in 1975.[12] The latter was exceptionally impressive: an immense purpose-built entertainment venue – pub, bingo hall, function rooms and ballroom with a capacity of 2000 – built as part of the adjoining Becontree Estate. Up until 1969 it operated as The Village Blues Club, putting on bands like Led Zeppelin and Pink Floyd and later hosting early UK shows by German acts Faust and Can. But to no avail. After a gig by Sailor on 8 November 1975 a poster appeared stating, *'We regret that due to objections from the G.L.C. the club will be closed after this Saturday because of complaints from local residents regarding the noise. We hope the club will be ready to reopen very shortly. Please watch* Melody Maker *for full details of reopening. If you would like to help with a petition please write to the Roundhouse.'* It didn't reopen.

It's interesting to note the preponderance of large suburban pubs in this network, and how they withdrew from the market first. Most of their gigs were by commercially successful bands with album deals. The demise of the Wake Arms – sited at a major road junction within Epping Forest, and not therefore likely to generate noise complaints – was particularly puzzling. Clearly, there were many factors, social and economic, driving these changes. But even success could be problematic, as the case of The Tally Ho demonstrates. Run by Lilian Delaney from the late 50s, it was one of three venues she managed with her husband Jimmy, the others being The Kensington, West Kensington and the extremely louche Mandrake Club in Meard Street, Soho.[13] Jazz was performed at all of them, with The Tally Ho being particularly noted for its casual, freewheeling Sunday jam sessions. Crowds would spill out onto the street listening to the many musicians who dropped by to blow. The performances there spawned a couple of live albums: *Jazz at The Tally Ho* (1963) and *Tally Ho Sunday* (1966) featuring various sidemen whose collected credits would include playing alongside Don Rendell, Alexis Korner's Blues Incorporated, Mick Mulligan, Graham Bond, Terry Lightfoot, Caravan and Soft Machine. Landlady Lilian Delaney sang with them too and was pretty decent as a vocalist. After US band Eggs Over Easy got a Monday night residency in 1971, crowds began flocking there to hear rock as well, encouraged by the free admission policy. Bands got a percentage of the bar takings, and so much beer was sold that the owners, Watneys, simply tripled the rent, resulting in Mrs Delaney quitting and the pub abruptly ceasing to feature live music. It was a thoughtless, self-defeating action by the brewery who really had no understanding of how to make the most of such a phenomenon.[14]

Leaving aside the likes of the Marquee, a small circuit of mainly inner-city venues were putting on live music at the beginning of the pub-rock period, and still doing so four years later as that scene shaded into punk and new wave. These were The Golden Lion, Fulham and The Greyhound, Fulham joined by The Kensington, West Kensington, the Hope & Anchor, Islington (both of which switched from jazz to rock in 1972), the Brecknock, Camden and The Half Moon, Putney. Moving a bit further afield there was the Winning Post, Twickenham, The Greyhound, Croydon and The Torrington Arms, Finchley. Added to this was a rare out-of-London gig: The Nags Head, High Wycombe. Here rock music had been a feature from 1968, promoted by Ron Watts, who also managed his own band, Brewers Droop, and acted as booking agent at Oxford Street's 100 Club.[15]

These were the constants. Alongside them, but with a less continual (or reliable) schedule of bookings could be found The Windsor Castle, Harrow Road, The White Lion, Putney and the Telegraph, Brixton Hill.[16] To which one could add the Fishmongers Arms, Wood Green, where the music was staged in the Bourne Hall: a long wooden building at the rear. Originally a jazz venue (Karel Reisz and Tony Richardson recorded the Chris Barber band in action here in their 1956 documentary *Momma Don't Allow*), by 1972 this was offering rock and roll revival acts as The Hound Dog Club. When not in use others used it as rehearsal rooms, with visiting journalist John Pidgeon considering that it was '*one of those legendary London music pubs where countless bands had played the blues, before they became famous... draughty hall in need of refurbishment, its décor untouched for at least a decade, judging from the scraps of posters here and there advertising bands that once must have packed the place. Wall-to-wall bodies would be the only way to have warmed this tatty venue, I speculated, because the stingy radiators weren't up to it*'. He was right, and it never recovered its preeminence, though trying to establish when it last offered live music has proved difficult. There were many other, lesser-known, haunts.

Once rock bands began performing somewhat more frequently in pubs, additions included Dingwalls Dance Hall, Camden Lock, a long narrow warehouse with few windows, and, unusually for the time, eating facilities,[17] The Lord Nelson, Holloway, where live music was provided by Tom Healey 1973-75 and a trio of Fuller's pubs, The Nashville, West Kensington, The Red Cow, Hammersmith and The Red Lion, Brentford all of which switched to rock circa 1974, after staging mainly country and western acts.[18] That year also brought in The Dublin Castle, Camden, run by the Conlon family from Mayo,[19] and Newlands Tavern, Peckham.

During 1975, with both Ace and Dr Feelgood enjoying commercial success, things expanded further with the reopening of The Bridge House, Canning Town. The landlord here was Terry Murphy, a former boxer, who had actually run music venues in the mid-60s, notably The Tarpot, Benfleet, which had staged acts like The Paramounts, the Southend band that would eventually evolve into Procol Harum.[20] No one would claim that Canning Town was in suburbia, but as a venue The Bridge House had similarities to places like Cooks Ferry Inn and The Village Roundhouse. A huge, mock-Tudor barn, its music and stage area had a capacity of a thousand, with often twice that many crammed in. Murphy was very precise about the economics: music was ok as long as the beer money covered the cost of the band. He was also clear that, by the 70s, large pubs needed live music to keep their takings at a level high enough to ensure their survival.[21]

By 1976, the impact of pub-rock, together with its London orientation, and the reconfiguring by various managers, booking agencies and record labels of how they launched a new act, led to the emergence of further venues. These included The Rock Garden, Covent Garden, The Pegasus and The Rochester Castle (both in Stoke Newington) and The Half Moon, Herne Hill which prior to then featured a mixture of folk and jazz. A couple of others reappeared too, such as The Moonlight Club[22] and The Castle, Tooting, shedding as it did so its Tooting Blues Club moniker. Finally, reflecting the politics of the era, a number of council-funded community centres appeared, some of which put on music regularly. These included The Albany Empire, Deptford[23] and Acklam Hall, Ladbroke Grove. Despite its name, the latter was a modern building, built on empty land underneath the Westway. Paid for by an Urban Aid grant sponsored by the GLC, it opened in 1975 with a benefit gig for North Kensington Law Centre, headlined by Joe Strummer's 101ers.

London in the first half of the 70s had an abundance of live music venues, many of which were pubs. There were similar networks elsewhere, up and down the country, but with the music press and record labels solidly domiciled in the capital these were the ones that got reported and these were the places where emerging acts were studied.

Notes

(1) Jimmy Power did play The Greyhound, but his contributions to this LP were recorded at The Little Favourite, off Holloway Road.

(2) Interview with Michael Harty, 29 January 2022.

(3) Interview with Frank McAweaney, 30 January 2022.

(4) Several of the albums noted here were heavy sellers: Savoy Brown's *Looking In* reached No 39 in the US and the Edgar Broughton

Band's eponymous release peaked at No 28 in the UK. The idea
that one might see them in a local pub – and simultaneously on TV
– without booking beforehand says a lot about how accessible live
music was at that time.

(5)   One that did was Evans Supper Rooms, 43 King Street, Covent
Garden. Dating back to 1856, the basement was used, 1967-68, by
the Middle Earth Club.

(6)   Literally as well as figuratively: it was at the end of a narrow, ill-lit,
cobbled street (Shepherd's Lane). An ideal location for discreet and
illicit encounters.

(7)   Side A was at the Deuragon. Side B was recorded at Peter Cook's
Establishment Club. Martine was considered 'a forgotten original of
British comedy'. See his obituary in The Guardian, 11 October 2002.

(8)   A compilation LP, Stars from Stars and Garters, reached No 17 in the
UK charts in March 1964. Kirby's own 16 Hits from Stars and Garters
peaked at No 11 a month earlier. The TV show seems to have taken
its name from The Star and Garter Hotel, Bermondsey, one of the
great nineteenth-century entertainment saloons. For confirmation
that bands played in such venues, note that The Searchers appear in
a pub in Poplar in the 1964 film Saturday Night Out.

(9)   Also below the radar screen were an increasing number of reggae
venues.

(10)   None of which should be taken as implying that landlords were
hard up. In the mid-70s they might typically be earning, before
overheads and deductions, between £800 and £2500 per week
(£6000-£18000 per week today). Managers were paid a wage, about
£80 a week (about £500-£550 a week now) but had various perks,
such as keeping any profit from food sales. Many landlords and
managers offered bands either a low all-in fee (£15-£40 for a gig) or
an unpaid slot and after gauging the upturn in business came to a
mutually beneficial financial agreement. Information provided by
Alan Hooper, 8 January 2022.

(11)   Klooks Kleek occupied the first floor of the Railway Hotel. The
premises here were brought back into use as The Starlight Club in
the late 70s.

(12)   This was despite the Tithe Farm House putting on Bees Make
Honey, Brewers Droop, Ducks Deluxe and Clancy up until 1974-75.
Clearly, the owners did not appreciate the potential to maintain a
high audience via live music shows.

(13) All of which implies that the Delaneys were quite sophisticated people. Footage of The Mandrake Club is shown in *Saturday Night Out*. Known as *'London's only Bohemian rendezvous'* it was frequented by Daniel Farson and went through many incarnations, later being known as Gossips, Billy's and Gaz's Rockin' Blues.

(14) See Sarah Jane Delaney interview at: https://www.mixcloud.com/FrenchSpurs1/retropopic-491-lillian-delaney-the-Tally Ho-of-kentish-town-the-birth-of-pub-rock/

(15) The Nags Head clearly gives the lie to any notion that pub-rock began in London in 1972. Watts, who is not widely recognised as such, was clearly a major figure in the UK music scene in the 70s and 80s. See his obituary at: http://www.chairboys.co.uk/history/2016_07_ron_watts_obit.htm

(16) The Telegraph was particularly opulent, having been designed by WM Brutton, an architect who did many immense nineteenth-century gin palaces, including The Fitzroy Tavern, Fitzrovia.

(17) Dingwalls was initially managed by Howard Parker, formerly DJ at The Speakeasy and road manager for Jimi Hendrix. He vanished in the Mediterranean in the mid-70s, see: https://www.youtube.com/watch?v=QPKi7XntdMs He was succeeded by Dave 'The Boss' Goodman, former road manager for Pink Fairies, who also doubled as chef and DJ.

(18) Hammersmith seems to have provided more music venues than any other London borough. There was also The Swan, Hammersmith Broadway, which had jazz up until 1977 and the Clarendon Ballroom, also Hammersmith Broadway, which did country and western until the late 70s and was the location for Dave Robinson's wedding reception. (According to Michael Harty, *'It had a bar next door that sold 'Ullage' to the 'Winos', which was basically the slops they collected, your feet would stick to the floor, as they never washed it!'*) And, of course, there was Mecca's Hammersmith Palais with its revolving stage and immense dance floor. The Palais staged many reggae acts from the mid-70s.

(19) According to vocalist Suggs, Madness obtained their critical early gigs at The Dublin Castle after this exchange with Conlon, *'He asked us what we played and we said country and western, and jazz – we thought that would be the thing to say when going in to ask for a gig at an Irish pub.'*

(20) The Bridge House had been a music venue in the late 60s. Bobby

Harrison, ex-Procol Harum, obtained a residency there for his group The Freedom in 1969. Geographically, it was where the Essex gig circuit met the London gig circuit.

(21) See Terry Murphy, *The Bridge House, Canning Town: Memories of a Legendary Rock and Roll Hangout* (2007) p109. Murphy was quite an operator, even running his own record label (the only pub landlord to do so) 1978-82. His book describes a world not dissimilar to that of Farson and Watts 10-15 years earlier, or even the recollections of John Osborne, whose grandparents had been publicans, recorded in *A Better Class of Person* (1981).

(22) The Moonlight Club was slightly downstairs and to the rear within The Railway Hotel, West Hampstead, and therefore within the same building that had hosted Klooks Kleek.

(23) The Albany was within The Albany Institute, a late nineteenth-century charitable endowment. Latterly owned by the GLC it was a community theatre project from 1972 and a music venue from about 1975 before being destroyed in an arson attack in 1978.

PETER BUCK

(PROMOTER: THE HARROW INN and THE SAXON TAVERN)

I promoted bands at the Harrow Inn, Abbey Wood from 1962 to 1974. After I'd done my National Service in the Army, I lived in Bermondsey and worked as a pipe-fitter and part-time musician, getting as far as being offered a slot in a TV orchestra. But my wife wasn't keen on me working as a full-time musician, so I opened an R'n'B club instead. My partner, Tommy Brown, and I approached the landlord of the Harrow Inn and just asked if their hall was available. I think Tommy knew about it because he came from Dartford. The hall itself was a large building, immediately to the rear of the pub itself. The brewery wasn't involved, and luckily for us we only dealt with two different landlords in the next twelve years. We paid them some money every time we used it – £5 or so – they ran the bar and kept the takings, and we kept the door money. We arranged a couple of bouncers, paying them about £2 each and rarely charged more than 4s (20p) to get in. The bands were paid about £15. It was licensed for 200 people by the London Fire Brigade, but we frequently went well above that, often as high as 700!

One of the first acts I had on there was Georgie Fame, with Ginger Baker on drums. Harry Starbuck, an 18-stone boxer, was one of my bouncers. He could knock someone out with one punch. There were fights, often when the band were playing, usually about something stupid, like someone knocking over a drink. But we never had to call an ambulance and the police were never involved. We did a couple of fundraisers for *Oz* magazine at the Harrow Inn. One with Pink Fairies and Skin Alley paying them £35 each. The Fairies drummer, Twink, did the entire set naked. There were 661 people there and after raising £132 for the cause, we still had £100 left to split with the promoter, John Carden. We did another with Hawkwind and they played so loud that the landlord was in a real state telling me to ask them to turn it down... I walked into the music room, and as I opened the door the soundwaves nearly knocked me over! We did well at the Harrow Inn but started to lose money towards the end, despite the building of the enormous Thamesmead Estate nearby. On 27 October 1972, for instance, we had 148 people to watch Supertramp, who got paid £60. After all the other deductions we ended up losing £23. Then, on 25 November, we got 594 people for the Edgar Broughton Band. We paid them £300, but still lost £100, of which £35 was down to the advertising costs.

So... I started promoting music at local colleges instead. I met the Student Union manager at Thames Polytechnic which had a fabulous hall, much bigger and better than the Harrow Inn, and we agreed I would book the bands there. Through him I also got involved with Bromley College. In 1976 I started doing bands at the Saxon Tavern in Catford but pulled out about eighteen months later as I was losing money. I started my own haulage business instead. I always wanted to be a musician, but failed, so putting on bands was my way of keeping in touch with the scene. There was no pressure on me to stop being a promoter, but I wasn't earning regularly and things became difficult.

KEVIN BURKE

(GLENSIDE CEILI BAND and sessions for ARLO GUTHRIE, CHRISTY MOORE)

In London during the 70s I would typically watch bands at the Marquee or Dingwalls, mixing this with Irish sessions, often on a Sunday, at pubs like The Favourite, Benwell Road or The White Hart, Fulham. My favourite bands on the scene were Chilli Willi and the Red Hot Peppers, Brinsley Schwarz and the Kursaal Flyers. The best gig I saw was probably one of the last that Chilli Willi did. It was at the Roundhouse and lasted all day with several supporting acts. A great vibe. The Brinsleys played too: all wearing red tartan jackets and ties. They looked like The Shadows and did the same choreographed foot movements during their set! After I went to Ireland, in 1974, I started to lose touch, and by the end of the 70s I had no contact at all with the London scene. My recollection is that it was pretty fluid: places closed, but new places opened.

I was playing in Irish music venues from the 60s, as a teenager. My father was involved with the Glenside Ceili Band, occasionally helping them organise their gigs. They were the all-Ireland champions in 1966, and put out an album on Transatlantic a year later. He'd bring me along and I'd sit in with them. We did all the big venues on that circuit. The ballrooms: the Galtymore, Cricklewood; the Hibernian Club, Fulham; the Gresham, Archway; the Harp at New Cross; the Shamrock Club, Elephant and Castle and various church halls and so on. The audiences in the big ballrooms were immense, up to a thousand people in places like the Galtymore. At that point I wasn't really playing for money. It was more like pocket money. Sometimes I got a few quid. Whatever the band was paid would be shared out amongst the men. Most of them had day jobs. In fact, not having a day job was frowned on, then. If you didn't work, you weren't respected. There was a real work ethic.

Later I did a lot of playing in pubs and folk clubs. In the pubs you might be watched by 70-100 people. The folk clubs were smaller, maybe 50-60 people, and more serious. I played at The Union Tavern, Clerkenwell when it was the Singer Club. This had been started by Ewan MacColl and Peggy Seeger and had been held at various locations since the late 50s. There was another place, the Kings Stores, Widegate Street, near Liverpool Street, a room above a pub, where I sat in with The Peelers, Tom Madden's band. They had a residency there. I was at school with Paddy Bush, brother of Kate. The Bush family lived in Welling, and their mother came, I think, from Waterford. Through Paddy I met Dave and Toni Arthur... I played on their 1971 LP *Hearken to the Witches Rune*.

I thought London had a really vibrant music scene back then. From the point of view of traditional music there were pub sessions all over the city. In fact, there was a bigger Irish music scene in London then than in Ireland, and as a young Londoner I had access to all these great players. There was music on seven nights a week, on top of which there were all the pubs with rock bands and all the bigger venues too up to and including places like the Lyceum and the Rainbow. I remember seeing BB King at the Hammersmith Palais!

Looking back, I would say that the Irish pub landlords were much more open to having live music in their bars. After all, it was a thing you got all the time in Ireland. You just didn't have the same approach in English pubs. In Eltham, where I lived at that time, the atmosphere was very different when you went out for a drink, compared to say Islington or Camden. Live music, of any type, wouldn't have worked so well in places like that.

THE MUSIC

Establishing that live music featured in pubs for a long time prior to 1972 is relatively easy. After all, we all remember the first time we drank in a pub – probably underage and buoyed by the thrill of the illicit – and likewise, we all remember the first band we saw. In many instances the two events may be related. A harder question to answer is if pub-rock really did exist as a discrete genre, when and how did it begin and what were its characteristics? To answer this, we need to answer another question: what was the UK music scene like circa 1971, between the disintegration of the Beatles and the emergence of David Bowie, Alice Cooper and Roxy Music?

The easy response to such a query is to reel off who was selling records then. The 60s behemoths – The Who, the Stones – strode on. There was the usual array of simple formulaic chart fodder, a huge amount of reggae, Tamla, soul and people like Tom Jones and Tony Christie who alternated between Saturday evening TV and cabaret. Then there were the album-selling acts. Singer-songwriters like Elton John and Cat Stevens and a whole slew of bands, from Atomic Rooster to Yes via Deep Purple, Led Zeppelin and Pink Floyd in the alphabetical compendium guides of the time.

What all these had in common was that, increasingly, they toured in large venues: the university and college circuit, town centre cinemas and ballrooms. The days of seeing any of them at your local pub were over. As for new acts, like Rod Stewart and The Faces and T. Rex, whilst their music was accessible with plenty of pop/rock and 3-minute songs, they too clearly aspired to all the trappings of fame: jets, limousines and overnight accommodation in immense hotel rooms. All of which came with a cost. Large PA systems, huge drum kits, massed ranks of amplifiers and speaker cabinets, possibly a light show as well, with a dozen or so roadies, drivers and general heavies needed to set it up, take it down and keep unwelcome interlopers at bay. Only good-sized venues could accommodate this, and touring, particularly if it included the US and Europe, with extended distances between gigs and multiple overnight stays, was expensive. By 1971, everything was much bigger in scale than had been the case only a few years earlier.

During the mid-70s, some bands began eschewing such trappings. A number of explanations were offered for this. Pete Frame, a shrewd observer, and editor of *ZigZag* magazine 1969-73, thought that the emergence of pub-rock was '*a chance for bands to play low-key gigs and return to honesty and reality*'. Specifically, he considered that Brinsley Schwarz were '*certainly the popularisers of the pub scene and were responsible for the media focus*' after they took a residency at The Tally Ho, Kentish Town in the summer of 1972.[1] In 1976, *The Encyclopaedia of Rock Volume 3: The Sounds of the Seventies* acknowledged this but took a cautious view, stating that pub rock was '*the convenient term used to describe a phenomenon of the early seventies in Britain*', whilst noting that, '*music has always been an integral part of pub life*'. As to what it sounded like, it offered the explanation, '*If "pub rock" had a typical sound, it was this: music best designed for jigging about, pint of beer in hand.*' The same article studiously, and correctly, notes, '*With the decrease in the number of small clubs (ironically, often in pub back rooms) it was becoming impossible for up-and-coming bands to gain exposure. Gradually, as more bars moved from jazz to rock (notably The Kensington) and breweries, or their managers, realised that a rock band would boost sales, a loose circuit of small venues arose.*'[2]

Towards the end of the decade Julie Burchill and Tony Parsons summed up what it had all been about with comments that were, in equal parts, inaccurate, debatable and reasonably fair. Writing in their slim volume *The Boy Looked at Johnny: The Obituary of Rock and Roll* they spoke about the '*emergence of Pub Rock in 1975*', stated that what audiences had been offered was '*revamped R & B cranked out in small sweaty venues who had taken to serving live music along with the brown ale. Mostly the music itself was dire and derivative'* and ascribed the relative lack of success enjoyed by most of the bands that came through the scene as being due to *'their inability to capture the live gig excitement on cold, hard, vinylised plastic'.* Clearly, neither Burchill nor Parsons were aware of what had been going on in 1972-75 and their view that everything played in pubs was *'revamped R & B'* is absurd... yes, there were some acts like that, but most couldn't be pigeonholed in that way. A variety of non-mainstream (for want of a better word) styles were on offer.

Had they wanted a bit more information, they could have spoken to Dave Robinson. Owner of Stiff Records, manager of several acts and at that point (1978) producer of Jona Lewie, he would have been, for a couple of *New Musical Express* writers like themselves, easy enough to reach. Speaking many years later Robinson was clear about his role in promoting pubs as music venues circa 1972, *'My career in London at the time was to open a lot of pubs up to rock 'n' roll music and to get the landlords who were mainly Irish and they didn't mind what the music was as long as there was a lot of people in front of the bar, they were happy.'* He was also forthcoming, up to a point, about what type of music he was looking for, *'I got the chance to get away from the prog-rock... I thought it should be New Orleans and it should be Louisiana, it should be short and sharp and Tamla Motown. So, I convinced a lot of the young bands that that was the style they should assume'.* [3] In fact, via his Irish connections, Robinson established, within a short space of time, a network of around 35 pubs in London where bands could play what they liked.

As it happens, Burchill and Parsons didn't even need to speak to him to confirm this. An extensive interview with *Street Life* magazine in November 1975 noted that he spent most of his nights in pubs listening to live music, visiting venues along Holloway Road, in particular, to listen to Irish country and western bands. The piece quotes him as saying, *'There are some really good bands, though they don't get the credit for it. If one of those bands was to play at the Hope people would love it, but because they're in Irish pubs...'* As to his own views about the music industry, and how it functions he is clear, *'Take football – any promising young player will be signed up by a club by the time he's 16 or 18, because there's such a good scouting system. Why aren't the record companies out round the pubs looking for new bands? Most people in record companies wouldn't get jobs in advertising agencies or straight business. Everyone sits around moaning that nothing's happening, but if nothing's happening it's because the record companies aren't making anything happen. You need a catalyst, there are a lot of good bands, good songwriters under the surface; but these people seem to think bands fall off trees.'* His role, and that of London's Irish diaspora, in acting as midwife to the emergence of both pub-rock and punk-rock is thus made very clear.[4]

All of which is fine. What Robinson did not spell out, though, were some of the basic economic factors that determined his views in 1972, and thereafter. At that point he was manager of Brinsley Schwarz, who, after releasing three albums for United Artists, had yet to achieve even a modest degree of commercial success. With high overheads and an expectation from their record company that they would tour in reasonably big venues, their expenses often outstripped their income. Understandably, Robinson and the band were looking to both cut costs and reboot themselves commercially. Finding a different sound was in some ways the easy part. In the years that followed the financial side of the business would only become more pressing. To take one example, there was a big hike in the price of petrol, from 35p a gallon in 1972 to 77p a gallon by 1976, an increase of 120%. The costs of everything else rose too and spending a lot of time out on the road, with a lorry for the gear and roadies, a coach for the band, and continual overnight stops in hotels meant incurring a level of costs that only the biggest hit record or highest selling LP could hope to redeem. The solution? Play smaller venues, with less gear, a van to carry everything and go home to your own bed each night. Even better, wherever you were playing would be within easy travelling distance of the London based A&R (Artists and Repertoire) men and music media scribes that you were seeking to impress. And finally, put out singles rather than LPs, this being much cheaper. LPs could follow if required.

Returning to Robinson's recollections about the sound he was looking for, '*I thought it should be New Orleans and it should be Louisiana... short and sharp and Tamla Motown*', clearly indicated his personal tastes. As an influential manager and producer, he was scarcely alone in having these thoughts, though. After all, the music industry is about selling records, and plenty of A&R men, producers and agents were having these ruminations in the early 70s. It was their job to do so: what would the next sound be... where would it come from... how would they sell it, and most importantly... could it be sold in the enormous US market? Indulging in this record industry futurology meant studying what was 'hitting' and assessing how this might develop over the next year or two. If you were doing this in, say, 1971, what might you have noticed?

Mainly, that US influences dominated. Firstly, there was country-rock, as exemplified by The Band, shading into the deeper and gutsier boogie and swamp-rock of Canned Heat and Creedence Clearwater Revival. This meant unpretentious 3-minute songs, arranged, played and sung in a straightforward manner. The overall ambience tended towards a 'classic rock' sound with an emphasis on Americana. (Particularly The Band; Canned Heat were clearly more of a blues act.) The rough UK equivalents of this were McGuinness Flint, who had a couple of big feel-good country-rock hit singles, 1970-71, with *When I'm Dead and Gone* and *Malt and Barley Blues*. Their eponymous debut album, which reached No 9 in the UK, featured shots of them in nineteenth-century garb, looking suitably rustic. Less obviously one might also note Lindisfarne, whose LP *Fog on the Tyne* was a massive seller, 1971-73, reaching No 1 and spending 56 weeks in the charts.[5]

Secondly, West Coast harmony rock; *Easy Rider* road-movie music, full of lightness and space. As exemplified by Crosby, Stills, Nash and Young, and James Taylor, this meant performers with long hair, t-shirts, sneakers and denim. The demeanour was serious with plenty of acoustic sets and an orientation towards the album market. Despite the lack of obvious cultural references for much of this material in the UK, it sold in immense amounts there in the early 70s. A local equivalent, ironically called America, and with a double irony... they were all Americans... emerged in mid-1971. Discovered and produced by Ian Samwell and managed by

Jeff Dexter (both of whom had been mod DJs at the Lyceum in the
early/mid 60s) whilst they did decently enough in the UK, but in
the US their debut LP *America* went platinum, and they were still
selling heavily more than twenty years later.[6]

A third sound that would have been noted as having potential
was the latinised rock-funk-soul mix popularised by Santana. As
with Crosby, Stills, Nash and Young et al this was immense in
the US... and big in the UK too. Their 1970 LP *Abraxas* spent 88
weeks in the US charts, and 52, an entire year, in the UK where
it peaked at No 7. Musically this was almost big-band territory.
A 7- or even 8-piece act, clad in flamboyant outfits, Santana were
augmented live with dancers and in the studio by session players
and guests. Trying to replicate their sound in smaller clubs and
venues around the UK would clearly have been problematic... but
several UK bands would appear down to the mid-70s, trying to do
just that.[7]

Then, and requiring much less effort on the part of the A&R
men, there were the US acts that arrived in the UK 1971-72.
Either having been jettisoned by their US labels, or seeking to relaunch their careers, this was an impressive list, led by Lou Reed
and the Velvet Underground, both of whom turned up separately
in the autumn of 1971, with The MC5, The Flamin' Groovies
and Iggy Pop and The Stooges all present by July 1972. Of these
Reed was particularly admired and successful, this period in his
career producing the big-selling albums *Transformer* (No 13 UK/
No 29 US) and *Berlin* (No 7 UK) together with one of the truly
great singles of the period *Walk on the Wild Side* (No 10 UK/No
16 US). He toured to promote these, notably with The New York
Dolls as his support band, in late 1972. David Bowie, the great
chameleon of UK pop, produced *Transformer* and its immediate,
and much less successful predecessor *Lou Reed*, and was also
behind the mixing desk for Iggy and The Stooges's *Raw Power*.
Collectively, the impact of these various US rock and roll acts
would ultimately be significant, and clearly obvious after 1976
with the rise of punk. Prior to that those imitating this sound,
or just inspired by it, had difficulty in getting heard by the UK
music industry.[8]

And finally, there was still the residue of the late 60s UK blues boom. Simple, unpretentious jug band/country blues acts like Mungo Jerry, who by virtue of their experience might suddenly come good with a string of hits. A number of these could still be found plying their wares on the small club and pub circuit, or as support acts on tours of the universities, colleges and ballrooms.

So... was pub-rock a sound that mixed a bit of Creedence Clearwater Revival, with a smidgeon of Crosby, Stills, Nash and Young, a dash of funk, some American guitar rock raunch and some latent English blues/pop? Quite possibly. But before any of these mini-genres had a time to take root and gestate, something else was rumbling about in the background and selling in immense amounts to the UK public.

In December 1970, to some expressions of surprise, *Elvis Golden Records Vol 1*, originally released in March 1958, reentered the UK charts reaching No 21. It was followed by Slade's debut hit, a cover of Little Richard's 1967 track *Get Down and Get with It* (No 16, June 1971), after which Elvis came good again with a reissue of *Heartbreak Hotel*. This hit No 10 and provoked something of a debate about what was happening, including a careful, detached explanation of the cultural mores at work, delivered by Kenneth Tynan on the 31 July 1971 edition of *Parkinson*. Alongside this Decca were exploiting the public's liking for classic Rolling Stones material with the albums *Stone Age* (No 4, April 1971), *Gimme Shelter* (No 19, September 1971) and *Milestones* (No 14, February 1972). Amongst these came a July 1971 rerelease of *Street Fighting Man* which reached No 21. Nor were Jagger, Richards and co alone. The Who's back catalogue appeared as *Meaty, Beaty, Big and Bouncy* in December 1971, peaking at No 9 in the UK and No 11 in the US, where it went platinum.

Thus, whilst the next sound was being sought, there was already a UK market for 'old', retro pop and rock. And the collective sales of this meant that finding new acts that could purvey it (or a 'sound' like it) duly became an objective within the industry. Chiming with this nostalgia about Elvis, the Stones, Little Richard and The Who came Dave Edmunds and his November 1970 single *I Hear You Knockin'*. Astonishingly successful, reaching No 1 in the

UK and No 4 in the US, this was New Orleans 1955, reimagined à la Canned Heat. As well as being retro, in two minutes and 48 seconds, it was surely a starting point for 'the pub-rock sound'.[9]

Notes

(1)　See *Pete Frame's Rock Family Trees* (1980) p28.

(2)　*The Encyclopaedia of Rock* appeared in 3 volumes 1975-76 and was edited by Phil Hardy and Dave Laing. Early chroniclers of rock history and authors of various compendium guides, they met at the University of Sussex in the late 60s. Laing had previously edited *Let it Rock* magazine 1972-73. Consultant editors for the series were Charlie Gillett, Greil Marcus, Bill Millar and Greg Shaw, probably the four best music journalists of that time. In *Volume 3: The Sounds of the Seventies* (published mid-1976) Hardy and Laing only provide entries for Ace and Brinsley Schwarz. Conversely, *The NME Book of Rock 2* (late 1976) has listings for both of these as well as the Kursaal Flyers, Kilburn and The High Roads, Dr Feelgood and Kokomo indicating how quickly the scene developed in its last few months.

(3)　See interview with Dave Robinson 25 July 2020 at: https://www.13thfloor.co.nz/interview-13th-floor-musictalk-with-dave-robinson-of-stiff-records-part-1/

(4)　See Dave Robinson interview in *Street Life* (November 1975) at: https://standupandspit.wordpress.com/2020/02/29/dave-robinson/

(5)　Between them, The Band, Canned Heat and Creedence Clearwater Revival had 9 UK chart albums, 1970-72. Of these, *Cosmo's Factory* (Creedence Clearwater Revival) was the biggest, reaching No 1 in November 1970. With 11 tracks, including Bo Diddley, Roy Orbison, Arthur Crudup and Marvin Gaye covers, it also yielded two UK Top 30 hits, *Up Around the Bend* and *Long as I Can See the Light*. One imagines that this approach inspired many of the later UK pub-rock practitioners. Note too that there was a revival of interest in The Byrds, 1970-71 whose album *Untitled* and single *Chestnut Mare* both sold heavily.

(6)　Singly, collectively or in duos, Crosby, Stills, Nash and Young had 10 UK chart albums in the early 70s, with *After the Goldrush* (Neil Young) being in situ for an astonishing 68 weeks. During the same time James Taylor's albums *Sweet Baby James* and *Mud Slide Slim and the Blue Horizon* spent a total of 94 weeks in the UK charts.

(7)   Oddly, Hardy and Laing's *Encyclopaedia of Rock* has no entry for Santana despite the band's popularity. Either this was an oversight or they couldn't work out how to categorise such music: a difficulty that afflicted some of the UK acts that played similar stuff a bit later.

(8)   They also played in pubs: The Velvet Underground at The Dagenham Roundhouse (19 October 1971) and The MC5 at The Greyhound, Croydon (13 February 1972) and the Wake Arms, Epping (18 June 1972). The MC5 also did a show at the Scala, King's Cross (10 June 1972) as did Iggy and the Stooges and The Flamin' Groovies (both 15 June 1972). Lou Reed played there too (14 July 1972; *'Back by popular demand'* 28 July 1972). His support band on 14 July were Brinsley Schwarz. After which, like The MC5, Reed appeared at The Greyhound, Croydon (30 July 1972). The idea of going to see The Velvet Underground in your local pub...

(9)   According to Edmunds he had originally intended to record a cover of Wilbert Harrison's *Let's Work Together* but abandoned this when Canned Heat put out their version in January 1970. If this was so, he waited at least nine months before picking *I Hear You Knocking*. Whatever the circumstances he certainly produced an effective facsimile of the Canned Heat sound.

DES HENLY

(FUMBLE)

I was originally in an R'n'B band, The Iveys, with Mario Ferrari, our bass player, and his brother. We were based in Weston-super-Mare and were at art school together. We recorded a single on EMI in 1966 which got released in Sweden and Denmark and toured over there doing gigs, residencies and even some TV. Around 1967 we hooked up with Sean Mayes and Barry Pike and formed an outfit called The Baloons. We played around Europe doing poppy stuff and writing quite a lot of our own material. We were a gigging band. Around 1970 we were doing some shows in Switzerland and our manager, John Sherry, suggested we adopt a retro/rock and roll image. We did and changed our name to Fumble.

We did quite well and signed to the Sovereign label, an EMI subsidiary, in 1972. There was no advance. John Sherry sold us to them as a rock and roll band, and it was his idea to do an entire album of cover versions. We enjoyed doing it... and we knew the songs anyway... and the album got noticed because of its really striking cover by Hipgnosis, which David Bowie thought was great. He booked us as his support act for his 1973 US tour, after seeing us on *The Old Grey Whistle Test*, which was quite something. He wouldn't fly... he got himself out to the US by boat. Our visas were late so we missed the opening show, at Radio City, New York. But it was fabulous. We drove everywhere from Philadelphia to Los Angeles including Route 66. A little boy's dream!

My favourite bands on the pub-rock circuit were Ducks Deluxe and Dr Feelgood and our favourite venue The Greyhound, Fulham. But the issue with most of the places like that was the acoustics weren't great: they hadn't been built as music venues.

There was a really big university and college circuit back then, and we tended to play a lot of those, alongside people like Thin Lizzy or Jon Hiseman's Colosseum. I enjoyed the universities rather more than the pubs: you had proper halls and stages. And we were always playing the Marquee. However, you could thrive in the London scene and the pub-rock circuit was certainly better than many of the smaller provincial clubs we played. I remember a gig in Bourne, Lincolnshire one New Year's Eve where we got paid £50, but the evening ended in a fight.

When Fumble started out, we would typically get around £25-£30 a night and would do around 4 gigs a week. Even though I was married with a child, I was a full-time musician. You had to be as you picked up a lot of gigs via cancellations... you had to be 'on call' so you could do them. It was difficult to get by. After we did *The Old Grey Whistle Test* in December 1972 things changed and took off a bit. Once you've been on TV you travel because people are waiting to see you. We signed to RCA in 1974 and got a £5,000 advance, with each of the band members getting £500, equivalent now to about £10,000. We had hit singles in Denmark and started recording our own stuff too. By 1974-75, we were being booked for about £250-£300 a night, on top of which I was getting some songwriting royalties as well. Our February 1975 single *Don't Take Love* is my favourite track from that time. *Time Out* put it in their alternative Top 10 (at No 1) for two weeks and John Peel said, '*I think this is Fumble's coming of age.*'

After that we did a couple of years as the band and performers in our own right in Jack Good's West End show *Elvis!* This had Shakin' Stevens and PJ Proby and was a bit weird, like having a proper job! We were given a flat to live in, in Wigmore Street, so we slept in our own beds every night and could walk to work each day. We got paid £125 a week to start with, rising to £225 as the show ran. Which was very good money then.

Looking back, I can't really be that specific about the period. But it did seem to be a time when there was a lot more live work. You always seemed to be meeting other bands on your way to and from gigs, and hanging out with other working musicians. That whole scene seemed to drop off a bit by the end of the 70s.

SPIRIT OF WOODSTOCK

But where did this retro rock and roll stuff come from? Edmunds clearly didn't start it himself, and like so much of pub-rock its origins were found more in the USA than in the UK. The earliest sighting seems to have come via Cat Mother and The All Night News Boys, who emerged out of Greenwich Village, New York in 1967-68. Initially managed by Mike Jeffrey, who also handled Jimi Hendrix, they ended up recording for Polydor, with Hendrix as producer. The upshot of which was a June 1969 US hit single *Good Old Rock 'n' Roll*, a nostalgic medley of 50s tracks by Chuck Berry, Little Richard, the Big Bopper, Jerry Lee Lewis, Carl Perkins and Buddy Knox. A month later their debut album, *The Street Giveth... and The Street Taketh Away* appeared, sold well, and saw them performing in a style midway between country and rock. With band members who had also played extensively in the US folk-rock scene (Roy Michaels in The Au Go-Go Singers, and with Bob Smith in The Dirty Shames) this type of sound would have been very familiar to anyone perusing what was on offer in the Torrington, Finchley 4-5 years later.[1]

Cat Mother dressed like a typical 1969 band, unlike Sha Na Na, who appeared 'from the streets of New York' a few months later. A 12-piece, dressed in a mixture of gold lamé suits and 50s streetwear and with much shorter hair than was usually the case back then (including several greased-back pompadours), these were retro rock and roll enthusiasts, with an elaborately choreographed act. At Woodstock in August 1969, they wowed the crowd with a 30-minute slot prior to Hendrix closing the festival, their set-closer *At the Hop* making it into Michael Wadleigh's documentary film of the event.[2] Sha Na Na also reached the UK, touring in June-July 1971 alongside Medicine Head and Uriah Heep. Which is an important point: they were not seen as being divorced from the mainstream of rock, but rather as part of a continuum that appealed to the same audience.

The same might be said of The Wild Angels, a band closely associated with The Nightingale Café, Biggin Hill, Kent. One of a number of roadside cafés on the outskirts of London that attracted fleets of motor bike-riding rockers and 'greasers', the Nightingale (or 'Gale) was actually inside a fully functioning RAF base and owed its popularity to its jukebox which still boasted, in 1967, an impressive range of 50s rock and roll hits. Much less extravagant than Sha Na Na, The Wild Angels took their name from Roger Corman's 1966 Peter Fonda and Nancy Sinatra biker-movie. They signed to Major Minor in April 1968, put out a single and hit the road with a prolific gig schedule. By the time the Dave Clark Five's cover of *Good Old Rock 'n' Roll* was tearing up the UK charts they were touring with Gene Vincent and had moved across to the B&C label. This resulted in 3 singles and a couple of albums, the first of which, *Live at the Revolution*, appeared in April 1970, with the second, *Red Hot 'n' Rockin'*, following only nine months later. Contemporary reviews note their exciting live shows and popularity. But in a foretaste of what would be typical of the pub-rock scene, on vinyl they seemed to be not much more than a highly efficient covers band. In an indication of the type of market they were pitching to, both LPs were cut-price releases, selling at 19s 11d (99.5p). Despite a promotional appearance on BBC2's prestigious *Disco 2* series on 14 February 1970, they failed to trouble the charts. Live, though, like Sha Na Na, they frequently appeared with prog bands. At the Revolution, a swish venue in Bruton Place, Mayfair, they were headlining at a club that also put on the likes of the Graham Bond Initiation and the London Radha-Krishna Temple, whilst other gigs have them bracketed with Genesis and Van der Graaf Generator. Indeed, their lead singer, Mal Gray, was so highly rated by 50s connoisseurs that he was poached by Sha Na Na as a 'guest vocalist' from 1971.[3]

It was a time when many of the major bands attracted gangs of bikers decked out in Maltese crosses, German WW2 helmets and even swastikas. The Wild Angels projected this image too, rather than the formulaic faux 50s teddy boy look that became common later in the decade. But whether at Hyde Park, Altamont or anywhere else, the uneasy alliance between album-buying, peace-loving hippies and much harder, 'greaser' elements, was always likely to unravel. *The Times*, reviewing a concert at the Albert Hall by The Who in July 1969, where the band were supported by Chuck Berry noted, *'Berry was uncomfortable with the playing order (he topped the Bill the night before) so he was allowed to close the 1st of the 2 Shows... Unfortunately, the 5th also coincided with the Stones Hyde Park Free Concert and therefore numerous Rockers and Teddy Boys took advantage of seeing Chuck Berry at the Albert Hall. When The Who appeared for their 2nd show a riot broke out and Townshend struggled to regain control launching into a raucous version of 'Summertime Blues'*. Playing a heavy rock version of the Eddie Cochran hit was probably a wise move by Townshend given that *'a small platoon of rockers turned up from the last show to mob Chuck Berry and even smash a chair or two, while The Who were received with calm enthusiasm'.* The paper concluded its review with the astute comment, *'Berry, an immaculate singer and guitarist, has a relaxed buoyancy in his music which seems to have been lost along the road to progress. Modern pop sometimes seems too dogged and hard working to be much fun.'* For a simple explanation of the surprising (for some) resilience of 50s music this could scarcely be bettered.[4]

There was less rioting recorded on 14 December 1969 at the Saville Theatre, Shaftesbury Avenue, where, in another example of the old-rock-meets-new-rock milieu, The Rolling Stones headlined, supported by Mighty Baby and Shakin' Stevens and The Sunsets. For the Stones this was ongoing promotion for *Let it Bleed*. For Mighty Baby, led by brilliant guitar interplay between Alan King and Martin Stone, it was one of many slots where their performance amazed the audience, who (if they could remember the evening) would wonder a couple of years later whatever had happened to them. For Shakin' Stevens and the Sunsets, though, it was an immensely important, and decisive, London gig.

The band hailed from Penarth, a faded Victorian seaside resort near Cardiff, and were put together earlier that year by local impresario Paul Barrett to back singer Michael Barratt aka 'Shakin' Stevens'. Their origins, as The Backbeats, were in the beat scene of the early 60s... think here matching outfits, brylcreemed hair and a set of US covers... with manager Barrett aka 'Rockin' Louie' often taking a turn as lead vocalist. Among the crowd at their Saville Theatre gig was DJ John Peel, who raved about them in his column in the following week's edition of *Disc and Music Echo*. At this point Peel's label Dandelion had Gene Vincent under contract, and a great deal of effort would be expended trying to persuade Barrett, Barratt and co to do likewise. Peel even produced a number of demos, with a view to releasing a 50s style 10" LP, only for the band to kick back with some vigour: they didn't see themselves as that type of novelty act and didn't think the quality of what they had in the can good enough. At the end of the day, all there was to show for Peel's enthusiasm would be a Shakin' Stevens and the Sunsets BBC session, recorded circa June 1970. The truth was, rather than Dandelion, both the band and their manager wanted a deal with a major label.[5] Which is where Dave Edmunds came into the story.

South Wales rock music was a small world. People knew each other and band line-ups drew most of their personnel from a pool of local musicians and singers. By 1967 the scene had produced Tom Jones, The Amen Corner and The Bystanders, the latter renamed Man a year later. In late 1968 Love Sculpture, the group with which Edmunds made his name, would be added to this list, after their massive hit with a rocked-up version of Khachaturian's *Sabre Dance*.[6] Originally Edmunds had been one of The Image, who put out 3 singles on Parlophone and two others in Germany 1965-67, though whether he played on any of the UK releases seems uncertain. Later, he was in The Human Beans, who evolved into Love Sculpture after their solitary offering, *Morning Dew*, flopped in July 1967. Offering a mixture of blues, pop and covers, John Peel was an early admirer, booking them for three sessions, and Parlophone invested money in five follow-up singles and, importantly, a couple of albums. The first of these, *Blues Helping*

(December 1968), was favourably reviewed, the second *Forms and Feelings* (January 1970) had a more mixed reception. Neither sold. Despite much promotion, including an appearance on BBC2's *Colour Me Pop*, a trip to the US to play The Fillmore with BB King, and an autumn '69 UK tour with Humble Pie and David Bowie, Love Sculpture never advanced beyond their initial hit.

Nevertheless, with *Sabre Dance* such a significant success, Parlophone trusted Edmunds enough to let him start producing the group's output. This, and his general connections at the label, led to an approach from Paul Barrett seeking a deal. Edmunds duly got Shakin' Stevens and the Sunsets a contract, with himself as producer, at around the time Love Sculpture broke up. For their debut single Barrett and the band selected *Spirit of Woodstock*, a cover of a September 1969 Ernie Maresca single. A driving, contemporary, US-inflected country rock number with clear rock and roll antecedents, this is surely another candidate for the prototype 'pub-rock' sound.[7] It appeared on 28 August 1970 and tanked. An LP, *A Legend*, did likewise after adequate reviews, at best. Significantly it was radical in its rejection of how most bands approached making an album then. To start with it had 18 tracks, 17 of which were cover versions, including one of Smiley Lewis's *I Hear You Knocking*. And then there was the cover... the epitome of glamorous retro: a backlit portrait of the band, shown in mid-distance on an elegant, curtained stage, wearing 50s teddy boy style outfits and with ludicrously short and swept back hair.[8] Even if you didn't rate the music, the photo was worth framing and keeping as an artefact. Alas, Parlophone dropped the band.

Much of *A Legend* was done at Rockfield Studios, Monmouthshire, where Love Sculpture and The Amen Corner had also recorded. It provided a residential arrangement: you lived and worked there whilst recording and had functioned since 1965 under the ownership of Charles and Kingsley Ward. Their back story included releasing a couple of singles as The Thunderbolts and The Charles Kingsley Creation. They had also been involved in Joe Meek's abortive *Space Symphony*.[9] By the late 60s Kingsley Ward was working, often alongside Edmunds, as either a producer, arranger or engineer and it was at Rockfield that Edmunds recorded his version of *I Hear You Knocking* in August 1970. Whether he decided to do so after hearing the Smiley Lewis rerelease, or after producing the Shakin' Stevens cover isn't clear... but the end result, on which Edmunds played every instrument, was a close facsimile of the Canned Heat sound with significant amounts of compression, particularly on the vocals, à la Joe Meek.[10]

Released on MAM it reached No 1 in the UK and No 4 US and was a massive international success. Much was expected to flow from this, but the problem was Edmunds hardly toured, electing instead to spend much of his time at Rockfield. Follow-ups – on EMI subsidiary Regal Zonophone – included a country rocker *I'm Comin' Home* and a cover of Fats Domino's *Blue Monday*. Both flopped in the UK and were only minor US hits. After which *Down, Down, Down* written by ex-Move man Trevor Burton did absolutely nothing. An album, *Rockpile*, on which Edmunds was assisted by a couple of Love Sculpture colleagues, appeared in May 1972, but didn't sell either despite generally positive reviews. As with *A Legend* it was mainly cover versions: just one original among 10 tracks with the remainder Chuck Berry, Dylan, Neil Young and blues standards. A great many subsequent pub-rock LPs would offer similar fare, in similar style, but this was the first such and, as with his single, could be considered something of a template.

Whilst Edmunds tried and failed to repeat the success of *I Hear You Knocking*, Shakin' Stevens and the Sunsets added guitarist Mickey Gee, formerly of Love Sculpture, to their line-up, adopted a scruffier denim/street wear image and signed to CBS for a 1971 album *I'm No JD*. This had 5 originals, out of 12, but like their debut still didn't sell. Donny Marchand, who also did The Wild Angels, produced, and a second LP with him *Rockin' and Shakin'*, consisting mostly of covers, appeared on the budget Contour label in early 1972, with a single, *Sweet Little Rock and Roller*, following on Polydor. None of these sold either, but despite this the band continued to play prolific numbers of gigs in both the UK and Europe.

Simultaneously with Edmunds putting together his smash hit at Rockfield, interest in the continued existence of teddy boys, and their peacock-like attire, was being noted by serious cultural observers. In a world where popular fashions were expected to change every couple of years, or even annually, it seemed to some almost outlandish that something first noted circa 1954 had survived. The notion that not everyone was signed up to the hippy/ counter-culture scene attracted attention as did the locations where the members of this select urban tribe could be discreetly observed. One such was The Black Raven, 185-187 Bishopsgate, London EC2, part of a long terrace of properties jammed up against the eastern side of the old Liverpool Street Station. In an extensive piece in *The Sunday Times* on 27 September 1970, landlord Bob Ackland stated, '*Nineteen fifty-six to fifty-eight was the great old days for real music. The Beatles and Stones was good at first, then they went out on a cloud. These* [sic] *type of old records will go on when The Who and that is dead and gone. That modern music, it's all the same, ain't it? Weak, like.*' Not that he booked bands to appear at his venue, explaining, '*I spend £6 a week on records, and I hire a jukebox – it's better than a group. The Top Twenty is obsolete in this pub: most of it's a load of rubbish. I've had six brand-new jukeboxes in three years – they're worth about £700 each, it wouldn't pay me to buy one. Dancing gets a thirst up – without that jukebox I'm a dead duck.*' [11]

Friday night sessions at The Black Raven were particularly popular with vintage US cars parked outside and a clientele that included Graham Fenton, singer of The Houseshakers, Charles Kray (brother of), Malcolm McLaren and Vivienne Westwood and Dave Clark: yes, the same one who had spotted the hit potential in *Good Old Rock 'n' Roll*. It was bracing company, much of which drifted over on a Saturday evening to the Fishmongers Arms, Wood Green, where live music was also on offer. A definable, retro, rock and roll scene was clearly emerging and within it, bands like Shakin' Stevens and the Sunsets were highly prized. The success of *I Hear You Knockin'* also saw The Wild Angels reboot themselves, adding Geoff Britton, formerly of East of Eden after the exit of Mal Gray. They signed to Decca in early 1972, with an LP, *Out at Last*, and 5 singles following. The LP did nothing, but one of the singles, *I Fought the Law*, was a Swedish No 1 in 1973, the same year that they covered some songs from the US stage show *Grease*. When this opened in the UK, they became the house band in a production starring Richard Gere at the New London Theatre, Drury Lane. There were new groups around too. The Rock 'n' Roll Allstars, a 5-piece with conventional teddy boy gear, signed to B&C in March 1971 releasing 2 singles and an album *Red China Rocks*, the cover of which had Mao in a drape jacket. Graham Fenton's band, The Houseshakers, backed Gene Vincent on his penultimate UK tour including a John Peel session with him in February 1971. With a line-up that included Irish saxophonist John Earle and guitarist Terry Clemson, late of The Downliners Sect, they signed to budget label Contour for an LP, *Demolition Rock*, which, as with the releases from Shakin' Stevens, The Wild Angels and The Rock 'n' Roll Allstars, failed to sell to a wider public.[12]

This blossoming interest in jukeboxes, 50s clothing, cars, bric-a-brac and records required, and got, servicing. November 1971 saw Malcolm McLaren and Vivienne Westwood take over a boutique at 430 Kings Road squarely aimed at this market. Named *Let it Rock*, it became the centre of their subsequent business activities. They weren't the first. Ted Carroll had already opened *Rock On* at 93 Golborne Road, Ladbroke Grove in August that year. Carroll co-managed Thin Lizzy and had come into the ownership of 1800 vintage singles on the highly collectable London label that were found languishing in a Dublin loft. They formed the core of his stock. By October 1972 there was a magazine, also called *Let it Rock*, which managed to run for three years, Elektra had released a double LP, *Nuggets: Original Artyfacts from the First Psychedelic Era, 1965-68* (copies of which were much sought after in the UK), and Skydog Records, specialising in hard to obtain blues and rock and roll material, had commenced business in France, with its releases gradually reaching the UK via import.[13]

On top of which, bands were arriving from America as well, for a variety of reasons. The years 1971 and 1972 were peak Nixon, with the draft in place, Vietnam ongoing and, in social and cultural terms, a noticeably colder wind blowing than had been the case a few years earlier. Various outfits and individual musicians crossed the Atlantic to avoid this and enjoy an easier-going climate in the UK. First to arrive were Detroit's The MC5, dropped by Atlantic after disappointing sales and invited over by pirate radio hustler Ronan O'Rahilly.[14] Despite key personnel drifting back to the US, and being replaced by session men, they managed to play 26 UK gigs, opening at the London School of Economics on 5 February (with The Houseshakers as support) and even slotting in a visit to Northern Ireland at Magee College, Derry on 5 June. One wonders in the context of Ulster and Derry, then, how their fiercely political blues-rock went down. They also spent time recording material for *Gold*, a film O'Rahilly had somehow acquired and been allowed to score.

Similarly, Andrew Lauder, head of United Artists records, brought The Flamin' Groovies over from the US after Kama Sutra cancelled their contract. The attraction was the chance to work with Edmunds. According to guitarist Cyril Jordan, *'When we heard 'I Hear You Knockin'' in 1969* [sic] *the sound on the record was so great that we thought Rockfield was the new Sun recording studios.'* On arrival in the UK, they just drove to Rockfield without telling United Artists or Edmunds, who was reading in that week's edition of *Melody Maker* that he would be producing their next record, when they arrived. Two singles, both produced by him, followed. The first, *Slow Death* (a reference to heroin addiction), was immediately banned by the BBC on its release in June 1972. The second, *Married Woman*, fared no better six months later, by which time the group had returned to the US. Both failed commercially, and if you owned either of these you were probably one of a group of no more than 1000 people in the UK at that time.[15] Nor did The Flamin' Groovies play anything like the number of live shows as The MC5.

What all of this eventually built up to was the London Rock 'n' Roll Show, staged at Wembley Stadium on 5 August 1972. A day-long event, rounded off by a decent set from Chuck Berry, those with the stamina to stay the course also got to see Bo Diddley, Jerry Lee Lewis, Little Richard (whose performance was widely regarded as inadequate and self-indulgent) and Bill Haley and His Comets. But... to get that far also meant watching The Houseshakers and UK stalwarts like Joe Brown, Emile Ford and

The Checkmates, Screaming Lord Sutch, Heinz and Billy Fury. Added to which the promoters clearly had a definition of rock and roll somewhat at odds with that held by much of the crowd, as elsewhere on the bill were Gary Glitter and The Glitter Band, Wizzard and The MC5.

Glitter (aka Paul Raven; first release 1960) got off lightly with just being booed. Major opprobrium was reserved for The MC5, despite their biker/outlaw credentials, with the band subjected to considerable hostility from part of the audience. Reviews of their performance were unanimous, *Sounds* noting, '*The MC5, who played some searing music, left the stage after twenty minutes, forced off by howls of derision*'. *Melody Maker* reported '*The MC5 were the only band to try and capture the feel of rock'n'roll, yet they shared the booing stakes with that incredible blunder head Little Richard. Severely limited on time, as were most of the acts, the MC5 did try to communicate with the audience of traditional rock lovers, but the lead singer, Wayne Cramer [sic] got pelted with beer cans for his pains. His big mistake was to run down to the audience, leaving the safety of the stage. Quite why singers try to make contact in this fashion has long been a mystery... They stomped through 'Gloria' which was greeted with ominous silence and a few slow hand claps, then came the famed cry of 'Kick Out the Jams' that would doubtless have most American audiences in hysterics and warrant at least five pages of comment in* Rolling Stone. *It was received with cold indifference, as the gold clad figure of Wayne bravely ducked a hail of cans like a Christian in the gladiator's arena. "Stop that you idiots – there are people here who want to stop the whole show", yelled a desperate announcer, as a bunch of same began a can throwing contest among themselves. They did stop, and there was no more trouble throughout. The MC5 were not exactly thrilling, but at least the band got it on'* and *Rolling Stone* concluded, '*Detroit's MC5, not a rock and roll band by any stretch of the imagination, was applauded with a hail of Coke cans and wine bottles from the crowd of 50,000. Real 1957 stuff. With Teds and Rockers, you either play it their way, or not at all.*'

Heinz, Joe Meek's faded Adonis, had a kinder reception. His backing band that day, a then unknown outfit from Canvey Island, Dr Feelgood, noted the treatment doled out to The MC5, with Wilko Johnson later remarking, '*Teddy Boys convinced us we didn't want nothing to do with classical rock and roll. It was so mindless... they thought if you didn't wear a drape suit it wasn't classical rock and roll, but no singers ever dressed like that. Chuck Berry never wore a drape suit'.* [16] The critics were clear that The MC5 actually played quite a good set, despite the band being in a poor place and breaking up four months later. Wembley showed very clearly how little real empathy most teddy boys, Hells Angels and the like had with anything beyond their own inflexible parameters. But it didn't change the attitude of the music industry as a whole towards retro acts.

One such was Fumble, who'd been together as a working band since circa 1965. [17] In 1971 their manager suggested they relaunch themselves as a rock and roll revival group, something they were happy to do. It quickly led to a burgeoning reputation on the gig circuit. Endorsed by John Peel, for whom they did a session on 27 June 1972, they signed to EMI, recording an LP *Fumble* on the Sovereign subsidiary at about the time the Wembley Festival was happening. Consisting entirely of cover versions and marketed with the strapline *'Feel at home with Fumble'*, it appeared to some acclaim in October that year. *Melody Maker* rated it *'a thoroughly enjoyable and singable album'* but what was really remarkable about it was the cover. Done by Hipgnosis and prefiguring Peellaert and Cohn's *Rock Dreams*, it was a perfect example of rock and roll iconography, showing an accurately attired and styled teenage couple listening to a stack of 45s on a Dansette and getting familiar with each other amid the debris of a typical 50s living room. As a piece of pop-art it was quite brilliant and made a huge impression. David Bowie loved it and after an appearance on *The Old Grey Whistle Test* (19 December 1972) they supported him on his US Ziggy Stardust tour. Back home they did a set at the 1973 Reading Festival where they *'got everybody going with their 50s rock and roll'* in a slot between jazz-rockers Riff Raff and French progsters Magma but neither the album, nor subsequent singles, sold in significant quantities.

Nevertheless, the rock and roll revival was up and running, the next step in its development being the film *That'll Be the Day*. Set in the late 50s with David Essex, at 26 years old, playing a teenager running away from home to pursue a career as a rock and roll singer. Filming started in October 1972, after about a year in preparation, with a supporting cast that included Ringo Starr and James Booth. Its attempt to reconstruct everyday life 15 years earlier was very hit-and-miss, and musically, this was like sitting next to a jukebox playing pre-1963 chart hits for 1 hour 31 minutes. Critics had mixed views about the end result, with *Time Out* being particularly sharp, *'Hugely overrated dip into the rock'n'roll nostalgia bucket... But good tunes, and worth catching for Billy Fury's gold lamé act'*. (Fury, who was in the film for no more than ten minutes as rock and roll singer Stormy Tempest, upstaged everyone.) The public adored it, though, making it the second most popular film of the year in the UK. A double album soundtrack was duly released on the Ronco budget label, reaching No 1 in the UK in July 1973. Which seems to confirm that one reason there was no market for cover versions by Shakin' Stevens and Fumble was because one could buy the real thing quite cheaply in Woolworths.[18]

One side of the soundtrack does in fact contain fresh material recorded especially for the film. It's worth listening to as an example of how rock musicians between the ages of 25 and 35 in 1972-73 sounded when attempting to write short accessible 'retro' style songs. Much of pub-rock was similar. Here we get six tracks by Billy Fury and one apiece from Vivian Stanshall, Wishful Thinking and Eugene Wallace. Fury's sessions were recorded in October 1972 by a band that included Graham Bond, Ron Wood, Pete Townshend, Jack Bruce and Keith Moon, whilst in the film Fury mimes a couple of tracks with Bond, Moon, two of Moon's roadies and John Hawken.[19]

Fury does a decent job singing straight rock, but it's a very mixed bag. His best effort is probably Pete Townshend's *Long Live Rock*. Vivian Stanshall's *Real Leather Jacket* works quite well as a tight parody of the period, and Eugene Wallace, who has a small role in the film, does ok with a version of *Slow Down*.[20] The remainder of the non-greatest hits selection has David Essex's *Rock On* (which sounds nothing like the 50s at all) and *What in the World* by Stormy Tempest. Written by Stanshall this is not a Fury track, unless he's playing the harmonica on it somewhere: it appears to be a girl group.

One major beneficiary from this high level of nostalgia about
the 50s was Dave Edmunds. With Rockpile defunct, aside from
his efforts with The Flamin' Groovies, he had been producing
albums for Man, Foghat and new band Brewers Droop. With the
chance to spend an abundance of time in a well-equipped studio,
he also knocked out a couple of facsimile versions of oldies himself,
releasing Phil Spector-like covers of *Baby I Love You* in December
1972 followed six months later by *Born to be with You*. Both were
big UK hits and led to his being hired to do the music for *Stardust*,
the sequel to *That'll Be the Day*. Set in the 60s this has Essex's
character (Jim MacLaine) ascending to rock stardom. Edmunds
appeared in the film too, as one of Essex's retro-band, writing and
arranging most of the music.

A soundtrack LP, *Stardust – 44 Original Hits from The Sound
Track of The Film*, appeared on Ronco in October 1974. Like its
predecessor it was 75% licensed 'greatest hits' and 25% newly
recorded material, including 10 tracks by either Jim MacLaine
or The Stray Cats, much of which was recorded almost single-
handedly by Edmunds. Buried in the 'greatest hits' section was a
cover of *Da Doo Ron Ron* by Dave Edmunds and The Electricians,
the latter turning out to be Brinsley Schwarz using an alias, and
the album closed – track 11, side 4 – with *Stardust*, the main title
theme, sung by Essex and a huge hit for him. Unlike *That'll Be the
Day*, the album didn't sell.

Which was odd, given the runaway success enjoyed from
1972 by obviously retro acts like Gary Glitter and the Glitter
Band, Wizzard, Alvin Stardust, Showaddywaddy, Mud, and The
Rubettes. There was plenty of gold lamé and faux 50s clothing
on show with all of these, and between them they raked up 73
Top 30 hits in the UK, most of which were increasingly aimed
at Saturday evening TV and cabaret tours. Exceptions might be
made for Wizzard whose 1974 album *Introducing Eddy and the
Falcons* and single *Are You Ready to Rock?* were the finest pastiches
released at this time, and Alvin Stardust, aka Shane Fenton
and originally a pre-Beatle pop star, who successfully projected
a stage persona that was clearly 50% Gene Vincent and 50%
Dave Berry.[21] Collectively, it amounted to a massive, commercial,

takeover of the rock and roll revival genre. It was no longer cool to automatically embrace such stuff and the cognoscenti moved on: in the spring of 1974, for instance, Malcolm McLaren and Vivienne Westwood relaunched their boutique as SEX.[22] Those still ploughing the rock and roll furrow, searching for originality and artistic integrity, found themselves part of a smaller, more authentic scene where bands struggled to get deals, many of them becoming more popular in Europe than the UK.

For Shakin' Stevens and the Sunsets, this was a period of popularity in the Netherlands. Despite a prodigious UK gig schedule their record sales remained low and in 1973 their LP *Shakin' Stevens and the Sunsets* (14 tracks, 5 originals) appeared on Willem van Kooten's Pink Elephant label. A 1975 follow-up, *Manhattan Melodrama,* was an attempt at a concept album with all-original compositions and the Sunsets augmented with Dutch session players. Produced by Antonius Schellekens, late of Amsterdam-based progsters Brainbox, like its predecessor it didn't sell. Nor did an April 1976 one-off single on Mooncrest. A cover of Hank Mizell's *Jungle Rock*, which had been successfully reissued by Charly a month earlier, it failed to piggyback on the success of the original and was their last release. In late 1977 Stevens went solo.[23]

It was a similar story with Fumble. Signing to RCA in August 1974, Shel Talmy, no less, produced their album *Poetry in Lotion*, but despite much promotion including a January 1975 slot on *The Old Grey Whistle Test* it flopped in the UK. They had hits in Denmark, but RCA weren't interested and dropped the band. There were further releases on Decca and DJM, but in 1977 they followed the route set by The Wild Angels four years earlier, taking the part of the house band in a West End musical. This was Jack Good's *Elvis*, featuring Shakin' Stevens as 'the King' in his prime. It ran successfully for a couple of years at the Astoria, Charing Cross Road.[24]

The Houseshakers split in 1974, with Fenton and Clemson forming The Hellraisers, one of whose members, Tommy Husky, had been in Earl Preston's Realms during the Merseybeat phenomenon. After a budget LP *Remember When?* on Contour, they folded in 1976 when Fenton joined Matchbox. It was similarly hard going for some of the new arrivals too. Like Shakin' Stevens and the Sunsets, Crazy Cavan and the Rhythm Rockers were part of the tightly knit South Wales scene. Cavan (aka Cavan Grogan) had even been, briefly, in a band with Dave Edmunds. For most of the 70s they played gigs for fees as low as £15 perfecting an authentic, sparse, menacing rockabilly sound. They wrote their own material, releasing a self-funded single and an EP in 1973. Favourably reviewed in the *New Musical Express* by John Peel, British record companies remained uninterested. Rockhouse in the Netherlands were, however, releasing an album, *Crazy Rhythm*, in 1975 after which they switched to Charly (a French label that relocated to the UK) for *Rockability* a year later. Like Stevens and the Sunsets, they were a terrific live act, albeit with violence prone to erupt at their gigs. One particular incident, 6 August 1976, at The Adam & Eve, Homerton degenerated into a massive brawl with a local motor bike gang, guitarist Lyndon Needs recollecting, *'there was a big fight, there was a lot of violence, it was the worst fight that I'd ever seen, it was just like a blood bath. It was the aftermath that concerned us all and Don (Kinsella, the band's bass player) was convinced that they would come back and get us. It even got in the NME, a bikers versus teds type of thing'*. (A mere two hundred yards away, The Dueragon Arms was a far less dangerous venue, which possibly endorses the view that establishments run by the Krays tended to be quite safe.) Another memorable, and somewhat calmer, show took place at the Roundhouse on 5 September 1976 with the Kursaal Flyers and The Clash. After this, The Clash asked them to tour as their support act... only for Charly records to refuse to put up any of the required funding. A deal with Stiff collapsed too, because of the length of the contract the band already had with Charly. Sadly, Cavan and his colleagues never recorded for a major label or had a significant UK hit.[25]

Others fared no better. Rocky Sharpe and the Razors, basically a homegrown doo-wop act, were prominent on the pub and club circuit for a couple of years, but only released an EP on Chiswick after they split... the problem being that some of their members wanted to finish university degrees rather than turn 'pro'. Another band, Bazooka Joe, based around Danny Kleinman and Stuart Goddard, both students at Hornsey Art College, were similarly popular for a while. They never released a record, despite 5-6 years of gigging and a line-up that at various stages included Pat Collier, John Ellis, Rick Wernham and Lee Kosmin. With connections like these some curiosity arose in later years about what their sound and image had been. Pete Frame noted at the time that their set 'comprised 90% original material... peppered with bizarre oldies, such as Teenager in Love, Apache and Pipeline' and in a 2009 interview, their bass player Chris Duffy confirmed, 'We were definitely influenced by bands from across the Atlantic, but it was mainly older doo-wop stuff such as Sha-Na-Na and American Rock and Roll stars like Frankie Valli. Our look was pretty Grease Lightning at the start, we slicked our hair and wore leather biker jackets.' They played St Martin's College of Art in November 1975 with The Sex Pistols as their support. It seems to have been a significant experience: shortly afterwards Goddard had assumed the moniker Adam Ant and gone punk. Collier and Ellis would follow this path too, in The Vibrators.[26]

Eventually, the wheel went full circle. What had started in the US with Cat Mother and the All Night Newsboys and Sha Na Na returned from the US in 1976 with the reappearance of The Flamin' Groovies. In their absence they had contrived to release an EP, Grease, and a single, Jumpin' Jack Flash, on Skydog in the Netherlands and two more singles, You Tore Me Down and Let the Boy Rock and Roll, in the US and France on Bomp! and Philips respectively. Now with a deal care of Sire Records, run by long-term habitués of the Brill Building Seymour Stein and Richard Gottehrer, they made their way once more to Rockfield to complete the work they had begun four years earlier.

Dave Edmunds produced, fitting it in after working on the final releases from Ducks Deluxe and Brinsley Schwarz, both of whom broke up shortly afterwards, as well as his 1975 effort Subtle as a Flying Malet (12 tracks, 10 of them covers) which, like its predecessors, didn't sell. What emerged was Shake Some Action, released to considerable critical acclaim in June 1976, and regarded as quite possibly the Groovies' finest hour. Of the 14 tracks, 6 were

non-originals, including a Beatles number. Strikingly, like Shakin'
Stevens' A Legend, the image the band projected on the cover was
immensely radical. They had short hair, matching, sharply cut
suits with drainpipe trousers and Cuban heels and were standing
alongside a Daimler Sovereign saloon, outside a modern office
building 'in City Road... right across the road from the tailor who made
our suits'. It looked like 1965, and was as comprehensive a rejection
of the denim, flares, greatcoat and tank-top uniform still worn
by many bands then as the mixture of fetish gear and teddy boy
clothing that Malcolm McLaren adopted for The Sex Pistols and
their ilk.[27]

In terms of sales Shake Some Action was niche in the UK and
rose no higher than No 142 in the US. (Although that still makes
it today their biggest selling release.) Whilst he was working on
it, Edmunds was signed by Swansong, Led Zeppelin's label, and
released a single, Here Comes the Weekend. Co-written with Nick
Lowe, this was original and fresh-sounding and brought him back
to the fore. Again, it didn't sell but another Lowe song, I Knew the
Bride (June 1977 No 26), finally gave him a hit.

One of the distinctive strands of pub-rock was retro rock and
roll bands, or if not exactly that, just the propensity by most of
the acts gigging on the circuit to include cover versions in their
set. Often to the point where the majority of their set was cover
versions. Whilst most of the 'authentic' rock and roll bands and
singers (such as Crazy Cavan) remained relatively restricted in
terms of their appeal, it was clear that smoother, commercialised
versions of this (Mud, Showaddywaddy, and so on) really did have
huge appeal, with this trend continuing after the demise of pub-
rock. By 1978 the membership split within Rocky Sharpe and
the Razors had produced two new groups, Darts (who included
John Dummer and Ian Thompson from the John Dummer Blues
Band) and Rocky Sharpe and the Replays. Between them they
had 10 UK hits from 1977, at the end of which Darts followed
The Wild Angels, Shakin' Stevens and Fumble onto the West
End stage, in this case the show Yakety Yak which ran until 1983.
Graham Fenton's Matchbox also came good, with 5 hits in 1979-
80. And finally, post-Elvis, so did Shakin' Stevens, racking up

5 chart albums and no fewer than 30 hit singles between 1980 and 1990. He was easily the highest-selling UK artist of the 80s.[28]

But, in terms of the sound that many people associate with pub-rock, much of it was based on a mixture of country-rock, blues-boogie and Americanised road-music. If that could be distilled into just one 2-3-minute piece of noise, then from *Spirit of Woodstock* to *Shake Some Action* it was created in the studio by Dave Edmunds between 1970 and 1976.

Notes

(1)   Their single reached No 21 in the US. The UK cover version by The Dave Clark Five peaked at No 7.

(2)   Sha Na Na's albums were only modest US chart hits, though, with their highest placing reached in 1973 with *The Golden Age of Rock 'n' Roll* (No 38). Which seems to suggest that audiences loved them live... but didn't buy their records (much). Perhaps UK bands that followed their path should have noted this.

(3)   On The Wild Angels see: https://nightingalecafe.webs.com/explanation.htm

(4)   On 4 July, Berry had headlined at the Albert Hall with support from Chicken Shack, The Misunderstood and The Alan Bown Set. Jeff Dexter was DJ. Both gigs were part of the First London Gala Pop Festival.

(5)   As did Roxy Music a little later, turning down Dandelion, and Peel, for Island.

(6)   One of a number of records that mixed rock and classical riffs at that time, others being Procol Harum's *A Whiter Shade of Pale* and The Wallace Collection's *Daydream*.

(7)   The Shakin' Stevens and the Sunsets version is at: https://www.youtube.com/watch?v=cfhIcaBxMwU Ernie Maresca's is at https://www.youtube.com/watch?v=CD5kfLbVvcw Curiously, Stevens' manager Paul Barrett claimed a writing co-credit for his band's version, as can be seen on the LP, *A Legend*. It is clear from the US release that Maresca co-wrote the track with Warren Gradus, formerly of Dion and the Belmonts.

(8)   For the cover see: https://www.discogs.com/master/318716-Shakin-

Stevens-And-The-Sunsets-A-Legend/image/SW1hZ2U6NjM
4NjIyNDM=

(9) See the rather peculiar instrumental *Lost Planet* at https://www.
youtube.com/watch?v=ggP6BMwVuvA

(10) The Shakin' Stevens version of *I Hear You Knocking* can be heard
at https://www.youtube.com/watch?v=ecmORA3RhY4. Track
six, side two of *A Legend*, it has manager Barrett on lead vocals,
apparently at the insistence of Edmunds. A faithful, almost note
perfect cover of Smiley Lewis, it lacks the drive and intensity of the
Edmunds version.

(11) See: http://www.edwardianteddyboy.com/page36.htm According
to Ackland he bought the pub in 1967 after a lucky win on the
horses. It closed in 1975 and was subsequently demolished when the
Broadgate office development was built.

(12) John Earle, from Dublin and ex-Odeon Show Band, would later
play in Kilburn and the High Roads as well as being noted for
sessions with Max Wall, Dave Edmunds, Graham Parker and the
Rumour, and Jona Lewie, most of whom came via Dave Robinson's
Stiff label. For an account of his career see *The Irish Times* 17 May
2008 at: https://www.irishtimes.com/news/versatile-and-highly-
rated-musician-who-supported-some-of-the-greats-1.1213508

(13) Skydog were started by Marc Zermati, who also ran a clothes/retro
shop, The Open Market. Their first release was a bootleg LP of The
Jimi Hendrix Experience jamming in the US with various other
parties in 1968.

(14) It was something of a return engagement, O'Rahilly having
originally brought them over to play the Phun City Festival, near
Worthing, in July 1970.

(15) They also backed Roger Ruskin Spear on a rather bizarre solo
album, *Electric Shocks*, which probably sold even fewer copies.

(16) The concert was filmed and released in 1973 as *The London Rock and
Roll Show*, directed by Peter Clifton. The footage includes a brief clip
of Heinz, backed by Dr Feelgood and shots of Malcolm McLaren
and Vivienne Westwood selling t-shirts from a stall.

(17) To the extent that, as The Iveys, they released a single *When Love
Meant So Much to You* on Columbia in Sweden in 1966. The existence
of another UK act with the same name (the band who later became
Badfinger) caused a 1968 name change to The Baloons, after which
they became Fumble.

(18) The success of the *That'll Be the Day* compilation was no real surprise to the marketing men. Other similar releases prior to its appearance (all on budget labels) were *20 All Time Hits of the 50s* (October 1972, No 1), *25 Rockin' and Rollin' Greats* (December 1972, No 1), *20 Flashback Greats of the 60s* (March 1973, No 1) and *40 Fantastic Hits from the 50s and 60s* (April 1973, No 2). Malcolm McLaren and Vivienne Westwood supplied the film with a considerable number of the costumes worn by the cast.

(19) Bond is clearly heard on 5 tracks, and, ironically, this album would end up being his only chart success. Incidental music for the film was done by Wil Malone.

(20) Eugene Wallace was an EMI act from Limerick who cut a couple of albums 1974-75 in the gravelly-voiced rock style of Frankie Miller. See: https://www.irishrock.org/irodb/bands/wallace-eugene.html

(21) Between them these acts had 14 Chart LPs as well. With the exception of Roy Wood's Wizzard, all were bands or singers active in the 60s, cashing in a decade later on a burgeoning trend.

(22) Their antennae must have already been twitching, as in 1973 they renamed *Let it Rock* as *Too Fast to Live, Too Young to Die*.

(23) For a while this was somewhat disguised with his band continuing to tour as Shakin' Stevens's Sunsets. The author saw them in this incarnation – with Paul Barrett as lead vocalist – in 1978.

(24) Given that Presley died on 16 August and the show opened on 28 November 1977, one can only marvel at the speed with which this was done. PJ Proby was cast as the late, Las Vegas version of 'the King'.

(25) See *50 Rockin' Years* by John Kennedy and Louise Barrell, the booklet accompanying the 2020 CD box set released by the band on their own label.

(26) On Bazooka Joe see Pete Frame's *Rock Family Trees Volume 2* p19 and https://anotherexistence.wordpress.com/2009/07/08 Their image appears to have been similar to that of Slik, a Scottish band who had a No 1 hit with *Forever and Ever* in January 1976. The Rocky Sharpe EP on Chiswick has a picture sleeve showing some of the band's fans: https://www.discogs.com/release/3856264-Rocky-Sharpe-And-The-Razors-Rocky-Sharpe-And-The-Razors/image/SW1hZ2U6NzY5NTY2Ng== Note too at this time the popularity of *Happy Days* (screened on UK TV from 1975), the 1973 film *American Graffiti* and *The Rocky Horror Show*, a retro-pastiche stage

production which ran at various venues in the Kings Road from 1973.

(27) Quote from Cyril Jordan in *ZigZag* 64 (September 1976). *ZigZag* 59 (April 1976) records rock journalist Nick Kent saying that he played on *Slow Death*. Jordan, however, states that *Slow Death, Shake Some Action* and *You Tore Me Down* were all recorded '*the first night at Rockfield*'. Kent also states re: The Flamin' Groovies, '*I don't think Dave Edmunds did them justice at all, and I'm very surprised they went back to him to record their Sire album (out soon)... he made them sound wet, I thought*'.

(28) For confirmation of which see *Record Collector* 22 October 2007: https://recordcollectormag.com/articles/shakin-all-over-again

HORACE TRUBRIDGE

(ROCKY SHARPE AND THE RAZORS, DARTS)

Rocky Sharpe and the Razors were put together by Den Hegarty from a group of people who were all at school together in the Brighton and Hove area. I joined a bit later. Originally, I played the clarinet around Brighton and was influenced by trad jazz. After seeing Roxy Music, I switched to saxophone, which was an easier instrument, and modelled myself on Andy Mackay.

In both Rocky Sharpe and the Razors and Darts our favourite venue was The Nashville. It was almost our home and Rocky Sharpe did their last gig there. People forget but in the mid 70s the rock and roll/retro scene was really huge. The Lyceum on a Saturday night was teddy boy heaven, particularly with bands like Crazy Cavan and the Rhythm Rockers. We tended, though, to attract a Hampstead-type crowd who wore 50s street gear and were into *American Graffiti* and *Happy Days*. I loved all the tribes back then, thought it was great.

Of the other bands around then I rated and liked the 101ers, The Stranglers and Be-Bop Deluxe, who I thought were really good. Very classy. We did quite a lot of gigs with Deaf School whose singer Bette Bright later married Suggs from Madness. Madness – who were just a bunch of skinheads from an Islington council estate really – used to come and see Darts at The Rock Garden, where they'd fight with the teddy boys, but they'd never cite us as an influence!

Until we got a deal, in either band, most of our gigs were in London. Darts made very little money from playing live. Don't forget: we were a nine-piece! We just hoped we'd get royalties and publishing money a bit later. Generally speaking, our best gigs were outside London. As people say, 'the further north you go, the better the gigs'. Places like Glasgow, Liverpool and Newcastle were all good places for us. We also toured Northern Ireland, which is where we met real trouble. We did a gig at Fivemiletown in Tyrone which was really rough. We were playing in this place that was like an enormous barn or hangar with no bar inside, so everyone got completely tanked before they came into the venue. As soon as we started our first number the audience – mainly young kids – started chanting 'Brits Out... Brits Out' and throwing bottles on the stage. We stopped after a couple of numbers, our roadies got beaten up and we ended up taking refuge in the caretaker's house. The caretaker said to us, 'Just lie on the floor.' But we completed the tour. At the last gig, at the Bantry Boys Club, a couple of men who looked like geography teachers came up to us and said, 'We really rate your band. Thanks for coming over here, not many people do now. We know about the trouble you had in Fivemiletown and we know who was responsible. They've been dealt with.' One of them was Martin McGuinness.

We didn't get paid much at all for gigs in Rocky Sharpe and The Razors, or in Darts in the early days. The problem with Rocky Sharpe and The Razors was that half the band were at university, and didn't want to leave... that's why we split up and some of us left to form Darts with John Dummer, Iain Thomson and George Currie from The John Dummer Blues Band. Everyone signed on. In fact, we were still signing on when we had our first hit in Darts and appeared on Top of the Pops! And, if I wasn't signing on, I would have been working in music shops as a day job.

When Rocky Sharpe and the Razors got a deal with Chiswick in 1976, we got no advance at all. With Darts, various labels were interested in signing us, including Stiff and A&M. We were offered a substantial advance by A&M but our manager, Bob England, thought that Magnet, who had people like Alvin Stardust and Chris Rea, were better. Magnet certainly had a remorseless focus on promoting their acts, but only as long as they had hit records. Once that started slipping, they got behind the next big act. In terms of what we recorded, I thought Daddy Cool, our October 1977 debut on Magnet, was a fantastic song. I also wrote material, including a Top 10 hit *Get It*, and 'death discs' like *Annual County Fair*. Bob England took on Chas and Dave in the late 70s and eventually had his own label, Towerbell Records. He ended up owing a lot of money to a lot of people, and left us with a substantial unpaid VAT bill. Darts later appeared in the West End show *Yakety Yak* at the Astoria, Charing Cross Road, and a version of the band continues to this day.

Looking back at that time, I don't think there has ever been a better period for how accessible music was, and what an extraordinary hodge-podge of styles you could see on a night out.

NICK HOGARTH

(CURTIS KNIGHT ZEUS, BLUE GOOSE)

The first band I ever played live with were The Blue Set, doing Yardbirds covers and so on. We entered a beat group competition at Streatham Ice Rink and came second... the band that won were Mud, long before they started having hit records.

I'm actually a classically trained musician, but my influences were blues and boogie-woogie after I discovered the blues as a teenager. In 1971-72 I was in Ray Owen's Moon with Chris Perry, Owen being ex-Juicy Lucy. I also played and recorded quite a lot with Mataya, an afro-rock band. They had a residency upstairs at Ronnie Scott's, and we did a lot of shows and recordings together. A little later, through Eddie Clarke, I got involved with Curtis Knight.

Curtis was a soul singer who'd had Jimi Hendrix as his lead guitarist before Hendrix was discovered. Because of this connection he was well known and had a contract with Pye Records' Dawn label. He put us on a retainer of about £20 a week, with a Mercedes truck for our gear that was fitted out with some airline seats. Eddie, Chris Perry and I would rehearse and jam in a studio near Shepherd's Bush and Curtis would come down, record us on a cassette machine and then go off and write lyrics to what we were doing, after which we would record the material properly at CBS studios at Whitfield Street, London. We did a couple of singles and an album, *The Second Coming*, as Curtis Knight Zeus. Curtis had a friend with a Rolls-Royce, and we often travelled to gigs in this! He had a completely OTT soul revue-type show, very much like James Brown, and we played a lot of places like Leicester; real chicken-in-the-basket stuff.

The engineer at a studio in Piccadilly had some downtime one night so Eddie, Chris and myself went there to do some stuff of our own. Curtis found out about it and got very irate and that was pretty much the end of the band. The demos from these sessions got us a recording contract with Anchor records, then part of ABC/Dunhill. This band became Blue Goose; we needed a singer for the band and both Speedy Keen and Steve Ellis were considered as possible members, but in the end Alan Callan, who was managing us, became the main singer. He was married to Clare from Deborah & Clare's shirt shop in Knightsbridge and they put us on a retainer of about £30 per week until the advance came through from Anchor Records. What happened was one of Alan's colleagues from Deborah and Clare's got a job at Anchor Records' label and they had just signed Ace. Alan gave him our demo tape and they liked it so they signed us with a huge advance of £250,000, to make 6 albums over 3 years. However, Alan and Eddie fell out quite badly and Eddie left, and we ended up recording our first album, which we were due to do on Ronnie Lane's mobile studio, with Anton Matthews producing. Steve Marriott was going to produce but was going through a bad time. Alexis Korner and Joey Molland (from Badfinger) both helped a lot making the album.

We did a couple of gigs and started work on a second album, but although Eddie was replaced by Mike Todman the band was not the same and fell apart. When we gave the finished tapes to Anchor, they wouldn't release it. We took out a case against them for breach of contract, backed by the Musicians' Union, which was eventually settled in our favour 3 years later. Whilst this was going on I spent some time in Mauritius and Paris as well as being part of Eddie's band Continuous Performance.

I used to spend quite a bit of time hanging out at Dingwalls, often with Eddie and Lemmy, who was Jimi Hendrix's roadie when he first came to the UK, which is probably when the Eddie-Lemmy connection started. I was aware of several of the pub-rock acts, and thought that Brinsley Schwarz, Ducks Deluxe and Bees Make Honey were all great bands, as were Dr Feelgood, whom I remember seeing in a tiny pub in Shepherd's Bush. I played a couple of times with Roogalator. Danny Adler was a brilliant guitarist. There was much more creativity. One of the things that helped was all the main studios had kitchens... when you were doing stuff and went to have a tea or coffee you'd bump into the other musicians and get talking. What a great scene it was! People went to gigs to witness something they knew you couldn't record. Today, people go to the pub and just want to eat.

All in all, with the retainers and the bits of extra money for gigging, I was a full-time musician. Looking back, I think the Curtis Knight Zeus album, *The Second Coming*, was probably the best stuff I released then.

STANDING ON THE PLATFORM

Electric blues wasn't invented in the UK. But it certainly became commercially significant there. In *Awopbopaloobop Alopbamboom* Nik Cohn, writing in 1969 at the age of 23, was pretty disparaging about it. *'Like you'd expect, most of our homegrown bluesmen were lousy. They'd come out of Surbiton, their hair down in their eyes...'* In some despair, he also went on to note the existence of *'a fad for 'heavy' groups (groups who played incessant twelve bar blues, as loudly and crudely as possible). At its worst this had led to awful excesses. In particular, heavy bands like Led Zeppelin and Ten Years After have reduced blues playing to its lowest most ham-fisted level ever'.* Harsh words from the father of pop criticism, a man whose attraction to the flamboyance, attitude, speed and dynamism of early rock and roll would lead him, within a few years, to embrace disco as its natural progression.

Up to a point he was right. Yes, a lot of them came from suburbia, with Mick Jagger (Dartford) leading the way. And yes, a lot of them were journeymen, even if the amount, and quality, of UK blues, rhythm and blues and hard rock that appeared from the early 60s onwards continues to impress decades later. Leaving aside trailblazers like the Stones, in commercial terms this style – electric blues played louder and 'heavier' than previously – was pioneered by Cream.[1] Following on from them came a succession of UK heavy blues/heavy rock bands who sold tens of millions of albums in the US. Beginning in August 1968 with the Jeff Beck Group and *Truth*, by 1970 this profitable sub-genre had expanded to include Deep Purple, Led Zeppelin, Blind Faith, Ten Years After and Black Sabbath. Despite immense sales and prodigious levels

of mayhem and misbehaviour on their many tours, all of these
lacked the mythology and iconography that appealed to Cohn,
and all were conspicuous by their absence from *Rock Dreams*, the
1973 book he co-authored with Guy Peellaert.[2]

If Cohn and like-minded souls were not interested, given
the returns, record companies were. It was simple accountancy:
between 1968 and 1976 these acts accrued 91 platinum and 10
gold discs in the US. End result? The labels kept signing bands
like them, hoping to strike lucky, with the result that some of
the artistes they promoted, whose ship hadn't yet sailed, were still
knocking about on the pub gig circuit well beyond the date this
kind of sound was regarded as cutting edge.

One such, and probably the most distinguished in that
category, were The John Dummer Blues Band. Formed in 1965
and led by Dummer, originally on vocals and later drums, early
line-ups featured Tony Topham, the man Clapton replaced in
The Yardbirds, on guitar.[3] A solid live act, by early 1968 they
had a coveted Sunday afternoon residency at Studio 51, in Great
Newport Street, as well as regularly backing visiting US bluesmen.
With the line-up stabilised to Dummer on drums, Ian 'Thump'
Thompson on bass, Tony McPhee and Dave Kelly as rival lead
guitars, John O'Leary on harmonica and Kelly's sister, Jo-Ann
Kelly, as a featured vocalist they contained a fair amount of talent.
McPhee had already led Groundhogs and both the Kellys had
released material on several different compilation LP 'samplers', a
format then common.[4]

Much was expected, and Mercury signed the group in May
1968. John Peel liked them; the first of several sessions for his show
being broadcast on 11 August, and their debut LP *Cabal*, released
at the end of the year, attracted uniformly good reviews. Words
like brilliant, great and excellent were bandied about. But sales
were lowish, and it didn't chart. Today it sounds tight, jazzy and
still worth a punt. Good live music, if perhaps ever so slightly too
conventional in its approach. Before the album appeared, though,
McPhee had left to reform Groundhogs, the band replacing him
with Adrian Pietryga. Stability would be a problem throughout
their existence. Adding Bob Hall on keyboards, they recorded an

October 1969 follow-up, *John Dummer Band*, to mixed but generally satisfactory reviews.

Extensive touring of Britain and Europe followed, often as the headlining act. By the time of their third set, *John Dummer's Famous Music Band* (June 1970), Dave Kelly and Bob Hall had departed with the band now based around Dummer, Thompson, Pietryga and multi-instrumentalist Nick Pickett. Again, the critics were positive, but UK sales remained low. They broke up shortly after its release, only to find that a single lifted from it, *Nine by Nine*, had become a huge hit across Europe. An elegant 30s-style violin-led instrumental, it was particularly admired in France due to its stylistic similarities to Django Reinhardt, Stéphane Grappelli and the legendary Quintette du Hot Club de France. It was certainly their most distinctive track.

Suddenly they were in demand. Dummer duly reformed them and they were showcased on *The Old Grey Whistle Test* on 28 March 1972 alongside Randy Newman. A fourth album, *Blue*, appeared on the prestigious and now collectable Vertigo 'swirl' label a month later. Credited to The John Dummer Band, it came with a Roger Dean cover, at that point the go-to man for such work.[5] Once more the reviews were mixed, veering to positive, and once again, it failed to chart. At which point Nick Pickett quit for a solo career, apparently advised to do so by Peter Green. Despite this, they persevered. John Peel booked them in for 4 sessions over the next eighteen months and following further line-up changes they rebooted themselves as John Dummer's Oobleedooblee Band.

By now the personnel were Dummer, Thompson and Pietryga, with Dave Kelly back on board. Sister Jo-Ann and Roger Brown were around to provide additional vocals and a violinist (Michael Evans, moonlighting from Stackridge) played occasionally too. Anxious to lap up its vibe, they headed down to Rockfield, where Fritz Fryer and Kingsley Ward produced their fifth album, *Oobleedooblee Jubilee* (March 1973). Regarded as their best work to date, like its predecessors it didn't sell in sufficient quantities to chart.

Further line-up changes ensued. Pietryga, Brown, Evans and Jo-Ann Kelly departed being replaced by guitarist Pete Emery and

Graham Bond, fresh from his stint as a suspiciously hirsute, and rather elderly-looking saxophonist in *That'll Be the Day*. Colin Earl joined from Mungo Jerry on keyboards. Another album was recorded at Rockfield during the course of which Dummer drifted away from the band, taking a job as a promotions manager at MCA records. They plugged the gap temporarily with Pick Withers, who did many Rockfield sessions. With Vertigo cool on the idea of a sixth album, Earl was despatched to the US where his brother Roger was touring (and selling records) with Foghat to try and get a deal. The pitch was simple: a year earlier Foghat's eponymous debut had been produced at Rockfield by Dave Edmunds. It had since gone gold in the US... did anyone want another chip off the same block? Apparently not. There were no takers and after Graham Bond, ravaged by drug addiction, committed suicide in May 1974, The John Dummer Band expired following a final gig in Liverpool with Brinsley Schwarz and Ducks Deluxe.[6]

There was a lesson here. However competent some bands were, and the various incarnations of John Dummer's Band were all highly competent, they just couldn't get sufficient traction within the UK to become commercially successful. Brinsley Schwarz had a similar experience. Would any record label today indulge a band with five albums and low sales? Probably not, but half a century later the music from Dummer and co still sounds good and their solitary hit, *Nine by Nine*, remains a unique fusion of blues, jazz and swing.

Brett Marvin and the Thunderbolts took over Dummer's residency at Studio 51 in the spring of 1969. A collection of teachers and pupils from Crawley, Sussex, led by trombonist Pete Gibson, their line-up included Graham Hine on guitar and John Lewis on keyboards.[7] Building on the reputation they built up at Studio 51, the band, Hine and Lewis contributed no fewer than seven tracks to the Liberty sampler LP *I Asked for Water, She Gave me Gasoline*, one of which, their take on Skip James' *I'm so Tired*, was played on John Peel's *Top Gear* on 11 October 1969.

A deal followed, with the band signing to Swedish label Sonet shortly afterwards. Having opened a London office run by Rod Buckle in 1968, Sonet were known mainly for obscure soul and

Scandinavian pop releases. Buckle would later write of Brett Marvin as, 'a totally co-operative group, despite their name, they had no leader which made negotiations a little protracted, but eventually they agreed to record for Sonet'. They were the label's first UK band and Sonet committed quite heavily to them, booking Orange Studios, New Compton Street for their debut LP and arranging TV appearances, notably in the Netherlands show Pop-Eye on 4 February 1970, alongside Roy Harper and Aynsley Dunbar.[8]

The LP, Brett Marvin and The Thunderbolts, appeared in January 1970, but didn't sell. Nor did a one-off single, Standing on the Platform, in April. The album had 13 tracks, almost all of which were 'traditional' pieces by obscure bluesmen. The single, a fine, stomping, blues-shuffle with plenty of slide guitar, was a group composition, but it seemed the music press, for the main, were bemused, Music Business Week noting, 'Some of the finest modern-day rhythm and blues can be heard on this album, but unfortunately the group indulge in some messing around that spoils the effect' and Record Retailer signing off with, 'A pleasing but inconsistent release.'

The problem appears to have been that important, and often self-regarding, arbiters of contemporary musical taste didn't quite know where to place Brett Marvin. Was this music? Or performance art? Why did they have such a retro name? At a time when bands were acquiring bigger and bigger PA systems and deploying maximum volume at every opportunity, Brett Marvin, with their eclectic collection of instruments (they often played without a conventional drummer), were (deliberately?) the polar opposite of what was expected. Their calling card was authenticity, and their sound a mixture of the Mississippi delta country blues circa 1920 and English eccentricity. Standing on the Platform, in fact, has a similar sound to Ken Colyer's Skiffle Group on their June 1956 release Downbound Train. The critics didn't really expect this from a new band in 1970. John Lewis had seen the band at Studio 51 before being invited to join them, and was knocked out by how radical their approach seemed, 'Here was Blind Lemon Jefferson meeting Robert Johnson and playing hypnotic delta boogie, right here in London!' He had a point, but however wonderful this sounded in a crowded basement club, it was niche.

For the moment, though, they continued to ascend. Peel had them on *Top Gear* on 30 May 1970, after which they toured as support group to Eric Clapton's Derek and The Dominoes, a slot to be envied given Clapton's reputation at that point. There was also *Bottleneck Blues*, a Graham Hines solo album, with backing from John Lewis and others, which appeared on the Blue Goose label in the US.[9] But, neither their second album *12 Inches of Brett Marvin and The Thunderbolts* nor its accompanying single *Little Red Caboose* sold in significant numbers. Which, in the case of the latter, was a shame. Written by Henry Thomas, an obscure ragtime blues singer-guitarist you might have encountered riding the railroad in Texas in 1895, it rattled along in an unpretentious and charming fashion.[10] One can understand Lewis's remarks about their sound being 'hypnotic' when you hear it. Sadly, in June 1971 not many of the record-buying public did.

A few months later, a slimmed-down version of the band recorded the John Lewis composition *Seaside Shuffle*, releasing it under the pseudonym Terry Dactyl and The Dinosaurs. Without much promotion from Sonet, it flopped too, only to have a curious afterlife. A couple of discotheques picked it up as a novelty number, one you could dance to, and Jonathan King, now running UK records and looking for talent, took note. He enquired about licensing it. Brett Marvin, with no manager and cooling on Sonet, agreed. Sonet acquiesced.[11]

Reissued by UK on 7 July 1972, and with King's hustling powers in full play, it snowballed into a substantial hit. The band were on *Top of the Pops* three weeks later, with the single eventually reaching No 2 in the charts. It certainly had a unique sound. The vocals were deadpan and laconic, much like Ray Davies, in their understated Englishness. Part 30s dance band, you could imagine it being sung by George Formby or Max Miller, part morris dancing music and part sea-shanty with lots of accordion, it was so popular that the Joe Loss Orchestra did a cover version. Terry Dactyl's nom de plume quickly blown, they more or less parked Brett Marvin to concentrate on their success. Sonet released a compilation of their first couple of albums plus the hit as *Alias Terry Dactyl and the Dinosaurs*, whilst King recorded another Lewis song, *On a Saturday Night*, as their follow-up for the UK. Released in November, and more square-dance than blues, it struggled to No 45 domestically, but did much better in Europe. Footage exists of Lewis performing the number on West German TV with a trio of musicians plundered from the Jawbone Jug Band, the caption for which notes, '*they were met at the airport by a limo complete with young ladies, provided by the studio. Apparently, the rehearsal for this broadcast produced a better performance (than) the silly dance being suggested by the studio director. Unfortunately, copious amounts of alcohol were available.*'[12]

After a third single, *She Left I Died*, on which they were billed as Terry Dactyl and The Dinosaurs featuring Jona Lewie (as John Lewis had now become), the inevitable split occurred. Lewis/ Lewie contracted glandular fever and couldn't fulfil a schedule of gigs worth £400 each (approximately £7500 today). The band were broke, and couldn't walk away from the work, so reformed Brett Marvin without him, bringing in as replacement Taffy Davies, the keyboards player from the Jawbone Jug Band.[13] For their third studio album, *Ten Legged Friend*, they used Kingsley Ward as producer, but it didn't sell and nor did three follow-up singles. By 1975 Sonet had dropped them.

At which point one would have expected them to disperse to more rewarding activities. But Brett Marvin stayed together. There was still a circuit they could play, they were good value as a live act, and could oscillate comfortably between pubs and colleges. From the mid-70s onwards you were likely to encounter them in secondary level venues like the Stapleton Hall Tavern, Crouch End. This was the type of pub that was common then and provided the local public with a lot of good live music. Like many other venues, it didn't advertise in the music press, so trying to assess its influence now is somewhat tricky as memory fades and non-digitalised documentary evidence slips away.

A large nineteenth-century 'gin palace' at a main road junction, it ticked a lot of boxes in terms of what constituted a typical 'pub-rock' venue: it was in North Islington, it had an Irish landlord (Jim, from Cavan), it had a substantial music room to one side of the saloon bar, and it served as a kind of testing ground for bands seeking to hone their acts and move on to better things. Admission was free. Pre-Eurythmics act The Tourists road-tested their set there, both The Pleasers and Landscape (of *Einstein A Go Go*) had residencies at one point and it was amongst these and the likes of Dick Heckstall-Smith's Big Chief that Brett Marvin and the Thunderbolts continued playing. They never got another deal, though, their only subsequent releases being a couple of self-financed EPs in 1980-81.

It only remains to record how John Lewis/Jona Lewie continued his career. Remaining on Sonet he released a string of singles, the first of which *Piggy Back Sue* appeared in late 1974, and was about as retro as you could imagine. A powerful piano led piece of boogie-woogie – the sort that you might see now done by the host of *Jools Holland Live* – it featured the Chris Barber Band, an outfit as long in the tooth as Ken Colyer. It didn't sell, and neither did any of the others, the most notable of which was *Hallelujah Europa* (July 1976). A paean to the joys of European unity, it clocked in at 9 minutes 28 seconds and was spread across both sides of a 45. Musically it veers into electronica with a repetitive keyboard riff and the chorus repeated throughout. A very 'European' sound in fact.[14] Nor did Lewie play too many live gigs to promote his releases, though he did appear 1975-76 as one of Martin Stone's Jive Bombers. At the end of 1977 he signed to Stiff, Dave Robinson noting *'Jona had songs coming out of his ears. He'd talk for hours about how every one of them was a work of genius.'* Some of them were. Who could forget the drollness of *You'll Always Find me in the Kitchen at Parties* and the effective anti-war sentiment of *Stop the Cavalry*, the big Christmas hit of 1980? The latter was his crowning achievement, peaking at No 3 in the UK, but reaching No 1 in Austria and France and No 2 in West Germany. Certified platinum, it has subsequently been rereleased on 15 occasions.

Ploughing a not dissimilar furrow to Brett Marvin and the Thunderbolts were Brewers Droop, two of whom, Steve Darrington and John McKay, had been part of the heavy blues band Mahogany a couple of years earlier, Darrington joining in 1969, whilst taking a sabbatical year from Sussex University. A

Buckinghamshire-based outfit, they quickly built up a head of steam, recording demos at Jackson Studios in Rickmansworth, where Dr Feelgood, Motörhead, the 101ers and Eddie and the Hot Rods would later venture. More to the point they had a manager who was prepared to pay a London promotions company £30 for 13 weeks (£390 then, about £11,000 now) to get them a record deal. He did. The best offer came from CBS, and they signed.

Astonishingly for a new band, consisting mainly of teenagers, CBS brought in Tony Clarke, whose credits included most of the Moody Blues huge US successes, as their producer. A debut album, *Mahogany*, emerged gaining a US release on Epic, but for some reason failing to appear in the UK, though it was available in the Netherlands. A tremendous, unaffected piece of work, eight of its ten tracks were written by Darrington and McKay and the sound is tight, the playing good and the material above average. It puts a lot of better-known bands to shame, but it didn't sell and they were certainly in no position to visit the US and tour. What work came their way came via Marty Wilde, who was looking for musicians to back him.[15] This brought them appearances on *Late Night Line Up* and quite a bit of live work as Wilde promoted his album *Rock 'n' Roll*, the cover of which has him astride a motor bike in black leathers amidst a crowd of greasers and Hells Angels.

But they weren't a retro rock and roll band. In late 1970 Darrington and McKay had been approached by promoter Ron Watts and asked to join Malcolm Barrett (bass) and Bob Walker (drums) in Brewers Droop. By virtue of the connections he'd developed booking bands into The Nags Head, High Wycombe, Watts was exceptionally well known throughout the industry. He almost got his new charges a slot at the June 1971 Glastonbury Festival only to have this cancelled at short notice, due to the organisers needing to minimise the number of acts appearing for safety reasons. What he did manage to do, apart from secure them a great many gigs, was get the band signed to RCA in early 1972. A debut single, *Sweet Thing*, appeared in May 1972, followed five months later by an album, *Opening Time*, launched at a champagne reception at RCA's offices in Curzon Street. Like the single this didn't sell, and in fact the album was quite widely panned, typical reviews being, 'An insignificant album, saved slightly by two tracks, The Way I Feel and Why, which reveal that the band possesses much talent, given the right material. It's all just a bit too self-indulgent, though' (Music Week 28 October 1972 and 'An album for those whose bellies have recently been filled with ale. Listening to it cold sober is not a very happy experience... Surprisingly, Tom McGuinness produced it' (Record Mirror 28 October 1972).

What caused such comments? Darrington is on record as saying, 'We were a bawdy, Cajun R&B band that was unaware of boundaries' and listening to the album today it does contain quite a few boozy singalong 12 bars, often with double entendre lyrics. (Sample songs: I Can See Your Public Hair and If You See Kay Tonight). And then there was the band's name: slang for erectile dysfunction brought about by heavy drinking. One of the album's tracks is a blues instrumental, Droopin', complete with much harmonica, a brass section and girl backing singers. Who was meant to buy this? What Watts and RCA appear to have believed was that, in a world where ex-wrestler Judge Dread was a pop star (he had 7 'rude reggae' hits between 1972 and 1976), there might be a similar market for risqué blues-rock. Despite the enthusiasm of their audiences, though, on vinyl much of Opening Time was like listening to a collection of rugby club songs, which were, admittedly, quite popular then.[16]

Whatever the intention, they were an accomplished band, and continued to tour, both in their own right and backing US bluesmen. Shrugging off the indifference to their debut, they headed down to Rockfield to record a follow-up. Dave Edmunds produced these sessions, but only a single Louise (September 1973), emerged. A pleasant Cajun song, with an accordion accompaniment, it didn't sell either and their second album was shelved. The economic realities of the mid-70s kicked in too, with Darrington noting, 'The climate for a self-financing touring band became unfavourable for us in 1974. Petrol prices went through the roof and new legislation requiring fire prevention measures caused the demise of the cheap B&Bs we relied on, living on the road and travelling from gig to gig. More money was going out than coming in. So, we split.' Both Pick Withers and Mark Knopfler were members of the band in its latter stages, and both would later be staggeringly successful in Dire Straits, but Brewers Droop broke up after a final show at The Golden Lion, Fulham in March 1975.

After which Darrington and drummer Bob Walker joined Shucks, Darrington stating some years afterwards they were, 'playing the same pub rock scene as AC/DC, Brinsley Schwarz, Dire Straits and the like, but also playing social clubs and country and western clubs... it was great fun'. Given that AC/DC made their UK debut at The Red Cow, Hammersmith in April 1976 and Dire Straits are on record as playing at the Hope & Anchor, Upper Street, Islington in September 1977, Shucks, forgotten now, were clearly a band that played that circuit for at least a couple of years. In late 1975 they recorded an album: *Two Days – Two Tracks* on the tiny Sweet Folk and Country label, the cover of which has the band, a five-piece, posing by an immense American car, wearing lumberjack shirts and what appear to be Stetson hats. As The Damned's Brian James would later state, 'All the bands in pubs wanted to be the Ozark Mountain Daredevils, wear the checked shirts and wished they were born up a mountain in Arkansas.' He had a point, and 1976-77 was a bit late in the day for this image.[17]

Like Shucks, Sweet Folk and Country, run by Joe Stead out of his spare bedroom in Shrewsbury Lane, London SE18, is largely a forgotten label today. A minor legend on the folk circuit, Stead had started out appearing alongside Pete Seeger in various Soho pubs in the 50s. A heavily-built, bearded man, usually wearing an immense woolly jumper, his repertoire ran from sea shanties to political protest. The latter category included *George Davis is Innocent OK!* an entire LP from himself and various colleagues about police corruption and the wrongful conviction of George Davis (a career criminal) for a specific crime that he didn't commit. His label, which started life as Sweet Folk All, had a huge roster of British folk singers and country and western bands, releasing no fewer than 105 albums between 1973 and 1979. A pioneering indie, predating Chiswick and Stiff by several years, it provided music for a tiny number of hardcore fans and specialist record shops. Much of its output was recorded in Wales, at Gordon Davis's Mid Wales Sound Studios, which like Rockfield was based on a farm. There was no question of Shucks getting an advance from Stead, and it goes without saying that their album only sold in limited quantities. But they got to record and release their stuff. After a 1977 follow-up, *Hillbilly Swing*, they broke up. It's worth remembering that, for every famous name that crops up in fondly remembered accounts of the pub-rock era, there are many others, now forgotten and submerged by time, who were so typical of what was on offer back then. Shucks are one such act.

Returning to electric blues and its long afterlife, one figure who continued to loom large after his demise was Jimi Hendrix. The UK LP charts featured six posthumous Top 30 releases by him between 1970 and 1972, and as late as 1975 an album, *Crash Landing*, went gold in the US. He still sold and was immensely popular. All kinds of people connected to Hendrix sought to capitalise on this, none more so than soul singer Curtis Knight. Born in either 1929 or 1945, according to which account of his life you read, Knight (aka Mont McNear) released 7 singles in the US from 1960, 3 of which, as Curtis Knight and the Squires, feature Hendrix as lead guitarist, and clearly anticipate his style. With Knight owning this material, an album of Hendrix's work with him, *Get That Feeling*, appeared as early as May 1968, and did quite well, reaching No 39 UK and No 75 in the US.

This fame by association gambit was energetically pursued by Knight, who recorded prodigiously. By 1973 he was based in the UK, working with a new backing band, Zeus, the membership of which included keyboardist Nick Hogarth and guitarist Eddie Clarke. Given Knight's standing as a former colleague of Hendrix, the band revolved – entirely – around its leader, who put his musicians on a wage and rehearsed them until '*you could actually play a tune in your sleep*'.[18] Knight was also credited as the sole composer of all their output, irrespective of his contribution, which was usually to write the lyrics. In Europe, where they were popular, they released an LP, *Sea of Time*, on Philips, after which a deal with the Pye subsidiary Dawn produced a couple of singles and a follow-up album *The Second Coming*.

Musically, what is on offer here is a mixture of soul, rock, blues and just a smidgeon of psychedelia. It's more than acceptable and they were clearly a decent live act... but sales weren't great. Whilst promoting *The Second Coming*, Knight wrote and published *Jimi: An Intimate Biography of Jimi Hendrix*, an account of Hendrix's life that had its fair share of detractors. Like his records, though, it sold, running to several editions. It seems possible things might have worked out quite well for him had he not fallen out badly with his own band. Finding out that they were privately rehearsing without him, Knight regarded this as tantamount to treason and objected so strongly that they upped and quit.

This seems to have ended Knight's period in the UK quite abruptly, as the next we hear of him is a brief stint as a record producer in the US four years later. His band – Hogarth, Clarke and drummer Chris Perry, joined by bassist Nick South – formed Blue Goose in mid-1974. Managed by Alan Callan, their demos got them an astonishing deal with Anchor Records: a £250,000 advance to make six albums. (The equivalent of £33.375m today, or about £5.5m to cover each album and all associated touring and promotional costs.) This was around the time Anchor signed Ace and were actively looking for similar UK bands. Given the scale of the advance, they must have thought Blue Goose would do really well in the US, and it was intended they would record at Ronnie Lane's Mobile, a large (26 feet long) streamlined US trailer converted into a mobile recording studio, and based at Lane's farm in Powys.[19] Like Rockfield, this was a highly prized location, used by megastars like The Who as well as aspiring acts like Chilli Willi and the Red Hot Peppers.

The future seemed – very briefly – full of opportunities. The band considered co-opting Callan as a second guitarist, and did so at early rehearsals. The problem was he had no amp of his own and had to plug into Clarke's. A blazing row quickly broke out, with Clarke accusing Callan of deliberately playing over, and drowning out, his solos. In a situation that might have made a memorable scene in *This is Spinal Tap*, Callan promptly sacked Clarke, replacing him with Mike Todman. They duly completed their debut album *Blue Goose* with this line-up, but neither it, nor an accompanying single *Loretta*, attracted too much attention. Listened to today it comes across as well played, efficient blues-rock, with, by virtue of the band having a keyboards player, some interesting interplay between the lead instruments. You can see why Anchor gave them such a large advance, and there seems no reason to think that given time they couldn't have made money on the US and European circuit in the same way that many other bands did. Instead, a follow-up was recorded only to be quickly rejected by Anchor who cancelled their contract, leading to a lengthy legal dispute that the band (which broke up) fought and eventually won.

In the meantime, whilst Blue Goose were stumbling towards their collapse, Eddie Clarke formed Continuous Performance. This band – which, unusually, had a female lead vocalist Ann McLuskie – gigged and did demos without securing a record deal. Even when Nick Hogarth was drafted in, no one was interested and by 1975 Clarke had all but given up music. Eventually, in late 1976, he was contacted by Ian 'Lemmy' Kilmister and asked to join Motörhead. He did so, and between 1979 and 1982 played on 5 of their big-selling albums. He might not have reached the same levels of critical acclaim as Hendrix (for whom Kilmister had roadied) but in time he certainly became a renowned figure in UK heavy rock and heavy metal.

Pub rock was a very male environment. There were few women musicians or singers and audiences mainly comprised beer-drinking men. But, like Ann McLuskie, there were exceptions, the best known of whom was probably Carol Grimes. An accomplished blues singer, Grimes' first recordings were with Babylon, a 1968-69 jazz-rock ensemble, after which she had a fair stab at being a UK version of Janis Joplin, recording an album, *Fools Meeting*, with Delivery. The extent of her versatility was shown on the 1971 B&C sampler *Battle of the Bands Volume 1* which has her backed by the Red Price Band on a cover of the 1967 Little Richard track *I Don't Wanna Talk About It*. Appearing on the same album were Shakin' Stevens and The Sunsets, Gene Vincent and The Houseshakers, The Wild Angels and The Rock and Roll Allstars. As for Red Price, if you were old, you might have seen him on *Oh Boy!* as one of Lord Rockingham's XI, and if you were really old, you'd have known him as one of the saxophonists in the Ted

Heath Big Band. (Not the Prime Minister, the trombonist with a residency at the Hammersmith Palais.) After this venture into the rock and roll revival market, Grimes reappeared in 1972 as one of Uncle Dog, a publicity flier for which refers to them as 'a band that has been credited as the first on London's 'pub-rock' circuit'. A six-piece, the other members included keyboardist and song-writer David Skinner, formerly of Twice as Much, and later one of Clancy, and drummer Terry Stannard, later in Kokomo. After gigging and cutting demos they secured a deal with Signpost, a new label set up by US executive Artie Mogull, and released their debut album, Old Hat, in September 1972. John Peel thought they were wonderful, they did three sessions for him, and the critics raved too but sales were low and when Signpost ceased trading in mid-1973 the band quickly broke up.

Another exception was Sandra Barry who reappeared in 1974 as lead singer of Slack Alice. One of the schoolgirls in The Belles of St Trinian's, she'd released a solo single on Oriole as far back as 1958. By 1963 she was combining singing with acting, mainly in TV stuff like Epitaph for a Spy. Today collectors pay a lot for her March 1964 single Really Gonna Shake, released as Sandra Barry and The Boys. The Boys, in this case, being the same group of Kentish Town mods who became The Action and, after drinking deeply in the well of the counter-culture, Mighty Baby.[20] A decade later, and with The Boys guitarist Alan King enjoying commercial success in Ace, Barry rebooted her career once more, this time as a bluesy rock-chick, not dissimilar to Suzi Quatro, but unlike Quatro not aimed at a mainly pubescent audience. The band name, Slack Alice, was drawn from the same lexicon as Brewers Droop and one wonders if it might have also owed something to the immense success, around 1974, of Larry Grayson, who included a character called Slack Alice in his outré monologues.

Alongside Barry in the band were keyboardist John Cook who had done a stint in Rice and Lloyd-Webber's Joseph and the Amazing Technicolour Dreamcoat as well as the prog band Octopus and guitarist Pete Finberg, previously one of many in Renaissance's ever-changing line-ups. They signed to Philips in May 1974, began gigging (an early show being at The Kensington) and released a couple of singles and an eponymous album. To promote the latter, they toured as support to The Sensational Alex Harvey Band... in some ways the perfect match. Both bands were theatrical (Barry often 'acted out' her songs) and both were led by troupers who'd been around since the very beginning of UK pop. Produced by Robin Freeman, who later did a lot of Herman Brood's stuff in Europe, one of their singles, Motorcycle Dream, charted in the Netherlands. Most of the material on the album Slack Alice sounds a bit like The Faces; boozy good-time music. Critics, then and now, couldn't work out how good it was and it didn't sell in the UK. After completing their contracted gigs, the band broke up in 1975 with Barry and bassist Michael Howard moving to France.[21]

Most people who went to pub gigs in the 70s probably never saw Blue Goose, Shucks, Uncle Dog or Slack Alice. One band they couldn't avoid, though, was Scarecrow, who played all through the decade, and beyond, claiming to consistently do upwards of 250 gigs a year. A hard-rock/heavy blues quartet, two of their members, guitarist John Stewart and drummer Dave Ramsey, had originally been together in The Information, a late period pop-psych group. Under this name they toured Europe and the UK, often as support to Manfred Mann and Jimi Hendrix, putting out a single, Orphan, on the Beacon label in March 1969. Based in Willesden, Beacon initially specialised in licensing US soul records. Dipping a toe into the market for UK bands, they signed The Information, and, a little later, UFO. By late 1970 this yielded some returns when UFO broke into the German charts with their third single, Boogie for George, and quickly moved on to greater things.

Which was not the case with The Information. Beacon did not commit to any further releases and the band's second single, Lovely to See You, appeared in April 1970 on Evolution, an obscure underground label run out of 63 Old Compton Street. A Moody Blues cover, written by Justin Hayward, it was arranged by Joe Moretti, a legendary UK session player whose work included rock and roll classics like Brand New Cadillac and Shakin' All Over, Donovan's Mellow Yellow and a great deal of Serge Gainsbourg's output. Sadly, like their first release, it didn't sell and Evolution ceased operating in July 1971, leaving them without a record contract.

Going through some line-up changes, they reemerged as Scarecrow at The Greyhound, Fulham, in March 1972. Hundreds of gigs followed, in the UK and abroad, and they became a name you saw in the music press, week in, week out, playing 3, 4 or 5 different venues. In November 1975 they appeared (in the prestigious Saturday night slot) at the first week of live music at the reopened Bridge House, Canning Town. According to landlord Terry Murphy, 'We went on for a few months, but then Scarecrow had to go. They were a good band with a good singer... but they were Heavy Rock which was beginning to phase out. It was too much the same, long solos, head bangers and dope smokers. I wanted to change our image...'[22]

Losing a slot at one pub when they were playing so many others probably didn't worry Scarecrow too much. The band all lived in London, travelled to gigs in a coach, had their own PA and van, arrangements that enabled them to travel easily to and from gigs and sleep in their own beds at night. They still played in Europe getting regular bookings in Germany and doing so many gigs, over such a long time, gave them a wide repertoire of original material as well as making them pretty tight musically. After demos that no label wanted and long after punk and 'new wave', not to mention the burgeoning mod revival scene, had ousted most of their contemporaries, Scarecrow took the plunge and recorded a live album, at the Brecknock, Camden Road and the Marquee, during Easter 1978. Elaborately packaged, with a six-panel wraparound sleeve, two stickers, a bio sheet and a fan club newsletter, only a thousand were pressed, ensuring it became a collector's item. The fact that a band without a record deal had a fan club ought to have said something to somebody. But, as the 80s dawned and synth-pop predominated, who wanted another UFO/Budgie soundalike, however competent? There were more abortive demos, and more gigs, until Scarecrow finally called time on their efforts at the end of 1982.

A common theme of all these acts was that they tended to enjoy greater popularity in Europe than at home. The reasons for this mismatch are not often explored. Quite simply, around 1971-72 a huge part of UK pop music was occupied by glam or retro bands, a trend that was mainly absent in Europe where there were few, if any, local equivalents of Gary Glitter, The Rubettes or Mud. The retro scene especially, on the scale seen in the UK, was unique to the UK. In contrast with this, all through the 70s conventional 'progressive' – and quite accessible – blues rock was still very much part of the mainstream in Europe, something that anyone who listened to the pirate stations Radio North Sea International (from 1970) or Radio Caroline (from 1972) can confirm. Here bands like John Dummer, Slack Alice, Curtis Knight Zeus and Scarecrow played prestigious gigs, and enjoyed a modicum of commercial success. In the UK, though, they found times harder, and in many cases were still scuffling around the pub circuit a decade or more after they started.

Notes

(1) Cream had their big breakthrough success in the US with the platinum albums *Disraeli Gears* (November 1967) and *Wheels of Fire* (August 1968).

(2) They do, though, have some fun with an image of Jethro Tull's Ian Anderson. But Tull were never quite heavy rock or heavy blues. Mention should also be made of John Mayall, Free and Peter Green's Fleetwood Mac who were all popular in the UK and Europe, but less so in the US.

(3) By coincidence Dummer hailed from Surbiton, Surrey... was Cohn thinking of him when he made his comment?

(4) Material by Tony McPhee, Jo-Ann Kelly and Dave Kelly can be found strewn across at least 10 sampler albums released between 1966 and 1969, mainly on the Liberty label. The purpose of such releases, which were assembled from demo tapes and sessions, was to give early exposure to acts and singers who might then move on to a proper deal of their own.

(5) Dean, 28, was a busy man in 1972, doing 13 intricately designed album sleeves. A generic designer, he had originally specialised in furniture and architecturally related projects. He moved into doing album sleeves after earning £5,000 (about £163,000 today) for the cover of *Gun*, by the band Gun, in late 1968.

(6) The final Dummer recordings were eventually released in 2008, as *The Lost 1973 Album*.

(7) For an account of Gibson's career, during which he was active in many areas of the arts, see his Guardian obituary at https://www. theguardian.com/music/2021/jun/30/peter-gibson-obituary?fbc lid=IwAR3F4ohmvNAN5yg19dn6PchU85B8ZmTP3Orm0WDil YVYwX6x20N0S7Ju0qI Sadly, he died shortly before he could be interviewed for this book.

(8) Orange Studios had been started by Cliff Cooper in 1968, and was equipped with Joe Meek's former mixing desk, acquired when Meek's effects were auctioned off. Cooper also ran Orange Records who released a string of singles from 1969 through to 1974.

(9) Blue Goose and its sister label, Yazoo, were run by Nick Perls, a New York-based enthusiast for country blues purists, who rereleased rare recordings by Blind Lemon Jefferson, Son House and many others. Graham Hine did a second solo album, *Bowery Fantasy*, for Blue Goose in 1976.

(10) Thomas, who recorded nothing after 1929, and whose date of death is unknown, was highly regarded by the blues cognoscenti, with Bob Dylan, The Lovin' Spoonful, John Martyn and The Grateful Dead all covering his work. He also appears to have been the originator of the 1968 Canned Heat hit *Going Up the Country*, so recording one of his tunes may have seemed quite a smart way to get a hit single.

(11) King signed 10cc to UK the same month that he licensed *Seaside Shuffle*. Commercially, they would be his most successful act with an album and 5 singles (including *Rubber Bullets*, a No 1) in the Top 30 through to 1974. Apart from promoting material released by himself under various pseudonyms – Shag, Bubblerock and One Hundred Ton and a Feather – UK also enjoyed success with First Class, Lobo and Carl Malcolm and was responsible for early releases by Gerald Thomas (GT) Moore and the Kursaal Flyers.

(12) See https://www.youtube.com/watch?v=Kunth54ZsVE The band also promoted the song on *Crackerjack* (a BBC kiddies teatime show) on 9 February 1973. The Jawbone Jug Band, as distinct from Jawbone, a completely different group, had played alongside Brett Marvin and the Thunderbolts at Studio 51 in 1971, releasing a couple of singles on the B&C label, including a cover of *Jailhouse Rock*, during this time.

(13) See http://www.brettmarvin.co.uk/taffy.htm

(14) There appear to have been quite a few covers of Lewie's songs released in Europe, particularly in Germany where *Stop the Cavalry* was reworked as *Das Lied von der Bundeswehr*, in the style of an oompah band. See: https://www.youtube.com/watch?v=ioJoHecGpM4

(15) See the entry for Paul Dobbs (Mahogany drummer) in *The International Who's Who in Popular Music 2002*, edited by Andy Gregory p233 and comments by Steve Darrington 6 July 2019, at https://m.facebook.com/groups/swanagebluesfest/posts/944511929345763/

(16) For just one example, see the LPs by The Shower Room Squad at https://www.discogs.com/artist/1168516-The-Shower-Room-Squad The 70s, of course, were also a time of phenomenal mainstream popularity for Benny Hill and Robin Askwith sex comedies as well as being a period when strippers were common in pubs, many of which were the same that put on live music.

(17) See *Mojo* magazine interview with Brian James (*Mojo* 225, August 2012).

(18) A comment attributed to Clarke at: https://m.facebook.com/fasteddieclarke10/photos/young-eddie-clarke-with-curtis-knight-zeus-he-always-said-it-wasnt-easy-working-/2332927383383947/

(19) For more on this see https://www.ronnielane.com/ronnie-lanes-mobile-studio-lms.html

(20) Footage of Sandra Barry and The Boys, recorded for *Pathe News*, can be seen at https://www.youtube.com/watch?v=IibayurVJXw

(21) Both returned in 1979 as members of the electronic pop act Darling. Barry also essayed a film career in France through to the mid-80s.

(22) See *The Bridge House, Canning Town: Memories of a Legendary Rock and Roll Hangout* Terence Murphy 2007 p7-8.

DAVE KELLY

(JOHN DUMMER'S BLUES BAND, TRAMP, ROCK SALT, DOGS)

I'd seen The Rolling Stones and the Downliners Sect at Studio 51, which was run by a couple of women, Pat and Vi. When John Dummer's Blues Band started, Bob Glass, the partner of my sister Jo-Ann, suggested we ask them for a gig, and they agreed. We ended up doing a Sunday residency there. Brian Shepherd signed us to Mercury and our managers, Olly and Tommy Vaughan, put us on a retainer. I can't remember how much it was, probably more than you got for sweeping the roads and far more enjoyable!

We did a lot of live work including tours with various blues legends as their backing band. I remember a gig at The Red Lion, Leytonstone where everything went wrong for us, amps blowing up, tuning problems and so on. The promoter refused to pay us, and said we *were the worst band in the world*. We bumped into him again a couple of years later, at The Toby Jug, Tolworth where we were supporting John Lee Hooker. He asked us to do a set of our own as a warm-up, and we refused, reminding him what he'd called us! Later we toured with Howlin' Wolf. Lee Brilleaux of the Feelgoods used to say that what originally inspired him was seeing Howlin' Wolf at a gig in Romford in the late 60s. We were the backing band that day. A bit ironic really.

I left John Dummer in 1969. We'd just come back from Scandinavia. It was July and I had a long-planned holiday. They wanted me to cancel it and do another string of dates. I refused and went on holiday instead, recommending Nick Pickett as my replacement. After that I was involved with a studio band, Tramp. This had Bob Hall, Bob Brunning, Mick Fleetwood and Danny Kirwan. We did a couple of albums. As well as this, sister

Jo-Ann and I played the folk clubs, and knew people like The Dubliners.

Later I was in a country rock outfit called Rock Salt, with Thump Thompson, Pete Miles, Cedric Thorose and Keith Nelson. We took our name from the bluegrass song *Rock Salt and Nails*. We did quite a few gigs and Mainman, who had David Bowie and Dana Gillespie, were interested in signing us. They paid for some demos. We did 4 tracks, but nothing got released and the band broke up.

Then, because *Nine by Nine* had been a big hit in Europe, the John Dummer Band reformed. But Nick Pickett was advised against rejoining, and opted for a solo career, so they asked me to come back. We did a couple of albums, recording them at Rockfield. It was a nice arrangement, living there and working at the same time. I can remember coming down one morning and finding Dave Edmunds slumped over the mixing desk fast asleep. He was doing the music for the film *Stardust* at that point and working through the night on it! The second album had Pick Withers on drums because John Dummer wasn't around much, as well as Colin Earl from Mungo Jerry and Graham Bond. Vertigo paid for it, but didn't release it and the Oobleedooblee Band, as it was called by that point, just kind of fizzled out.

Around 1975 I got together with Wilgar Campbell, Rory Gallagher's drummer, and formed Dogs. Wilgar lived near me in Streatham, and we just thought let's do some pub gigs. The other members were George Currie and Thump Thompson, who was depping at that point with Rocky Sharpe and the Razors.

We had a bluesy, rocky set and were just playing live. I didn't earn my living playing music. I would do a few solo gigs in folk clubs, but at one point I was driving a laundry van as my day job. My wife worked as a teacher and we had two young kids. But I kept playing and eventually Keith Nelson recommended me to Tom McGuinness and I joined The Blues Band.

I enjoyed this period. I was in my mid-20s and there were a lot of good bands around: Chilli Willi and the Red Hot Peppers, Brinsley Schwarz, Bees Make Honey, Roogalator and, of course, Dr Feelgood.

MO WITHAM

(THE FINGERS, LEGEND)

When I was 10 years old, a neighbour who played and taught me guitar gave me two EPs. One was by Big Bill Broonzy, the other was by Django Reinhardt. He said, *'learn to play like that'*. I played them to death and fell in love with both of them.

Eventually I joined The Orioles, Mickey Jupp's band. We were supporting Lulu at the Cricketers, Southend some time in 1965. I was asked if I would be interested in joining her band, The Luvvers, but learned later on that she didn't like the tattoos on my hands, so I didn't get the job! The Orioles actually had an audition with Tony Hatch at one point. He was producing The Searchers and Petula Clark at the time and was interested. Mickey was supposed to attend a recording session in London, but didn't go. He never explained why. We were very popular around Southend and had a manager for a while, but discovered that he was taking more money than he should have, so we dumped him. I didn't record anything with Mickey until Legend were formed.

When I joined The Fingers, they were already signed with EMI where Peter Eden was a resident producer. We would record at Abbey Road a couple of times a month, usually a Geoff Stephens song. Unfortunately, the band wasn't writing much at the time, so we were totally at the mercy of Pete and his associates to record their songs. We did, but none of them were hits. Our gigs at the Cliffs Pavilion, Westcliff were great. There would be three bands. A top touring group (like The Move), ourselves and another support act. We really held our own on those nights. We did a lot of work in those days and consequently were very tight. Our act was very much like The Lovin' Spoonful. We split after doing a couple of months in Germany playing in Frankfurt and Cologne, after which I got married, and lived in a flat in Balmoral Road, Southend, with my wife and son. I didn't touch a guitar for years. I wasn't interested in the Doughnut Ring.

In the meantime, Mickey started another band, Legend, with Chris East and a couple of others. I wasn't involved with it, until one day he knocked on my door and wanted me to join. We recorded 'Georgia George' with Robin Trower producing and B J Wilson (Procol Harum) on drums in a little studio on Denmark Street. That was fun, although I got electrocuted using an American Fender amp that wasn't earthed. Apart from that, it was great!

David Knights, the former bass player with Procol Harum, was Legend's manager. He dealt with Vertigo. We weren't privy to the details. He paid me £10 per week and told me that I needed to stick with Mickey as he needed me. He said we would have several bass players and drummers but I needed to stick with Juppy. I had a lot of catching up to do as shortly afterwards we were rehearsing for the Red Boot Album. That was a serious wakeup call when I realised that Tony Visconti was producing it and engineer of the year Eddie Offord was in the chair! Visconti mixed it. We weren't invited as he didn't get on with Mickey. After listening to the album now, I wish I hadn't stopped playing. My playing was not good.

We did several universities around the country and went down well. The only problem was that Mickey refused to play any of the Red Boot Album that we were promoting! When we were asked by the social secretaries to play some of the songs, Mickey said, 'we only play Rock 'n' Roll' which is probably why it didn't sell. However, Moonshine was a different deal. We had total control over the album with freedom to choose the songs and the arrangements. It was a wonderful experience, even Mickey enjoyed it. We mixed it as well. Great!

The end came when we were offered a new deal by CBS. We had a meeting with Maurice Oberstein who said that he had been watching our progress and was impressed with Mickey's songwriting. He offered us a 5-year contract with a £100,000 advance. Mickey said, 'I just want to play Rock 'n' Roll and darts in the pub in Southend.'

I looked at David... he looked at Mickey... and I left the band. Legend was no more.

After that I decided to work as a session player. I was working with John Kongos who had his own studio in the basement of his house. I did many sessions there with lots of different producers. I also worked for some Christian publishers doing an album every week in a studio in Eastbourne. I did a single with Cliff Richard at Abbey Road called 'My Kinda Life' composed by Chris East. It was a top ten hit and we performed with him on Top of the Pops. I worked with Mike Vernon on some blues albums with black American artists that he would bring from America. He was probably the best producer that I worked with. Eventually, I married Kellie who wrote her own songs which we recorded in several studios. We were working with Suzi Quatro, I played guitar, Kellie as a backing vocalist. We did a couple of world tours with her over a period of 9 years. I did a few years with Chris Farlowe which was great.

In 1977 I was asked to join Dr Feelgood when Wilko left, but to be honest, I didn't want to tour for eleven months of the year playing the same thing. They offered me £25,000, a new house on Canvey and 3% royalties, but Kellie had just given birth to our son and I just didn't want to tour.

I believe that Mickey, Gary Brooker and other similar musicians established R'n'B as a style in the south east, and were responsible for many of the bands that followed. To work with Mickey was two-fold. His songwriting, piano and guitar playing and his voice were, and still are, second to none. But he is a nightmare to work for. He's rarely happy with his band. In those days he would throw his guitar across the stage, or attack the piano. He would run away to Bath or Cumbria and not turn up for gigs. But this is quite normal behaviour for people as gifted as him.

There were great times, though.

DOWN BY THE JETTY

For a couple of years in the mid-70s, Southend-on-Sea, and its various satellite towns, were regarded by many in the UK music industry as being the centre of a new sound. A trio of bands – Dr Feelgood, the Kursaal Flyers and Eddie and The Hot Rods – seemed to be sweeping everything before them and were, week after week, the subject of laudatory gig reviews and admiring multi-page spreads across the trade press. Their authenticity, accessibility, ruggedness, 'no nonsense' playing style and sharp, streetwise image were much admired. When it came, and for most people it came when Dr Feelgood's third album, *Stupidity*, reached No 1 in the autumn of 1976, it confirmed everything that had been said about them, their material and the venues they played over the preceding years. It was a full, and ringing, endorsement of the centrality of pub-rock, for all those who might have had doubts.

A trickier question, and one not really put, was why Southend? Or, if Southend, why not somewhere else as well? Were there other places, across the UK, producing tight, aggressive music circa 1975? Is it possible that there were, and time has just washed away all trace of them? If there were, we have yet to find them. When considering the Feelgoods, the Rods and the Flyers, the first thing to acknowledge is that they didn't emerge fully formed from a vacuum. Whilst Southend and its surroundings were fertile soil for young (or youngish) musicians seeking to start a band and make a decent living, the area also had distinct advantages that other places lacked.

Firstly, there was its proximity to London. With the city only 42 miles away, commuting was feasible and people didn't have to 'move down/up to London' like they did everywhere else. Rather, for 40 years after 1945, much of London moved out to Essex. A new town, with a population eventually in excess of 100,000, was built at Basildon and the routes into Southend would eventually be packed full of major developments at places like Brentwood, Billericay, Wickford, Rayleigh and Canvey Island. Especially Canvey Island, with its oil refineries. There was a lot of employment here, added to which the proximity of Tilbury Docks was analogous to that of Liverpool with its waterfront. In both places the crew of returning boats brought US records back with them.

Secondly, being adjacent to London, and on the coast, meant that Southend and its surroundings were full of hotels, ballrooms, enormous nineteenth-century public houses and theatres, which continued, despite the growth in continental holidays, to fulfil a role as London's seaside. A place for cheap holidays, day trips and weekends away. Millions went there every year. It was to London what Coney Island and Atlantic City, New Jersey were to New York. And bigger than both as well, with a population of 183,000 against 38,000 (Atlantic City) and 25,000 (Coney Island).[1] Thus, like any large provincial town, Southend was big enough to have its own identity, but where it really scored was in its closeness and shared culture with London, which gave it a vibrancy and scale you wouldn't have found elsewhere.

Thirdly, because it was a place people came to be entertained, live music was always being performed there. By the early 60s it had a huge mod scene, as big as Brighton's, with hundreds of scooters parked outside dance halls on a Saturday night. An array of local groups developed, playing mainly in Southend but also venturing as far into London as Romford and Canning Town and as far out into Essex as Chelmsford and Maldon. There were plenty of places to play. As well as the big ballrooms and function rooms, there were youth clubs, church halls, established music venues (where the headlining act would be a band with a recording contract, and the Southend group would be the 'support') and pubs, pubs, pubs.[2]

The first band to emerge locally, in late 1963, were The Paramounts. After which came Force Five, from Canvey Island and The Cops 'N Robbers, actually from Hatfield, but big in

Southend. Mention should also be made of The Golden Apples of
the Sun and The Powerpack, both of which featured drummer and
ex-pro footballer Bobby Harrison. Finally, there were The Fingers,
formed in 1966 by the remnants of The Orioles after that group's
leader, Mickey Jupp, had been imprisoned for failing to maintain
alimony payments. So far, so like any UK town during the 'beat
boom' years. All sizeable urban areas then had at least a couple of
bands that made it on to vinyl. But Southend had other aces up
its sleeve. Unlike most of its provincial rivals it was also home to
two of the 60s' most significant songwriters and producers, Geoff
Stephens and Peter Eden.[3]

Stephens, whose parents owned a bed and breakfast hotel
in Westcliff-on-Sea, was in many respects a pretty conventional
Tin Pan Alley operator, albeit one with the useful gift of writing
massive international hits. His solo credits included *The Crying
Game* and *Winchester Cathedral*, the latter a US No 1 for The New
Vaudeville Band, and so successful that it was covered by Sinatra.
With John Carter, Les Reed and Tony Macaulay respectively, he co-
wrote *Semi-Detached, Suburban Mr James*, a brilliant faux Dylan hit
for Manfred Mann, *There's a Kind of Hush*, for Herman's Hermits
and, for Scott Walker, *Lights of Cincinatti*. In terms of record sales,
he peaked in the mid-70s with David Soul, and although gone
from the area by then he could still be spotted driving around
town in his Rolls-Royce. Further, until Mickie Most took over,
Stephens and his colleague Peter Eden co-produced Donovan's
early hits, and despite their association with an awful lot of very
straight, route-one 'pop', both retained an interest in innovative,
high-quality music.[4] Locally, they were closely associated with
groups like The Cops 'N Robbers, whom Eden managed, and The
Fingers.[5] Eden, from Hadleigh, had originally been a musician
backing actor-singer Mike Sarne. When this came to an end,
he helped run one of the area's top venues, the Studio Club, at
Westcliff-on-Sea.

Finally, unlike many other towns and cities outside London,
Southend had its own immensely well-connected booking agent:
Barry Collings. Operating out of a semi-detached Edwardian
house in Claremont Road, Westcliff-on-Sea, at various times

Collings acted as sole agent for Elkie Brooks, Legend (whom he recommended with 'Here's something different. Legend led by composer Mickey Jupp in what can only be described as a cross between Bob Dylan, Johnny Cash and Jerry Lee Lewis') and, interestingly, a pre-Brinsley Schwarz Kippington Lodge. A national figure, he found his huge roster of acts every type of live work... pubs, clubs, colleges, cabaret and package tours. Clearly, if you were in a band based in Southend in the 60s and 70s you didn't need to travel far to get access to the upper levels of the music industry. A bus trip to Westcliff-on-Sea would suffice. With Collings, Eden and Stephens in town anyone competent and determined might pick up quite a lot of gigs and, eventually, release a record.[6]

It was from these substantial foundations that Procol Harum emerged in May 1967. Though not initially a Southend band, their original line-up included Gary Brooker from The Paramounts and Bobby Harrison from The Powerpack. By March 1969 repeated changes had revised this to Brooker, BJ Wilson, Robin Trower and Chris Copping, the same membership The Paramounts had circa 1962-63.[7] Despite being authentic rock stars with significant touring and recording obligations, like Stephens and Eden, Brooker and his colleagues remained connected to their hometown. Part of that connection included an admiration for Mickey Jupp, long regarded as the most outstanding prospect locally, a man who could sing, play guitar and piano, and – unusually then – write his own material.

Given the colossal sales enjoyed by A Whiter Shade of Pale, Homburg and Procol's first couple of albums, Peter Eden briefly entertained the idea of floating another 'Southend supergroup', via an amalgamation of Force Five and The Fingers. Known as The Crocheted Doughnut Ring, this band gave birth to one of the greatest non-hits of the era, Maxine's Parlour, on the Deram label in March 1968. A gorgeous, slow, elegant ballad, despite an appearance on Dee Time it went nowhere in the UK.[8] Maxine's Parlour was written by Bill Fay, another of Eden's artists, and one for whom record collectors now die.

As with The Crocheted Doughnut Ring, few people back then bought Fay's brilliant debut single, Some Good Advice, and fewer

still either of his albums. For Eden, this was scarcely the point:
he was interested in the music, and the higher the quality, no
matter how rarefied the record-buying public might find it, the
better. British jazz was another field he excelled in, and from the
late 60s he produced many highly sought after albums by John
Surman, Mike Gibbs, Mike Westbrook, Mike Osborne, Norma
Winstone and Alan Skidmore. All sold poorly, but vinyl editions
of them are now immensely valuable. In 1970, being all of 27 years
old, he scaled back his chores, opening a record store on London
Road, Southend.[9] Among the commitments he maintained were
production work for Sonet, where he produced Brett Marvin and
Heron, a folk-rock band led by Gerald Moore.[10]

All the key participants in the later Southend groups – people
like John Martin, Wilko Johnson, Mickey Jupp, Will Birch, Graeme
Douglas, Vic Collins, Lew Lewis and John Higgs – arose from this
shifting pool of musicians who constantly formed, dissolved and
reassembled around various bands from the early 60s onwards.
Like Procol Harum they shared the consensus that Mickey Jupp
was the man most likely to make it, despite his somewhat peculiar
attitude towards his own career. A perfectionist, who claimed
to have bought no records after 1961, Jupp had no particular
ambition beyond wanting to play good music, and by 1965, had
already avoided committing himself to deals with Decca and Tony
Hatch.[11] After his release from prison, he spent a few weeks in
1967 rehearsing with Robin Trower for a postulated blues group
that never got off the ground. (As did John Wilkinson aka Wilko
Johnson; Trower opted instead to join Procol Harum.) After
which he lived out of the area in Bath, writing songs and sticking
to a day job. The songs led to a publishing deal, however, which
in turn led to a contract with Bell and the formation of his next
group, Legend.

The earliest publicity photos for the band, taken in late 1968,
show Jupp and his colleagues, Chris East (guitar), Steve Geere
(bass) and Nigel Dunbar (drums), looking amazingly unlike any of
their contemporaries. No long hair, no kaftans, no beards, bells,
tie-dye t-shirts, greatcoats or granny glasses, they resemble instead
extras from *Performance* or *The Italian Job*. A debut single, *National*

Gas, appeared in February 1969, followed by an LP, *Legend*. Neither sold. The single had a tight, unique sound that would have taken listeners, used to Led Zeppelin, Ten Years After et al, by surprise. Reviews of the album noted its reliance on acoustic instruments (a double bass and a 12-string guitar were used) with comments that the end result was like a *'cross between Country Joe, Fairport and the Spoonful'* (*Melody Maker* 8 March 1969). To be honest, today it doesn't sound much like Fairport Convention, though there are similarities to The Lovin' Spoonful. The clue to its sound probably lies with producer Sandy Robertson, who in 1969-70 recorded Robin Scott, Keith Christmas and Shelagh McDonald using musicians from Mighty Baby to back all three. The tenor here, then, is rocky and folky rather than bluesy as well as being exceptionally well played. *Legend* is part of that canon, a route English music could have taken had it not been knocked off course by glam as represented by Bolan, Slade and Bowie, circa 1971-72.[12] Prior to that, though, and after just one appearance, a promotional event for Bell on a barge on the Thames, the group disbanded.

At this point, his admirers rode to the rescue. Dave Knights, who had just left Procol Harum, became his manager and Robin Trower produced a second single for Bell with BJ Wilson on drums, Matthew Fisher on bass and ex-Oriole Mo Witham on second guitar.[13] The outcome was *Georgia George*, which appeared to equally little effect in October 1969. Every bit as good as *Spirit of Woodstock* and *I Hear You Knocking*, it preceded both and had a very tight electric country boogie sound that sounds remarkably like Edmunds's hit.

This time Jupp persisted. By January 1970 another version of Legend had taken shape with Witham, John Bobin (bass, and like Witham formerly one of The Fingers) and Bill Fifield (drums).[14] Even better, the new line-up started gigging regularly. After an early show backing Billy Fury at the Country Club, Haverstock Hill[15] they appeared on the premier BBC music show, *Disco 2*, on 1 May 1970, played most of the pub venues around the London circuit, as well as colleges, the 100 Club, and even the Winter Gardens, Cleethorpes.

Knights worked hard as their manager and secured a deal with Vertigo, with Tony Visconti producing. A debut single, *Life*, appeared in November 1970, followed by an album, *Legend*. Despite fair reviews ('A *light-hearted, casual attempt to recreate the sounds of the late 50s and early 60s... Quite pleasant and nostalgic, but hardly distinctive; an hour after I'd played it, I could not recall a single number' Melody Maker* 6 February 1971), it didn't sell. On the other hand, interest in the group was strong amongst fellow musicians. Dave Edmunds wanted Witham and Fifield for Rockpile, which both declined, though Fifield did eventually quit when he joined T. Rex after getting a better offer from Marc Bolan.[16] Quickly replaced by Bob Clouter, another ex-Oriole and also once of The Fingers, the new line-up did a John Peel session in March 1971, with a follow-up single, *Don't You Never*, appearing the same month. Like its predecessors, it didn't chart.

For their second Vertigo album, *Moonshine*, Matthew Fisher did the string arrangements, after which some degree of commercial success finally came their way. *Life*, a slowish, bluesy ballad with a quasi-operatic treatment, became a hit in Italy, reaching No 12. They toured there and lost a lot of money. When the LP failed to sell too, Clouter left and when Jupp famously, and unilaterally, turned down a stupendous deal with CBS, the group broke up.

After this Jupp worked as a duo with harmonica player Frank Mead,[17] a project that gradually morphed into The Mickey Jupp Big Band, a 10-piece outfit that began playing the London pub rock scene in July 1975. Led by Mead, now on saxophone, this had horn players, backing vocalists, keyboards, Bob Clouter back on drums and singer Bob Fish, from Rochford. Jupp's role here was writing the material and anchoring the sound on rhythm guitar. During a busy ten months, both The 101ers and The Sex Pistols appeared as their support band and they also did a couple of sessions with Peter Eden for Sonet, two tracks of which eventually appeared on a sampler LP, *Southend Rock*, in 1979. As an exercise in obscurity, it couldn't have been bettered. Released as a benefit record for the Billericay Hospital Burns Unit, few people bought it.

In many ways, The Mickey Jupp Big Band, like Martin Stone's Jive Bombers, were an absolutely typical pub-rock ensemble.

Extraordinarily entertaining, not costing much to see, accessible via your local pub or college, they worked up a good reputation, got some decent reviews... and then vanished before very much (if anything) could be committed to vinyl. After they broke up in May 1976, Fish joined Darts and Clouter became Lew Lewis's drummer. Once again Jupp's friends came to his rescue: this time he was offered a publishing contract by Gary Brooker and Keith Reid at £30 per week, a significant sum in 1976, and one which allowed him to concentrate on music full-time. He eventually reemerged, on Stiff, in 1978. Much was made of Jupp's waywardness both before and after 1976, and he certainly turned down a number of deals that might have brought him considerably more wealth and fame than he subsequently accrued. But he was no Syd Barrett. By and large he kept playing live throughout, even as a solo act at local folk clubs in the Southend area, honing his songwriting and searching for ways to do something on his terms. Between 1969 and 1983 he released 7 albums and 14 singles on major labels, securing as he did so his place in UK musical history, whilst never becoming a household name.

In their final stages Legend often appeared with Dr Feelgood as their support act. Like their contemporaries, Dr Feelgood had origins back in the mid-60s, though the initial version of the group – Lee Brilleaux (vocals and harmonica), Wilko Johnson (guitar), John Sparks (bass) and Terry Howarth (drums) – didn't come together until the spring of 1971 when they secured a Sunday residency at The Railway Hotel, Pitsea. Acquiring Chris Fenwick, a 19-year-old TV actor, as their manager they did some gigs in Holland (apparently Fenwick told promoters they were 'a famous UK band') after which they were approached by Heinz, an early 60s pop star seeking to capitalise on the rock and roll revival circuit, and asked to act as his backing band. When Howarth, a former bandsman, opted to rejoin the army, John Martin ('the Figure'), who had been in an unsigned teenage R'n'B act, The Roamers, with Johnson back in 1964 was quickly drafted in as his replacement.[18]

Adding a keyboards player, John Potter, they appeared with Heinz at the August 1972 London Rock and Roll Show, Sparks noting, '*I remember we shared a dressing room with Gary Glitter, who we hadn't heard of at that time, and we were next door to Little Richard. We also bumped into Chuck Berry, standing next to his Rolls-Royce; he was filming all the goings on backstage. He autographed Wilko's Telecaster. We had a hard time on stage, because the monitors weren't working. We'd played a small club the night before to about 100 people, so it was a big jump to play to 80,000 at Wembley Stadium. We were promised £25 for the gig, but never received it... But I remember that Bo Diddley was great!*' [19] The arrangements with Heinz included appearing at the Kursaal Ballroom, Southend on 23 September 1972 with Screaming Lord Sutch, The Flamin' Groovies and Shakin' Stevens and the Sunsets, a significant gig and one much less remarked on than the Wembley show. But they ceased shortly afterwards – it was never going to be a permanent thing – and with Potter also leaving, the classic line up of Brilleaux, Johnson, Sparks and Martin emerged. They made their debut on the London pub circuit on Wednesday 11 July 1973 at The Lord Nelson on the Holloway Road, and built their reputation slowly and steadily thereafter.

A year of hard work followed, not least because the band were all still part-timers at this point: Johnson a schoolteacher, Sparks a bricklayer and Brilleaux a solicitor's clerk. A critical factor in their rise was a change of image. Photos of the band in 1972-73 show them looking very typical for that period: longish hair, denims, generally scruffy. By the start of 1974 this had changed to shorter hair and the kind of crumpled, faux smart business suits worn by bouncers, bookmakers and the owners of seedy nightclubs. In photographs they project back at the camera a studied indifference with overtones of menace. They were not considering the cosmos, nor were they joking amongst themselves in the self-deprecating way 'good-time' country-rock bands were supposed to do. This new look was the kind of 'look' that was common in TV crime dramas of the period. Perhaps we should note, by way of a possible explanation for this switch, that their manager, Chris Fenwick, made appearances in *Villains*, *Dixon of Dock Green* and *Softly, Softly* as well as the June 1973 reboot of *Jack the Ripper* in which DCS Barlow and DCI Watt attempt to solve the Whitechapel murders. [20] It also meant that the band were identifying with how a great many working-class men still dressed. A kind of deliberately unfashionable, and yet fashionable, chic that set them apart from the vagaries of teenage fashion and the conventions of the music industry. The message that came across was: these are serious grown-ups. Their music complemented this perfectly: sharp, well-drilled and unpretentious. And they now had a stage act too. Guitarist Johnson in a black suit manically walking back and forth like a psychotic about to pick a fight (most pubs had one then) whilst vocalist Brilleaux, in a white suit, hand in pocket, smoked between verses and blasts of harmonica.

The gigging, the well-drilled set and the change of image worked. They signed to United Artists in June 1974, and immediately went out on tour with Brinsley Schwarz and Dave Edmunds. Surviving an attempt by the band Sparks to poach Johnson (he declined, and Sparks opted instead for Trevor White; as a result, we never got to hear Wilko's take on *Never Turn Your Back on Mother Earth*),[21] United Artists booked them into Rockfield. Here, with Vic Maile producing, and Kingsley Ward as main engineer, they began assembling their debut album.[22] Further recordings took place at Jacksons in Rickmansworth with the last couple of the 14 tracks being done live at Dingwalls.

Whilst this was underway, *ZigZag* 45 (September 1974), in a lengthy piece headed *Canvey Island Rock*, noted approvingly, '*instead of blowing their advances on a 3-ton van and a prestige 'limo', they've bought a coach and fitted it with bunks, tables and an enlarged boot for equipment as well as recruiting... a demon driver from Canvey bus station*' before concluding, '*these guys... mostly look like androids on amphetamine*'. To promote their November 1974 debut single, *Roxette*, the flipside of which was the ubiquitous *Route 66*, they went on tour with Hawkwind, but insufficient copies were sold to get anywhere near the charts. Nevertheless, United Artists' Head of A&R Andrew Lauder believed, correctly as it turned out, that the band could still break through into the mainstream market. It was all quite logical as he confirmed some years later, '*In a sense the pub bands were straitjacketed by their success in London and it was very difficult getting people out of town interested in them... We had* Down By The Jetty *in the can and really believed the Feelgoods could do it if they had the right exposure. So, putting them on alongside two other really good bands, with none of them saddled with the ultimate responsibility of pulling in the crowds? That was what we'd now call a no-brainer.'* [23]

What he devised to meet these requirements was the Naughty Rhythms Tour, which kicked off on 11 January 1975 showcasing Dr Feelgood alongside Kokomo and Chilli Willi and the Red Hot Peppers. It was an interesting combination, and not necessarily one that would have occurred to most people. Kokomo, like the Feelgoods, were new kids on the block, whereas the Peppers were on their second album without yet achieving commercial success. Each were with a different label. One wonders if part of Lauder's initiative was down to simple economic circumstances... spreading the cost of touring for three bands that weren't selling in huge amounts. Whatever the intention, the gigs were memorable, as anyone who saw one will readily admit. There were attempts to record it for posterity and the BBC filmed them all at Plymouth Guildhall on 2 February 1975, but sadly the tapes appear to have been either wiped or lost. The consensus was that, if anyone did well out of the tour, it was Dr Feelgood. They recorded a John Peel session on 10 February, and released their album, *Down By the Jetty*, together with a second single, *She Does it Right*, a few weeks later. An appearance on *The Old Grey Whistle Test* (14 March 1975) occurred to promote both events.

Sadly, the critics were hardly ecstatic. Even *ZigZag*, usually strong supporters, considered it *'must inevitably remain a second-best alternative to seeing them 'live'. That's not to put the album down, however, it just emphasises how good they are onstage and how difficult it is to capture the essence of rock 'n' roll on vinyl'.*[24] The response in the US was particularly poor, with United Artists happy to drop the band.[25] Back home some thought the decision to record everything in mono was being overly reverential towards the recent past. Others thought the songwriting a bit pedestrian, which, given Johnson authored 9 of the tracks, including the single, was clearly not ideal. The album's non-Johnson tunes included John Lee Hooker (*Boom Boom*), Larry Williams (*Bony Moronie*), *Tequila*, Mickey Jupp's *Cheque Book*, and, in a homage to Johnson's other guitar hero Mick Green, *Oyeh*, a November 1964 instrumental by The Dakotas. Where a consensus developed was that Maile had done a good job at conveying their high-energy approach, and the monochrome album sleeve, with its shot of them on the waterfront at Canvey, captured their essence.

Fortunately, as Lauder had intended, the tour definitely increased their audience, and they came out of it a headlining act. A month later *ZigZag* carried a multi-page interview with Johnson, who concurred with Lauder's views about the limitations of pub-rock, '*We can't go on forever doing what we were doing, which is just one-nighters all over, because it brings you down bad, the work's so hard, and you go out night after night, and give yourself totally, and there's no real kind of end in sight, just gigs stretching on for infinity. It's not really very healthy... it's a great situation at first, and then it gradually turns around*'.

By now, though, they were on an up, appearing on Granada TV's *Rock on with 45* on 20 July 1975 and releasing their next single, *Back in the Night*, shortly afterwards. A second album, *Malpractice*, came out in October 1975, and this time it did sell, reaching No 17 in the UK. They produced half of it themselves and the material was still a mixture of originals (6 tracks, all written or co-written by Johnson) and 5 covers with Bob Andrews from Brinsley Schwarz around to assist on a couple. It was all terribly well done, and contemporary opinion was that this was a better set than their debut. In some ways, the fact that a thuggish-looking band playing a significant number of R'n'B covers could chart at all said more about the changing mores of UK music at this point than the actual level of success *Malpractice* achieved: the tectonic plates were starting to shift.[26]

To promote it they toured with GT Moore and the Reggae Guitars as their support, after which they finally visited the US. Here they got to play with Journey in Detroit, The Ramones in New York and Bad Company in San Francisco, a somewhat random selection, though the two nights at the Bottom Line, Greenwich Village with The Ramones sound fun. Nothing else appeared until the release of their third album, *Stupidity*, in September 1976. Recorded live in Sheffield, Southend and Aylesbury it came with a free single, *Riot in Cell Block No 9*. Out of the 15 tracks, 8 were covers (by the usual suspects, Chuck Berry, The Coasters,

Solomon Burke, Bo Diddley, Sonny Boy Williamson, Rufus Thomas) and 7 Johnson originals, one co-written with a renascent Mick Green. The choice of material, band image and production values made for an interesting comparison with *Shake Some Action*, which appeared at more or less the same time. Unlike that album, though, *Stupidity* reached No 1 in the UK charts, an astonishing feat for a live set. It secured their reputation as the hottest band in the UK, with their next tour being sold-out well in advance.[27] The year ended with a sort of official validation, footage of them playing live being shown on Janet Street-Porter's London Weekend TV show *Punk Rock* on 28 November 1976. This also had The Sex Pistols, The Clash and Siouxsie Sue on display as well as an interview with the highly prescient Ron Watts.

Even at this late stage it wasn't clear who would emerge top dog. Would it be the hardened rockers from Canvey Island, or the King's Road products of McLaren and Westwood's clothes shop? Most would have backed Dr Feelgood to have had a very long and profitable career but that reckoned without the psychological factors at play within the band, and the additional pressures that kick in once success rears its head. Required to constantly produce new material, matters came to a head when a decision was taken – by Brilleaux, Martin and Sparks – to include a Lew Lewis song on *Sneakin' Suspicion*, their next album. The band had backed Lewis on his Stiff single *Boogie in the Street* in October 1976, so it looked logical enough to record one of his other songs, except Johnson was against it, and quit the group in April 1977, bringing an abrupt end to their classic line-up. When *Sneakin' Suspicion* appeared it had 10 tracks, of which 5 were by Johnson, 1 by Lewis and the rest covers. At the time Johnson's exit caused genuine shock. Looked at today one wonders why things got so strained. Did he feel marginalised? That his songwriting would gradually be reduced as a component within the group?

In the end, both parties picked themselves up, dusted themselves down and continued, with Dr Feelgood doing rather better, in commercial terms, than Johnson. *Sneakin' Suspicion* sold well, reaching No 10 in the UK. Henry McCullough was drafted in to fulfil gig obligations and a couple of months later Johnson was replaced on a more permanent basis by John Mayo. They finally had a big UK hit single in 1979 with *Milk and Alcohol*, co-written by Nick Lowe, but they never became the immense success that some predicted in the mid-70s. The band spluttered to a halt in 1982. Brilleaux reformed it in 1983 with three new recruits, and after he died in 1994, they kept going without him. They still exist now, like the Glenn Miller Orchestra, a ghost band with none of their original members. Their website, curated by Chris Fenwick from his address in Canvey Island, continues to record UK tours, the most recent of which kicked off at The Half Moon, Putney.

Dr Feelgood's longevity suggests that the music (and attitude) they offer, as a classic, stripped-down guitar band, has a deep and continuing resonance with quite a fair proportion of the public. They have rarely, if ever, deviated from this template. Which is not something you could say about the Kursaal Flyers. Like Jupp, Johnson, Witham and Martin, this band could trace its origins back to the mid-60s and consisted of some of the most experienced musicians in town. So much so that their initial line-up of Paul Shuttleworth (vocals), Vic Collins (steel guitar), Graeme Douglas (guitar), Dave Hatfield (bass), Richie Bull (banjo) and Will Birch (drums) might be considered the 70s equivalent of what Procol Harum were in the 60s: a Southend 'supergroup'.

Of these, Bull, from Corringham, started out in The Clay County Travellers, a band featured on the 1969 sampler *Britain's Third Country Music Festival Volume 2 Live!* After which he joined Natchez Trace for a couple of albums followed by a spell in the final gigging-only line-up of Mr Fox. A prolific session player he'd also recorded a solo album, *World of Country Music Volume 4*, on Decca. Hatfield had been in bluegrass act The Morris Boys 1968-69, and Vic Collins, from Benfleet, was one of The Cardboard Orchestra (great name for a band!) who put out a couple of singles on CBS, the second of which, *Nothing But a Sad Sad Song* (November 1969) is, like *Maxine's Parlour*, another example of a fine late 60s record that sold in minute amounts and is now, half a century later, hugely collectable. For their part Shuttleworth, Birch and Douglas had been in Surly Bird, a local Yes, King Crimson and Family type group playing five, six and seven minute songs with complex arrangements. Most of their gigs would be as support to visiting touring bands, with occasional forays to London.[28] They must have had some proficiency, though, because they got as far as auditioning for Tony Hall and Peter Meaden at the Fishmongers Arms, Wood Green, in October 1970. Always on the look out for talent, Meaden had started out producing The Who in 1964 before moving on to Jimmy James and The Vagabonds whilst Hall, a Radio Luxembourg DJ, had scored successes with The Locomotive and Arrival.[29] Some gigs were booked and demos recorded but nothing substantive happened, Hall preferring The Real Thing and Meaden – eventually – opting for The Steve Gibbons Band.

Taking their name from a ride at Southend's main amusement park, the new ensemble rehearsed for several months prior to doing their first live shows, in a local pub, in February 1974. After a brief hiatus when Birch quit to join Cornwall-based Charlie and the Wide Boys (he returned two weeks later) they began honing their act, offering a set of incredibly well-played country rock originals, studded with covers like *I'm a Believer*, *Route 66*, *Twenty Flight Rock* and *Six Days on the Road*. By the summer of 1974, Dr Feelgood had recommended them for a slot at The Kensington, after which things snowballed. Pete Thomas, drummer in Chilli Willi and the Red Hot Peppers, saw them. He invited Charisma's Steve Conroy to their next gig. Conroy became their manager, throwing himself into the role with some gusto, Paul Shuttleworth noting, '*He was getting us so many gigs – 5 or 6 nights per week – that it was getting silly... We'd do London gigs through the week, we couldn't go outside the Home Counties, because we all had to get home as we were almost all doing day jobs. Then at weekends we'd dash off to Liverpool or somewhere, drive back on Saturday night and sleep it off on Sunday*'.[30] At one of Conroy's bookings, the 100 Club, where Ron Watts held sway, Jonathan King caught them and signed the band to UK.

They had already started to accumulate good notices in the music press with *ZigZag* 49 (January 1975) noting their '*unlimited potential... good-humoured rapport with the audience, the same lunatic sense of theatrics*'. The following month John Peel had them in for a session after which they started a tour of Europe as support to The

Flying Burrito Brothers. Slimming down to a five piece (Hatfield dropped out and Bull switched to bass) a debut single, *Speedway*, and an album, *Chocs Away!*, appeared in July 1975. Both were produced by Hugh Murphy, who also worked with Kilburn and the High Roads around this time, but neither were hits. *Speedway*, in particular, though immaculately played and sung, was too singular a sound, with its tempo changes, steel guitar and narrated verses, to do well. But they continued to rise, with great things expected. A second John Peel session (October 1975) was followed by another single, the poppy *Hit Records* and an appearance on the Granada TV show *Look Alive* on 2 December 1975.

Whilst this was being prepared for release BBC TV filmed them on the road for an episode of *2nd House*. Unlike *Look Alive*, which went out at 4.25pm (and was aimed, like *Crackerjack*, at kiddies coming home from school), this was a flagship arts programme presented by Melvyn Bragg, and the equivalent of being canonised by the establishment. The BBC, with its immense budgets, was heavily interested in rock music at this time, following the success of Pennebaker's *Don't Look Back* which followed Dylan around the UK in 1965, and Tony Palmer's *Cream's Last Concert*. Palmer, in particular, did a lot of lengthy rock documentaries for the BBC, some of which also got a cinema release. It was a time when evening TV often screened programmes about both up-and-coming performers, like Elton John, on LWT's *Aquarius* in April 1971, or established stars like David Bowie, profiled in *Cracked Actor*, screened on BBC's *Omnibus* in January 1975. But there were also studies of the hard slog experienced by new bands out on the road, of which this was one.[31]

Bragg, wearing a white polo-neck top, introduces the programme by stating the Kursaal Flyers are *'a band tipped for success this year'* after which an explanatory narrative, over shots of the band members being picked up one by one for a drive north, confirms that their manager pays them a salary of £40 per week. We follow them in their transit van on a trip to play gigs in Aberdeen, Glasgow (where Slack Alice were support) and Middlesbrough. Over the next 80 minutes we see them drinking, smoking, preparing to go on stage, coming off stage, entertaining female admirers in their dressing room, eating takeaways, sitting in motels whilst talking and arguing amongst themselves. There's a fair amount of swearing and sexist banter (it's 1975), intercut with live footage filmed at the Marquee. No particular point is made, other than this is what being a rock musician out on the road is like, day after day: brief bursts of extreme excitement followed by long spells of mundane activity.

The film, entitled *So You Wanna Be a Rock 'n' Roll Star*, was broadcast on 21 February 1976.[32] That Bragg and the BBC put them on at all was clearly an indication of how big an act people thought they might become. It coincided with the release of their second album, *The Great Artiste*. Produced by themselves, Bob Andrews and Brinsley Schwarz helped out on one track and there was a Nick Lowe song, *Television*, in the mix too. It was a fine record with plenty of well written and well played pop songs, but once again, it didn't sell. With Jonathan King's time being taken up with recording cover versions of *Una Paloma Blanca* and *It Only Took a Minute*, the band released a third and final single on UK, *Cruisin' for Love*, in April 1976. After it flopped, they signed to CBS.

Here they were paired with Mike Batt, whose other work at that point revolved around The Wombles, the furry puppets from Wimbledon Common who racked up 7 hit singles and 3 chart albums, 1974-75. A canny producer, his credits stretched back to 1968 and included working with Groundhogs and Steeleye Span. He had a wealth of experience he could deploy, and this was shown to some advantage on their October 1976 debut single, *Little Does She Know*. Complete with an elaborate string and horn arrangement, and with less of a country-rock feel, it sold heavily. CBS also got them out gigging, with Burlesque as their support, in city halls, cinemas and universities, branding these dates the *Annual Works Outing Tour 76*. The result was a hit with the band appearing twice on *Top of the Pops* (25 November and 9 December 1976) as *Little Does She Know* reached No 14 in the UK charts.

At which point, as the second Southend-on-Sea band to break through commercially, great things were predicted. Except for one thing. As we know now, and as could be observed at close range then, things changed very suddenly at the beginning of 1977. The sales expected for their third album, *Golden Mile*, failed to materialise and, with much of the attention span of the music press suddenly taken up by punk rock, with its antics, attitude and ability to convey outrage, 'quality' pop acts like the Kursaal Flyers suddenly seemed much less interesting. Four more singles (and a live LP) appeared through 1977 but none replicated the success of *Little Does She Know* and the group broke up.

The final act to emerge, as *ZigZag* 60 put it, '*from the windswept depths of the Essex marshlands, from the bars and backstreets of Rochford*' were Eddie and The Hot Rods. Originally named Buckshee, two of their members, Lew Lewis (harmonica) and Dave Higgs (guitar), had played alongside Lee Brilleaux, Wilko Johnson and John Sparks in various unrecorded ensembles as far back as 1969. Barrie Masters (vocals), Rob Steel (bass) and Steve Nicol (drums) completed the line-up. Changing their name to Eddie and the Hot Rods, early performances were noted for displays of manic, Chicago blues harmonica from Lewis, which together with their frenetic set didn't endear them too much to promoters. Masters would later note, '*We did all the little Working Men's clubs, getting banned and thrown out from every single one. Every time we played one, there was a fight – that's just the sort of scene it is.*'

After Steel had been replaced by Paul Gray, the band's image took shape, as part 70s football hooligan (braces were on display) and part American teenage gang, with many of the trappings of the latter: bomber jackets, sunglasses, tight-waisted flared trousers and medium-length hair. Sartorially, there was nothing extreme here – certainly no fetish gear or soiled gangster suits – and musically they played very tight R'n'B with plenty of wailing harmonica. Like the Kursaal Flyers, Dr Feelgood (to whom they were younger cousins) gave them a break by recommending them for a slot at The Kensington in July 1975. Everything happened very quickly thereafter. Island signed them after seeing them at The Nashville on 7 October 1975 with The 101ers, and a debut single, *Writing on the Wall*, appeared in February 1976. They gigged heavily to promote this, an early show being at the Marquee on 12 February, with The Sex Pistols as support. It was an interesting evening with media opinion divided about the outcome. Paul Kendall (*ZigZag*) siding with Eddie and the Hot Rods and Neil Spencer (*New Musical Express*) contriving not to mention them at all.

Their next single, a cover of Sam the Sham's 1965 hit *Wooly Bully*, appeared on 25 June 1976. By this point Lewis had left, replaced on the record by Andy Mackay of Roxy Music, and with him in situ they made their TV debut on Tony Wilson's *So It Goes* on 17 July. As ever, Wilson, adept at spotting the next big thing, introduced the band as '*the hottest new band on the small club circuit, teen anthems, rhythm and blues, the Southend sound... Eddie and the Hot Rods, ladies and gentlemen*'.[33] The music was fine, and the assumptions not inaccurate. But who needed another version of an eleven-year-old Tex-Mex hit? Not many; like *Writing on the Wall*, it didn't chart.

Still, their ascent continued. After a trip to France to headline at the 1st European Punk Rock Festival, they played at Reading where they followed Nick Pickett (late of John Dummer) on the Saturday afternoon, doing a 45-minute set before giving way to Moon. The rest of the entertainment that day included solid traditional fare like Jon Hiseman's Colosseum, Manfred Mann's Earth Band, Van der Graaf Generator, Camel and Rory Gallagher. Accounts of the event record a by no means pleasant experience, two such being, '*The other memories I have are of rain (some, but not lots in 1976, as I recall), mud, lots of drunkenness (by us, and everyone else as I remember), and lots (and I mean lots) of can fights, which seemed fun at the time, but were probably actually pretty dangerous. If you got a half-full can of Watney's Red Barrel on the back of your head, you really knew about it, and several people must have come home from the festival with pretty nasty cuts and scars. The festival was moving from a friendly, hippy vibe to a drunken, laddish, almost aggro vibe*'[34] and '*The reggae acts apparently received a mixed reception, with a tinge of racism creeping into the audience response, which was unfortunate to say the least. Apparently ace drummer Sly Dunbar was nearly hit by a can, a sign of the burgeoning division and acrimony that would increasingly pervade British society and which led to the establishment of the Rock Against Racism campaign of the early 80s. For some reason, Reading had turned into "can alley", with increasing numbers of can fights – due no doubt to the tendency of larger and larger portions of the audience to render themselves semi-comatose due to massive binge drinking. Alcohol was taking over from pot smoking as the drug of preference, or people were mixing both to excess, which is never a good idea. The racist taunts were worrying as they occurred in front of an audience that should have appreciated reggae.'* [35]

John Peel was compering that day, and hugely impressed by Van der Graaf Generator. Whilst he played Eddie and the Hot Rods on his radio show, he was not initially forthcoming with any offers for a session and only seems to have concluded there was *'something afoot'* when the band's *Live at the Marquee* EP dented the singles chart a month later.[36] Consisting of four covers, *Get Out of Denver, 96 Tears, Gloria* and *Satisfaction*, it rose no higher than No 43 but got them slots on *Top of the Pops* (9 September) and *Multi-Coloured Swap Shop* (9 October), the latter a Saturday morning children's TV series presented by Noel Edmonds. The following month they released their debut album, *Teenage Depression*, and there were further TV appearances. The album, with 11 tracks (eight originals and covers of Sam Cooke, Joe Tex and The Who) was produced by Vic Maile, clearly the go-to man for Southend acts, given he was in the chair for Dr Feelgood previously and the Kursaal Flyers subsequently.[37]

The new year duly brought a February 1977 John Peel session, and in a recognition that times were changing, an image change to shorter hair, straight trousers and leather jackets. They achieved their biggest hit in August 1977 with the single *Do Anything You Wanna Do* which made No 9 and closed the year with a hit album *Life on the Line* which climbed to No 27 in the UK. After line-up changes and a label switch from Island to EMI in 1980, the band folded in 1982 without further success. Like Dr Feelgood it restarted, and like Dr Feelgood still exists today without any of the original members.

What one remembers now about 'the Southend sound' are the high-energy, manically performed hits by Dr Feelgood and Eddie and the Hot Rods and the Kursaal Flyer's elegantly written pop songs. The two former bands in particular laid down parameters that greatly simplified what audiences expected from a live band.

Great musicianship was no longer completely central: being competent and very, very tight would suffice along with a dose of attitude. This made things much easier for the punk bands that followed them.

Between them the Southend bands managed to accrue 3 hit singles and 4 hit albums between 1975 and 1979, hardly evidence of a huge musical movement. They did nothing in the US. Could they have done better had Malcolm McLaren not been on the scene? Quite possibly. And they would have lasted longer too. The fact that two of them still exist as gigging bands today clearly demonstrates their lasting appeal.

Notes

(1)   In terms of distance Southend-on-Sea is 42 miles from London. Re: proximity to New York... Atlantic City, New Jersey is 126 miles and Coney Island 22 miles

(2)   Nor was it just a question of live music. There was also a club and DJ scene, involving Chris Hill. An avid London mod in the 60s, he had a residency at a pub in Orsett from 1969 and ran soul nights at The Goldmine, Canvey Island from 1972. The latter included 40s swing music sessions (this being the era of Bette Midler and *The Rocky Horror Show*) and were hugely popular, with coachloads of adherents arriving from all over the UK. Hill also had two hit records, *Renta Santa* (1975) and *Bionic Santa* (1976), and ran a record shop in Westcliff-on-Sea at one point. See: https://nationaljazzarchive.org.uk/explore/jazz-in-essex/1277633-chris-hill

(3)   Between 1963 and 1967, The Paramounts, Force Five, The Cops 'n' Robbers, The Golden Apples of the Sun, The Powerpack and The Fingers released 19 singles and an EP. Harrison's footballing days were spent 1954-58 as a youth and reserve player at West Ham United, playing alongside Bobby Moore.

(4)   Notably their work as co-producers of protest singer Mick Softley.

(5)   Via The Cops 'n' Robbers Eden met Scottish folk singer Donovan Leitch, who had returned from busking in Europe, and was sleeping on Southend's beach whilst performing solo at the group's gigs. Eden and Stephens liked Donovan's songs, and agreed a management and production deal, that effectively launched Donovan's career.

Initially in partnership with Stephens, Eden later worked as an independent producer and adviser for Pye, EMI and Decca.

(6) Information supplied by Peter Buck, including circulars from the Barry Collings Agency dated May 1969 and March 1971.

(7) This version of the band recorded *Ain't Nothin' to Get Excited About*, an entire album of rock and roll covers at Abbey Road in September 1970 under the pseudonym Liquorice John Death and The All Stars. Not released at the time, it finally appeared in 1997.

(8) All was not lost, though, as an earlier single by the band, *Havana Anna*, reached No 11 when released in Japan in June 1968.

(9) By all accounts a very discerning establishment that Eden ran as a salon for the curious. It is fondly remembered by many. He later relocated to Leigh-on-Sea and eventually retired circa 2010.

(10) Eden produced the 1969 sampler album *Firepoint* that includes material by both Dave Kelly and GT Moore, and also produced Kelly's side project Tramp. For more on his career see an interview dated 21 February 2017 at https://www.loudersound.com/features/the-managers-that-built-prog-peter-eden

(11) For a biography of Jupp see *Hole in My Pocket: The True Legend of Mickey Jupp: The Rock and Roll Genius who Refused to be a Star* Mike Wade 2015.

(12) For more on Robertson see: https://www.goldminemag.com/columns/well-kept-secrets-sandy-robertons-uk-folk-treasure-trove

(13) Witham was rated the best guitarist to come out of Southend by Wilko Johnson.

(14) Fifield, from Hockley, had previously been in The Epics, who released 3 singles 1965-68. Two other members of The Epics later found their way into Christie, who had a massive international hit in April 1970 with *Yellow River*.

(15) The club itself was in the entrance area of a massive deep-level air raid shelter. The gig took place on 29 March 1970 when Fury was still contracted to Parlophone. At this time Barry Collings was Fury's sole booking agent, and suggested to the band, who declined, that they back Fury on a permanent basis.

(16) Where he would be known as Bill Legend and would play on 11 hit singles and 4 hit albums.

(17) For an account of Frank Mead's career see http://www.frankmead.com/fabout.html Post Jupp, Witham worked as a session player for producer John Pantry (from Leigh-on-Sea) playing on a great many

Christian folk-rock records, including Cliff Richard's March 1977 hit *My Kinda Life*, which was written by Chris East. Pantry wrote *Try a Little Sunshine*, a great 1969 psych-pop release by The Factory. Working with minor labels like Dovetail, Key, Myrrh, Gideon and Pilgrim. In an interesting comparison with Sweet Folk and Country, he produced 34 albums of religious themed folk-rock between 1972 and 1976.

(18)   Immediately prior to joining the Feelgoods, Martin drummed in a late version of 60s pop group Cupid's Inspiration. Promoter Barry Collings had acquired the rights to the names Nashville Teens, Cupid's Inspiration and The Love Affair and kept various line-ups of these working in cabaret for many years. (At one point Wilko Johnson was considered for a slot in The Love Affair.) However, as Terry Murphy noted when he booked The Nashville Teens into The Bridge House, Canning Town in 1978, '*it ended up a really disastrous night... The band were good... but they had become a cabaret band... when you're playing for money that old vibe goes and you get the same worn-out old jokes in between the songs*'.

(19)   See *Record Collector* December 2014 *Prophets from the Pub.*

(20)   The obvious comparison here would be with *The Sweeney*. But this was first broadcast in June 1974, with the series not starting until January 1975. Still, Dr Feelgood's image switch certainly caught the zeitgeist.

(21)   See *ZigZag* 51. The approach probably took place in August 1974.

(22)   Maile had previously produced Brinsley Schwarz and Man and was assisted on this by David Charles and Pat Moran, both of whom worked as producers at that time. Bob Andrews and Brinsley Schwarz also play on a couple of tracks on the album too. United Artists clearly put a lot of money into launching Dr Feelgood.

(23)   See *Record Collector* November 2004.

(24)   See *ZigZag* 50 March 1975.

(25)   See *ZigZag* 61 June 1976. This has a big feature on Dr Feelgood touring the US, '*Apparently, when their first United Artists album was released, the bosses of the American company decided it was too crappy to sell in any quantity and gave Chris Fenwick carte blanche to sign to another label if he chose.*' Both Swan Song (Robert Plant having seen them live) and CBS were interested, with Dr Feelgood opting for CBS as their US label.

(26)   More recent opinion (see *The Great Rock Discography* Martin C

Strong 2002) rates *Down By the Jetty* and *Malpractice* quite highly. For a contrarian view see *ZigZag* 59 (April 1976) which quotes Nick Kent: *'I enjoyed the Feelgoods for a time, when they were playing clubs – in fact I still enjoy seeing them in big halls, but I think they're crap... they're the English J Geils Band'.*

(27) Their support on this tour were the George Hatcher Band, a US 'southern rock' outfit whose leader came from South Carolina.

(28) They were one of the acts at the Eastwood Free Festival, Southend on 1 August 1969 alongside David Bowie, the Edgar Broughton Band, Michael Chapman, Roger Ruskin Spear and Formerly Fat Harry.

(29) Hall in particular had a tremendous career, rooted like Peter Eden in UK jazz, that stretched over six decades from the 50s.

(30) See *ZigZag* 67. Conroy had originally been Social Secretary at Ewell Technical College, after which he moved, in 1971, to working as a booking agent for the Terry King Organisation, at a salary of £18 a week. Based in Soho he handled some of the new acts from Tony Stratton-Smith's Charisma label. See: https://www.aylesburyfriars. co.uk/introspaulconroy.html

(31) For examples of this see Annie Nightingale presenting *On the Road*, an episode of *Search* on 28 April 1971, about the tribulations experienced by Affinity, a band who broke up after being filmed, at https://www.youtube.com/watch?v=7wvry4hKspo&t=268s   There was also the 1968 documentary about The Mike Stuart Span, done as part of the series *A Year in the Life*.

(32) It can be seen at https://www.youtube.com/watch?v=xQKNeWlQzdI Both the overall format, a serious fly-on-the-wall observation, and the length (75 minutes), would not be broadcast on a mainstream channel today.

(33) Footage of Wilson and the band can be seen at https://www. youtube.com/watch?v=rYBDfHqdgxI

(34) See https://myvintagerock.com/2014/02/16/the-reading-festival-27-29-august-1976/

(35) See https://www.ukrockfestivals.com/reading-76.html

(36) See https://peel.fandom.com/wiki/Eddie_And_The_Hot_Rods It appears his producer John Walters remained unimpressed, *'They're just doing all the old stuff.'*

(37) He also produced The Pirates after their 1977 reunion.

PAUL GRAY

(EDDIE AND THE HOT RODS)

The first record I bought... the cool answer would be *Ride A White Swan*, but I think it was probably beaten by either *Bridge Over Troubled Water* or *The Joy of Living* by Cliff Richard and Hank Marvin for the flange guitar solo.

I never thought of becoming a musician; I learned the piano, taught myself bass, and just seemed to become one. Bass players always seemed to look the coolest and most mysterious, they had the longest hair, longest guitar necks, and I was always drawn to the bottom end parts on the keyboard so it seemed perfectly natural.

I saw the Feelgoods during my year at Southend Tech in 74, who were fab, along with Hustler and Stray. Before that I'd only seen a few other bands at the Kursaal in Southend – Hawkwind, who I saw on the '72 Space Ritual tour and who blew me sideways, and Alex Harvey spring to mind. My first show was Atomic Rooster when I was about 13, I guess. Eddie and The Hot Rods were my first proper band. After leaving Southend Tech I had a day job for 5 months pushing bits of paper around at the tax office. Then in January 1976 we signed with Island and were put on the grand sum of £15 a week. I lived at home so had no bills. Of the others in the band, Barrie was a glazier, Steve a labourer and Dave a roofer. They were a few years older than me.

Lots of labels were interested but Island were the coolest and their A&R guy Howard Thompson completely got us, loved the same kinda music as we did and besides was only a few years older than us. And he didn't dress in a suit like the other ones. The A&R men all used to pile along to The Nashville and try and impress us. We'd get them to buy us loads of beers then unceremoniously sling them out of the dressing room. Only Howard gave as good as he got, that was the main reason we went with them. Blackwell produced our 2nd single, *Wooly Bully*, and did such a dreadful job on it that it was dumped. Nice chap, though. Island was so laissez faire back then they just let you get on with it, which suited us just fine.

Our retainer went up to £25 a week after a bit, but even at the end it was still only about £75. The Hot Rods' finances were a disaster, there was some terrible financial mismanagement along the way. I got some publishing money too... you could just walk into Island Publishing and tell them you'd written the next single or something and score an advance of a few hundred. I did that loads of times! They never checked...

We were very aware of the changes that were taking place in music throughout 1976... we were spearheading it, although we get little credit for it these days. Over that year probably The Damned, The Hammersmith Gorillas and The Count Bishops were the bands I saw most. When all the punk fashion bollocks kicked in, we laughed. It had nothing to do with us but, of course, we went from being called an R'n'B band to pub-rock to new wave to punk and pop/rock too. Punk to us was The Seeds, The Shadows of Knight, The Stooges. They were the original punk garage bands. And early Kinks. Punk was just a word recycled again by journalists. Rock and Roll has always been loud and snotty and about rebellion – just reinvented by a new generation. The only new band called punk I really liked was The Damned. The Stranglers were great too, but they were never really punk either. It's all the same 3 or 4 chords at the end of the day.

In terms of favourite venues, I'd say the Marquee when we first started. The Nashville was great too. Hot Rods gigs were never violent.

DEKE O'BRIEN

(BLUESVILLE, BEES MAKE HONEY, NIGHTBUS)

My key influences were Otis Redding. Soul music. Aretha before she became famous. Both of these led on to Mr Love: Marvin Gaye. Early on I listened to Radio Luxembourg, hearing Elvis and Jerry Lee Lewis. The impact of Carl Perkins and *Blue Suede Shoes* can't be denied, either. In terms of technique, Wes Montgomery took my breath away.

My first band was the Alpine Seven Showband. This coalesced around Mick Cummins, a guy who had a van, a PA and a string of gigs that needed playing. The line-up included Ian McGarry on drums who later played with Bluesville, and Gerry Ryan, bass, who was a precision guitar builder. (He built Mick Molloy's first electric guitar.) Myself and Mick Molloy took to hanging around the Irish Federation of Musicians to get a gig. The band leaders and promoters would come in there looking for people whenever they were short. This was whilst I was still at school. I ended up failing most of my exams, but I was earning up to £35 a night, a huge amount then. I ended up with a 1600 E Ford Cortina, bought for cash, and a wardrobe of mohair suits. The gigs were long, and you played nothing but covers. Mostly hit parade. In the Alpine Seven we did country and western stuff too, but also rock and roll in the form of Chuck Berry, Gene Vincent and Little Richard, whereas other showbands would mix in rocked-up trad material. Showband members often earned enormous amounts. I knew people like Fran O'Toole and Paul Ashford (originally from The Chosen Few) in the Miami Showband who were on £120 per week, a colossal amount at the time. But it meant being on the road 5-6 nights a week most of the year.

I first crossed paths with Barry Richardson when he was playing in another of Mick Cummins's groups, The Crickets. He was at Dublin University at the time, as was Ian Whitcomb. Neither were Irish: Barry was from Ealing, Ian was from Putney. They hung out with Peter Adler, son of Larry, who later played saxophone in Bluesville. Ian really wanted to be George Formby. I played on *You Turn Me On*. It was only ever done as a demo, recorded live on 2-track with *This Sporting Life*, but Ian sold the tapes to a label in Seattle, who packaged him as the next Mick Jagger. When it was a big hit, I never got a penny from it... back then I didn't know anything about ongoing royalties. I knew you got paid for gigs, got session fees and mechanicals if you were a songwriter. But royalties from sales? I wasn't even aware of it. None of us in the Bluesville line-up that gigged around Dublin in 1964-65 were invited to join Ian in the US. We were paid $1000 each by Jerden Records to walk.

Mick and I ended up in The Chosen Few. The line-up went through numerous changes, and at one time we were calling ourselves The Limited Company, possibly because of the existence of a UK group also called The Chosen Few. We recorded a live album with Alex Harvey at the Cavalier Club in Dublin in 1966, but the tapes got lost and it failed to appear. I played with The Chosen Few for quite some time, but towards the end we lost our way. We had residencies at clubs that were like prototype discos, arranged around DJs and bars. One day around 1970 I got a call from Mick Molloy saying he was in the UK and had hooked up with Barry Richardson. They were putting a band together. Was I interested? I was. I sold my Mercedes to finance my trip over and spent six months living with Barry in Ealing, after which Bees Make Honey were born.

I saw Eggs Over Easy at The Tally Ho. They were awesome. The simplicity of their show and the ease with which they changed instruments was fantastic. Jake O'Hara was the one with the presence. They were very like The Band, and I think they'd be as impressive today as they were then if they were still around. I went around their house a couple of times, one of the rooms had mattresses pushed up against windows, for soundproofing. It was a well-lived-in abode!

Bees Make Honey got a residency at The Tally Ho. We also played the Delaney's Club in Meard Street, and had a hell of a job getting our gear, including a Yamaha upright keyboard, down the spiral staircase into the basement area. Dave Robinson was our manager, and got us a deal with EMI, who paid an advance. They launched us at a reception with Queen, their other big signing at that time, and one to which they provided far more resources. We went out for pretty good money live, £1500 a night at big colleges and even £450 or so at The Torrington. Throughout it all, though, Robinson was paying us a retainer of something like £20 per week. I think we made more money playing The Tally Ho and The Kensington where we split the takings with the owners. Barry was very much the band leader, and wanted us to morph into The Average White Band. The best times with Bees Make Honey were the live gigs. The worst moments were in the studio. We never really developed an ability to adapt to the studio environment. In the end both Mick and I were sacked by Dave Robinson!

There was no point staying in London, and I got an opportunity to put a band together in Ireland. This was Nightbus. It was a funk band, along the lines of Little Feat with John Ryan on keyboards and TJM a truly awesome bass player. We just wanted to make people dance. We did an album which Ruan O'Lochlainn and Fiachra Trench played on and a couple of singles in Ireland, and visited the UK too. We played Dingwalls and the ballroom opposite The Tally Ho. The one that doubled as a bingo hall. It was owned by a guy who was connected to the Delaneys. They were from Mullingar. We were offered £1000 to play there, and it covered the costs of coming over from Ireland. Back home we did a package tour in 1976, with Cheap Thrills and The Boomtown Rats. Each of us took turns at headlining. It was the first such organised in Ireland, and it didn't really pay. Bob Geldof was a hugely industrious and committed performer. We'd be in the bar after the gig and he'd already be in the next town putting up posters for the following night. The Boomtown Rats set was all originals, even then. Their only cover was *It's Only Rock 'n' Roll*, the Stones number.

If I could do any of this again, I'd sort out the management of bands, make it into something that you feel more comfortable with. More honesty and empathy towards the artist and a rigorous diligence in pursuit of the artist's goals from the labels, publishers and promoters etc. The recording process would be more technically creative whilst retaining the live element for which the Bees were famous, so obviously the right producer is crucial. Looking back, the best venues were the Hope & Anchor and The Nashville. John Eichler ran the Hope & Anchor. He was a lovely guy, he made it a musician's nirvana. You could even sleep there if you were short of somewhere to stay. But being Irish in London in the 70s could be pretty awful. The police were hard. I had an Irish reg car, so I got stopped quite often. On one occasion they made me put all my gear – guitars and all – out on the pavement whilst they searched the car. Because of the IRA they were really aggressive. When I asked them to help me put the stuff back, they just said *'Fuck Off'*, which inspired me to buy a UK reg car within days.

MUSIC EVERY NIGHT

On a Monday evening in April 1971 Jack O'Hara, an American musician living with two others in a damp house in Alma Road NW5, had a wash, changed his clothes and combed his long dark hair. Going out he walked up Anglers Lane, reached Kentish Town Road and turned left. Past The Oxford Tavern, past the entrance to the railway coal yard and past the empty street level buildings of Kentish Town Station, whilst a diesel train rattled through the cutting below. Past the empty shops and tall Dublinesque terraces divided into flats. A solitary fish and chip shop was doing good business. Buses rattled by on long cross-London journeys, their illuminated headboards listing Plumstead Common, Potters Bar, Crystal Palace, Barnet and Victoria. He passed The Assembly House where a few months earlier Richard Burton had shot scenes for the gangster film *Villain*. Moments later came the Forum cinema where crowds of middle-aged and elderly women waited patiently for the night's bingo to commence. After The Bull and Gate, he turned into Fortess Walk and entered The Tally Ho.

He put 11p on the counter and ordered a pint of bitter. It was quiet. There was one barman serving. They had a brief conversation and the barman went to speak with the owner upstairs. O'Hara drank some bitter. The barman reappeared and asked how he would describe his music in one word. *'Fun'*, said O'Hara. The barman went back upstairs, came down a few minutes later, and said, 'OK, *come around next weekend and do a show.*' O'Hara thanked him, gave contact details and went to sit in a quiet corner, drinking and studying the layout of the music area and its stage. Then, leaving his pint half-finished, he went to the payphone on the wall by the bar, called the house, spoke with one of his colleagues and told them the news.[1]

Many popular accounts of UK pub-rock stress how it all stemmed directly from an American band playing at The Tally Ho. This is clearly not the case and people knew as much at the time, and really ought to know better now, despite the many accounts that start from this premise. Even O'Hara dismisses much of what has been said subsequently as 'complete bullshit'. But what were three US singer-songwriters doing in London in the first place? And why were they asking to play in a pub?

Well, it had an awful lot to do with the immense success of the 1969 film *Easy Rider*. A massive international hit, it took one hundred and fifty times its budget at the box office, was nominated for Academy Awards, BAFTAs and won a prize at Cannes. Even better, its soundtrack album, with material by The Byrds, Jimi Hendrix and Steppenwolf, sold in vast amounts, charting at No 6 in the US and No 11 in the UK. Suddenly, production companies everywhere developed an interest in making similar youth-orientated, counter-culture films with a significant musical element. One such company was Cannon Films.

Incorporated in October 1967, and run by Dennis Friedland and Chris Dewey, both at that point in their early 20s, Cannon produced mainly low-budget horror and sex films, some of which were Swedish co-productions.[2] As early as 1968 they dipped a toe into the UK, backing *The Velvet House*, a gothic thriller starring Michael Gough, to the tune of £55,000. A co-production with Abacus, it eventually reached US audiences in 1971 as *Crucible of Horror* and finally turned up in the UK a year later as *The Corpse*. By the beginning of 1970 they had produced 13 features and, by virtue of their ownership of a network of cinemas, had begun distributing films by other directors and producers in their theatres, usually material that major distributors shied away from. After the success of *Easy Rider*, they made a play for the youth market, recruiting Peter Kauff, one of America's top music agents, to help them achieve this. *Cash Box* reported this on 21 March 1970, stating in an article headlined *Cannon Group Forms Music Publishing Company* that 'Kauff joined Cannon six weeks ago and was

previously vice-president of Premiere Talent Associates, a talent agency
specialising in the representation of pop music groups including The Who,
Led Zeppelin, Jimi Hendrix and Joe Cocker.'

Kauff and Cannon didn't have to wait long for their approach to
pay dividends. In July 1970 the company's latest film, *Joe*, became
a surprise hit. Directed by John G Avildsen, and starring Peter
Boyle and Susan Sarandon, this was a counter-culture film with
an intriguing twist, having a virulently anti-hippie, anti-hero as its
central character. It caught the post-Altamont, post-Manson mood
in the US perfectly, made 25 times its outlay and was the 13th
biggest US film of the year. The screenplay, by Norman Wexler,
was nominated for an Oscar and it also came with a soundtrack
album on which Kauff was credited as Executive Producer, albeit
one suspects he wasn't around too much in the mixing room. The
actual production duties and much of the music itself were handled
by Bobby Scott, writer of *A Taste of Honey*, a song so endemic
throughout the 60s that it was part of the audio-wallpaper of the
era.

Such acclaim took things to a different level and Cannon made
plans to exploit their success. To do this, they needed a band... an
outfit that could write and perform their own material, release
albums and tour whilst providing a stream of songs for the films
the company would now produce. *Joe* had barely been out a month
when Kauff found what he was looking for. He saw a trio, Eggs
Over Easy, consisting of Jack O'Hara, Austin De Lone and Brien
Hopkins, performing at a venue in New York. He was knocked out
by their show and signed them immediately.

Over half a century later, and with only the slenderest of their
work committed to vinyl, establishing why Kauff was so impressed
is not immediately obvious, but by all accounts, the band were very,
very good live. They were also well connected, their careers having
already intersected with a number of legendary figures. O'Hara
and De Lone had arrived in New York in late 1969, after meeting
up in the San Francisco Bay area. Prior to this O'Hara had played
on albums with David Blue and Ramblin' Jack Elliott,[3] and De
Lone had co-written, with Allen Silverman, an August 1967 single
by The Stone Poneys. Via Silverman, De Lone was connected to

Grootna, a post-Jefferson Airplane/Marty Balin side-project who lived in a communal house in Los Angeles. There was more too. After they teamed up De Lone and O'Hara were in The Minx, Alice Stuart's backing band. An early member of The Mothers of Invention, Stuart had origins in the US acoustic folk-blues-protest world before, unusually, striking out on her own as the leader of an electric group.[4]

Kauff moved quickly with his proteges, *Billboard* announcing on 12 September 1970 '...*Eggs Over Easy is the first CG (Cannon Group) act, which is into films, the first to be working in the media mix concept that is expected to produce big dividends for the Cannon Group as well as for the young talent...*' because, as Kauff put it in somewhat mangled grammar, '*many artists have film ideas through increased interest in different media*' by which we may assume he meant that musicians generally wanted to break into films.[5] The next step was to get them lined up with a producer, something that turned out to be quite simple. To quote O'Hara, '*Our manager took us to audition for Chas (Chandler)... we put on a show and just basically played our songs as a three-piece band. Chas said, 'Yeah, let's do it.' So, we went to England because it was cheaper to record there. It was an exciting adventure for us*'.[6]

By October 1970, Chandler and the band were in London, where time was rented at Olympic Studios, in Barnes, for the recording of an album. Everything seemed auspicious. Cannon had committed to two more UK films, *The Blood on Satan's Claw* and *The Beast in the Cellar*, and Kauff, now listed as President of Cannon Music, continued to extol the virtues of *Easy Rider* and *Woodstock* in *Billboard*.[7] For the sessions De Lone, Hopkins and O'Hara shared duties on guitar, keyboards and bass and were augmented by Les Sampson on percussion and John Steel, formerly a bandmate of Chandler's in The Animals, on drums. By the time work concluded in January 1971 they had cut 12 tracks: 9 written by the principal band members, 2 De Lone-Silverman compositions that predated Eggs Over Easy and one Robert Fraker song.

As produced by Chandler this is well written, well played and unpretentious material. Good-time music with prominent honky-tonk piano and multiple vocal parts; more than a bit like The Band. There were plenty of nice moments, with *111 Avenue* C, a very cool jazz-blues number featuring scat singing from Rahni Raines, being particularly outstanding.[8] But for whatever reason, nothing happened. Cannon, who had paid for the sessions and owned the copyright, declined to release the album. Whether they had cash flow issues, or thought that it wasn't quite that distinctive, however technically competent it might have been, is hard to say. Nor did Cannon use any of it in their films. Kauff, who was not around very much at this point, organising music industry seminars in Montreux, among other things, seems to have fallen out with Cannon too, whilst maintaining good relations with the band. He advised them to stay in the UK.[9]

It fell to Chandler, who acted as their manager at this point, to arrange whatever live work he could find. Seemingly unable to get them work supporting Slade, his main act, he found them instead some dates performing incidental music at poetry readings, much of this coming via the US Embassy, who were funding UK appearances by Marilyn Hacker, Dennis Boyles and Louis Simpson. Of these Simpson, who won the Pulitzer prize in 1964, was probably the most eminent, whilst Hacker was a regular contributor to *Ambit* magazine and Boyles the founder of Wanda's Factory, a co-operative of poets and literary magazine editors who arranged readings and musical performances at places like the Institute of Contemporary Arts and St. Mary's Church, Paddington Green.[10] This was all interesting stuff, but far from what the band had imagined they would be doing when they set out for the UK. By the spring of 1971 they were effectively biding their time in Kentish Town on a retainer of $100 a week (about £41.67p then, £340 per week now) '*to drink beer*'. Hence, O' Hara's reconnaissance of the area to source a venue where they could play live.

The arrangements at The Tally Ho worked well. The band had a small PA of their own, borrowed from the Robert Stigwood Organisation, and used the piano on the pub's stage, '*a baby grand because it was a jazz club,*' as O'Hara noted. The guitar and bass were played through portable amps, neither of which was a fashionable make, and there was a minimum of effect pedals. John Steel joined them for the live appearances and provided a solid backbone to their sound. They played two sets an evening (a common practice in pub gigs) and audiences grew exponentially. For Austin De Lone it was because, '...*When we played, we were just having so much fun that people dug it so much... It was loose, unpretentious...*' whilst in separate interviews O'Hara would recollect, '...*we just didn't give a fuck, and we did whatever we wanted to do... we did Ray Charles songs, old rock'n'roll, Sam Cooke songs, and we did our material, whatever we wanted to do. There were no lines drawn, it was just a true, natural organic experience... There was no barrier between us and the audience. They just responded. There was nothing they had to intellectualise at all... we just had little amps and a grand piano, so we weren't loud, we were just rockin'...*'

What the punters saw was something quite different from a typical 1971 rock show. There were no Marshall stacks, banks of amplifiers or huge mixing desks, no batteries of effect pedals and no array of keyboards jammed in at right angles surrounding their player. There wasn't a PA that required separate scaffolding or a massive light show. Nor was the drum kit a bewilderingly vast structure. Eggs Over Easy didn't play at a deafeningly high volume and there were no bombastic, aimless guitar solos.

For the cognoscenti, who quickly began gathering, what also resonated were the connections to Zappa (via Stuart), the Dylan circle (via Blue and Elliott) and the Jefferson Airplane entourage (via Grootna). All of this, playing at the local pub for free! Even more impressive was the scale of their repertoire. With De Lone, Hopkins and O'Hara all being songwriters they had something like 50 originals between them, and any number of covers. With such an archive at hand they would often ask the crowd to name a song, and then play it... as they did memorably one evening with *Brown Sugar*, The Rolling Stones chart topper, the same week it was released. The word got out, and amongst those beating a path to NW5 to check them out were John Peel, Loudon Wainwright III and various members of the Procol Harum and Ten Years After road crews.[11]

Other work came their way. On 15 June 1971 they supported Hardin and York at the Marquee. Dave Robinson, manager of Brinsley Schwarz, saw them here, was heavily impressed, and after a backstage discussion drove the trio to meet his band in their communal house in Northwood. Arriving very late, with only Nick Lowe still up, Robinson proclaimed that O'Hara, Hopkins and De Lone were *just like Clover*, and represented the type of direction that Brinsley Schwarz, then treading water after two albums that failed to sell, might profitably follow. Clover, like Creedence Clearwater Revival, were signed to Fantasy, and had released a couple of albums, *Clover* (1970) and *Fourty Niner* (1971) noted for critical plaudits and low sales. They'd put out a couple of singles as well, *Wade in the Water* and *Shotgun* (both covers) and, like Eggs Over Easy, did accessible original material of their own as well as eschewing the live paraphernalia of major rock bands: they played with small amps too.

It was an interesting comparison, given that outside the US Clover were hardly known, had made no commercial impact and hadn't played a single gig in the UK. But now there was the chance to see somebody just like them, and, presumably gauge whether Brinsley Schwarz might be remodelled in this image. Accordingly, Lowe and Billy Rankin, the drummer in Brinsley Schwarz, made their way to Kentish Town to catch the next Eggs Over Easy show. Lowe noted, *'it was a wild neighbourhood'*, but came away knocked out by the music and general ambience. Taking the same approach as Eggs Over Easy was the ladder that Brinsley Schwarz would use to climb out of the hole that their overblown launch in 1970 had pushed them into.[12]

For O'Hara and his colleagues, things improved when Chas Chandler found them a bit of studio work – backing Steve Ellis, formerly of The Love Affair, on his solo single *Have You Seen My Baby*. A very polished and well written Randy Newman number, this was released on CBS in August 1971, but failed to chart. Ellis would later recollect, *'I bumped into Chas Chandler in a nightclub and we got chatting. He made the right noises. I stayed with Chas for a couple of singles, including* Take Your Love. *Then I did* Hold On, *with Howie Casey and his big brass section, Johnny Steele from the Animals* on drums, little Jimmy McCulloch on guitar, Zoot Money on piano and a Canadian band, Eggs Over Easy, who were over here touring with Loudon Wainwright. That was a bloody good band. We did a few gigs.' [13]

It's a confusing account. Chas Chandler didn't produce *Take Your Love* (it was Keith Mansfield and Martin Clarke), *Hold On* was the chorus of *Have You Seen My Baby*, not the name of the single and there is no evidence of Eggs Over Easy (who weren't Canadian) touring the UK with Loudon Wainwright III, though they might have done a bit of unobtrusive backing for him. Did Ellis and his ensemble do any gigs? It's not impossible, but if they did, evidence of any is hard to come by.

Nevertheless, it was a great single and turned out to be the only piece of vinyl featuring Eggs Over Easy to be publicly released then in the UK. With George Butler now on drums, things came to an end after some slots supporting John Mayall in September-October 1971, because, as O'Hara said, '...our visas had run out, we were laying low, and we wanted to get a record deal and our management was in the US... It was just difficult to stay, and we were homesick. Basically pub-rock didn't happen for a good amount of time, a year or nearly two, after we left...' He might have added too that, by the autumn of 1971, Chandler was increasingly engaged in managing the ascent of his charges Slade to mega stardom. There was nothing to keep them in the UK and they returned to the US.

Here they added Bill Franz on drums and signed to A&M. With Kauff back as Executive Producer, they headed to Tucson, Arizona where Link Wray did the actual knob twiddling, to record an album *Good 'N' Cheap*. Released in August 1972, it was only available on import in the UK, an unhappy conclusion to their brief sojourn in the country. Veering from amiable, pleasant, country-rock to decent rock-blues, the most striking track was probably *Song is Born of Riff and Tongue*, ironically the only one the band didn't write. A folk tune by Robert Fraker it could almost be a madrigal. The album sleeve had artwork in the style of Edward Hopper's *Nighthawks*, echoing in its use of mythic Americana the Fumble album that appeared the same year.

And like the Fumble album, it didn't sell. At which point the trail goes rather cold. Circa 1975, Dave Robinson got back in touch, trying to get them to return to the UK. Possibly he saw them as an early signing to Stiff, but it didn't happen. There was a 1976 US-only single, and a third album five years later, after which they broke up. The tracks that they cut at Olympic with Chas Chandler finally appeared in 2016, but in terms of trying to understand why they made such an impression fifty plus years ago, only the memories of a diminishing number of people who saw them live at the time remain, together with a reputation where the legend seems to have somewhat obscured the bigger picture.

One person who definitely caught them at The Tally Ho and thought they were 'quite remarkable' was Barry Richardson, a 31-year-old saxophone, clarinet, bass and harmonica player on the jazz scene. Like many, his musical experience went back quite some way, in his case to the early 60s as part of a rhythm and blues group at Trinity College, Dublin, with fellow UK undergraduate, Ian Whitcomb. Known as Ian Whitcomb's Bluesville, it was modelled on Alexis Korner's Blues Incorporated, and included Deke O' Brien and Mick Molloy from The Alpine Seven Showband, another outfit Richardson was playing with. In the early summer of 1964 Whitcomb travelled to Seattle – not an obvious choice for a vacation – where he visited Jerden records. The logic here was that, in July 1963, Jerden had issued The Kingsmen's version of *Louie Louie*. It did well and was quickly rereleased on a bigger, national label (Wand), where it sold over a million copies, reaching No 1 in the US and No 23 in the UK. With America in the throes of Beatlemania, Whitcomb pitched Jerden some Bluesville demos and they signed the band.[14]

Soho, an instrumental featuring Richardson, was released on Jerden in July 1964. Credited to Ian Whitcomb, it has since acquired historic status by virtue of being the first record by an Irish group to be released in the US, as well as the first original rhythm and blues recording from an Irish band to be available anywhere, beating the debut single from Belfast's Them by about two months. In January 1965, Jerden released a follow-up single, *This Sporting Life*, credited to Ian Whitcomb and Bluesville. The flip, another instrumental, *Fizz*, was listed as being by Ian Whitcomb and Barry Richardson.[15] It took off commercially, quickly becoming a regional hit in Seattle, and sensing another British invasion sensation Tower, a newly formed subsidiary of Capitol Records, leased the master and succeeded in hustling it to No 87 in the *Cashbox* charts.

Next, Tower released *You Turn Me On*, a Whitcomb original, on which he was backed by Molloy, O'Brien, Gerry Ryan (bass) and Ian McGarry (drums). There was an album too, with Richardson playing saxophone on a few tracks. The single reached No 8 in the US, and to exploit this Whitcomb toured extensively at Tower's suggestion with a completely different set of musicians, leaving his Dublin-based colleagues to separate, less lucrative careers. By this point, Richardson was back in London, having completed his degree at Trinity College. Stardom was not on offer and he returned to the jazz world where he is mentioned as a regular at The Tally Ho later in the decade, usually accompanying either Brian Lemon (keyboards) or Johnny Richardson (drums, no relation), or both.[16]

By the time Eggs Over Easy turned up, Richardson was still doing Sunday jamming sessions, but having caught O'Hara and his colleagues live saw the potential in forming a similar band. He invited O'Brien and Molloy over from Ireland, and after introducing them to multi-instrumentalist Ruan O' Lochlainn,[17] took them to see Eggs Over Easy. They agreed to form a band, and recruited their drummer, Bob Siebenberg, via an ad in *Melody Maker*. Initially they performed at The Tally Ho without a name, in the same informal way that Richardson and fellow musicians had for years, but began calling themselves Bees Make Honey around January 1972.

As one might expect from a band whose core had been playing together as far back as 1963, they advanced in an assured manner. Dave Robinson became their manager and they were admired by both Charlie Gillett and John Peel (for whom they did two sessions on 23 January 1973 and 20 March 1973). Following a tour with Frankie Miller, EMI signed them that June. Their debut album, *Music Every Night*, had Robinson producing, with Vic Maile and Kingsley Ward as engineers. Like their demos, and so much else in the pub-rock oeuvre, it was recorded at Rockfield. Preceded by a single, *Knee Trembler*, it appeared in November 1973.

With ten tracks (7 originals, 3 covers), it was the latter that were revealing, the album opening with Louis Jordan's 1945 hit *Caldonia*, swerving into country-swing with Hank Penny's 1956 *Bloodshot Eyes* and closing with Kenny O'Dell's *My Rockin' Days*, covered not long before by The Crickets.[18] Very Americanised, very competent, this was an enjoyable set, where the musicians had a lot of fun. In that respect, it was similar to both Alexis Korner's Blues Incorporated and The Tally Ho All Stars. The reviews were generally ok, *Music Week* opining, '*Wonderfully refreshing to return to basics, where band and audience share the buzz of merry-making*' and by way of promotion they did a slot on *The Old Grey Whistle Test*.[19]

But neither the single nor the album sold. Worse still, there were personnel changes during its recording with O'Lochlainn and Siebenberg departing. Robinson brought in Malcolm Morley as a temporary stopgap on keyboards and Fran Byrne joined on drums. Around this time Richardson switched to saxophone with Rod Demick taking over on bass. Further changes happened in the spring of 1974: Molloy, O'Brien and Morley all quit and were replaced by Kevin McAlea, Ed Deane and Willie Finlayson.[20]

A second album was recorded for EMI, who weren't keen. DJM were, and a third album got recorded for them, only to be left on the shelf too. Throughout it all they kept up a steady schedule of live work, Richardson insisting, '*There is no way the Bees can make it on an image basis. We want to be known as a playing band.*' A more serious and fundamental split happened in October 1974, when most of their line-up departed, Byrne joining Ace, Finlayson Meal Ticket, Deane Frankie Miller and McAlea (with Deane) later turning up in the French outfit Il Barritz.[21]

A final version of the band – Richardson, Molloy, Demick and Paul Atkinson (drums) – emerged a little later. Taking a leaf out of the approach that had worked for Dr Feelgood, Ian Gomm, late of Brinsley Schwarz, produced a live album recorded at The Nashville. Out of the 13 tracks, 4 were released on a Charly EP a few months later. They kept going for a while thereafter but Richardson finally called it quits after a 1978 gig at The Pegasus, Stoke Newington. When this happened Demick joined Finlayson in the final line-up of Meal Ticket, a group similar to Bees Make Honey to the extent that they even recorded a couple of Richardson's songs. With a membership that was even longer in the tooth, they lasted down to 1980, their final task being to record some music for *The Flipside of Dominick Hide*, a BBC *Play for Today* that attracted record viewing figures.[22]

If Bees Make Honey were Richardson's effort to make it as a rock musician (and one presumes it was, after his early experience in Bluesville and recognition of what might be possible after seeing Eggs Over Easy) then it is worth pondering why it didn't work out for him. Musically the band were fine, and like Eggs Over Easy, they had an extensive set list. On the night you might see them open with The Byrds' *You Ain't Going Nowhere*, follow that with their take on the 1955 Sun Records release *Red Hot* and then spend the remainder of their set mixing originals, Chuck Berry covers, Louis Jordan's *Caldonia* and a few boogie numbers. But as for their appearance... they looked like a semi-pro band playing a pub gig after work. There were no quirky outfits, no visual boundaries were pushed and their attire was casual and very unlikely to make waves. They never really established themselves beyond the pub circuit, where catching a band like this after a day at work yourself was a welcome, inexpensive diversion. As Richardson admitted some years later, '*It did not work out for us financially.*'

Which is not to say that several of those who passed through the ranks of this most Irish of clearing houses didn't achieve greater success elsewhere. By the mid-70s, Siebenberg was in Supertramp, where he collected a vast number of silver, gold and platinum discs, Byrne in Ace and Morley in Man. Later, Kevin McAlea was much in demand as a backing musician, enjoying success with Barclay James Harvest and Kate Bush. He also wrote the English language version of Nena's big 1983 hit *99 Red Balloons*.

Richardson's lineage, which took in UK jazz, Irish showbands and the first early flutings of Irish rock, marked him out as something of a veteran in the mid-70s. But it was nothing compared to Max Merritt, who went back even further, to the very beginnings of Antipodean rock and roll. From New Zealand, Merritt fronted The Meteors who released 17 singles, 4 EPs and 2 albums in their home country and Australia between 1959 and

1966. Playing mainly cover versions of prominent US hits, with a scattering of originals, their image changed after a 1967 road crash which saw the key members of the band severely injured, Merritt losing an eye. Recovering, they switched to a mixture of country-rock and soul and after enjoying a big hit locally with their cover of Jerry Butler's *Hey! Western Union Man* (1969) and seeing their third album, *Max Merritt and The Meteors*, chart in Australia (1970) a move to London was arranged.

Here, a slimmed-down version of the group, minus most of its brass section, began slogging around the pub and club circuit. The database shows them playing the Marquee that May, doing an *Oz* magazine benefit a month later (one of many for the Australian-owned and permanently troubled magazine), and headlining The Greyhound, Fulham in January '72. Today, no one would think a band in their 30s that unusual. Half a century ago, middle age struck early, and was usually deeply unfashionable. Rock was a young man's game, young meaning under 25, and preferably around 21-22. If Bees Make Honey struggled with an average age of about 27, Max Merritt and The Meteors looked positively antediluvian. Merritt himself was in his mid-30s; his drummer Stewart Speer a full decade older. They made Bees Make Honey look like teenagers. Their image, the polar opposite of glam-rock and the artistic flourishes of Bowie, Reed and Roxy Music, was equally nondescript. Massively hirsute (though Merritt had quite short hair and was clean-shaven), visually this was all beards, long hair, Afros, baggy overcoats, flares and an abundance of denim.

Musically though, they ticked the box with very competent, very unpretentious, short accessible songs. A deal with Bell produced an April 1972 single, *Let it Slide*, which, like most pub-rock era releases, flopped. A bluesy, country-rock with gravelly vocals it was typical of the genre. And John Peel – always able to spot something worthwhile – really liked them. They did a session for him as early as May 1972, after which they toured with Slade and Juicy Lucy.

An abundance of live work followed, with the group seemingly moving towards clinching a major contract, only for disaster to strike in 1974, when their manager Peter Raphael decamped, leaving them stranded without funds. Forced to sell their van and move into cheaper rented accommodation, they lost their saxophonist Bob Bertles to jazz-rockers Nucleus, with Merritt obliged to take up his old day job, as a bricklayer, to make ends meet. Eventually a new line-up emerged, Merritt and Speer being joined by Barry Duggan (saxophone, and ex-Dada), Martin Deniz (bass), Dave McCrae (keyboards) and John Gourd (steel guitar).

Returning to the circuit, things finally worked out for them. In May 1975 Clive Davis, head of Arista Records, arrived in London to establish a UK division of the company. He was taken to The Nashville, West Kensington by *Rolling Stone* journalist Andrew Bailey, to see one of their gigs. Hugely impressed, he signed them on the spot, making them the first UK-based act on the label's roster. Arista brought in Del Newman to produce them, Newman being noted then for his success with Brian Protheroe's September 1974 hit *Pinball*.[23]

The album that resulted, *A Little Easier*, sold well in Australia where it reached No 10, and an accompanying single *Slippin' Away* did even better in the Antipodes, reaching No 2 in Australia and No 5 in New Zealand. Despite continued endorsement by John Peel, who gave them another session in October 1975, their lack of UK success continued. Duggan left, and was replaced by Lance Dixon from Gonzalez. They continued their sorties around the pub circuit, a slightly odd angle for a band that were having top ten hits elsewhere in the world, making numerous appearances at The Nashville, the White Hart, Willesden Green and The Windsor Castle on the Harrow Road.

A third Peel session came and went in May 1976, and a second Arista album, *Out of the Blue*, released that July was another hit down under whilst doing little in the UK. What finally did for them was the burgeoning punk scene. By early 1977, it was clear they couldn't compete as the music industry rapidly realigned to accommodate this phenomenon. The band broke up, with Merritt pursuing a solo career.

Researching them today, and trying to gauge their impact, one is struck by how absolutely typical of the pub-rock scene they were. And, how overlooked they remain. With the music media still, for the most part, absurdly US-centric and Anglocentric, Max Merritt and The Meteors have no entry in either the three-volume *Encyclopaedia of Rock* (1975-76) or *The NME Book of Rock* (1976). Nor do they feature in contemporary reference works like *Tapestry of Delights* or *Galactic Ramble*. It's almost as if some kind of rock music version of the Ministry of Truth has been at work rectifying the past and writing them out of history.[24]

Among those impressed by Eggs Over Easy was Declan McManus, at that point a 17-year-old would-be singer-songwriter oscillating between London and his mother's home in Liverpool. Even at this early stage, McManus had a band, Rusty, who covered songs by Crosby, Stills, Nash and Young, Dylan, and Van Morrison as well as attempting a few numbers of his own. Like many other ensembles slowly making their way in the rock music world, they made a stab at getting somewhere (88 gigs over two years), before folding after two dates supporting Steve Harley and Cockney Rebel in Coventry in June 1973. Interestingly they also managed a slot at The Half Moon, Putney, and having sampled this, and seen what was on offer elsewhere in the capital, London was where McManus gravitated after departing Merseyside.

By this point he had appeared, with his father Ross, in a TV commercial for R Whites Lemonade, an absurd, but entertaining film clip in which an actor sings *I'm a Secret Lemonade Drinker*, faux-Elvis style. Several different versions of this were made, in one of which a band, with Ross McManus on keyboards and son Declan on bass and backing vocals, can be seen. The advertisement won a silver award at the 1974 International Advertising Festival.[25]

Father and son were never going to perform live together, though had Ross McManus done so he would have only been as old as Max Merritt's drummer, and not much older than Alex Harvey. Nevertheless, his background is worth sketching in, if only to underscore how much his son owed to his influence at this stage in his career. From Liverpool, McManus Snr sang with the Joe Loss Orchestra from the early 50s, made an appearance on *Six-Five Special*, had a hit in Germany with a cod-ska number *Patsy Girl* in 1966, left Joe Loss and went solo mixing acting with singing, appeared in a couple of episodes of *Z Cars* and had a second hit in Australia in 1970 with a cover of *The Long and Winding Road*. By 1972, he had climbed on board the rock and roll revival scene, releasing an album *Elvis Presley's Golden Hits Sung by Big Ross & The Memphis Sound...* which led to the R Whites gig. On occasion he performed as Day Costello (this being his mother's maiden name; the family were solidly Liverpool Irish), and the combination of 'Elvis' and Costello would eventually be appropriated by his son.[26]

This was still a few years off, and for the moment Declan was concentrating on his new band, Flip City. As with Rusty, his father's background and the R Whites stuff, details of this were kept deliberately sketchy for some years. They seem to have had a reasonable career progression, playing a significant number of gigs around London in 1974-75 including a couple of top billed shows at The Greyhound, Croydon, and were in some demand as a competent support band... among those they opened for were Eddie and The Hot Rods, The 101ers and Slack Alice.

What were they like? Well, footage of one of their early performances has surfaced and shows a 4-piece outfit, in dungarees, denim, flares and check shirts (and longish hair) doing a set composed 50% of covers like *I'm A Hog for You* and *This Old Heart of Mine*.[27] Charlie Gillett thought they had something and they did a session on his radio show in March 1975. Others were less sure. Rock journalist Nick Kent had vague memories of them as a bluegrass act, and Dave Robinson, who got them in to record some demos in the Hope & Anchor, thought '*they were just the weirdest fucking band*', amateurish and ragged. (Under-rehearsed, and possibly not that good.)[28]

On the other hand, McManus wrote a lot of songs: and many of them weren't bad. At around the time he was trying to entice Eggs Over Easy back from the US, Robinson considered making Flip City's recording of *Third Rate Romance* an early release on Stiff records (or Street as the label was then known). He decided against and Flip City broke up.[29] After this Declan plugged away submitting demo tapes to all and sundry and eventually made headway with Robinson and his colleague Jake Riviera. In August 1976 an offer was made. Stiff wanted him as an in-house songwriter, specifically to provide material for Dave Edmunds. A few months later, after further demos, and despite reservations about him having a bad case of verbal diarrhoea, Robinson and Riviera relented further and made McManus the first act signed by Stiff, with an advance of £150, a new guitar amp and a tape recorder.

Sessions for a proposed single began almost immediately at Pathway, a tiny, cramped studio at the end of an alley off Grosvenor Avenue, Newington Green. Wedged between tall, thin Georgian houses and the back yards of shops with dingy living accommodation above, it was located in Mildmay Park, one of London's then unfashionable areas, but came with an interesting backstory, and was favoured by labels who wanted emerging acts recorded in a 'live', informal manner. Its owners, Mike Finesilver and Peter Ker, had both been musicians themselves before moving on to write and produce stuff for Love Sculpture and Arthur Brown. They already had a relationship with Robinson and, just prior to McManus turning up, had recorded several of the early Stiff singles, including *New Rose*, by The Damned, which ended up being the label's first release.[30]

Nick Lowe, who doubled up on bass, was nominated as producer, with John McFee (guitar) and Mickey Shine (drums), being drafted in from Clover to complete the band. Yes, the same band Robinson had raved about after seeing Eggs Over Easy at The Tally Ho five years earlier had finally made it to the UK at his instigation to benefit from the burgeoning pub-rock scene. This was a session stint for them, between recording their two Vertigo LPs. By the spring of 1977, and at a cost of no more than £2,000, enough of McManus's material had been laid down to release an album, at which point it became necessary to decide what name it would be released under. There was agreement on blotting out the family connection to the Joe Loss Orchestra, and erasing the R Whites Lemonade episode too. And so emerged Elvis Costello, born into the UK music scene with an elaborately disguised background.

His debut, *My Aim is True*, was released in July 1977. It sold well, reaching No 14 in the UK. By December, it had charted in the US where it eventually went platinum. Early publicity stated that Costello was backed by 'The Shamrocks', Clover not being mentioned for contractual reasons. It seems that they made little financially from it and they had no further involvement with Costello, who recorded his first hit single, *Watching the Detectives* (No 15 in the UK, November 1977), with Steve Nieve (keyboards), Andrew Bodnar (bass) and Steve Goulding (drums), the latter two being members of Graham Parker's Rumour. Eventually, a permanent backing band, The Attractions, was sorted out, with Nieve joined by Bruce Thomas (bass, from Quiver) and Pete Thomas (drums, late of Chilli Willi and the Red Hot Peppers).

Ultra-competent, ultra-professional and very, very mainstream 70s pop/rock, they did Costello proud. Over the next 45 years, playing much of the time with them, he accrued 24 chart albums and 14 Top 30 singles. He was particularly big in America where he earned 3 platinum and 9 gold discs. The logical outcome of the ingredients that went into pub-rock, not all the assumptions made early on about him by Robinson, Nick Kent and others were necessarily wrong. Yes, he was driven, chippy and wrote a lot of songs, many of which sold. But cover versions of his work were often sublime: Dave Edmunds *Girls Talk* (1979) and Robert Wyatt *Shipbuilding* (1982) to name but two.

About four and a half miles south-west of The Tally Ho, in an area regarded then as being on 'the wrong side' of Holland Park, could be found the Duke of Clarence. Where Kensington met Shepherd's Bush, this was an old Victorian pub, rebuilt in the 30s, on a busy main road, traffic roaring past night and day with a steady stream of red buses carrying passengers to and from Oxford Street and all points east. By the early 70s, its setting and appearance were typical, a rather frayed-looking building in an area where rapid change was underway. The GLC had opened the West Cross Route not quite opposite – as part of the never-to-be-completed Inner London Motorway Box – and new, brutalist, council estates had emerged on the land cleared to enable this. There were demolished sites, lingering bomb damage and unkempt old houses split into bedsitting rooms in the vicinity. A hundred yards to the west, one of British Rail's major arteries carried around 80 freight trains a day.

Although never accorded the sacred status of the Hope & Anchor and the Nashville, or awarded the retrospective accolades enjoyed by The Tally Ho, the Duke of Clarence was a locally significant music venue, where live bands of various types were enjoyed by a diverse community. Recollections of this can be found online[31] where John Woodsford comments, '*I married my wife from Trinidad in 1971. We went, along with my wife's 3 sisters, to the steel band sessions at the Duke of Clarence, held every Sunday lunchtime, off and on, from 1972 to 1976. Always a great atmosphere, laidback and cosy. We would meet other Trinidadians there, then go on to house parties after 2.30pm when the pub closed*', and Dave Clemo, a musician, notes, '*in 1972 I was living locally and popped in one Wednesday to be confronted by a huge folk music session. The musicians set up around a table in the middle of the room and as more musicians arrived the circle would get bigger. The audience would stand or sit nearby and would join in all the songs. It was great. So great that I joined them a few weeks later and stayed for about 18 months. The pub had a small stage in the corner which the other bands would use. I remember that another Irish band played on Tuesday nights. They were a four- or five-piece band with a female singer and someone played the uilleann pipes. Our band (now renamed as Captain Swing) played on Wednesdays, an avant-garde jazz group played on Thursday nights and a band called Starry Eyed and Laughing played on one of the other nights*'.[32]

Possibly the most accomplished and interesting of the country-rock bands to emerge after 1972, Starry Eyed and Laughing were originally Tony Poole and Ross McGeeney, both guitarists, playing as a duo. It seems they made their first appearance at the Duke of Clarence on 28 May 1973, and went down so well that they landed a residency, pleasing the audience with their covers of Byrds, Dylan and Beatles songs. Within a few months they'd become a band, adding Iain Whitmore (bass) and Nick Brown (drums).[33]

They started to get noticed. *Record Mirror* advised their readers there was '*...something exciting happening at the Bush...*' and by April 1974 they were sufficiently regarded to be included in the line-up for *The Amazing ZigZag Concert*. Held at the Roundhouse, this celebrated the magazine's fifth anniversary and saw them opening for Michael Nesmith, John Stewart, Help Yourself and Chilli Willi and the Red Hot Peppers. The concert was recorded, with the intention of releasing the material as a live album, but remained in the can until appearing as a 5-CD set in 2010, when it appeared with no fewer than 10 tracks by Starry Eyed and Laughing. Back in 1974, an event like this was a really big deal. Contemporary reviews, and recollections from those there, all say what a great night it was, with the centrality of country-rock as the sound of the future being very much confirmed. It mattered not that Nesmith (ex-The Monkees) and Stewart (ex-The Kingston Trio) sold in only respectable amounts in the US and hardly at all in the UK, or that Chilli Willi would never even dent the UK Top 50. What it represented was a coming of age. Rock was now serious, focused and played by bands and singers for audiences somewhat older than a decade earlier.

Starry Eyed and Laughing impressed so much on the night that ZigZag editor, Pete Frame, became their manager. After replacing Nick Brown with Mick Wackford, they did a John Peel session on 18 July 1974, and signed to CBS, who allocated Dan Loggins as their producer, Loggins then riding high after successes with the semi-eponymous albums Mott and The Hoople. With a big label and big-name producer behind them, things looked promising and their debut releases appeared that October: a single Money is No Friend of Mine and an album, Starry Eyed and Laughing, containing 12 originals. Both were nicely played and well-produced, but neither sold. What they sounded like was The Byrds circa 1967 (both Poole and McGeeney played Rickenbackers à la Roger McGuinn) with lots of twelve-string guitar and excellent harmonised vocals.

Peel had them in for another session on 9 January 1975, after which a second single, Nobody Home, also failed to chart. By the summer of 1975, they were down at Rockfield recording their second album, Thought Talk, in the midst of which they managed a third visit to Peel's studio. The album had 10 originals, but neither it, nor the accompanying single Good Love, did anything much in terms of sales. At which point CBS began pondering their investment. The first album hadn't had a US release. It was now decided to remedy this with a 110 date US tour, promoted as one of the label's New Faces of '75. After well attended appearances at The Nashville, Friars Aylesbury and the Roundhouse, the band flew across the Atlantic and commenced live work in the US.

It was a disaster. The gigs stretched over three months with substantial travelling between them. The costs ended up outweighing the income quite considerably, with the band making nothing (CBS paid the difference) and on their return to the UK they expanded to a 5-piece with the addition of Roger Kelly (guitar). This line-up did a live set for *Rockpalast* on West German TV on 24 February 1976. Effectively a fourth album, it ran to 17 tracks and included Jackie DeShannon's *When You Walk in the Room* as well as 3 Dylan covers, one of which, *You Ain't Goin' Nowhere*, was also a staple of Bees Make Honey's live set.[34]

In the summer of 1976, there was an attempt at a relaunch. The band's name was shortened to Starry Eyed, and Flo and Eddie, late of Zappa's Mothers of Invention and later still of The Turtles, were brought in as producers. A couple of singles ensued, *Saturday* and *Song on the Radio*, and when both of these failed, they folded at the end of 1976.

As Tony Poole says, *'The band split mostly for economic reasons, we couldn't sustain the band without hits, but also for personal reasons. We had a very intense 2 years playing and living together, and the different pressures affected us in different ways... The worst memory, really, is of all the time spent travelling in cold vans that broke down, no luxury tour buses at that level!'* Most groups come to an end for fairly mundane reasons, and for Starry Eyed and Laughing it was no different. What made it slightly ironic, though, was that they ceased to exist at around the time The Flamin' Groovies started making some headway. Like their better-known US counterparts, an evening watching Poole et al meant lots of harmonies and jangly melodies. Their cover of The Byrds' cover of Dylan's *Chimes of Freedom* was really quite exquisite, even if today we might think it more akin to something by a tribute band.

Like The Flamin' Groovies, their vinyl offerings didn't sell, but there was more to it than that. From today's perspective, Starry Eyed and Laughing had a real lack of image. They looked ordinary, unlike the Groovies in their sharp suits and short hair, and their set had no quirky covers. There was nothing that journalists could play one-upmanship games with. Slightly too early to pick up on the interest The Flamin' Groovies generated, they were also 10-15 years too early to cash in on the revival of interest in classic 60s sounds. After they split, Kelly had some success in the Streetband, and the others cropped up from time to time elsewhere, but their output between 1974 and 1976 remains their finest hour.

Expertly played good-time country rock was also purveyed by Charlie and The Wide Boys. Formed in Cornwall in 1972, they were built around the songwriting and singing abilities of Charlie Ainley and the drumming of Guy Evans, Evans having previously been in Van der Graaf Generator, one of the great prog-bands of the late 60s/early 70s.[35] Richard Worthy (guitar), Simon Fraser (guitar), Nigel Chappell (bass) and Greg Phillips (percussion) completed their line-up. After significant acclaim in their home county, they headed to London for an assault on the pubs, clubs and colleges. By all accounts, they were a great live band, similar in style to Bees Make Honey and Brinsley Schwarz.

It helped that Richard Worthy was a friend of Tony Cox, a noted producer and arranger, who had been in The Young Idea, a Peter and Gordon-type act who had a 1967 hit with a cover of *With a Little Help from my Friends*, as well as The Bunch, who released a rock and roll revival album, *Rock On*, in 1972.[36] Cox had also worked with Family, Yes and Jonathan King and owned Sawmill Studios in Fowey, Cornwall, which was residential, like Rockfield. He had immense music industry contacts, and via these Charlie and The Wide Boys got a deal with Anchor, the third such band to do so after Ace and Blue Goose.

Work began immediately on a debut album. For a while, possibly about six months, things looked good and they were widely expected to become a major fixture on the UK circuit. Then, problems emerged. Evans quit in October 1974, as soon as discussions started about reforming Van der Graaf Generator. He was replaced by Will Birch from the Kursaal Flyers who found things not entirely to his liking, *'The Wide Boys had a very laidback lifestyle... They were unambitious. I rehearsed with them for four days and it was completely loose, and I sussed I wasn't good enough, but I did a couple of gigs with them, and at the end of the week, because they hadn't said they wanted me, and I wasn't completely enamoured with them from the professional point of view, I said goodbye. They were great, though, they should have made it... they were just lazy'.*[37]

Exactly what the problem was is hard to establish. Maybe they didn't like working or living in London? Possibly there were shades here of Mickey Jupp? A desire to remain in one place and find inspiration from familiar surroundings? With their act minus a drummer and unable to perform, Anchor pressed ahead anyway and released an EP, *Gilly I Do*, to reasonable acclaim. John Peel played one of the tracks on his show on 28 November 1974 and *ZigZag* 48 (December 1974) reviewed it as the *'first release from an up-and-coming band with rock 'n' roll aspirations... a few steps away from the real nitty gritty... more good timey really, but very enjoyable nevertheless'.* However, as Ainley later admitted, *'the band can't concentrate long enough to make a record. We spent most of our time trying to live up to the fact that we're all wide boys'.*[38]

Which is how it ended. With the weeks turning into months and nothing very much happening Anchor abandoned plans to release the album, which eventually appeared on the budget label Music for Pleasure as *Great Country Rockers* in 1976. It did nothing commercially. During the winter of 1976-77 Ainley spent two months depping for Shakin' Stevens in Shakin' Stevens and the Sunsets whilst Stevens was in hospital, after which he and Richard Worthy went back to auditions and recording demos. Several months later a deal came with Nemperor, a US jazz label, formed many years earlier by Brian Epstein, that had now branched out into rock. Two albums and three singles followed, all credited as Ainley solo releases. They did a fair amount of live work too, which saw them through to the end of the decade but nothing charted and both drifted away from music shortly afterwards.

Like the rock and roll revival scene, the brief flickering of UK country-rock was a highly Americanised genre. In some ways it provided a missing link, a connection between classic rock and roll – Cochrane, Presley, Perkins, Jerry Lee Lewis, Chuck Berry – and the hirsute outlaw images of the late 60s counter-culture. A lot of people back in the early 70s thought this had real integrity and that it represented some kind of genuine force within rock that was refreshing and unpretentious. Both John Peel and Charlie Gillett believed so, as did Dave Robinson. There were a couple of critical single releases too that made a great impression at the time, finding a place in the record collections of many of those who followed the latest trends: *Saturday Nite Special* by The Sundown Playboys, released by Apple in November 1972, and Johnnie Allan's cover of *Promised Land*, put out by Charlie Gillett on Oval in December 1974. The former was an accordion-heavy quickstep dance piece by a Louisiana band that had been together since 1945. The latter, a 1971 cover of Chuck Berry's 1964 Chess original, done in hard, tight, driving cajun style. Both were tremendous and explain why UK musicians and critics thought that, if only this sound could somehow be distilled and reproduced domestically, a new, authentic era in music would emerge.

But for many there was another side to this. The downside was the image, and the absolute lack thereof. And the age of those playing the stuff. Teenagers don't want bands and singers in their 30s. All those plaid shirts, flared trousers, beards, shoulder-length hair, moustaches, tight t-shirts, cowboy boots, medallions and so on were easy to deride. It was no coincidence that, midway between *Saturday Nite Special* and *Promised Land*, Philips released an eponymous album by the duo Jehosophat and Jones. Produced by Peter Raphael, among the musicians credited on this were Max Merritt, Stewart Speer, Richie Bull, Gordon Huntley, probably the busiest UK steel guitar player (he was part of Matthews Southern Comfort and had a lineage back to the mid-60s), and Roger Churchyard, formerly in bluegrass outfit The Orange Blossom Sound. It was very well done... but on close inspection turned out to be the work of Ronnie Corbett and Ronnie Barker, comedians and satirists who knew a good opportunity to mock when they saw one. You had to listen to it quite closely before you realised it wasn't the latest pub-rock act.

Notes

(1) Paraphrased with artistic licence from https://americana-uk.com/
     interview-jack-ohara-on-how-eggs-over-easy-accidentally-helped-
     punk-to-develop

(2) Cannon Films produced, co-produced or distributed 29 films
     between 1967 and 1972, including *Sam's Song* (69), one of Robert
     De Niro's early screen appearances.

(3) O'Hara plays on Elliott's 1968 LP *Young Brigham*. Originally from
     Pennsylvannia, he headed to San Francisco where he met De Lone
     who had dropped out of Harvard to pursue a career as a singer-
     songwriter.

(4) See: https://www.keranews.org/2016-06-21/how-the-band-eggs-over-
     easy-kicked-off-londons-pub-rock-movement According to Zappa,
     Stuart was sacked from The Mothers of Invention because she
     couldn't play *Louie Louie*. (Possibly a deadpan joke, given how few
     chords are needed to play *Louie Louie*.) Stuart's backing band on
     her 1970 *Full Time Woman* album included Vic Smith of Grootna.
     Interestingly, she was in London in 1971 too, appearing on BBC
     TV's *Old Grey Whistle Test* on 28 November 1971.

(5) Quoted at https://books.google.ie/books?id=kCkEAAAAMBAJ&
     pg=PA4&lpg=PA4&dq=cannon+films+%2B+kauff+%2B+
     eggs+over+easy&source=bl&ots=27-K6kV2ST&sig=ACfU3U32
     YAlnvtGl7XR2FBcVKOKs9C24Jw&hl=en&sa=X&ved=
     2ahUKEwj76N6f4dv_AhWTNcAKHXRSDJ8Q6AF6BAgsEAM#v
     =onepage&q=cannon%20films%20%2B%20kauff%20%2B%20
     eggs%20over%20easy&f=false

(6) See: https://aquariumdrunkard.com/2016/07/11/eggs-over-easy-
     the-aquarium-drunkard-interview/ As to why Chandler in the first
     place, see *Look Wot I Dun*, Don Powell's 2013 autobiography, 'Chas
     had an American partner named Peter Kauff... Chas had met him in
     his Animals and Hendrix days and they were really good friends. Peter
     Kauff used to be a booker at the Premier Talent Agency, the biggest agency
     around...'

(7) See the article *Filmrock* written by Kauff (as President of Cannon
     Music) in *Billboard* 14 November 1970.

(8) Raines had an extensive career as a backing vocalist in the San
     Francisco area, and was associated at one point with Kingfish, a
     band regarded as a Grateful Dead offshoot. Fraker died in 2017. His

obituary can be read at https://bluegrasstoday.com/robert-fraker-passes/

(9)   See *Billboard* 13 March and 20 March 1971. In the end, Eggs Over Easy were not required on either *The Blood on Satan's Claw* which had music by Marc Wilkinson or *The Beast in The Cellar*, a Cannon-Tigon co-production, which used an Edison Lighthouse song as its main theme. Kauff was also credited as musical director of *Maid in Sweden* which was shot May-July 1971. This has 'CSN-*esque music*' according to a review at https://www.thespinningimage.co.uk/cultfilms/displaycultfilm.asp?reviewid=8815 Alas, this isn't Eggs Over Easy either. It seems the musicians used for this were John Tippet, Tony Bird and Paul Burchill (see: https://ringostrack.com/en/movie/maid-in-sweden/58138) formerly in a Bristol based folk-rock outfit Dawn, who '*mixed original material with Byrds and Dylan covers*' according to an entry in *Bristol Folk* by Mark Jones. Why Cannon chose not to use Eggs Over Easy after paying to record them, house them and giving them a monthly retainer is puzzling.

(10) *Ambit* is still published today. Wanda's Factory was responsible for producing *Poetry Workshop*, one of the first literary programmes broadcast on BBC Radio London, 1971-72.

(11) According to Loudon Wainwright III, '*There were nights spent hanging out at The Tally Ho in Kentish Town, a legendary pub-rock venue. I was buddies with the American expat country-rock trio Eggs Over Easy, who played there regularly, as did the Eggs-influenced English band Brinsley Schwarz, which featured Nick Lowe.*' See his 2017 autobiography *Liner Notes: On Parents & Children, Exes & Excess, Death & Decay & a Few of My Other Favorite Things.*

(12) For more see: *Cruel to be Kind: The Life and Music of Nick Lowe* Will Birch (2019).

(13) Quoted at http://www.steveellis.co.uk/?Action=AboutSteve The Howie Casey brass section referred to here was most likely Howie Casey (tenor sax), Alan Townsend (trumpet) and John Lee (trombone), all of whom played on a July 1971 LP by Curtiss Maldoon whilst members of the Roy Young Band. Other musicians involved with Curtiss Maldoon included Roger Powell and Ian Whiteman from Mighty Baby and Bruce Thomas, then in Quiver, and later one of Elvis Costello's Attractions. Pub-rock was a small world.

(14) There was also *The Kingsmen in Person* album, which had a two-year run in the US charts from January 1964, peaking at No 20.

(15) *This Sporting Life* aka *The Sporting Life* was originally recorded by Brownie McGhee in 1946 and covered by Ken Colyer's Skiffle Group (August 1957, credited as 'Trad'), The Chas McDevitt Skiffle Group (September 1957, credited to McGhee), The Mickey Finn (March 1965), The Lovin' Spoonful (June 1966), Jackie Lynton (April 1967) and Caroline Munro (May 1967). Whitcomb claimed he wrote it.

(16) See recollections of Mike Hogh at https://www.sandybrownjazz. co.uk/profilemikehogh.html By 1969 both Lemon and Richardson were alternating between the two Delaney pubs, The Tally Ho and The Kensington. At the latter, ensembles led by luminaries Kenny Napper and Phil Seamen were also featured.

(17) O'Lochlainn was also a photographer, taking many of the cover shots used on jazz and rock albums, including releases by Jethro Tull.

(18) Live footage of Bees Make Honey performing *Caldonia* at The Nags Head, High Wycombe can be seen at: https://www.youtube.com/ watch?v=boSKRgH0vKM

(19) On 20 November 1973, the following week the show featured The New York Dolls.

(20) The extent to which Bees Make Honey relied on Irish musicians was astonishing. Byrne, McAlea and Deane were all from Dublin, and between them had played with The Creatures, The Sands Showband, Some People, The Real McCoy, Granny's Intentions and The Woods Band. Demick, from Belfast, had been with The Wheels (a legendary 'garage' outfit on a par with Them) and Demick and Armstrong. Finlayson, from Edinburgh, had previously been in The Writing on the Wall.

(21) Il Barritz released an album on Atlantic in 1975 and were a second attempt at rock stardom by wealthy French playboy Phillippe DeBarge. Co-produced by Phil May and Wally Allen of The Pretty Things, it followed an earlier 1969 attempt with that band to promote DeBarge's ambitions, the fruits of which would not appear for 40 years.

(22) In many ways a typical pub-rock outfit, Meal Ticket existed slightly outside the time frame covered by this book. Gigging from July 1976 they were originally a 6-piece, led by Finlayson, with Rick Jones (previously a 60s folk singer as well as co-presenter of *Play School*), Steve Simpson (ex-Ronnie Lane's Slim Chance,

and formerly a colleague of Ritchie Bull), Ray Flacke (ex-Third World War), Jack Brand (ex-The Factory) and Chris Hunt (ex-Mayfield's Mule). Hugely experienced and extremely competent, they were signed by EMI after The Sex Pistols had been dumped and recorded two albums for that label, followed by a third (on which Demick appears) for Logo. In their later stages they also had a lyricist, the 45-year-old Canadian poet David Pierce. Lyricists had been big in the late 60s with bands like Procol Harum, King Crimson and Renaissance. It was surprising to find one writing for an outfit playing the Hope & Anchor and similar venues a decade later.

(23) Newman also arranged the wonderful 1967 Focus Three single *10,000 Years Behind My Mind* as well as producing Scott Walker's post-1973 releases.

(24) For more on Max Merritt and The Meteors see http://www.milesago.com/artists/merritt.htm

(25) Footage of the 1973-74 R Whites lemonade add with McManus Snr and Jnr can be seen at: https://www.youtube.com/watch?v=lK26bP0M7BQ

(26) Between 1974 and 1979 Ross McManus also provided theme songs for 5 of the UK's execrable soft-porn films, something his son may not have wished widely known at the time.

(27) Footage of them playing at the 1974 E1 Festival can be seen at: https://www.youtube.com/watch?v=kNgdRc0Hzus

(28) See Nick Kent's *The Dark Stuff* p206-207 (1994) which quotes McManus as saying a few years later, '*Course nobody wanted to know back then... None of yer rock hacks were around, then! And neither were you! I remember the time you came down to the Marquee when we were supporting Dr Feelgood and you spent all your time in the dressing room talking to Wilko Johnson. You didn't even bother to check us out. Oh No!*' For more on this period in his career see Graham Thomson *Complicated Shadows: The Life and Music of Elvis Costello* (2005).

(29) *Third Rate Romance* was a No 14 US hit for The Amazing Rhythm Aces in July 1975. Typical country rockers, it is interesting to consider where McManus was anchored musically until quite late in the day.

(30) For more background on Finesilver and Ker see https://www.britishmusicarchive.com/artists/elli/

(31) At https://www.closedpubs.co.uk/london/w11_hollandpark_dukeofclarence.html)

(32) Clemo was later in Left Hand Drive, a 5-piece country rock outfit based mainly in the Northampton area. An album of their recordings emerged in 2012.

(33) Of these Whitmore had some prior experience in Patches, a Brighton-based outfit whose singer, Leo Sayer, was quickly whisked off to better things after they released a single on Warner Brothers in 1972. For a full account of Starry Eyed and Laughing's career see https://www.starryeyedandlaughing.com/Starry_Press.htm

(34) The material was released on CD in 2019.

(35) The transition from Van der Graaf Generator's unique prog-rock to the high-energy Americana of Charlie and The Wide Boys is hardly an obvious one. Evans also did sessions with The Misunderstood in 1968 and, interestingly, played on Colin Scot's 1971 solo LP on United Artists with members of Brinsley Schwarz, Yes, Van der Graaf Generator and King Crimson.

(36) The Bunch included Richard Thompson and Dave Mattacks from Fairport Convention, Sandy Denny, Pat Donaldson and Gerry Conway from Fotheringay, Linda Peters (later Thompson), then a solo folk act, and Ian Whiteman from Mighty Baby. Folkies getting nostalgic about rock and roll was quite in vogue at the time. The author remembers seeing Steeleye Span live in 1973; for their encore they changed into 50s outfits and did half a dozen pre-Beatle pop/rock and roll hits.

(37) Quoted in *ZigZag* 67 December 1976.

(38) See Ainley's notes on the sleeve of his July 1978 single *You Tell Me Lies* on Nemperor.

ROD DEMICK

(THE WHEELS, BEES MAKE HONEY,
MEAL TICKET)

The Wheels came from Belfast and secured a residency at the Queen's Ballroom, Cleveleys, near Blackpool in 1964. It was regular wages for 2 nights a week and allowed us to work the NE and NW until we got a recording deal. We never did any package tours but our agent had us travelling all over the place. Most of the time we earned about £20 a week which was a lot of money then. EMI signed us to their Columbia label in May 1965, after we sent them a demo tape. We put out 3 singles, but only gigged in London once, in 1965 at The Starlight Club, which was owned by our agent. As far as I can remember, The Walker Brothers, Them, PJ Proby and Twinkle were all in attendance and enjoyed our show, which was pretty manic.

But despite that, we remained outside London. Another band on the same circuit as us were The Rockin' Vicars. I remember when Lemmy joined them as lead guitarist. They were playing The Palatine Hotel in Blackpool. He was given a solo and promptly held his guitar against his amp causing howling feedback for 24 bars! I would run into him many times in London over the following years and we'd always have a laugh. After a few drinks and other substances, he would call me *Demwick* and I called him *Motormouth*. A hell of a man.

Even after The Shadows of Knight hit big in America with *Gloria*, which had been our debut single, and then covered our follow-up *Bad Little Woman* as their follow-up, there was no talk about The Wheels doing an LP. At one point we thought of bringing in Van Morrison as our singer just after Them split. Herbie Armstrong spoke with him, and he was interested, but said that he was waiting for a call from Bert Berns. He got that call and the rest, as they say, is history. After 3 years Herbie and I wanted the band to move to London, but none of the others wanted to take the risk.

So, The Wheels broke up and Herbie and I came to London. We were writing for publishing companies and also landed a gig backing Screaming Lord Sutch with drummer Howard Davies. The best thing about working with Sutch was the complete madness of every show… but some nights you also got the worst of it, such as when he set fire to the drums onstage in Germany during *Great Balls of Fire*. We never recorded with him but we had some wild times. He did talk about going to America with us, but as usual nothing happened so we went back to doing our own thing. By the summer of 1968, Herbie and I were recording as The James Brothers and put out a couple of singles on Page One. We didn't do any live gigs, though as a trio we did back a few soul acts at places like The Ram Jam Club. During the day both of us worked in boutiques in and around Carnaby Street, Herbie at Mates, where he was approached by Glenn Cornick and asked at one point to join Jethro Tull as replacement for Mick Abrahams. I didn't get any overtures like this, but I was asked to join the Riot Squad. Both of us declined.

In 1970, we were signed to Decca, by the same producer who'd had the big hit *Jesamine* with The Casuals. We recorded two albums as Demick and Armstrong, the first one, *Little Willie Ramble*, came out on MAM which Decca distributed. It's a mixture of country-rock and pop songs, but a bit harder hitting than many others around at that time. The second, *Looking Through*, was released on A&M. We wanted Van Morrison as producer but the label insisted that we use Chris Demetriou who'd worked with John Kongos. Around this time, we did TV and opened for people like Leon Russell and Steeleye Span as well as gigging on the college circuit. Despite good reviews, neither album sold particularly well and Herbie and I went our own ways.

I got back to playing music after a couple of years as a roadie. I knew the Brinsleys from playing with them at various gigs like the Roundhouse and the Marquee a few years earlier… so when I needed a gig, I spoke to Nick Lowe and he suggested I call Dave Robinson who was managing Bees Make Honey. I did and he invited me to an audition at the Hope & Anchor. I showed up and there was another bassist there (Norman Watt-Roy). Dave Robinson walked in, sent him home, turned to me and said '... *you've got the gig. You can sing and play bass at the same time!*' I played a few numbers with Barry Richardson on sax, Deke O'Brien guitar, Mick Molloy guitar and Fran Byrne drums. It was really refreshing to be part of the pub-rock scene because it was about bringing the music back to basics as opposed to bands like Yes and ELP.

During my time in Bees Make Honey we recorded two albums. One for EMI, which Nick Lowe produced, another for DJM with Albhy Galuten, who went on to produce the Bee Gees. For some reason neither were released, but we had a ball playing live in both Bees Make Honey and a little later with Meal Ticket. As far as regrets, I only have one. I turned down the gig with Kiki Dee not long after joining the Bees because I was earning good money and happy. The next thing that happened was Kiki and Elton John had a big hit with *Don't Go Breaking my Heart* and some of her band ended up working with Elton for years. That's life, I guess.

I'm philosophical about these things. Back in the 60s we didn't earn any royalties when The Shadows of Knight covered our song *Bad Little Woman*. It wasn't until years later, when it appeared on compilations like *Nuggets* and *Nowhere Men*, that some payments were made. In the 90s I licensed The Wheels recordings to Ace Records and since then money has been coming in. BETTER LATE THAN NEVER!

BILLY RANKIN

(BRINSLEY SCHWARZ, DUCKS DELUXE)

The first drumming I did was in my living room, sitting in front of the TV and playing along to the Z Cars theme. My mum paid for drum lessons with Frank King at Footes Drum Shop in Denman Street, Soho and I became a professional musician at 17 when I went to Munich as part of The Luther Morgan Relationship, an 11-piece James Brown-type soul revue. They ripped me off and a few months later I was back in the UK as part of the house band at the Wunderbar in Leicester Square. The other guys in that later became Hackensack.

I joined Kippington Lodge for their last six months and it was me who saw the *Melody Maker* ad that Dave Robinson had placed. About Famepushers, Stephen Warwick was what he said he was: a film editor. Eddie Moulton was 'the money man' but it turned out he was borrowing money to pay off people he'd borrowed from previously. A bit like a ponzi scheme. He just disappeared at the end. They didn't actually pay us anything. We got expenses and beer money and they paid for accommodation and studio time but in terms of actual pay... we got nothing.

Did we make a film with Omar Sharif? Yes! We didn't meet him, but the film was made and we did all the music for it. I remember us playing along to the footage in Olympia Studios. It was completely instrumental and very jazzy, lots of stuff in 11:8 time and so on, like film music often is. Neither the film nor the music ever got released. The documentary of our trip to New York never appeared either. Tony Palmer – the guy who did *All You Need is Love* and *Cream's Last Concert* – did it. He shot some footage of us in Tunbridge Wells and filmed me on the flight over

BRINSLEY SCHWARZ. In typically lo-fi mode with their Vox amplifier, Brinsley Schwarz were much-loved exponents of the trend toward informal good-time music. They were also prolific: between 1970 and 1975 they appeared on 10 albums, 7 of their own and 3 as backing musicians, but success eluded them.

THE FLAMIN' GROOVIES. Seen here during their 1972 UK visit. That July their gig with Iggy Pop and the Stooges at the Scala, Kings Cross, was one of the formative evenings in the emergence of punk rock.

JOE STRUMMER performing with The 101'ers at The Nashville in April 1976, shortly before he quit the band to help form The Clash.

ROBERT "ROCKIN' LOUIE" LLEWELLYN. Drummer in Shakin' Stevens and the Sunsets, pictured in 1971, modelling an early Malcolm McLaren-Vivienne Westwood t-shirt.

ACE. The classic line-up of the band, who, unusually for a pub-rock act enjoyed a massive international hit with How Long. Alan King (lower left) was a particularly fine guitarist with over a decades experience prior to this with Mighty Baby and The Action.

STARRY EYED AND LAUGHING were typical of the acts that populated the pub circuit. Playing a mixture of rock, pop and country-rock, musically they were exceptional. Visually, their image was indistinguishable from dozens of other, lesser, bands.

BURLESQUE Led by Billy Jenkins, Burlesque were a musically clever band that offered jazz-rock orientated material. Based in Bromley, they were largely overtaken by many of the punk rock groups that emerged after 1976.

THE DAMNED. The much loved first line-up. As with The Stranglers and The Jam, their meteoric rise owed little to the publicity campaigns waged through 1976 by Malcolm McLaren.

ROCKY SHARPE AND THE RAZORS. A 10-piece doo-wop outfit, Rocky Sharpe and the Razors were unusual in having a black female vocalist. Note their outfits: a mixture of 50s retro and 70s street chic. The band split in 1976, with both its successor groups Darts and Rocky Sharpe and the Replays, enjoying considerable success.

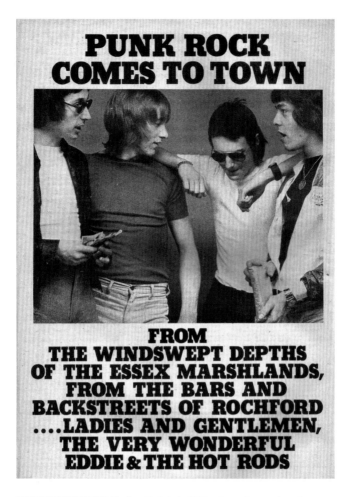

PUNK ROCK COMES TO TOWN

FROM THE WINDSWEPT DEPTHS OF THE ESSEX MARSHLANDS, FROM THE BARS AND BACKSTREETS OF ROCHFORD ....LADIES AND GENTLEMEN, THE VERY WONDERFUL EDDIE & THE HOT RODS

EDDIE AND THE HOT RODS. Until quite late in 1976... the epitome of punk.

KEVIN AYERS AND 747. Rated an exceptional act on the pub-rock scene, 747, seen here with Kevin Ayers (centre), failed to secure a recording deal.

DUCKS DELUXE. Formed by roadies, Ducks Deluxe played energetic material, much of which was written by their leader Sean Tyla. Bass player Nick Garvey (centre) and guitarist Martin Belmont (right) would later enjoy success with The Motors and Graham Parker and The Rumour respectively.

LEGEND. Mark One. No other new band looked like this in 1968. Guitarist Mickey Jupp teetered on the verge of stardom for many years.

DR FEELGOOD. A 1975 publicity shot, taken at a wind-swept Thames estuary oil refinery. Dr Feelgood exemplified the back-to-basics approach of the majority of pub-rock acts.

BEES MAKE HONEY. On stage at one of their many pub gigs. Led by Barry Richardson (left) the core of the band had played together in various incarnations, including an Irish show band, since the early 60's. (Photograph courtesy of Rod Demick)

THE WILD ANGELS. A considerable number of the acts that played the pub circuit through the 70s were rock and roll revival bands, of which The Wild Angels, pictured here in 1970, were typical. Singer Mal Gray (centre) was later poached by Sha Na Na.

ENO AND THE WINKIES. Not noted for his expertise as a rock and roll front man, Brian Eno poses with his backing musicians in an early 1974 picture. The Winkies continued without him, and were highly rated purveyors of simple 3-minute pop songs.

KOKOMO. An impressive soul-funk outfit, Kokomo had their origins in Arrival. Seen here playing an open air festival at Hyde Park, many of their early critical gigs were on the London pub circuit. Keyboardist Tony O'Malley (left) had begun his career as one of The Skyliners from Enniskillen, an Irish showband.

WILKO JOHNSON in action with Dr Feelgood after his 1974 image makeover. A noted figure on the Southend on Sea music scene, his manic stage demeanour would be a significant influence on the emerging punk scene..

THE SEX PISTOLS. February 1976, The Sex Pistols do a set at Andrew Logan's Valentine's Day Party at Butler's Wharf, London SE1. A semi-nude Jordan ensures the maximum publicity is generated.

to New York. I flew over on an earlier plane, so didn't get held up in Toronto with the others. When it came to filming them, and the audience we brought with us, everyone was so late, and so smashed, that the film never got completed. At Glastonbury we played incredibly well. But our set was interrupted in mid-flow by the Guru Maharaj Ji, who turned up in a Rolls-Royce with his orange-robed followers and made an appeal for money.

The idea for a circuit of pubs that put on live music came from Dave Robinson. He saw Eggs Over Easy in The Tally Ho, an Irish pub. They were a sweet band. Very tight, very funky and great vocal harmonies. Dave asked landlords he knew for unfashionable evenings where they weren't putting on music. Many of the venues were usually putting on jazz but they were happy to deal with him, and via that we got a number of residencies. We worked hard as a band... in one year we did 234 gigs and recorded 2 studio albums. We did sessions too, including the first Chilli Willi LP. They were lovely guys. You got £36 a time for session work, but I found it a bit dry. The people who make money out of sessions are the songwriters!

Our tours of Ireland were amazing. Derry was the scariest... explosions and gunfire outside the hotel. We were stopped by the army and had our van searched and at one point the landlady of our usual digs was kidnapped and held hostage for two days. She was never the same afterwards. In the South you'd play a place like Tullamore and not start until 11pm when the pubs closed. Then the place would be rammed. The men and women would stand on opposite sides of the hall, like a youth club dance years earlier, and the gig itself would go on to about 2am. Rather like a night with a showband playing.

The worst incident we had in the UK was in Mansfield where Nick Lowe – Nick Lowe of all people – knocked out some bloke's teeth with his bass guitar after he climbed up on stage. You got stuff happening at gigs back then but because I sat at the back as the drummer I wasn't as much in the front line as the other band members, fortunately.

I think the best song Brinsley Schwarz did was (What's So Funny 'bout) Peace, Love and Understanding. Some of our cover versions were great too, particularly our take on Sam and Dave's *You Got Me Hummin'*, which was eventually released on an album of BBC sessions in 2001. Our big mistake was not agreeing to do *Top of the Pops* to promote *Country Girl*. Towards the end Elton John wanted us to tour the US as his support band. He'd heard from Wings that we were really good. This would have been a huge step forward, and we wanted to do it. But it got bogged down in an argument about us only playing a set lasting 30 minutes. Our management insisted on 45, and we lost the gig to the Sutherland Brothers. I think the most difficult moments, for me, in Brinsley Schwarz were the sessions for *Silver Pistol*. Nick was incredibly depressed during them.

In 1975 Brinsley and I joined Ducks Deluxe and toured France and the Netherlands with them. Sean Tyla was a curious man. When we did a Ducks Deluxe reunion years later at the 100 Club, he sang his own songs but couldn't remember his own lyrics. After that I was in Tiger, a very pompous heavy rock band fronted by Big Jim Sullivan. Technically, that was the best drumming I ever did. But I didn't like it. I preferred Brinsley Schwarz much better. I dropped out after a spell with the Sutherland Brothers. I did a tour with them, and we had recorded half an album, when the record company dropped us. By then I was fed up with the travelling and the insecurity of the earnings. One month you might get £500. Then nothing for the next 3-4 months. I also got dropped by Nick Lowe which hurt me. He said, '*I can't play with you anymore because you make me sound like Brinsley Schwarz!*' So, I learnt instead to be a carpenter.

I think things are easier today than they were then. I did some sessions a few years back and it was much less stress than when we were doing them in analogue studios. The bands I really liked were Kokomo, the Average White Band, the Grease Band and Dr Feelgood. Kilburn and The High Roads too. Best venues? In London the Marquee and The Kensington. Outside London, probably The Black Swan, Sheffield.

(WHAT'S SO FUNNY 'BOUT) PEACE, LOVE AND UNDERSTANDING

Pub-rock wasn't just about country rock enthusiasts taking over a few select venues from folk and jazz enthusiasts. It was also about how a number of bands, and musicians, who having missed the boat in their first incarnation, found a way to keep themselves in the game as the 60s changed into the 70s. Mention pub-rock today and most people think automatically of Brinsley Schwarz. Regarded as pioneers, and fondly remembered, they were a band that stubbornly sold in limited amounts, despite being forever on the verge of a commercial breakthrough. Two of their personnel, Schwarz himself and keyboardist Bob Andrews, were much involved in the subsequent success of Graham Parker, and a third, Nick Lowe, was later a star in his own right as well as a go-to producer and songwriter for others. Like Dave Edmunds, Shakin' Stevens and Bees Make Honey, the story of how they came to be iconic pub-rockers begins in the 60s.

To be precise in March 1969, when Stephen Warwick, a sound editor on films like *The Bed Sitting Room* and *The Italian Job*, the latter quite possibly the apogee of Swinging London, met Eddie Moulton. A scientific executive who had been working in Canada, Moulton had been injured in a car crash, but had access to funds. The two hatched plans to become movers and shakers on the London scene, still the coolest on the planet at that point, and set up a network of companies to fund their objectives. Others were doing likewise at the time, notably David Hemmings (via Hemdale) and Robert Stigwood, but the obvious comparison would have been with Apple. Like them, Warwick and Moulton aimed to set up a brand. One that roamed around the pop world promoting music, film production, magazine publishing, fashion and graphic design. They named themselves Famepushers, and set up base at 295 Portobello Road W11, above the hippy 'head' shop *Forbidden Fruit*. This had a mural by The Fool, salvaged from the Apple boutique on Baker Street, across its frontage and was a noted venue for buying clothes, incense and antiques as well as a place for staging photoshoots.[1]

Top of their list was a plan to take over Red Sands Fort, an abandoned WW2 anti-aircraft bastion in the Thames Estuary and convert it into a huge entertainment centre, complete with light shows, music, dancing, overnight accommodation and performance areas. The location selected had been used by Radio 390, one of the 'pirate' radio stations that proliferated around the UK between 1964 and 1967. Warwick and Moulton's proposal would have been astronomically expensive, required licensing by the authorities (the fort was within territorial waters) and would have entailed partygoers travelling 50 miles out of London followed by an 8 mile trip by boat to their destination. The idea was quickly abandoned.[2]

Next up – and here they were on to something – was a 13-part TV documentary about Omar Sharif and his 'bridge circus', a group of wealthy card players who toured the world's casinos and luxury hotels putting on exhibition matches and tournaments for the wonderment of the masses. The end product would have resembled a Bond film: lots of exotic locations, richly detailed, plush interiors, opulently dressed men and fabulous women in the latest haute couture gazing in fascination as millions changed hands. Budgeted at $250,000, they hired Ned Sherrin to make the series. Finally, they sought to sign a band, partly to help out with the music for their film ventures and partly because, well, that was what you did, and where you made serious money. At which point enter Dave Robinson, former tour manager for Jimi Hendrix, introduced to Warwick and Moulton by John Eichler, with whom Robinson shared a house in Barnes. Robinson advised Famepushers to advertise in *Melody Maker* to recruit the required musicians.[3]

They did so, specifying they were looking for, '*a young songwriting group with their own equipment*', and out of the 80 or so applicants selected Kippington Lodge, a 4-piece band from Tunbridge Wells. As a harmony/pop act they had signed to EMI's Parlophone label in August 1967, where Mark Wirtz produced their first couple of singles, Wirtz being 'hot' at this point after his success with Keith West's *Excerpt from a Teenage Opera*. Their third single was written by one of Herman's Hermits, after which came two more produced by Gentry Records who also handled Vanity Fare. The last, released in April 1969, was a cover of Lennon and McCartney's *In My Life*. None of these sold and the band had latterly discovered a somewhat broader musical palate via the music of Chicago and The Band. They also shed some of their personnel. Drummer Peter Whale being replaced by Billy Rankin and keyboardist Barry Landeman opting for commercial success, and cabaret, with Vanity Fare.[4]

They were looking for a fresh start and impressed Robinson, who explained initially he wanted a group that wrote its own songs, would work hard and gradually reach the top of the music industry. After finishing their bookings as Kippington Lodge, Brinsley Schwarz made their live debut on 14 December 1969 at the Town and Country Club, supporting US country rockers Formerly Fat Harry.[5] Warwick and Moulton dug into their pockets and paid for them to do some demos with Mickie Most. By the standards of later years, when Schwarz were seen as a cool, niche act, and Most was noted for vulgar pop successes with Hot Chocolate and Suzi Quatro, this would have seemed the epitome of naff. But not so in 1969. Warwick, Moulton and Robinson were well aware of Most's success in the US, particularly the huge numbers of albums and singles sold by Donovan and Jeff Beck, the latter blazing a trail for Led Zeppelin. Alas, after an abortive session, where Most edited down one of the band's lengthier pieces to 3 minutes, he departed and Robinson took over production duties.[6]

Famepushers were up and running. Next, they moved into publishing, part funding *Friends*, a magazine which aimed to replace the UK edition of *Rolling Stone*. Then, they installed graphic designer Colin Fulcher (aka Barney Bubbles) in premises at 307 Portobello Road, with a brief to produce posters, album sleeves and general imagery for the burgeoning counter-culture. The TV series moved forward slightly too, with a press conference at the Mayfair Hotel on 1 January 1970 announcing, 'On *January 6th through January 10th, Omar Sharif will play a leading role with a difference in a remarkable new series of televised bridge games to be recorded at London's Piccadilly Hotel.*' [7] This sounded like game on for Ned Sherrin, but all of this cost money, and there was not much coming in.

At which point, with recording ongoing at Olympic Studios and enough material in the can for an album, Warwick and Moulton decided they needed to up their game. They couldn't afford Brinsley Schwarz doing a slow-burn... they needed to get them a deal immediately and sell them as the next big band to emerge out of England. Robinson thought he could do this. Specifically, he would get them a launch event at the Fillmore East in New York before an invited audience of music journalists, socialites and well-connected hangers-on, with a film crew present to record the event. He had been Hendrix's tour manager when Hendrix had played there in 1968. Attempts to persuade owner Bill Graham to do business by phone foundered, however. He wasn't interested. Not to be refused, Robinson crashed over to San Francisco, bearded Graham in his office, and played him some of Schwarz's demos. They were enough for Graham to cautiously agree the band could do two nights opening for Van Morrison and the Quicksilver Messenger Service on 3 and 4 of April 1970. This done, Robinson reversed back to the UK, called '*a friend of mine at Aer Lingus*' and arranged the hire of a Boeing 707, to ferry the band and their target audience there and back. [8]

It was a break but actually Graham wasn't giving them that much. Both his Fillmore venues often had nights with 3 or 4 bands, with the opening acts varying between unknown, obscure but interesting and a few who became recognised names. It's likely he thought he might as well have a third band on the night, and it was no big deal to him either way but to Schwarz and Robinson it represented a huge chance. In the weeks that followed they began selecting their guests and extracting as much music media interest in the event as possible. Andrew Lauder, who had seen them at the Town and Country Club three months earlier, was persuaded to sign them to a long-term multi-album contract with

United Artists. Announced in *Music Now* in late March 1970, this commented, '*A fantastic $30,000.00 advance is reputed to have been agreed, which is quite something for a group whose previous takings amounted to some £60 for a one-night gig. Negotiations are also in hand for the U.S. recording rights and the group's management Famepushers are quoted as having already turned down a six-figure fee. It looks like the signing could be an all-time world record.*' [9]

Next came the guest list. Half a century on, no definitive schedule of who made the flight exists, but other than Robinson, Warwick and the band it is known that the following were all invited and present: Jenny Fabian and Johnny Byrne (co-authors of that well-thumbed exposé of the hippie scene *Groupie*), Pete Frame (*ZigZag*), Charlie Gillett (*Record Mirror*), Richard Neville (*Oz*), Jonathan Demme (*Fusion*, and at that point 'music co-ordinator' for the film *Eyewitness*, in which capacity he engaged the services of Fairfield Parlour and Van der Graaf Generator), Royston Eldridge (*Melody Maker*), Tony Norman (*Music Now*), Keith Altham (*NME*), hippie heiress Olga Deterding and her partner Jonathan Routh, Routh's son Jodi, just 19 and heading the film crew tasked with making a documentary of the event. There were journalists from *The Evening Standard* and *The Guardian* along for the ride too. On the day they all arrived at Heathrow on time, took off three and a half hours late, made an emergency stop at Shannon Airport to check the aircraft's brake system, stopped again at Toronto (they couldn't fly direct to New York because they lacked the visas to do so) and eventually reached the US – with two engines out of commission, the 707 was barely airworthy – just an hour before the band were due on stage. [10]

Miraculously this wasn't an issue. Robinson had pre-booked a couple of dozen chauffeur-driven Cadillacs (provided by Head Limousines; he knew the company's owner) to get them to the Fillmore in a convoy escorted by NYPD motorcycle cops. [11] They reached the Fillmore with minutes to spare, to find Graham fuming and threatening to throw the band off the bill. Robinson sorted that too, getting Van Morrison to plead that Schwarz be allowed to do their set. Which they did... some were impressed, some not with most of the guests who'd come over from the UK too tired to comment or watch the two headlining acts. The exhausted entourage retired to the Royal Manhattan Hotel, then David Frost's New York HQ, where Famepushers had block-booked a couple of floors for the weekend. Few bothered to watch the band on the second day, when by all accounts their performance was much better, Pete Frame remarking, 'Actually, I saw it. The band was more relaxed, tighter and at the end of their set there were cries for more.'[12]

After which everyone returned home, to find that debts were piling up. Famepushers were in trouble. The morning-after-the-party feeling kicked in with a vengeance. Viewed by many as a gigantic hype, coverage of the event started appearing the Thursday prior to the gigs with Robert Partridge, then with Record Mirror, writing a lengthy piece headlined Once upon a time there was a group called Kippington Lodge. This is the never before told story about how they changed their name to Brinsley Schwarz and found fame, pushers and pop. Partridge, like other commentators subsequently, seemed as interested, if not more so, in the machinations of Warwick and Moulton than whether the band were any good. Along the way he noted the New York jaunt had cost £35,000, that, 'In return the group got saturation coverage in everything from the Financial Times to IT' and that Warwick and Molton (note the slightly different spelling here) were running 11 companies. 'Molton' was stated to have 'been at public school and had later gained a degree in physics'. Their business dealings were described in some detail... the abortive attempt to buy a pirate radio station, the publication of Friends, Barney Bubbles studio, the ownership of Forbidden Fruit, the 13-part TV series with Omar Sharif as well as an assertion that, '...a forty-minute documentary of Sharif was also made – in colour and with music by Brinsley Schwarz'. One wonders how this might have looked. Sharif, attired in evening dress in grand surroundings, dealing out the cards to music from Robinson's charges? Was there somehow, in someone's head, a meeting point between these unlikely opposites? Possibly Sharif's recent starring role as that totemic figure of the counter-culture, Che Guevara, in the 1969 biopic Che!

It was clear that Partridge had researched Famepushers in some detail. He noted that it had cost £8,500 to hire the Boeing

707 from Aer Lingus, that about £20,000 had been spent on the film crew who had made the trip, *'headed by Stephen Warwick... who... also made the Sharif film'* and that *'the final figure should come to anything between £25,000-£50,000'.* He cites, accurately, that they had a £12,000 advance when signing for United Artists who secured them in competition with Mickie Most's RAK and Warner-Reprise and concluded by urging readers to *'wait for the album to know whether it was all worth it'.*

Once everyone was back in the UK, *New Musical Express* (11 April 1970) reported the Fillmore shows in *The Schwarz Caper – Or How to Register a Name.* This namechecked Olga Deterding, Jonathan Routh and Jodi Routh, mentioned the malfunctioning plane and then commented on the music. Nick Lowe *'has so much hair it covers his face'* but *'sings lustily'.* Brinsley Schwarz *'plays a domineering lead guitar'.* Bob Andrews *'does some frantic run-ups with his flashing hands. And drummer Bill Rankin is not to be outdone'.* They note that the band opened with 12 minutes of *'a volume filled marathon called* Indian Woman' which *'only received lukewarm applause',*[13] comments that appear ominous only for the column to continue, *'They are getting better as it goes on and by the last number, Life is Death... the repetitive lyric and theme gets excitement mounting and... big applause'.* All in all, quite a fair review.

A week later, *Melody Maker* ran a piece by Royston Eldridge entitled *Brinsley from Kippington Lodge to the Empire State.* This barely mentioned the concerts, preferring to note that, *'Famepushers, the company behind the £30,000 promotion have been accused of perpetrating the biggest hype of all time.'* It quoted Brinsley Schwarz himself as saying, *'It would be a hype had we flopped at the Fillmore but we really enjoyed the whole thing. American audiences are really weird compared with English audiences because they groove on completely different things but it went well. All the pressures were on us that first time and none whatsoever the second time. We weren't screaming with paranoia but naturally it affected the play the first time but after we'd finished, we thought it's over, it's finished, let's go out and get it together, and it went better.'* In other words, as Pete Frame noted, the first show was pretty average, and the second a considerable improvement. Eldridge concluded with, *'The British public will be given a chance to hear Brinsley in concert. The group hope to make their first appearance at the Albert Hall, either on their own or with one or two big name bands, before starting a British tour. Whatever the criticisms of their music ability, Brinsley Schwarz have overnight reached a stage which takes many rock bands twice as long to attain. They have got to American and British public alike through one performance. From here on in it's all down to the music.'*

Between the two reviews Eddie Moulton (or was it Molton?) disappeared. He was never seen again, and no one ever found out what his real name was. The band's debut album, *Brinsley Schwarz*, appeared on 17 April. Wrapped in a nice gatefold sleeve by Barney Bubbles it had 7 tracks, all originals with 6 written solely by Lowe. The production credits were shared between the band and Robinson. The critics seem to have been reasonably impressed with typical comments including, *'A most pleasing first release... If not exceptional, still very worthwhile'* (Record Retailer), *'basically good, with excellent lead guitar and organ, and several interestingly original songs'* (Music Business Week), *'although this isn't the Pearl of the Pacific, it is very, very good'* (Record Mirror), *'this young band have produced one of the most encouraging albums to come out of a new English group for some while'* (Friends) and *'a first-rate album of the softer, more subtle kind of progressive music, laced with a very prominent C&W influence... Certainly, if they maintain this standard they will become a very, very important group'* (Record Buyer). It sold fairly well for a debut release but didn't chart. A single lifted from it, *Shining Brightly*, appeared a few weeks later and led to the band appearing on *Top of the Pops* on 28 May 1970, alongside Christie, Marvin Gaye and Cat Stevens. Quite how they managed this isn't clear... given that it came nowhere near the charts. Perhaps it looked for a week or two as if it might and was treated as 'bubbling under' or a 'breaker' in the parlance of the time. More prestigiously, they also did a slot on BBC2's *Disco 2* show on 6 June with Tony Joe White.

As the dust settled it seemed things had gone quite well for them after all. Dave Robinson would later comment, *'Despite the bad press, the Fillmore trip actually achieved what I most wanted. The band name was now known, they had a profile and some income.'* His take was shared by drummer Billy Rankin who recollected, *'We went from a local band earning £50 a night to a £200 headlining band with an album.'* Which was true, but possibly not how it would have seemed in 1970. A hype of the extent perpetrated by Moulton and Warwick was regarded as something of a scandal then, so much so that *The Sunday Times* Insight Team picked up on it and ran a major investigatory piece later in the year. And you couldn't escape the debt. Brinsley Schwarz had been launched with costs that were over four times their advance. Although the band stayed together – the sales of the album were sufficient to justify doing so – everything else connected with Famepushers crashed in ruins. Brinsley Schwarz didn't play the Albert Hall. Barney Bubbles lost his studio. Ned Sherrin's TV series was never made, the 40-minute Omar Sharif documentary was never seen and Jodi Routh's footage of the band's trip to New York is presumably still sitting on a shelf somewhere.[14]

Moving on rapidly, Robinson put them up in a large communal house in Northwood, Middlesex, and got them gigs and session work. In July 1970 they went into the studio with legendary US singer-songwriter Jim Ford, known now, by some, as *'the Godfather to Pub-Rock'*. Nothing was released and a month later they were working with PJ Proby, then seeing out his Liberty/ United Artists contract with a series of dud singles. Little if any of that material saw the light of day either.[15] In the meantime, they knocked out a second album of their own, named *Despite it All* in an obvious reference to the events of a few months earlier. Released in December 1970, this saw them augmented on selected tracks by John Weider (Family), Dave Jackson (Van der Graaf Generator) and Brian Cole (Cochise). The critics liked it, with *Sounds* proclaiming it was *'quite an improvement on their first... an excellent, relaxed feel'* and *Record Mirror* regarding it as *'a gem of an album'*. *Beat Instrumental* thought it *'excellent for removing depressions'* and *Friends* concluded, *'It might not shake the earth, but will certainly keep my home and heart warm this winter.'*

It was a very country-rock outing and after recording it they added a second guitarist, Ian Gomm, to their line-up. By way of promotion, they did a John Peel session on 5 December 1970 followed by the next stage of Robinson's recovery programme, a mini-package tour (marketed as the Down Home Rhythm Kings) alongside two of his other acts, Help Yourself and Ernie Graham. Both of these secured deals with United Artists, with Ernie Graham (formerly of Eire Apparent, a Belfast group Robinson had been involved with in the 60s) using Brinsley Schwarz as his backing band on his April 1971 eponymous debut. After which Rankin, Schwarz and Andrews found the time to take part in the sessions for an album by folk-rocker Colin Scot, the results of which were released to muted reviews, typical of which was 'A mellow, low-key exercise in introspection', Melody Maker (10 July 1971).

This was the position when Robinson, amazed by Eggs Over Easy's set at the Marquee, arrived at the band's communal residence in Northwood in the early hours of 16 June 1971. His band had found a niche, were still together and were being used wherever possible for session work. But could they do more? Get some real traction, sharpen themselves around the edges? He thought so; hence the suggestion to be 'just like Clover', which in practice meant slightly shorter songs, some cover versions, and everything (venues, amps, attitude) on a smaller, less pretentious scale. This may have been the intention, and the seeds were certainly sown when Lowe and Rankin headed down to The Tally Ho to watch Eggs Over Easy, but it still took a bit of time to adjust fully, as the next we hear of Brinsley Schwarz is their appearance at the Glastonbury Festival the following week.[16]

A fondly remembered event, this ticked all the boxes required for a late 60s/early 70s counter-culture happening: 7000 people in a large field, some with tents, many not, an abundance of nudity, drugs and sex, much improvised dancing and the famous triangular tent generating its earth energy and karma above the stage. The list of those appearing was truly impressive and included Melanie, The Edgar Broughton Band, David Bowie, Hawkwind, Arthur Brown, Fairport Convention, Family and Traffic. It wasn't pub-rock and, despite its mystical trappings, was better organised than Robinson's New York jaunt, producing both a feature film and a commemorative album. The former, under the jurisdiction of Peter Neal and Nic Roeg, doesn't include Brinsley Schwarz, but the latter, a tie-in live triple album à la Woodstock does... they have one track on side two, doing *Love Song* from *Despite it All* just prior to 16 minutes of Mighty Baby's epic *A Blanket in My Muesli*.[17]

After which it was back into the studio again, for their third album, *Silver Pistol*. This had shorter songs, 12 in all, of which 2 were Jim Ford covers. And, as part of moving away from being solely reliant on Nick Lowe, 4 tracks were written by Ian Gomm. In this case the studio was the rehearsal room in the band's communal house in Northwood, which meant, logically, that they had plenty of time to get things right, at much less cost than would have been the case elsewhere. The results were mixed. Their cover of Ford's *Niki Hokey* (ironically a US hit for PJ Proby four years earlier) is truly shambolic. Both *Melody Maker* and the *NME* commented on the similarities with The Band. *Disc* thought, *'I know Brinsley fans who love the album through their blind loyalty, but I found it a drag'* and *Frendz* commented, *'They're writing good tunes you can hum along with, but the lyrics are nothing to get excited about.'* It didn't chart, but as an exercise in finding themselves and sorting out a new sound it worked well enough. As did a general cleaning up of their image, part of which involved Robinson taking Lowe to see Dr Samuel Hutt, physician to the stars, to wean him off LSD.[18]

This accomplished, they finally played The Tally Ho on 19 January 1972, about a week before *Silver Pistol* appeared, the conjunction of the two events meaning that some critics, then, and some commentators, now, label it as the first album to be released by a pub-rock band. This clearly isn't the case... a better description might be that it was the first album to appear by an established mainstream band that had decided to play accessible material in smaller venues. Nor, for that matter, is it the case that Brinsley Schwarz played mainly pub gigs from 1972. It was something they dipped in and out of, with most of their live shows continuing to be on the university and ballroom circuit.

Indeed, on 13 February 1972, they played the Roundhouse with Man and Hawkwind as part of *The Greasy Truckers Party*. Like Glastonbury this was a major hippie event and was supposed to raise funds to build a hostel in Notting Hill Gate that would recycle its income into worthwhile causes. Running from 3pm to circa midnight, it took place 4 days after Prime Minister Edward Heath had declared a State of Emergency, as a national miners' strike reached its climax with spectacular power cuts across the UK, plunging most cities into darkness for several hours each evening. Although Brinsley Schwarz and Man got through their sets ok, the power failed shortly afterwards. As the audience milled about in the cavernous dark of the Roundhouse, there were attempts by the London Fire Brigade to evacuate the building. Many refused to leave, however, and eventually ad hoc temporary lighting was set up. Proceedings kicked back into life with Hawkwind taking the stage to *This is Your Captain Speaking*. They closed the evening with a memorable set that included the original take of *Silver Machine*, their biggest hit. But the chaotic atmosphere, less than a year after the bucolic bliss of Glastonbury, was very much a reflection of the changing social (and political) mores in the UK.

Like Glastonbury there was an album of the event released on United Artists a couple of months later. It contained 5 Brinsley Schwarz tracks, culled from the 16 they played on the night, of which no fewer than 7 were covers. By the time it appeared they were at Rockfield, where Kingsley Ward was producing their fourth studio album, *Nervous on the Road*. Not so countryfied, what was on offer here was more soul-inflected and not unlike Van Morrison. Critics reckoned that they had finally found their sound, and musically it had a consistency that their prior albums lacked. It also contained one of their best-known numbers, Nick Lowe's *Surrender to the Rhythm*. Released in September 1972, like its predecessors it failed to sell. This inability to shift vinyl, and linked with that, a lack of significant Radio One airplay, did not diminish their standing as a live act, though. They supported Lou Reed at The Scala, King's Cross in July 1972, a gig that was warmly commended by Charles Shaar Murray in the *NME*, and, as ever, they remained in demand as a pick-up band. Returning to Rockfield they backed Frankie Miller on his debut album, *Once in a Blue Moon*, after which Andrews, Lowe and Rankin were part of the crew assembled for Chilli Willi and the Red Hot Peppers' *Kings of the Robot Rhythm*. The latter was released on Revelation, the same label that did the Glastonbury Fayre triple album and was a peculiar offering, much of it consisting of manic, crazed bluegrass-style music. They rounded off 1972 with a second John Peel session on 12 December. It had been a busy three years: 4 studio albums of their own, a further 3 as a backing band and 2 extensive live sets recorded for release. No one could fault their work rate.

Through 1973 they built on their new lo-fi, dance band image. Their fifth album, *Please Don't Ever Change*, encapsulated this perfectly. Mostly recorded at Jackson Studios, Rickmansworth – no distance at all from Northwood – and co-produced by Vic Maile, this had a cover shot of the band playing on a modest-sized stage with a modest-sized backline, PA and drum kit, a retro late 50s typeface and graphics and a back cover picture of them next to their suitably unpretentious transit van. There were 10 tracks (4 covers and 6 originals), one of which was a live recording from the Hope & Anchor of Ronnie Self's 1967 single *Home in My Hand*. *Record Mirror* reckoned it was, '*the perfect illustration of bar-band music 1973 – good-time, neatly performed, and with flavourings of humour and nostalgia*'. Two singles were culled from the material, the first of which, *Hypocrite*, appeared in April 1973 under the pseudonym of The Hitters. A very capable cover of The Heptones' track of the same name, it was possibly the first attempt at the kind of white reggae that The Police would perfect.[19] The second, *Speedoo*, originally a 1955 doo-wop number by The Cadillacs, came out in August. Like the album, neither charted and sales continued to flatline... but in terms of credibility, particularly with the cognoscenti, they were doing fine, and an appearance on *The Old Grey Whistle Test* followed on 6 November 1973.

From there they took part in the filming of *Stardust*, having a brief, blink-and-you'll-miss-it scene where they perform *Da Doo Ron Ron*, credited on the soundtrack album to Dave Edmunds and The Electricians. A non-album single, *I've Cried My Last Tear*, a cover of Ernie K-Doe's 1962 Louisiana soul track, flopped in March 1974, after which the band returned to Rockfield for their sixth album, *The New Favourites of Brinsley Schwarz*. Dave Edmunds produced. There seems to have been some care taken over how to present and market this, an effort to build on the image they had now established. There was the title, which sounded like something from a decade before and a cover, by Pierre Tubbs, which looked deliberately like a K-Tel greatest hits LP. Image-wise, the band had changed too. They were now unrecognisable from the quartet that played the Fillmore in 1970. The vast amounts of hair were long gone, replaced by shorter locks. Their clothing too was different, no immense flared trousers or greatcoats but workaday outfits and (mainly) straight trousers. They made this sartorial shift at about the same time as Dr Feelgood. The album had 10 tracks, of which two were covers: Otis Clay's 1972 soul hit *Trying to Live My Life Without You* and The Hollies' *Now's the Time*, originally the b-side to their 1963 hit *Stay*. The latter, all clanking rhythm guitars and harmonies, sounded positively antiquated. Affectionate it may have been, but it was as if the band were regressing to their Kippington Lodge days, or even earlier.

But there was no doubting that it was very well done, and in Nick Lowe's *(What's So Funny 'bout) Peace, Love and Understanding*, it contained their pièce de résistance. A paean to how the times had changed for the worse since the late 60s, in the UK of 1974 it might almost have been an attempt to diagnose the state of the nation:

And as I walked on
Through troubled times
My spirit gets so downhearted sometimes
So where are the strong
And who are the trusted?
And where is the harmony?
Sweet harmony

'Cause each time I feel it slippin' away, just makes me wanna cry
What's so funny 'bout peace, love and understanding? Oh
What's so funny 'bout peace, love and understanding?

The critics liked it... the public were indifferent. Released as a single in June 1974 it failed to sell, as did the album.

For the moment they kept going. John Peel had them in for another session on 25 July and they were back at Rockfield once more to record a seventh album that autumn. This had Steve

Verocca producing, best known then for his work with Link Wray and iconoclastic UK songwriter Kevin Coyne. It may have been an attempt to fashion something for the American market, but little of it would be released at the time. A single, their take on Tommy Roe's 1963 hit *Everybody*, duly appeared in January 1975. It didn't sell. And neither did a cover of The Beatles *I Should Have Known Better*, released by them as Limelight the same month.[20] After a fifth John Peel session on 20 February 1975 and a final single, *There's a Cloud in my Heart*, as The Brinsleys, they went their separate ways in March 1975. The album remained on the shelf for another 13 years.

What came next? By April, Schwarz and Rankin could be found in the final line-up of Ducks Deluxe. This lasted until July, coming to an end with a gig at the 100 Club. Here Lowe and Andrews joined them for a couple of numbers, and the proceedings were eventually released as a live album, *Last Night of a Pub Rock Band*, in 1979. By the end of 1975, Schwarz and Andrews had both been recruited by Robinson as members of The Rumour, Graham Parker's backing band. Signed to Vertigo, and afforded heavy promotion, they finally enjoyed commercial success in both the UK and US in 1979-80.

Ian Gomm built a 16-track recording studio in Wales with Hawkwind's Dave Anderson. Here he produced and mixed the final live set from Bees Make Honey and also oversaw early demos by The Stranglers. In 1978, he returned to live music, releasing a single, *Hold On*, which charted in the US.

The most curious afterlife, though, lay with Nick Lowe. Initially, he busied himself recording half a dozen tracks, mainly in the style of The Bay City Rollers, accompanied by John Fee and John Ciambotti from Clover and Chris Miller, drummer in Rot, an obscure south London rock band.[21] The first of these, *Bay City Rollers, We Love You* credited to The Tartan Horde appeared on United Artists in July 1975. It did quite well in Japan – where it outsold anything Brinsley Schwarz had done – and led to the appearance of similarly embarrassing material, this time by The Disco Brothers, on which Dave Edmunds was listed as producer.[22] Whilst doing these Lowe also made his debut as a solo artist, with the single, *Keep It Outta Sight*, released in the Netherlands in 1976.

One hopes that Lowe made something financially from this. But even if he didn't, monetary rewards were not long in coming. By 1976 he was producing Graham Parker and was also involved in that capacity in the launch of Stiff Records, where he worked with Elvis Costello and The Damned, the band Chris Miller joined using the moniker Rat Scabies. Like Gomm, Lowe also kept his hand in as a musician. In fact, his single, *So it Goes*, was the first Stiff release in August 1976, and a follow-up, *I Love the Sound of Breaking Glass*, hit No 7 in the UK charts in 1978. A year later, he scored even better when *Cruel to be Kind*, co-written with Ian Gomm, hit No 12 in both the UK and the US, with the album it came from, *Labour of Lust*, making the Billboard Top 40. Thereafter, he worked successfully as a composer, producer and performer in both the UK and US.

A decade on from the foundation of the band, then, most of its members finally had the commercial success Robinson would have wanted when they started. One of the oddities about them, though, was the extent to which they remained famous, basically for not being famous, long after they ceased to exist. Most of the rock reference books of the 70s contained entries about them, and as early as 1976 Nick Kent was lamenting, '*I really miss Brinsley Schwarz; they were great – I always enjoyed seeing them... one of the last great British bands*'.[23] They were always acknowledged as being seminal, and their reputation has remained high long after their demise. When the pre-internet cataloguing craze of the mid-90s was at its peak, they could be found listed in Martin Strong's *The Great Rock Discography* (1994, several editions, with a foreword by John Peel) and several other breeze-block-dimension volumes. More recently (2014 and 2021) multi-CD collections of their studio and live work have appeared.

In essence, their fame rested on what they didn't represent when compared with many of their contemporaries. Once they had moved on from their initial heavy blues + hippy trappings, they were a band that established that it was ok not to have extravagant stage shows or elaborate costumes. It was also ok not to have an immense backline and PA, not to have a huge road crew and not to have a set of articulated lorries to transport your gear. Most importantly it was ok not to play a set consisting 100% of originals written by the band. The latter was an important point. Up until circa 1965 everybody played covers in their set, and many acts had sets that were almost entirely covers. Many bands hardly wrote any originals at all. The trend for writing all your own material began in the mid-60s, whereafter it became de rigueur for everyone to attempt this. With the exception of obvious retro acts, such as Shakin' Stevens and his contemporaries, recording a Hollies b-side or 50s doo-wop or a Ronnie Self cover simply wouldn't have been entertained. Brinsley Schwarz changed this. They made it ok for bands to provide their audience with something they would enjoy in an uncomplicated, non-cerebral fashion. It was a change from the intensity and intellectualisation, some might say pretentiousness, that marked much of the music produced in the 70s. At the end of the day none of these traits added up to much for them, in terms of record sales. But they cleared a path that many others followed.

Looking back, it is also clear how their career was shaped by three emblematic events: the New York shenanigans, Glastonbury Fayre and the *Greasy Truckers Party*. Although it wouldn't have been clear at the time, each of these represented a moment in the unwinding of the optimism of the 60s into the travails of the 70s. They start with a jamboree halfway around the world, billed as the next big rock band from London, pass through the short-lived bliss of a free festival, and end up in an immense, poorly maintained mausoleum of a venue, the Roundhouse, with their audience milling around in the midst of power cuts and industrial disputes.

You could make a very good drama documentary about the UK in the 70s, centred on Brinsley Schwarz, with it set against the events of the time and highlighted with key incidents from their career. Perhaps somebody will.

Notes

(1)   For an interesting account of this see https://retrochbabe.wordpress.com/the-brinsley-shwartz-hype/ Pictures of Ten Years After playing

on the pavement outside the shop can be viewed at https://www.
ibiblio.org/mal/MO/philm/ten_years/

(2)   See Will Birch *Cruel to be Kind: The Life and Music of Nick Lowe*
Chapter 5 (2019).

(3)   See https://www.psychedelicbabymag.com/2022/03/help-yourself-
interview-paul-burton.html This describes Famepushers as '*a film
production company who were also involved in music production*', and
that John (Eichler) '*was really into film making and he had friends who
were working on a film about Bridge – the card game. It starred amongst
others Omar Sharif, the well known film star... John was living in Barnes
with Dave Robinson... He had persuaded the people at Famepushers to
move into music, ostensibly to produce music for the film, but this had
expanded into band management and record production.*' Eichler and
Robinson remained close for many years, with Eichler later installed
as manager of the Hope & Anchor. In *Classic Rock* 4 April 2017
Robinson is quoted, '*I'd been tour manager with Jimi Hendrix, then in
1969 I got involved with two guys, Eddie Moulton and Steve Warwick, who
had set up a conglomerate of small companies known as Motherburger. They
were looking for somebody to start a management company. It was decided
to advertise for a group to be managed by the new company, Famepushers.*'

(4)   In their final year, Kippington Lodge were being booked out by the
Southend-based Barry Collings agency, whose pen portrait of them
on a May 1969 flyer states, '*Latest release on Parlophone 'In My Life' a
Lennon-McCartney composition. Plenty of plugs arranged.*'

(5)   Where they were seen by Andrew Lauder of United Artists records,
who thought '*They sounded a bit like The Band...*'

(6)   Most produced albums that enjoyed immense sales 1968-69,
notably The Jeff Beck Group (*Truth* No 15 US, *Beck-Ola* No 15
US) and Donovan (*A Gift from a Flower to a Garden* No 13 UK/
No 19 US, *The Hurdy Gurdy Man* No 20 US and *Barabajagal* No 23
US). Between them these earned 3 gold records and the success
of the Beck releases was a significant factor in the decision by Led
Zeppelin to concentrate on the US album market.

(7)   For the Mayfair Hotel press conference see: https://www.alamy.
com/jan-01-1970-press-conference-to-announce-omar-sharifs-bridge-
circus-image69445386.html

(8)   See: https://www.loudersound.com/features/brinsley-schwarz-press
trip-from-hell-new-york where Robinson states, '*There was a night
about three months later, with Quicksilver Messenger Service and Van*

Morrison, which needed a bottom-of-the bill act. Graham said, "We'll give it to you." Now we had to sort out the press trip. I got on to a friend of mine at Aer Lingus and they were interested in chartering a 707 which could hold 140 people. Suddenly I had a gig and a plane, neither of which I had paid for.'

(9) The advance was roughly equivalent to £12,100 then, about £219,000 today. This wasn't actually that remarkable, and the publicising of such details may have led some music industry insiders to conclude, even at this early stage, that this was a scam (or hype) perpetrated by amateurs.

(10) Most of the guests are listed at https://thebluemoment.com/tag/famepushers-ltd/

(11) Given that the NYPD has a significant Irish quotient, one wonders if Robinson pulled strings there too.

(12) On the gigs see https://thebluemoment.com/2020/04/04/a-night-at-fillmore-east-1970/ where an anonymous guest (who confirms the attendance of Deterding and Routh) states, *'sadly, we were unanimous: their subdued country-rock was best described as nondescript'*. At https://www.loudersound.com/features/brinsley-schwarz-press-trip-from-hell-new-york Brinsley Schwarz says (re: the second night), *'The best show we did, probably because the pressure was off and we could just enjoy ourselves, was the second set on Saturday, which no one saw.'* The same article confirms the comments made by Pete Frame.

(13) Brinsley Schwarz actually opened their set with a 12-minute-long version of *Ballad of a Has Been Beauty Queen.* They later performed this on the West German TV show *Beat Club,* the footage of which can be seen at: https://www.youtube.com/watch?v=R9Env3GEsWg Released as a single in France in 1970, one can see why comparisons with the heavy rock bands of the time were justified.

(14) Steve Warwick didn't vanish and carried on working as a sound editor in films, though no credits for him are listed after *Emerson, Lake and Palmer on Tour* in 1973. A comment at https://www.loudersound.com/features/brinsley-schwarz-press-trip-from-hell-new-york states that, *'he ended up as a postman living in a corporation flat in Acton'.* Bubbles' work for Famepushers was quite impressive and included album sleeves for Red Dirt, Cressida, Gracious and Dr Z. He later did many of the Stiff picture sleeves.

(15) For more on the Jim Ford sessions see: https://www.rocktownhall.com/blogs/jim-ford-godfather-to-pub-rock/ which states, *'Somebody*

got the idea that Ford should go to London and record a second album with Brinsley Schwarz as his backing band. These sessions were apparently a total failure, and I don't think any of it has ever been released. Nick Lowe has said that his band was simply not up to the task, and Ford was never the most stable or reliable character.' With Proby they were in good company: Led Zeppelin had backed him on his September 1968 LP *Three Week Hero.*

(16)   It wasn't their first. In July 1970 they were at the Euro-Pop 70 Musikfestival in Munich, West Germany with, among others, Taste, The Edgar Broughton Band, Black Sabbath, East of Eden, Can, Juicy Lucy, Status Quo, Deep Purple, Traffic, Free, Atomic Rooster and Black Widow.

(17)   The film was co-produced by Sanford Lieberson (*Performance, The Pied Piper, That'll Be the Day, Stardust*), Si Litvinoff (*A Clockwork Orange, The Man Who Fell to Earth*) and David Puttnam (*Melody, The Final Programme*) with photography (and uncredited direction) from Nicolas Roeg. After a short period on the circuit, it lapsed into obscurity until a 2018 rerelease.

(18)   Hutt was also a musician. As leader of Boeing Duveen and The Beautiful Soup he released a single, *Jabberwock,* in May 1968. A longstanding friend of Pink Floyd he was well known as '*the underground community's defacto house doctor'*, a description made by David Wells some years later. Lowe is quoted in Birch's book (op. cit.), *'I didn't speak and I was covered in lice and I had gonorrhoea... I was a horrible hippie case.'*

(19)   There is a suggestion that this is a Bob Marley song; however, the Marley track (of the same name) appears to be completely different.

(20)   Confusingly, United Artists released a cover of *Day Tripper* by The Knees at the same time, which led many to think this was Brinsley Schwarz too... it isn't. It's Man, using a pseudonym.

(21)   As well as Miller, Rot included Simon Fitzgerald, later in Johnny Moped, and Phil Mitchell, bass player in Dr Feelgood from 1983. The band broke up at the beginning of 1976 when Miller, by this point calling himself Rat Scabies, joined The Damned.

(22)   One of The Disco Brothers tracks, *Everybody Dance,* was co-written by Lowe with Danny Adler of Roogalator.

(23)   See *ZigZag* 59, April 1976.

IAN GOMM

(BRINSLEY SCHWARZ)

I was in bands in the 60s. I did 5 years as a mechanical and electrical draughtsman, working at EMI, and in 1967 I wrote to Sir Joseph Lockwood, the Chairman, asking for an audition. He wrote back agreeing and Norman Smith recorded us but asked me to get rid of the other two band members, so nothing came of it at the time.

I joined Brinsley Schwarz after they advertised in the *Melody Maker*. They couldn't replicate the sound of their first album live, particularly the vocals. I didn't want to stay working in an office of middle-aged men, so I applied. They asked me along and I played some stuff after which Nick Lowe said '*That's great man, you're in!*' What I didn't know was that they were all tripping on acid! I was very straight compared to them. Dave Robinson made them do the audition again, after they'd come down. This was just prior to their recording *Despite it All*. For contractual reasons I wasn't on the album, but my Telecaster was: Brinsley Schwarz plays it.

We all lived in a communal house in Carew Road, Northwood. There were about 11 people there at one point. It was an enormous place, with space for a rehearsal room. All our earnings went into a pot, but the band were very low on funds so my wife and I gave them our life savings, £500, which was quite a lump of money then. Living in Northwood meant we were quite near the big NATO base. A trio of young US guys, whose fathers worked there, took to calling around the house. They were in a band and one night they played us some of their songs... it was America, and we were hearing *Horse with No Name*, which later became a massive international hit.

Because of my work at EMI, I was often called on to fix amplifiers and cables. A little later I made Martin Belmont of

Ducks Deluxe a guitar, based on a Telecaster body. Called it the Gommcaster! In *Stardust* we make a brief appearance doing *Da Doo Ron Ron*. I don't know why Dave Edmunds called us The Electricians, but maybe it was down to my knack for repairing and building new gear from scratch.

I built the band's PA. At Glastonbury in 1971 we played for free, the crowd got in for free, and we lent the festival our PA. We did our set early evening, and went down fantastically well. But halfway through, the Guru Maharaj Ji arrived and we were asked to stop playing... this so angered us that we quit, packed up the PA when we left the stage and let them sort it all out.

I saw Eggs Over Easy at The Tally Ho. Everyone thought they were just like The Band. They used to swap instruments during their set, and had a much more extensive repertoire than was common at the time. We got bookings at The Tally Ho ourselves after seeing them, but the real change happened when the fuel crisis of the 70s kicked in. It became less economic to travel around the UK doing the college and ballroom circuit, so we compensated by doing more pub gigs. When we played them, we got a share of the bar takings and just lived on whatever we earned. Our favourite was probably The Kensington, a fantastic place.

Dave Robinson had good connections in Ireland and we toured there a couple of times. We were booked to play in Derry immediately after Bloody Sunday. I remember staying in a hotel in Belfast where there were bullet holes in the wall behind the reception desk. We got stopped at Newry in 1972 by the army. They lined us up against a wall with our hands up and searched the van. Most of the pubs we played in London had an Irish connection, again through Dave Robinson. He seemed to know everybody. Later, during the IRA bombing campaign in England, I remember a nervy night at The Kensington: there was a call saying a bomb had been placed there and everyone, the band, the audience, had to wait outside in the street while the pub was searched. I remember going back in to collect my guitar, which probably wasn't too clever a thing to do.

Gigs were often quite violent anyway. When I started playing, we used to take bets on what time the fights would start! It had toned down a little by the mid-70s but in Brinsley Schwarz we did a gig at Mansfield Civic Centre that ended in a brawl with some Hells Angels who kept shouting *Play Rock and Roll!* Nick Lowe hit one of them in the face with his bass guitar and knocked out most of his teeth, and our roadies, both Glaswegians, chased them off.

We toured with Wings, which was very prestigious, and got the gig via Henry McCullough, who'd known Dave Robinson from his time in Eire Apparent. Our best work at Brinsley Schwarz was done at Rockfield, with Dave Edmunds producing. Particularly *(What's So Funny 'bout) Peace, Love and Understanding*. Towards the end of our time together Island wanted to sign us and send us over to the US. The intention was to release *It's All Over Now*, with the original version of *Cruel to be Kind*, as part of a big push to break us there. But United Artists kicked back saying we still owed them 2 albums. Faced with this we split up.

It took me about a year to get my studio in Wales up and running. I bought a plot of land with Dave Anderson, one of our roadies, and formerly the bass player in Hawkwind. It had 2 cottages and a cow shed that I converted into the studio. It cost us £3,500. I mixed and overdubbed the tapes there for a live LP by Bees Make Honey, who'd toured Ireland with us. The first proper sessions we did were with The Stranglers; I think they were still called The Guildford Stranglers at that point. They turned up in an ice cream van: that was Jet Black's business! They drove all the way to Wales in it.

Looking back, it wasn't as big a scene as people seem to imagine now. Everyone knew each other. I really rated Ace, Chilli Willi and the Red Hot Peppers and Dr Feelgood. We were the first band to play live on *The Old Grey Whistle Test*. Our philosophy was *Keep it Real*. We didn't dress up either. In fact, our agency, NEMS, were always asking us to dress up more, like the rest of their acts. But we wouldn't do it. Could we have done something that might have changed our fortunes? We declined an appearance on *Top of the Pops*, because we wouldn't mime, and I think that maybe the name of the group was a bit of an issue. People couldn't spell it or pronounce it.

MARTIN BELMONT

(DUCKS DELUXE, GRAHAM PARKER
AND THE RUMOUR)

I was at art school in Bournemouth in the 60s. It was a great town to live in, you could get by on virtually nothing. Whilst I was there, I sang in a band – Sunday in St Petersburg – for a few months, and also spent quite a bit of time playing in folk clubs. I was heavily into Bob Dylan. After I left in 1970, I spent about a year trying to get a job in film/TV. I had one interview at the BBC for 'Assistant trainee film cameraman' but nothing. When I was told that I was 'overqualified' for a £7 a week job as a messenger for an editing company in Wardour Street I thought, 'well sod this'. The only other thing I was interested in was music so I decided to follow that path. A chap I was at college with was working as a photographer and had got to know Brinsley Schwarz (the band). He told me they were looking for a roadie and so...

I lived with them, Dave Robinson, another roadie and various wives and girlfriends in the big house in Carew Road, Northwood. I still wanted to be in a band, though, and Dai Davies, the PR man for Brinsley Schwarz, introduced me to Sean Tyla who was similarly motivated. He wrote songs and had the qualities needed to front a band. I was a half-decent guitar player and we shared many musical tastes. Dai wanted to be a manager and the whole thing was cooked up by the three of us – I think the name Ducks Deluxe was Dai's idea.

When we started, we lived together in a squat on Prince of Wales Road, Kentish Town. It was a three-storey town house that today would sell for a few million. We had almost no expenses while we lived there. Later we rented a house together in Hendon (handy for the M1!) I don't really remember how the day-to-day finances worked. None of us had day jobs and we were a full-time gigging band almost from the off. Did Ian Gomm build me a guitar? Yes! I played it for quite a few years. You can see me using it in the clip filmed for *The Old Grey Whistle Test* at The Lord Nelson, Holloway Road.

It was probably Dai's doing that we got to appear in a BBC *Play for Today*. Our segment was filmed at The Tally Ho, one of the main pubs on the circuit. It was in Kentish Town. We also got an advance from RCA. I've no idea how much. I believe it was a two-album deal. The split in the band in 1974 was due to musical differences to use a cliché. Andy and Nick wanted a more 'pop' direction I think whilst Sean and I were more rock'n'roll. But we were kind of inconsistent. One night we were great and the next a bit of a train wreck. I would say the first album, *Ducks Deluxe*, was the best thing we did and on a good night it was a great live band.

After Ducks Deluxe ended I lived and worked at the Hope & Anchor pub in Islington. Brinsley had been playing in Ducks Deluxe for the last couple of months and we had talked about having a new band together. Bob Andrews also wanted to do something and through Dave Robinson we met Andrew Bodnar and Steve Goulding who had been in a band called Bontemps Roulez. We started rehearsing, trying out different songs, covers and a few originals. We sort of knew what we didn't want to do – be in just another band playing in pubs – but didn't really know what we did want to do.

Then, once again through Dave Robinson, we met Graham and started rehearsing with him. That was around September 1975, I think. We did a couple of very low-key gigs and recorded demos at Dave's 8 track studio in the Hope & Anchor. Graham got signed to Phonogram and we started recording his album in December. We worked hard and gigged a hell of a lot for 5 years. It paid off. We got a degree of commercial success and were an untouchable live band.

Comparing the music scene then with now is like chalk and cheese. It's totally different. The entire music business is different. As for the music itself I'll take the 70s but even more I'll take the 50s and 60s. Today? Forget about it! By the way whatever

Wikipedia might say I am still working today and my mainstream recording and gigging career is still going (although more minority interest music) right up to today.

The bands on the circuit that I rated back then were all the usual suspects: The Brinsleys, Chilli Willi, Dr Feelgood. Post pub-rock then there were 3 GREAT outfits – Elvis and The Attractions, Ian Dury and The Blockheads and GP and The Rumour. Do I need to say who I think was the best of the lot? I don't have a favourite venue, there were too many – too long ago and too bad a memory!

TIME FOR ANOTHER

In their early incarnation Brinsley Schwarz had more than a little in common with Mighty Baby. Both bands had a prior life on EMI's Parlophone label, Schwarz as Kippington Lodge, Baby as The Action. Both had a core membership that stayed together as musical tastes changed and matured. Both mixed country-rock with heavier material. Both played Glastonbury Fayre, and both appeared on the Revelation Records triple album commemorating that event. Both were highly regarded as musicians, and in demand as session players. The output of the Brinsleys during their existence, appearing on 13 albums in just over 5 years, was surpassed by Baby with 14 in not quite 3, the core of the group, Ian Whiteman, Mike Evans, and Roger Powell appearing on releases by Robin Scott, Gary Farr, Shelagh McDonald, Keith Christmas, Reg King, Curtiss Maldoon and Andy Roberts. Both bands were also, for a while, expected to be the next 'big' act to emerge from the UK scene. Neither did, and in some ways (looking at this from the perspective of many in 1970-71) the failure of Mighty Baby might have seemed the more surprising. So, what went wrong, and what were the long-term effects of their demise?

First, though, let's be clear: Mighty Baby were not a pub-rock ensemble, though like everyone else they played such venues. Originally a quintet of sharply tailored Kentish Town mods, they had actually been together since 1963, originally as The Boys, backing Sandra Barry at one point. Things changed for them in late 1968 when they recruited guitarist Martin Stone, regarded then as one of the most promising in the UK. With his contributions well to the fore, their sound developed from

pop-soul to brilliantly played acid-drenched psychedelia, and
they released, to rave reviews, a debut album *Mighty Baby* on the
small Head label in 1969. Produced by Guy Stevens it opens, side
one, track one, with *Egyptian Tomb*, one of the great masterpieces
of its time.[1] In early 1971 Mike Vernon, sharing the consensus
that they were going to be huge, signed them to Blue Horizon.
It was a considerable step in the right direction, given that both
Fleetwood Mac and Chicken Shack had started out there and
Vernon had just taken on production duties for Dutch band
Focus.

Martin Stone took a lunch break during rehearsals in April
1971, in the course of which he met Ian Dallas, a Muslim convert.
Dallas took Stone to a meeting at the Islamic Cultural Centre,
Regent's Park, where he introduced him to various Sufi adherents.
Amongst these were a trio of US converts – Conrad Archuletta,
Susan Archuletta and Daniel Moore – all of whom were heavily
connected with the San Francisco music and theatre scene. Both
Archulettas were members of the Floating Lotus Magic Opera
Company, an outfit founded by Moore that performed regularly
at the Avalon Ballroom and the Fillmore West, and prior to this
Susan Archuletta (then Susan Graubard) had played flute on Pat
Kilroy's 1966 psychedelic folk album *Light of Day*.[2]

By the summer of 1971 the whole band had met Dallas and the
US trio. As when people encountered Eggs Over Easy, they were
knocked out by the musical depth Susan and Conrad Archuletta
brought with them, Ian Whiteman noting, 'We didn't have that
influence... which is why when California suddenly came to London, it was
a breath of fresh air'. Just as importantly, Dallas was an impressive
figure and incredibly well-connected. Starting out as an actor, by the
late 50s he was a TV scriptwriter, adapting both *Jane Eyre* and *Vanity*
Fair for the BBC. Becoming steadily more bohemian, he hung out
in Paris, where he counted Edith Piaf as a friend, was cast by Fellini
in a supporting role in *8½*, appeared in the legendary (and now lost)
BBC TV play *The Madhouse on Castle Street* alongside Bob Dylan
and David Warner, adapted Lermontov's *A Hero of our Time* for TV,
with Alan Bates starring, and then, in 1967, converted to Islam. By
this point he was friendly with Eric Clapton and George Harrison,

and via the latter was slotted into a bizarre scene in *The Magic Christian*.[3] This brought him to Hollywood, pitching a script, and it was here, after reading about them in *Rolling Stone*, that Dallas checked out the Floating Lotus Magic Opera Company. Having met him Mighty Baby thought their fortunes might change. To quote Ian Whiteman again, *'I think there was a secret desire fluttering that he was going to somehow open new doors in our careers.'*

Most of the band duly visited Morocco, an awkward arrangement given their recording and gigging schedules, and on their return their second album *A Jug of Love* appeared. A pleasant set of country-rock originals heavily influenced by The Band and The Byrds, it got ok reviews, but was so different to their first that the audience they had would have been puzzled at the transition. By this point Dallas was exerting an influence within the band itself, which alienated guitarist Alan 'Bam' King who quit in November 1971. Despite this, they continued to rise. Chris Blackwell had been noting their progress and offered them a deal with Island *'to make an album of whatever they wanted'*. Like Mike Vernon, he probably thought Mighty Baby were destined for greatness.[4]

At this point Martin Stone was still with the band. But with no live shows lined up, and it becoming clear that Dallas was establishing a cult-like control over his colleagues, he departed in February 1972.[5] This left Whiteman, Evans and Powell who now joined with the Archulettas and began recording as The Habibiyya. Their album, *If Man but Knew*, appeared in October. It was another significant shift in direction, this time towards devotional, introspective Islamic music played on traditional eastern instruments. Reviews were dismissive, *Melody Maker* remarking, *'one for those who collect albums of North Vietnam peasant songs... not of much interest to the average rock fan – except possibly those heavily into Quintessence'*. Sales were minute. It was world music, but twenty years too early. Chris Blackwell was happy to do more but the band disintegrated with Evans and Powell vanishing into Dallas's cult. Only Whiteman continued his musical career, appearing on albums by Marc Ellington and Richard and Linda Thompson for a few more years.

Looking back at this now, it's interesting to compare Mighty Baby's failure to deal with Ian Dallas with Brinsley Schwarz's gradual recovery from their encounter with Eddie Moulton. The collapse of Mighty Baby was certainly a waste of talent, and they might have achieved much had they stayed together. Importantly, though, both their guitarists survived, and emerged from the wreckage leading bands that were central players on the pub-rock circuit.

The first to reappear was Martin Stone, which was perhaps not that surprising given his reputation. Prior to his stint in Mighty Baby, he had played on *Shake Down* the 1967 debut album by The Savoy Brown Blues Band, after which he backed US bluesman Walter Horton on his 1968 set *Southern Comfort*. His standing was high, and in around May-June 1969 he was seriously considered – recommended by Alexis Korner, no less – as a replacement for Brian Jones in The Rolling Stones.[6] That didn't happen – it's a great what-if to consider – and three years later, having exited from Mighty Baby, he put together Chilli Willi and the Red Hot Peppers with Phil Lithman, a long-standing friend who had just returned from a spell in San Francisco where he recorded as one of The Residents, an avant-garde, multimedia and some might say deliberately obscure, collective.

The two of them decamped to a farm in Wales owned by Tom Crimble, who had been involved with staging the 1971 Glastonbury Fayre. Through him they met bass player John Fox, and percussionist Barry Everitt. Fox and Everitt had been at Glastonbury too and Everitt, also a pirate radio DJ with Radio Geronimo, had set up Revelation Records with John Coleman to issue the much admired triple album of the event.[7] Coleman, a music journalist, became the band's manager. Very much a continuation of the spirit that had propelled the festival, things slowly came together and they began recording an album. Bob Andrews, Nick Lowe and Billy Rankin from Brinsley Schwarz all provided assistance, as did Jo-Ann Kelly and Dave Vorhaus. Vorhaus was also part of White Noise, an experimental electronic outfit with Delia Derbyshire of the BBC Radiophonic Workshop. Like The Habibiyya a couple of years later, they too had been funded by Chris Blackwell to make an album of whatever they chose.

The outcome of this collaboration, *Kings of the Robot Rhythm*, was released on Revelation in March 1973, and rated as '*a happy, unpretentious album*' by *Disc and Music Echo*. Pete Frame described Stone and Lithman, the core of the group, as an '*acoustic bluegrass/ country blues/dope and madness duo*', and it was undeniable that the material had an energy, but like so much of what was produced by the pub-rock bands it didn't sell.

As he did for so many others, John Peel spotted their potential and they did a session for his show on 9 April 1973. The group was rebuilt. Fox and Everitt departed with three young recruits – Paul Bailey (banjo and saxophone), Paul Riley (bass) and Pete Thomas (drums) – joining in their place. Andrew Jakeman, otherwise known as Jake Riviera, became their manager, replacing John Coleman. They left Revelation Records and its ethos behind, and by September 1973 were gigging regularly. Peel had them in again on 21 February 1974, after which they were one of the acts at the Roundhouse benefit gig for *ZigZag* magazine, the recordings of which were eventually issued in 2010. Their set, 15 tracks in all, captures a band in transition, with their closing number being a cover of Dave Dudley's 1963 country-rock hit *Six Days on the Road*.

They were an impressive live act, as was to be expected of any band featuring Martin Stone on lead guitar. Following a third John Peel session (25 July 1974) they signed to Charisma subsidiary Mooncrest and began recording an album at Ronnie Lane's mobile studio. Both were auspicious developments: Mooncrest were enjoying considerable success with Nazareth and Lane's studio, in Hyssington, Powys, had numerous top-end clients on its roster. Among those recording there in 1973-74 were Eric Clapton, Rory Gallagher, The Who, Rick Wakeman, Bad Company and Peter Frampton. There must have been hope that the Peppers had joined the pantheon of greats.

Mike Nesmith, whom they'd supported at the Roundhouse, produced 5 tracks, of which only 2 were used. There was assistance too from Carol Grimes, Jo-Ann Kelly and Jacqui McShee (all on backing vocals) and Red Rhodes on pedal steel guitar. If Americana was your bag, you couldn't do better than have Rhodes on board. His list of credits, stretching from Van Dyke Parks through Nancy Sinatra to Gene Vincent, was truly astonishing. Finally, the band were augmented by Will Stallibrass, formerly with The Sky Rockets, on harmonica and practically a sixth member. The end result, *Bongos over Balham*, appeared in October 1974.

The reviews were good. It was endorsed by *ZigZag*, and if you liked them live, which many did, you'd like the album. But neither sales nor airplay followed. Perhaps it was too eclectic. Although there were 8 Lithman originals, including *Breathe a Little*, which sounded like Django Reinhardt and the Hot Club de France circa 1935, the set included a Jesse Winchester track and kicked off with a cover of Louis Jordan's 1946 classic *Choo Choo Ch'Boogie*.[8] For Riviera this wasn't good enough, and along the way he made his views known to the band. According to Dave Robinson, '*...they were more country, they were more country style and I believe from talking to them that Jake harassed them, harangued them, he was quite a tough geezer and he harangued them into wanting to be more like the Brinsleys who were pulling big crowds and playing more interesting music, so they were browbeaten by their manager into that area...*'

To address the specific issue of faltering sales a package tour with Dr Feelgood and Kokomo was proposed, both of whom had albums scheduled for release in January 1975. Given the economics faced by managing a band with low sales at a time of general austerity, it was hardly surprising that Riviera took the route of pooling costs whilst going for the maximum possible exposure. To ensure large crowds ticket prices were pegged at 75p, and to make everything as attractive as possible to venue owners the fee for booking all three bands was a mere £450... good value for them, but rather underselling the acts themselves. Dubbed the *Naughty Rhythms Tour*, with the strapline *Watch Out! First Time Ever! Non-Stop Real Music Coming Your Way At 1000 Smiles an Hour!*, it opened at Watford Town Hall on 28 January 1975. Live reviews were excellent and the BBC filmed the show at the Guildhall, Plymouth on 2 February 1975, intending to broadcast it as a rock documentary.[9]

Alas, at midpoint in the 19 dates, Riviera, seemingly without consulting either his charges or Mooncrest, announced that the band would be breaking up. Quite why he did this baffled many, but according to his account it was a last-ditch attempt to get the label to put more effort into breaking the band.[10] (Either that or he felt like giving up; he became Dr Feelgood's tour manager shortly afterwards.) Perhaps as compensation, Chilli Willi and the Red Hot Peppers topped the bill on the final night of the tour, at North London Polytechnic, Kentish Town on 28 February 1975. They closed their set with *Choo Choo Ch'Boogie*, after which Dr Feelgood, Kokomo and Messrs Schwarz, Andrews and Lowe joined them for a jammed-out 15-minute version of Bo Diddley's *You Can't Judge a Book By the Cover* by way of an encore.

By this point *Breathe a Little* had been released as a single. It did nothing, and the BBC never got around to screening their documentary of the tour. The footage for it is now lost. As predicted by Riviera, the band broke up. Paul Bailey and Paul Riley played on various Graham Parker demos later that year, after which Riley and Pete Thomas did similar sessions with Elvis Costello. Thomas subsequently became one of The Attractions and remained Costello's drummer of choice for many years, as well as fitting in work with Nick Lowe, Graham Parker and many others. Out of all the members of Chilli Willi and the Red Hot Peppers he has had the most successful musical career.

The duo who started the band struck out, almost defiantly, in very different directions. Phil Lithman returned to the US and renewed his membership of The Residents. He played on their legendary June 1976 deconstruction of the Rolling Stones hit *Satisfaction*, and as 'Snakefinger' remained with them, both touring and recording for many years thereafter. But the avant-garde didn't claim him 100% of the time. His solo career brought him back to the blues, notably on his 1984 set *Snakefinger's History of the Blues Live in Europe*, an album of covers that saw him leading a 9-piece band. He died in a hotel room in Linz, Austria in 1987, the same day that he released the single, *There's No Justice in Life*. He was 38 years old.

Martin Stone responded to the collapse of Chilli Willi by putting together another band, Martin Stone's Jive Bombers, the other members of whom were ex-Pepper Will Stallibrass, Jona

Lewie, Iain Thompson, later in Darts and Wilgar Campbell, formerly with Andwellas Dream and Rory Gallagher. Between July 1975 and April 1976, they did about 30 gigs, and by all accounts were a fantastic live act. But, as with The Mickey Jupp Big Band, nothing happened and the band soon went their separate ways. They left little by way of legacy, bar a solitary track, credited to Stone's Masonry, that crept out on a Stiff sampler in 1977.[11] By then Stone had been in Pink Fairies for about a fortnight in May 1976, playing on their single *Between the Lines*, which also appeared on Stiff. He'd even done a stint in The 101ers, recruited by Joe Strummer to replace Clive Timperley. This too rapidly became a dead end when Strummer walked out to join The Clash, and The 101ers folded.[12]

Which must have been pretty disheartening. In seven years Stone had gone from being touted as Brian Jones's replacement in The Rolling Stones to a 30-year-old without a regular income adrift in a world where punk was sweeping everything away. It was at this point he set in train a completely separate career as a 'book runner': locating rare books, many of them first editions, for specialist book dealers, and a select circle of wealthy private clients. It was a time when many such works could be found by diligent scouring of junk shops, house clearances and even jumble sales, picked up for 5p and sold on for much, much more. He proved good at it, and his own tastes in esoterica, much of which came via such arrangements, helped.

For a while he kept up a musical career too, with a Sunday night residency at Dingwalls, Camden alongside Paul Riley, Will Stallibrass and Chris Youlden, the latter formerly lead singer in The Savoy Brown Blues Band. This ran through to 1980, and proved astonishingly popular with Jo-Ann Kelly, Jona Lewie, Phil May, Paul Jones and Lew Lewis, among others, dropping in for a jam.[13] But it too fizzled out and Stone lived mainly in Paris thereafter concentrating on his increasing volume of commissions to source rare manuscripts.

Forgotten by the mainstream music media, he remained an enigmatic presence: a slight, painfully thin figure, coming and going from obscure locations at all times of the day or night as he sought out Holy Grails for discerning collectors. Much admired by writers like Michael Moorcock and Iain Sinclair, to the extent that he appeared as a walk-on character in some of Moorcock's fiction, he seemed to represent some kind of eternal vibrant current running through London life.

There were further recordings too. A single and an album with Wreckless Eric in the early 90s, followed by a live album in 2000 backing Billy Boy Arnold with Wilgar Campbell and Steve Darrington. Later there were releases in Denmark and France before his final sessions with Michael Moorcock and The Deep Fix shortly before his death. *The Times* ran an obituary (7 December 2016) describing him as a *'rock guitarist and rare book dealer'* and failing to mention his membership of either Mighty Baby or Chilli Willi and the Red Hot Peppers. It would seem that in death his literary reputation eclipsed anything he'd done musically, and 2017 saw a limited-edition commemoration of his life – 150 individually numbered copies only – published. A hefty purchase at £220 for 52 pages, it included contributions from Moorcock and Sinclair as well as James Fox and Marianne Faithfull. It was a remarkable memorial.

Stone never had a hit record, which was not a failing that would ever be levelled at his Mighty Baby colleague Alan 'Bam' King. Not long after Ian Dallas entered that band's life, King began appearing as a second guitarist in the gigging version of BB Blunder, a group that had arisen from the ashes of Blossom Toes, a highly regarded, and now highly collectable, quartet who released two albums on the Marmalade label 1968-69. Blunder had shrunk to a guitar-bass-drums power, augmented in the studio by session players on their May 1971 release *Workers' Playtime*, only to find that once out on the road they couldn't replicate the sound. With King's namesake, and former colleague in The Action and Mighty Baby, Reg King, already onboard as vocalist, it was no big deal for 'Bam' to sign up too.

His first appearance with them was at the Roundhouse on 20 August 1971[14] (when Brinsley Schwarz topped the bill) and he became a full-time member a few months later after his formal departure from Mighty Baby. The two Kings' version of BB

Blunder played 17 gigs and recorded two sessions for BBC Radio One's *Sounds of the Seventies* down to the end of January 1972 when Reg King, who was '*a bit prone to drink*', departed. Only 4 more gigs followed before they broke up in May 1972, the process eased on its way by the collapse of Sahara Records, their management company.[15]

Accounts of what happened around this time are somewhat vague, but it seems that after BB Blunder ground to a halt, Alan and Reg tried to put together another band, Clat Thyger, with guitarist Phil Harris. This came to nothing when Reg King fell down a flight of stairs and received a head injury which necessitated neural surgery.[16] By the end of 1972 King and Harris had formed instead Ace Flash and The Dynamos with bass player Terry Comer, from Warm Dust, and drummer Steve Witherington. The wacky, retro name, culled from the same lexicon as Chilli Willi and the Red Hot Peppers, was quickly shortened to Ace and after keyboardist and songwriter Paul Carrack (also ex-Warm Dust) joined in April 1973 they began a heavy gigging schedule.

As stated in *The NME Book of Rock 2*, a great many of these appearances were on the London pub circuit where they acquired a reputation as a '*polished white funk outfit*'. Critics took notice. Roy Carr (*New Musical Express*) caught them in Wandsworth in November 1973 and further reviews, all favourable, followed. As a band they were very professional, very unpretentious and enjoyably low-key. Their songs – there were few if any covers in their set – were rocky, bluesy pieces between 3 and 5 minutes long delivered in a style that mixed soul and country-rock. In May 1974 they became the first band to sign to Ian Ralfini's Anchor label. For Ralfini, setting up Anchor, which was a subsidiary of the US giant ABC, had been a triumph given the circumstances then prevailing in the UK music scene, '*I think it was a fantastic achievement to get into the record business at the time we chose. If you remember, there was a fuel crisis, three-day week, a vinyl shortage... But most important of all was the growing concern within the record business itself as to the future of the record business and what 1974 had in store*'.[17] Given these factors, it is quite telling that he scouted his first major act in the type of venues that in former years would have been overlooked.

Once the contract with Anchor was confirmed, the band brought in Fran Byrne from Bees Make Honey on drums, and began recording their debut album at Rockfield with John Anthony in the producer's chair. A strong choice if you wanted to enjoy major commercial success, Anthony's other credits around that time included Queen and Roxy Music. He didn't disappoint here. Their first single, *How Long*, appeared in September 1974 and quickly entered the UK charts, climbing to No 20. Written by Carrack, the band had originally wanted to do it like a Motown number: upbeat, very much a piece of white soul. It was reworked instead as a medium-speed study in weary resignation, and, as such, seemed to fit the mood of the times perfectly.[18] Released in the US in February 1975, it generated enormous amounts of airplay, peaked at No 3 in the *Billboard* charts and reached No 1 in the *Cash Box Top 100*. It became emblematic of 'the pub-rock sound', and turned out to be the only song from that genre (if one could say that pub-rock had a single genre) to produce numerous cover versions, including some done disco style. It still turns up on film soundtracks and when used in a TV commercial for Amazon Prime in 2020 generated sufficient downloads to send it to No 1 in the UK.

Against this background they did a John Peel session on 12 November 1974. Even if Peel hadn't rated them as highly as he did, he could hardly fail to appreciate, as a vigorous supporter of Liverpool FC, that the cover of their debut album, *Five-a-Side*, which was released almost simultaneously with this appearance, showed the band amongst the crowd at the Kop, Anfield.[19] The album itself had 10 originals, all but one written or co-written by Carrack and was a very tight, solid country-rock edged with funk set. Its favourable reviews led to an appearance on *The Old Grey Whistle Test* on 31 December 1974, performing 4 numbers. (Leo Sayer, on the same show did no fewer than 6). By February 1975 *How Long* was starting its ascent of the US singles chart, and, remarkably, *Five-a-Side* had begun to do likewise in the album chart: it would eventually peak at No 11, and remain in the Top 200 for nearly six months.

All of which suggested, for a brief moment, that pub-rock might prove a fertile hunting ground for A&R men looking for

UK bands that would enjoy significant commercial success in the US. John Peel gave them another session on 31 March 1975, and although their next single, the enjoyable loose-limbed country-rocker, *I Ain't Gonna Stand for This No More*, failed to do anything in the UK, they departed to the US a few months later, supporting Yes on an immense stadium tour. Much was expected of their follow-up album, *Time for Another*. Like *Five-a-Side* John Anthony produced and it was partly done at Rockfield. Alarmingly, a single lifted from it, *No Future in Your Eyes*, flopped everywhere when released in November, and the album itself did nothing in the UK and climbed only as high as No 153 in the US. Which is not to say that it was actively bad. The 10 originals had been put together by a much more considered group effort (Carrack was credited on only 5 of them), and it was well-produced and impeccably played. Possibly the issue was that by late 1975 audiences, especially in the UK, wanted a bit more Dr Feelgood and a bit less country-rock/funk. Suddenly, Ace looked (and sounded) a bit dated.

After returning to the UK for a slot on *The Old Grey Whistle Test* (16 December 1975) and a dozen or so gigs, they moved to Los Angeles. Harris left at this point, replaced by John Woodhead, formerly guitarist with John Stewart, and the band now applied themselves to the challenge that so many UK acts had faced: breaking America.[20] Scarcely seen back home anymore, a third album, *No Strings*, appeared in January 1977. Produced by Trevor Lawrence of the Paul Butterfield Blues Band, like its predecessor it was very well done... but this was 70s soft-rock, and considerably removed from anything that might have worked at The Lord Nelson, Holloway Road. It didn't do badly (No 170, US) but with the band in debt, two further singles failing, and musical tastes clearly shifting quite significantly, they came home and broke up after a gig at the Roundhouse in May 1977.

Carrack, Comer and Byrne all joined Frankie Miller's band, playing alongside Ed Deane, formerly of Bees Make Honey. They all appeared on Miller's big 1978 hit *Darlin'*. It would be Carrack, though, who would turn out to be the major beneficiary of the post-Ace years. His keyboards, vocals and songwriting skills would be heard in years to come with Roxy Music, Squeeze, Mike and the

Mechanics, a substantial solo career and finally with Elton John on the biggest record of all time: 1997's *Something About the Way You Look Tonight*, with accredited sales of 33 million and rising. As for Alan King, like Martin Stone, he continued musically much as he had started. In the early 80s he turned up in Juice on the Loose, part of a shifting line-up that also included Byrne and Deane. They played small venues like The 101 Club, Clapham, The Dublin Castle, Camden and The Half Moon, Putney as well as backing visiting US R'n'B players, but with the gig circuit collapsing under them, vinyl beginning to give way to CDs and music getting ready to go digital, the chances of making headway receded at speed and, like Stone departing for Paris, King eventually left to live in New Zealand.

Soon after Ace and Chilli Will emerged from the wreckage of Mighty Baby, Ducks Deluxe came together as an outgrowth from Brinsley Schwarz, the connection here being that Dai Davies, who did PR for Schwarz, introduced Martin Belmont, who roadied for them, to Sean Tyla who did likewise for Help Yourself, another of Robinson's bands. Belmont and Tyla were both guitarists, and both wanted to be in a band rather than humping gear about. They agreed they'd form one with Davies as manager.

Tyla had some prior musical experience, and an ability to write songs. In the late 60s he'd had a publishing deal with Apollo Music (Lionel Bart's company, sold to Hemdale in April 1970) and had also been involved with Tigon Film Music, whose primary function was to record 'library' material that could be used in the films they produced. In March 1971, as Third World, Tyla and a colleague Chris Money put out a single, *Miracles*, on CBS. There were no offers of further releases, hence Tyla's frustration at being at roadie.[21] Ken Whaley, the bass player in Help Yourself, was interested in joining and for a while Belmont, Tyla and Whaley rehearsed in Whaley's squat on Prince of Wales Road, NW5; there was a derelict piece of land at the rear and they could be found out there on summer evenings, jamming.

By July 1972 they had a drummer, Tim Roper, recruited via a *Melody Maker* ad, and gigging started shortly afterwards, with regular appearances at The Tally Ho. Whaley returned to Help

Yourself after a few months and was replaced by Nick Garvey, who'd roadied for The Flamin' Groovies during their brief UK sojourn. The fact that three of the band had been roadies drew some comment, but did them no harm at all as their rise was pretty rapid once they'd settled on their line-up. On 19 December 1972 they appeared with Man, Help Yourself and Dave Edmunds at the Patti Pavilion, Swansea, the recordings of which were released in July 1973 as the live album *Christmas at the Patti* by United Artists.[22]

By then they'd appeared in *Blooming Youth*, a BBC TV *Play for Today* screened on 18 June 1973. Produced by Tony Garnett, this was written and directed by Les Blair, and was a largely improvised study of three young men and a woman sharing a flat in Kentish Town. The characters were students at a local polytechnic, living away from home for the first time, and the situations that develop between them play today like a perfectly preserved time capsule from the mid-70s. The band appear performing in the background in a sequence shot at The Tally Ho, making this an unusually valuable historical record. It deserves to be more widely seen. After recording a John Peel session (26 June 1973) they signed to RCA.

A single, *Coast to Coast*, appeared in November, and was an extraordinarily striking record: fast, simple, unpretentious and as good a slab of original UK street rock as one would have heard around that time. It was quite as accomplished as anything The Flamin' Groovies would have released and it predated Dr Feelgood by twelve months. Their album, *Ducks Deluxe*, was in the shops just after Christmas, featuring 10 originals and 2 covers, the latter being *Nervous Breakdown* (previously essayed by The Wild Angels back in 1968) and Bobby Womack's *It's All Over Now*. They enlarged to a 5-piece by adding keyboardist Andy McMaster immediately after the sessions. A significant move in adding variety to their live sound, McMaster brought experience too: he'd been around since the mid-60s, including one band with Frankie Miller, and had written songs recorded by Anita Harris and Alex Harvey as well as releasing a single of his own in 1970. As constituted, they appeared on *The Old Grey Whistle Test*, playing live at The Lord Nelson, Holloway Road, on 20 January 1974. A second single,

Fireball, appeared in April, but as with the first and the album, the reviews were fine but the sales didn't follow.

Despite this, they maintained momentum. Granada TV had them on *Rock on with 45* (9 May), John Peel booked them for a second session (4 June 1974) after which they headed down to Rockfield to record their next album, *Taxi to the Terminal Zone*. Produced by Dave Edmunds, a single from this, McMaster's *Love's Melody*, was released in November. With twangy guitar interludes and catchy lyrics, it did that rare thing of creating its own atmosphere and should have been a huge hit. Despite another slot on *Rock on with 45* (7 November) it wasn't, and RCA even decided not to release the album in the US, a sad turn of events for what was a well presented, distinguished set.

Sadly, their decline and demise matched their rapid ascent. Early in 1975 McMaster and Garvey left. Reverting to a 4-piece they brought in Mickey Groome on bass.[23] A non-album single, *I Fought the Law*, appeared in February 1975, but flopped and after a third John Peel session (27 March) RCA declined to extend their contract. Popular in Europe, they released an EP on Skydog in France, the tracks on this including an interesting white reggae cover of *Here Comes the Night*, three years before The Police made millions with a string of hits done in the same style. Now Roper left and they completed their last tour with a line-up of Tyla, Belmont and Groome augmented by Billy Rankin and Brinsley Schwarz. The string of dates ended at the 100 Club in July 1975, the recordings of which appeared as *Last Night of a Pub-Rock Band* in 1979.

Anyone wanting to understand pub-rock should listen to it. A double album, with 18 tracks, the sound quality is no more than adequate, the playing acceptable, the singing mainly in key. Most of the material consists of cover versions: Creedence Clearwater Revival, Chuck Berry, The Rolling Stones, Bob Dylan and Them among those raided. It could have been mixed better, but that's hardly the point. The audience lap it up and its rough and ready nature was all part of the attraction. Why did they fail? It's possible that they were just a bit too eclectic, and that their image – t-shirts, denim jeans, baseball caps, beards and so on – was insufficiently sharp compared to, say, Dr Feelgood.

Their various members were not unemployed for long.
Belmont and Schwarz were with Graham Parker by the end of
1975. Nick Garvey (switching to guitar) formed The Snakes with
drummer Richard Wernham from Bazooka Joe, vocalist Robert
Grey and bass player Rob Smith. They released a terrific cover
of The Flamin' Groovies' *Teenage Head* as a single on Dynamite
in the Netherlands before breaking up in June 1976.[24] After this
Garvey began writing material with Andy McMaster. Bringing in
Wernham on drums and Peter Bramall on bass they made their
debut as The Motors in March 1977 and quickly secured a contract
with Virgin. Playing the kind of up-tempo melodic pop that might
have brought commercial success to Ducks Deluxe, they had a
couple of UK Top 30 hits in 1978.

Like Belmont, Garvey and McMaster, Tyla quickly found
himself another band. Unlike them his record sales remained
modest. By the end of 1975 he was leading The Tyla Gang, a
4-piece guitar band whose membership went through a number of
changes. A debut single, *Styrofoam*, appeared on Stiff in September
1976, and a year later with the line-up now incorporating Brian
Turrington and Michael Desmarais from The Winkies they
secured a deal with Beserkley. It was fortuitous timing. Jonathan
Richman and The Modern Lovers had three UK hit singles on the
same label 1977-78 and much was expected of their other acts like
The Rubinoos and Greg Kihn. Alas, despite his ability to write
songs and front a band, Tyla was unable to make this work, and
after a couple of albums the Gang went their separate ways. In
fact, the only real commercial success they enjoyed would be a
couple of live tracks, recorded at the Hope & Anchor, which made
it onto the compilation LP *Hope & Anchor Front Row Festival*. This
reached No 28 in the UK charts in early 1978, the only time Tyla
had anything resembling a hit.

The early years of pub-rock produced one more band from
the collection of musicians and roadies orbiting Dave Robinson:
Clancy. They were built around the singing and songwriting
skills of Ernie Graham, who intersected with a number of the
key individuals in this scene, and whom Robinson had known
since the 60s. From Belfast, Graham was originally one of The

People, who made it onto vinyl, appearing on the 1966 Ember compilation *Ireland's Greatest Sounds (Five Top Groups from Belfast's Maritime Club)*. With this under their belt they decamped to the UK, changing their name a year later to Eire Apparent. Under this moniker they toured with Jimi Hendrix and Pink Floyd and released three singles and an album down to March 1970. Robinson then signed Graham as a solo artist, during which period he lived for a while at the big house in Northwood and toured with Brinsley Schwarz and Help Yourself. Members of both bands backed him on his April 1971 solo album and a stint in Help Yourself followed – he appears on their album *Strange Affair* – but by late 1971 he was once again looking for a fresh start.

Assistance eventually came from Ian Gomm, who introduced him to Colin Bass. Gomm and Bass had played together, briefly, a couple of years earlier. Bass had also been with The Velvet Opera and had even appeared in a version of The Foundations playing the cabaret circuit across the north of England, including a tour of Northern Ireland during which all the band's gear was stolen from outside their hotel in Belfast. They were both looking for something new, and slowly a band coalesced around Graham, Bass and Jonathan Glemser, another Help Yourself outcast. Dave Vasco, from the same version of The Foundations was an early recruit, and the line-up gradually expanded to include Dave Skinner (keyboards, from Uncle Dog, replacing Glemser) and finally, by early 1974, percussionist Gasper Lawal and drummer Barry Ford. The last two were quite considerable additions. Lawal, from Nigeria, had done sessions for Graham Bond, Stephen Stills, Funkadelic and Carol Grimes.[25] Ford had played in an all-black heavy rock band, Noir, in 1971.

They quickly began appearing at many of London's pub-rock venues, attracting attention not only for their music but their multiracial line-up. If there were few women band members in the mid-70s, the same was true of non-white, non-UK musicians. Like The Equals (and The Foundations) some years earlier, Clancy had a mixed black/white membership... which may have endeared them to Island Records with whom Skinner already had a publishing contract. They were briefly signed to Blackwell's label only to be dropped after differences arose between themselves and producer Muff Winwood.

Instead, they got a deal with Warner Brothers, and like so many beat a path down to Rockfield where they recorded their debut album, *Seriously Speaking,* with Island producer Steve Smith. Smith was American and had worked with Bobby Womack at Muscle Shoals as well as with The Supremes. A single, *Back on Love,* appeared in December 1974. Playing a highly competent mixture of rock, funk and jazz-rock, they toured with Manfred Mann's Earth Band, but sales for either the single or the album failed to materialise. Two more singles *Baby Don't You Do It* and *Good Judgement* followed in 1975, after which came a second LP *Every Day* in early 1976. Like the first this was mellow, late-night music. You could imagine being entertained by this in a pub somewhere in inner London... good unwinding-after-a-hard-day-at-work music. Listened to now it comes across as being better quality than many other 'established' bands, particularly in the US, at that time. Sadly, not enough people thought so and after a fourth single *You Have Made My Life So Sweet* (June 1976) Clancy broke up. Ernie Graham managed just one more release, a 1978 single on Stiff, before drifting away from music.

By the summer of 1975 three of the main standard-bearers of pub-rock – Brinsley Schwarz, Chilli Willi and the Red Hot Peppers and Ducks Deluxe – had all disintegrated. A fourth, Ace, had migrated to the US. For most people including many avid readers of the music press their legacy amounted to a solitary hit single, *How Long.* History has been kinder, though, and their many albums today repay listening and are often cited as an influence by many of the musicians and bands who came later. More immediately their demise meant that there were spare musicians to be had, the main beneficiaries of this being Graham Parker and Elvis Costello.

Parker's backstory was not unusual for the time. He'd lived and busked around Europe for a couple of years, rising no further than low level gigs in cafés and restaurants. By 1972 he was back in the UK, working in a petrol station in Surrey, and writing more songs. Some of these were demoed for Stuart Johnson's Tower Bridge

Music circa 1973-74 after which Parker used the route one method for putting a band together: he advertised in *Melody Maker*.

Noel Brown, formerly guitarist with The Sky Rockets, responded, and via him Parker met Paul Riley, late of Chilli Willi and the Red Hot Peppers. Adding a drummer, Brian Neville, they did some more demos, which Riley took to Dave Robinson. Robinson considered these had potential, and arranged for further recordings in the small studio above the Hope & Anchor. One track from these, *Back to Schooldays*, later emerged on the 1977 Stiff compilation, *A Bunch of Stiff Records*. Another, *Nothin's Gonna Pull Us Apart*, had a more immediate effect, being played on Charlie Gillett's BBC Radio London show *Honky Tonk*. Nigel Grainge, an A&R at Phonogram, heard this and made enquiries.

No longer having Brinsley Schwarz to worry about, Robinson quickly became Parker's manager and reached a deal with Phonogram. Part of this meant dumping Brown, Riley and Neville. One wonders how they felt.[26] By September 1975, Robinson had recruited Bob Andrews, Brinsley Schwarz and Martin Belmont (who was actually living at the Hope & Anchor at that point and working in the bar) together with Andrew Bodnar (bass) and Steve Goulding (drums), latterly the rhythm section in Bontemps Roulez and previously colleagues of Noel Brown's in The Sky Rockets. Parker and his new band tried out their material at the Newlands Tavern, Peckham, in October. Like their rehearsals it went well and recording sessions for Phonogram, with Nick Lowe in the producer's chair, began around Christmas.

Billed as Graham Parker and The Rumour they began touring from January 1976, with a debut single *Silly Thing* and album *Howlin Wind* appearing in March and April respectively. Both got favourable reviews. *Sounds* (3 April) judged Parker to be better than Springsteen, whilst the *New Musical Express* (17 April) said he had '*a limited voice... You can tell, though, that Morrison is a predominant influence*' and on the whole thought the album '*remarkably excellent*' even if a bit derivative of Van Morrison, Springsteen and Dylan.

A year before the emergence of Elvis Costello this was laudatory stuff. The reference to Springsteen is revealing. There were obvious similarities: both sang in a fairly high-pitched register, both had an emotional delivery, both wrote material that was played at a high tempo and both wrote from an outsider point of view about backstreets, being cheated, failed relationships, a longing for home and trying to find a way out of life's difficulties. Springsteen made his first impact on the UK charts in November 1975 with his album *Born to Run*. It rose no higher than No 36, but it featured in the charts for 20 weeks and sold consistently. (In the US it went to No 3.) Springsteen headed a 5-piece band, augmented by a substantial horn section, and in the studio, strings. Parker didn't go for the strings but had a 5-piece band too and also made use of horn players, in his case almost entirely when recording and very rarely live.[27]

In 1975-76 this was very much how the future of rock was envisaged: extremely well played and produced albums of original material that expounded and enlarged on classic rock themes in an energetic no-nonsense style. The personnel you would expect to see on stage would be hardened professionals, between 25 and 40 years old. They would be dressed and speak like rock musicians, in the same elegant, nonchalant way adopted by the Stones, the Doors and others from the late 60s. Without any inkling that change was about to engulf the industry, Parker and The Rumour were heavily endorsed particularly by *ZigZag* magazine, John Peel (two sessions, June and November 1976) and the wider media, with an appearance on Tony Wilson's *So It Goes* (24 July 1976), alongside Mott and Lou Reed.

Looking back, it's easy to be a bit over-analytical. Appearing in venues that were smaller and more intimate than the functional stadiums that host established bands now, Graham Parker and The Rumour were a very exciting night out... one of the outstanding live acts of their time, or any time for that matter. By the end of 1976, it had been agreed that one of their songs would feature in the US film *Between the Lines*, an interesting ensemble drama, with John Heard and Jeff Goldblum, about the staff on an underground newspaper that's about to be taken over by a corporation.[28] They began selling records too, having a 1977 hit in the UK singles chart with *The Pink Parker* EP (No 24), followed by two UK chart albums, *The Parkerilla* (1978, No 14) and *Stick to Me* (1979, No 19). These were followed by *Squeezing Out Sparks* (1980, No 18) and *The Up Escalator* (1981, No 11) both of which peaked at No 40 in the US. Parker never became another Springsteen, but he and his ensemble enjoyed more commercial success post-1976 than they had done on the pub-rock circuit beforehand, and their recordings remain enjoyable today.

Notes

(1) The sleeve notes of the 2007 reissue of *If Man but Knew* have Ian Whiteman commenting, '*When Martin came in, he brought with him the I Ching, Aleister Crowley, and Gurdjieff – particularly Gurdjieff – and much more.*'

(2) On the performances at Avalon Ballroom and Fillmore West see: https://dangerousminds.net/comments/be_glad_for_the_song_has_no_ending_taking_a_trip_with_the_incredible_string which states, '*In September of 1969 I saw The Incredible String Band perform at the Fillmore West. I attended the concert with a theater company I was a member of called The Floating Lotus Magic Opera (yes, it's true). The concert was sparsely attended, the Floating Lotus making up a good part of it, and there was a real sense of communal intimacy in the Fillmore that night, with the audience singing and chanting along with Mike Heron, Robin Williamson, Licorice McKechnie, Rose Simpson and various other members of the String Band's extended family. The air was thick with incense, pot smoke and patchouli as the audience (gathering) repeated together the mantra from 'A Very Cellular Song'.*

(3) In both *8½* and *The Magic Christian*, Dallas plays some kind of magician figure, playing with the central character's sense of reality.

(4) It may have helped that Whiteman played on 7 tracks on Sandy Denny's 1971 Island album *The North Star Grassman and the Ravens*.

(5) Dallas, latterly known as Dr Abdalqadir as-Sufi, died in 2021. He issued a fatwa against Pope Benedict XVI in 2006. At https://www.overgrownpath.com/2017/08/untold-story-of-countercultures-islamic.html Ian Whiteman comments that his film roles '*presaged much of his projects in later life which were ambitious and radical but too often collapsed leaving people stranded and traumatised. Despite this his communities still survive in Norwich, Granada and Cape Town. But like*

him, they are strangely disconnected from mainstream Islam. The same could be said of his books which never appear in the bibliographies of the many books published in the Muslim world'.

(6) On Stone see: https://ianwhiteman.blog/2016/12/25/the-passing-of-martin/

(7) Interview with John Greene (aka John Fox) 10 August 2022. Greene/Fox stated, *'I don't know very much and can remember less but I was on a few of the tracks. I met Phil and Martin thru* [sic] *Tom Crimble in the aftermath of Glastonbury Fayre. We played together in Wales and they invited me to be on the album.'* (Crimble had formed an ad-hoc ensemble, The Worthy Farm Windfuckers, to entertain the crowd at the Festival. This included Fox.) On Everitt, see: https://hqinfo.blogspot.com/2017/05/barry-marshall-everitt-life-in-music.html Radio Geronimo was a pirate radio station set up in 1970 with funding from Tony Secunda and Jimmy Miller. They recorded their shows in a studio in Harley Street, and then sent tapes of them to Monaco where they were broadcast across Europe on 205 metres, medium wave. They were present at Phun City with Ronan O'Rahilly, and recorded the various acts at the Glastonbury Festival. Everitt was later involved with Radio Seagull 1973-74, broadcasting out of O'Rahilly's increasingly dilapidated ship.

(8) The author remembers Emperor Rosko playing the Louis Jordan original several times on his show in the mid-70s. MCA eventually released a single version of this in February 1976. Forties swing/kitsch had quite a vogue at the time with Bette Midler scoring a huge US hit in 1973 with her cover of The Andrews Sisters' *Boogie Woogie Bugle Boy.*

(9) See *Record Collector* 19 October 2007 where Paul Conroy, who worked for Charisma in the early 70s, states. *'I'm certain Jake got the basic idea from a tour we did with Genesis, Van der Graaf Generator and Lindisfarne under a Charisma Records banner a couple of years before.'*

(10) See *Melody Maker* 6 August 1977, where Allan Jones, in an article that kicks off, *'Jake Riviera reminds me of a hip Hitler',* records Riviera as saying, *'I presented them with all kinds of wild schemes... but no one had the imagination to suss what we could do. The whole thing was a lot more off-the-wall with the Willis, though. I mean, if you're a band with a name like Chilli Willi and the Red Hot Peppers and you release an album called* Bongos Over Balham, *it's going to strike a few people as eccentric.*

It's not exactly Frampton Comes Alive, is it? But, at the same time, there were people we could have got that record to, people that would've been interested and would have enjoyed it. We didn't have a chance, though, because no one would take the kind of risk involved'.

(11) The original version of Stone's Masonry released a single on Purdah in 1966. The members at that point included Peter Southworth (later Peter Shelley) who went on to be involved with Magnet Records and Keith Tillman later with Aynsley Dunbar's Retaliation and John Mayall's Blues Breakers. The 1977 line-up included Bobby Irwin (drums) whose later career included working with Roogalator, Lene Lovich, Paul Carrack and Nick Lowe.

(12) On 17 March 1976, in almost the ultimate live show by two pub-rock bands, Essex University had The 101ers (Stone's next band) supported by The Jive Bombers (Stone's current band). It appears that Stone completed the following gigs with The 101ers: Bromley College (28 May 1976), The Golden Lion, Fulham (30 May 1976) and Clare Hall, Haywards Heath (5 June 1976).

(13) For more on this see the recollections of Malcolm Mills at https:// www.lastmusic.co.uk/labelnews/chris-youlden-the-slammers https://www.pbfa.org/books/the-remarkable-martin-stone

(14) An Implosion event, a series of fondly remembered gigs often with Jeff Dexter as DJ. See: https://50.roundhouse.org.uk/content-items/ great-education-rock-roll-sunday-afternoons-roundhouse

(15) For more on this see the 2005 CD reissue of the *Reg King* LP. Sahara had been launched with funding from The Rolling Stones. The final days of BB Blunder were far from happy. At https://www.45worlds.com/live/listing/b-b-blunder-sirius-1972 Pat Martin from the band Unicorn, who supported BB Blunder at a gig on 14 January 1972 states, *'I remember jamming in the dressing room with Alan "Bam" King playing "Apache" from the Shadows and their Avis Hire rental van was driven away by Avis because their record label were behind with paying the rental.'*

(16) See Reg King's *Guardian* obituary 7 November 2010 at https://www. theguardian.com/music/2010/nov/07/reg-king-obituary

(17) See *Music Week* 14 February 1976 at: https://worldradiohistory. com/hd2/IDX-UK/Music/Archive-Music-Week-IDX/IDX/1976/ Music-Week-1976-02-14-IDX-14.pdf

(18) The song actually has no political or emotional background: it was written by Carrack about Comer playing privately with the

Sutherland Brothers and Quiver, without the knowledge of his band members, and his subsequent return.

(19) In the picture, though, Ace are waving blue and white scarves: Everton colours.

(20) Woodhead was recommended by Pete Thomas, then Stewart's drummer after the break-up of Chilli Willi and the Red Hot Peppers.

(21) Tyla (born John Tyler) claimed at various times to have been a member of Geno Washington and the Ram Jam Band, to have played with Freddie 'Fingers' Lee, and even to have recorded an unreleased album with Maynard Ferguson. The first of these was dismissed by Richard Treece of Help Yourself, 'Sean told us he had been a member of Geno Washington's Ram Jam Band and showed us a photograph to try to prove it... but even though the picture was badly blurred, we could see it was Pete Gage on guitar, and not Sean. We got used to Sean's stories and he became a sort of court jester'. Despite this, as Sean Tyler, he wrote the sleeve notes for their elaborately packaged 1972 album Strange Affair. An odd thing for a roadie to do. In an interview with the author (3 September 2022) Chris Money confirmed that he met Tyla at teacher training college in Oxford in 1969. They wrote songs together and recorded demos in London with Mike Noble, a recording engineer and songwriter involved with John Kongos and Ralph McTell. He confirmed that he co-wrote with Tyla the b-side of the 1971 single by Third World, the publishing credits of which are attributed to Tigon Film Music. Tyla never mentioned any other activities to him during this period, but his connection to Lionel Bart, and Apollo Music (Bart's publishing company, purchased by Hemdale in 1970) is mentioned in various accounts, including https://louderthanwar.com/sean-tyla-pub-rock-pioneer-1946-2020-2/ Did any of Tyla's material get used in films in the early 70s? It's possible that it did, and it wouldn't have been unusual for the musicians/composers concerned to be uncredited. Between 1970 and 1973 Tigon produced 13 films, including Black Beauty (1971) which has a title theme by Lionel Bart.

(22) Help Yourself feature throughout this account and intersect with many of the bands in this book but were not really a pub-rock band. The details of their formation, however, confirm much of the back story around the early period of Brinsley Schwarz. At http://www.terrascope.co.uk/MyBackPages/helps.html Richard Treece (guitar) states, 'About that time Famepushers was getting under way with Stephen

Warwick, ex-Sam Apple Pie manager... I went back to Walthamstow after decisions were made to start up Help Yourself as a full band. Dave Charles had become disillusioned with Sam Apple Pie and was coming round to the flat with various records (including jazz) and was well into the idea of a new band... Dave Robinson managed to get us a joint contract with Ernie Graham and Brinsley Schwarz for seven years, I think it was, which for an unknown band who'd never played a gig was really something'. At https://www.psychedelicbabymag.com/2022/03/help-yourself-interview-paul-burton.html Paul Burton (guitar) is quoted as stating re: keyboardist Malcolm Morley, '*Malcolm was involved with a film production company who were also involved in music production. Malcolm had written a bunch of songs and the company – Famepushers – had suggested he go and record the songs, so he was looking for musicians to back him. We met Malcolm... and he played us some of his songs. They were quite folksy tunes but really good. Malcolm then explained that he got involved with Famepushers through John Eichler... John was really into filmmaking and he had friends who were working on a film about Bridge – the card game. It starred, amongst others, Omar Sharif, the well-known film star. Anyway, John was living in Barnes with Dave Robinson who had been a road manager for Jimi Hendrix... He had persuaded the people at Famepushers to move into music, ostensibly to produce music for the film, but this had expanded into band management and record production... The problem was Malcolm didn't have a band, and Dave Robinson thought it would be better if he got a group together to support him... At some point we drove up to Famepushers' office which was located on Park Street, just by Regent's Park at the continuation of Baker Street, for a meeting with John and Dave Robinson and Eddie Moulton who was the MD*'. The mention of Stephen Warwick as a former manager of Sam Apple Pie (whose drummer, Dave Charles, would join Help Yourself) is interesting, given that Sam Apple Pie appear in the 1969 film *Toomorrow*.

(23) Frame says that Groome '*was in The Nashville Teens for a while*' which he may have been in 1973-74 when they used '*various deps*' on bass. See http://www.nashville-teens.com/Main07.htm Groome's later career included stints with both Psychic TV and The Barron Knights.

(24) Dynamite Records was a Dutch offshoot of the Amsterdam-based Real Free Press. Wernham, Grey and Smith were all later, at different times, members of The Art Attacks.

(25) Lawal had also been in Colin Young's Development, another Foundations link.

(26) Riley and Nevill were later in The Dyaks, who released a couple of singles later in the 70s. Riley also had a brief spell in Roogalator.

(27) On *Howlin Wind* Parker and The Rumour were augmented by John Earle (saxophone, from Ian Dury and The Kilburns), Dave Conners (saxophone), Danny Ellis (trombone), Herschell Holder (trumpet, from FBI). Earle and Ellis were both Irish.

(28) The majority of the songs in the film, though, are provided by Southside Johnny and the Asbury Jukes, a US act similar to Springsteen who were heavily promoted circa 1976.

COLIN BASS

(CLANCY)

The Velvet Opera were my first significant band. I answered an ad in *Melody Maker*, went to the audition and joined. We did a single that came out on Spark and I played on a lot of songwriter demo sessions in Southern Music's Denmark Street studio around 1969-70. Later I answered another ad in *Melody Maker* – that was how most bands were put together then – and ended up in The Foundations. Eric Allandale, from Dominica, was the main guy, leading the band on trombone with Pat Burke, from Trinidad, on flute. We did a lot of weekly gigs in cabaret, playing alongside comedians like Charlie Williams, and used to open our set with a cover of Curtis Mayfield's *Move on Up*. I remember a lot of driving up and down the motorways, in a truck with all our gear and us sitting in airplane-type seats, often jamming away whilst we travelled. Our drummer, Tim Harris, had a flat in Stockwell, and we used to rehearse there in an almost soundproofed room.

I first saw Ernie Graham at the Saville Theatre, Shaftesbury Avenue in 1967 when Eire Apparent were supporting Jimi Hendrix. I was 16. Ernie was at the centre of everything for a while, connected to Dave Robinson and Hendrix manager Mike Jeffries. He had so many stories about touring the US with Hendrix, and I heard them all many times. I finally met him through Ian Gomm. I'd been in a band with Ian when he was working at the EMI factory in Hayes before he joined Brinsley Schwarz. They had a Sunday night residency at The Tally Ho. I was there one night and Ian came over with him during a break in their set and said *"Ere... this is Ernie... get together!'* So, we drank some Guinness and started jamming at his house.

I'd just left The Foundations, and was sleeping at Martin Belmont's squat listening to a lot of Dylan, The Band, Sly Stone, Van Morrison and King Curtis. We agreed to put together a band. Various people were in it, including Martin briefly. Some, like drummer Twink, for no more than a photo-session. Eventually we had Jonathan Glemser on guitar, and Steve Brendell on drums. Jonathan had been with Ernie in Help Yourself and before that had played with *Barış Manço*, the biggest rock star in Turkey. Steve was personal assistant to John and Yoko... at one point we were rehearsing in their place in Berkshire whilst they were over in New York! We couldn't seem to get a deal, though. Ernie and Chris Gabrin, our manager, flew out to LA to take our demos to various record companies but came back empty-handed.

The line-up changed. Dave Vasco, who was in The Foundations with me, joined, Jonathan left and Dave Skinner arrived from Uncle Dog. George Butler took over on drums, and we all lived in a house in Putney. We started playing gigs and did really well at The Kensington. It was our stamping ground and at one point seemed full of A&R men, which led to us getting a deal with Island. But Muff Winwood, who was set to produce, wanted us to get rid of the drummer. We refused and the deal didn't happen. Ironically, we sacked George a little while later, which is when Barry Ford and Gasper Lawal came in.

Martin Jennings signed us to Warner Brothers, where I think we were known as 'Martin's Folly'. They paid us a weekly wage, I can't remember how much now, and we got booked into weekly slots at Ronnie Scott's opening for Maria Muldaur and Al Jarreau. I think we felt a little out of our depth! For the main part, though, we were happy to play anywhere. We enjoyed The Torrington, the Hope & Anchor (though the sound was terrible, just a brick cellar) and a little later, The Rock Garden. We did some good stuff in the studio and did tours supporting Argent and The Jess Roden Band, but I think we lost the plot a little on our second album. We were into Little Feat, Dylan, funk and soul and were pulling in too many directions. I'd say stylistically we were a bit confused!

I loved Brinsley Schwarz, they were a favourite. They were a notch up musically from everyone else and Nick Lowe was writing some great songs. I remember Dave Robinson saying, 'Nick just soaks up influences like a sponge.' I liked Kilburn and the High Roads too, and Bees Make Honey. The difference between then and now is that in those days you could not only pay your dues by being in a band, you could also pay your rent too (given that most of the places I lived in were not much more than £15 a week). There isn't really a circuit of gigs like that anymore. Record companies had more money too, so they'd be prepared to invest a little. They threw some money at us... it didn't work... but we still got to do a couple of albums. I also think that playing together, rather than remotely and mixing everything digitally online as seems to be the norm for most these days, makes a huge difference. It's what makes it special. After all, pub-rock was a return to a kind of grassroots approach to rock and roll and provided the breeding ground for the punk scene.

TONY O'MALLEY

(ARRIVAL, KOKOMO)

My father came from Louisburgh, near Westport, Mayo. He settled in London, on Devonshire Road, Harrow and worked at the Kodak factory. My sister was Mary O'Malley, who later became a playwright. We had a very Catholic upbringing. For me it came to a head when I was 14. The headmaster at my school wanted to beat me for copying my homework. I refused to accept this and left that year. I got a job quite easily as a telex operator and was glad to be in the outside world.

I'd been playing music since I was about 12 and joined my first serious band a little while after this. They were The Skyliners from Enniskillen, an Irish showband based in Luton. We played all the major Irish halls across London, places like the 32 Club and the Gresham Ballroom, as well as a lot of gigs in and around Luton. After about a year we went to an audition in the West End at the end of which Ian Samwell approached me and asked if we could meet. Eventually we did, and I joined The Blues Healers, who had a residency at the Bag O'Nails, a club run by Rick and Johnny Gunnell on Kingly Street, Soho. We did a lot of West Indian venues, including Count Suckle's Q Club, on Praed Street, Paddington. Our singer Malcolm Magaron was replaced by Ronnie Jones at which point we became Ronnie Jones and the Q-Set. My recollection is that we were on a weekly wage of £18 each. We did a lot of work with Ronnie Jones, including six months in Europe, but didn't play on any of his records. The band broke up in 1968 and I joined The Counts, who were basically the remnants of Jimmy James and the Vagabonds, with Phil Chen on bass and Count Prince Miller doing his MC stuff.

At the beginning of 1969 the Gunnells called me and asked if I'd join this band from Liverpool that Tony Hall was producing. This was Arrival. They did 4-part harmonies but needed backing musicians. I agreed and initially it was with Mac McCarthy on bass and Mick Hough on drums, though both were replaced, Mac by Don Hume and Mick by Lloyd Courtenay. We had a couple of hits and played the 1970 Isle of Wight Festival, and met on the morning at Battersea Heliport to travel down by helicopter with Richard Williams, a big music journalist, who later presented the first season of *The Old Grey Whistle Test*. We landed at midday, were on stage at 2pm and went down well. We got the helicopter back and did a gig the following day in Devizes.

We left Tony Hall and moved to CBS. But they didn't really want to know and things started to fall apart. I wasn't on a retainer so I asked CBS to release me from my contract, after which I sang the vocals on an album by The Mick Cox Band. Shel Talmy produced it in a big studio, but not a great deal happened and eventually myself and the drummer, Terry Stannard, decided to put together our own band. By that point Arrival had broken up, so Frank, Paddy and Dyan joined us. We started auditioning and gradually a 10-piece band coalesced, originally with Rosko Gee on bass, later replaced by Alan Spenner. We did a huge number of gigs around town and CBS were interested. We were a co-op band – with no leader – and all of us went to see them, but they only offered an advance of £10,000, which was nothing. Miles Copeland wanted to sign us to BTM and Steve O'Rourke, Pink Floyd's manager, loved us. He went back to CBS and got us an advance of £100,000 for the first year, increasing annually at £25,000 a year thereafter.

Which is not to say we were well-off. The overheads for a 10-piece band are colossal and we were all on a weekly wage. A lot of our gigs were at places like the Hope & Anchor. Later we toured with Dr Feelgood and Chilli Willi. We got on well with Chilli Willi but the tour really made Dr Feelgood. I think we were too American-sounding for UK audiences and the press gave us a hard time because we'd signed with CBS and were managed by Steve.

Both our albums sold well in the US and we spent quite a bit of time there. One day we were called to the studio where Bob

Dylan was recording *Desire*, all 10 of us. There were lots of other musicians present and we did several tracks that day, Dylan and I even discussing the keyboard part at one point! We were touring with the Average White Band and didn't think we were up to their standard, so we dropped Terry and replaced him with John Sussewell. But the band was floundering. Steve was spending most of his time with Pink Floyd and we just ground to a halt.

I think the single most exciting gig we did was with Kilburn and the High Roads, at the New Victoria Theatre in March 1976. Live we did lots of originals but our best number was probably Allen Toussaint's *Yes, We Can Can*. The best thing we released was Bobby Womack's *I Can Understand It*. My biggest regret is that I didn't take more control of Kokomo in 1977. I should have been more of a band leader. But musicians by nature are insecure people, and I was too.

Looking back at that time, on the one hand it's still the same now: to get anywhere you have to be dedicated. But the difference now is that it's much harder for young people to make the grade. It's a lot more corporate these days.

CINCINNATTI FATBACK

By acclamation, John Peel was the hippest DJ through the 70s. His career ticked every possible box: brought up on American rock and roll, involved with pirate radio, writing columns in the counter-culture press, free festivals, his own record label and an evening show *Top Gear*, which no matter how much the BBC shunted it around the schedule, retained a large and fanatical audience. If you could distil what Peel offered it would be anything unpretentious, musically interesting, subversive and (often overlooked) funny. He preferred the obscure to the already famous and most of all he looked for stuff that might just happen if given a bit of a push. From 1972 he was run a close second by Charlie Gillett.

A lecturer in film studies at Kingsway College of Further Education from 1966 and a journalist at *Record Mirror* from 1968, Gillett secured his reputation with his 1970 book *The Sound of the City: The Rise of Rock and Roll*. One of the first academic studies of rock and roll's origins, he dropped the manuscript off at his New York publisher whilst in town for the Brinsley Schwarz Fillmore East jaunt. Being a published author rather than a mere weekly columnist gave him kudos in the broadsheet press, and his reputation as a chronicler and curator of interesting sounds was further enhanced when he compiled and wrote the sleeve notes for the album *Blues from the Bayou*. Culled from recordings owned by the Jewel and Paula labels of Shreveport, Louisiana, none of which had previously been released in the UK, this was the type of material he would consistently champion.

From 1972 he presented *Honky Tonk*, a show on BBC Radio London, whilst acting as consultant editor to *Let It Rock*. The latter position lasted three years with the magazine, which appeared monthly, struggling to maintain a circulation of 20,000. Which in 2022 would be great, but half a century earlier was hardly considered worth getting out of bed for. With founding editor Dave Laing, he put together a compilation album of obscure Atlantic tracks in 1973. The continuing difficulties experienced by UK admirers in obtaining classic Americana vinyl, whether it was soul, blues, R'n'B, western swing, country rock or rockabilly, were shared by his radio listeners, and eventually led to him proactively exploring the US southern states in search of records he could bring back and get released in the UK.

There was a lot to get your hands on – Louisiana state alone being roughly the size of Bulgaria – but no takers among A&R men and record company managers back home for peculiar material with an abundance of accordions and much singing in French patois. So, Gillett and his business partner (and dentist) Gordon Nelki took the radical step of setting up their own label to release it, with Richard Branson's Virgin distributing. Named Oval Records – after their local tube station – it was run for many years c/o The Basement, 11 Liston Road SW4. The stuff they collected appeared in 1974 on the album *Another Saturday Night*, rated by many as a definitive compilation. Gillett's enthusiasm for authentic, simple and exciting Americana, rooted, ultimately, in the blues, was shared by a number of bands that played the pub-rock scene. Whether they were directly inspired by him, or whether his tastes were being confirmed, and inspired, by their live shows is hard to say, and doesn't really matter. What is true is that a sub-group of acts appeared – embracing guitar driven R'n'B, funk and white reggae – that were distinctive from their country-rock, rock and roll revival, estuary rock and late blues competitors. Gillett's shows and compilation albums acted as a kind of midwife to the birth of these sounds.

The first such were Roogalator, led by guitarist Danny Adler, who arrived in the UK in 1971 after a spell playing with Elephant's Memory in New York.

Originally from Cincinatti, he'd previously backed blues alumni like Arthur Crudup and John Lee Hooker, which coupled with his ongoing admiration for the bands that had led the 'British invasion' of the US pop charts circa 1965, set him apart from many of the other musicians trying to put a career together in the early 70s. Shortly after arrival he found himself part of Smooth Loser with fellow US expatriates Chris Gibbons and Jeff Pasternak.[1] Pasternak's brother, Emperor Rosko (aka Mike Pasternak), produced their recording sessions, and like Peel was a highly regarded DJ with prior US and pirate radio experience. Like Gillett he also had a great liking for classic American rhythm and blues and rock and roll, often featuring selected examples of this music on his programme. With playlists mixing current chart hits with carefully selected (and exciting) 'blasts from the past', against a background of wild noises and madcap dialogue, Rosko's Saturday lunchtime show on Radio One, which ran until 1976, was required listening for many adolescents before they hit the local High Street with its coffee bars, clothes shops, bookshops and record stores.[2]

By the time Adler joined Smooth Loser they were being co-managed by Henri Henriod, an associate of Don Arden, with Rosko's patronage extending to the provision of a communal house at Easter Compton, six miles north of Bristol, and a retainer of £10 a week each. In their later stages they were augmented by drummer Malcolm Mortimore after his departure from Gentle Giant. Rosko's recording sessions included some produced by Graham Gouldman and Lol Creme at Strawberry Studios in July 1972. Nothing was released at the time and by the autumn of that year the band had broken up with Mortimore eventually joining GT Moore and The Reggae Guitars.[3]

Adler then put together Roogalator with *'Michael Angelo Franchesco from Philadelphia and another Yank named Stuart on drums'*. Following their November 1972 debut at the Marquee they struggled to maintain a consistent line-up, or even get live work. A rapid turnover of personnel was something that would afflict Roogalator throughout their existence, with Adler later stating, with some regret, *'Ian Dury 'stole' a Roogalator rhythm section that I'd been grooming in 1973'*, this being a reference to Mortimore and bass player Giorgi Dionisiev, both of whom would turn up in Ian

Dury and The Kilburns circa 1975-76. Putting the band on ice for the moment, Adler went to Paris to study jazz theory, whilst keeping his hand in with live work and sessions for Kevin Barry and the Echo's. An Irish 4-piece, they mixed Brett Marvin-style country blues with material like *Whisky in the Jar* and *Come Out Ye Black and Tans*. He plays on their 1974 album *Real Home Grown Stuff Boys*.

After which, following much rehearsing and auditioning and with his guitar-playing skills honed to perfection, Adler relaunched Roogalator with Nick Plytas (keyboards), Paul Riley (bass, from Chilli Willi and the Red Hot Peppers) and Dave Solomons (drums, a jazz-percussionist). This line-up made their debut at The Nashville in September 1975, and quickly attracted attention. Robin Scott – who had been backed by Mighty Baby on his 1969 album *Woman from the Warm Grass* – became their manager, demos were recorded and in December *New Musical Express* proclaimed, 'My first impression of Roogalator was one of total disbelief. If such a band really does exist, they aren't just the most important thing to come out of Britain in years, but out of anywhere at all.' This would be a common reaction to their live work: Roogalator were unbelievably good. They played a set of tight, jazzy, funky, bluesy originals that really swung in a way that UK bands were rarely able to achieve.

United Artists were interested, and slotted them in as support to Dr Feelgood at the Hammersmith Odeon on 23-24 January 1976. It should have been a formality... a couple of decent sets and then a contract for several albums. For whatever reason, though, it didn't happen and the soufflé collapsed that night, as did that version of Roogalator. Adler and Plytas persisted, however, and progress of a sort was maintained. In *ZigZag* 59 (April 1976) Nick Kent is quoted, '*I saw Roogalator; I enjoyed them and liked their attitude*' and John Peel felt likewise, booking them in for a session, the first of three, on 13 May. Some European dates followed, during which most of their possessions were stolen from their van, and further line-up changes occurred. Finally, with Adler and Plytas augmented by Julian Scott (the manager's brother, bass) and Justin Hildreth (drums), they signed to Stiff and released the single *All Aboard*.

It did nothing and a year passed before a follow-up, *Love and the Single Girl*, appeared on Virgin in September 1977. They gigged all the time to promote it and remained an impressive, razor-sharp live act. But the contracts they were being offered failed to impress, and the next release, the album *Play It By Ear*, would be on Do It, their manager's label. When this didn't sell Plytas left and after a final round of gigs as a trio they broke up after a show at The Pegasus, Stoke Newington in August 1978. It was a sad end for a band that had briefly flashed so brilliantly across the firmament. Had they carried on a second album was planned, instead, much of the material planned for this appeared on Adler's 1979 solo outing, *The Danny Adler Story*.

By now times had changed. Peel had moved on, embracing inscrutable 'Peel bands'. Politically aware music was in vogue – with large amounts of spleen vented at Thatcher and Reagan – and much of the former pub network was shutting down as an economic recession swept the UK. But Adler persisted. In 1980 he bobbed up as one of The Deluxe Blues Band alongside Bob Hall, Bob Brunning, Micky Waller and Dick Heckstall-Smith. They recorded five albums, the first of which, *Live at The Half Moon Putney*, appeared in 1981. This in turn led to a stint with Rocket 88, a kind of Rolling Stones side-project with Ian Stewart, Charlie Watts and Alexis Korner. He isn't on their 1981 album, but the sleeve notes, curated by Stewart, confirm, *'as mentioned earlier, this has to be an occasional band formed from a pool of players as nearly everybody involved is the leader or permanent member of another group... so I would like to take the opportunity to thank some of the other musicians... and last but not least, Cincinnati's own Danny Adler'*. In a last hurrah for pub-rock, both Rocket 88 and The Deluxe Blues Band kept going to the end of the 80s, the latter managing to slot in a number of gigs at The Dublin Castle in Camden. Surrounded by luminaries who rated his playing immensely, Adler was a musician's musician not at all outclassed by the company he kept.

The same was true of Gerald Moore. Starting out as the teenage leader of a local mod-soul band in Reading, he went via Maidenhead Art School to recording demos for Peter Eden. One of his songs was included on the 1969 Spark folk-blues compilation

Firepoint alongside contributions from Duffy Power, Dave Kelly, TJ Robinson and Bob Hall. Shortly afterwards he joined Heron, a 4-piece band Eden was producing. With Vic Maile as engineer, they released two albums on Dawn, both of which consisted of rustic, hippies-in-a-field material, very well played, understated and quite nicely done. The first, *Heron* has no drummer, the second, a double, *Twice as Nice & Half the Price*, has them augmented by a number of session players. John Peel gave them a live session in June 1971 but the band made little commercial impact, and after further abortive recordings they stuttered to a halt.

Eden encouraged Moore to record as a solo act. An album's worth of material was laid down, the end result of which was a solitary single release, *Song of America*, on Jonathan King's UK label in the autumn of 1972. Not long after this appeared, Moore and fellow guitarist Martin Hayward (who had been in Heron prior to the Dawn deal) worked as backing musicians for Iranian folk singer Shusha Guppy in a documentary film she narrated, *Bakhtiari Migration: The Sheep Must Live*. About the annual journey nomadic sheep-herding tribes made across southern Iran, this was written and produced by David Koff and directed by Anthony Howarth, whose prior work included *The Black Man's Land Trilogy*, a very 70s, and very serious, examination of the nature of white colonialism. With stunning photography from Mike Dodds, *Bakhtiari Migration: The Sheep Must Live* was screened as part of the BBC 2 series *The World About Us* in June 1973.

The music provided by Moore and Hayward – guitar-based country blues blending into eastern style ragas – overlaps somewhat with the type of sounds made by Heron. It's also not unlike The Habibiyya's *If Man but Knew* or *Brian Jones Presents the Pipes of Pan at Joujouka*. The film was much liked and off the back of it, Shusha, who had already released a couple of UK albums as well as an earlier set of Persian folk songs in France back in 1958, secured a recording contract with United Artists.[4] Her debut for the label, *This Is The Day*, appeared in early 1974. Produced by Jerry Boys, noted then for Steeleye Span's breakthrough hit *Gaudete*, it's an eclectic collection. Side one alone contains covers of Captain Beefheart, Chuck Berry, Jacques Brel and Bob Dylan; side two gives us WB Yeats's *The Lake Isle of Innisfree*. Two tracks are co-written by her with Moore and Roy Apps, formerly of Heron, and the set closes with her cover of Moore's *Song of America*.[5]

Moore and Hayward were amongst the array of musicians who backed her on these sessions. From amongst these Tim Jones (keyboards) and Tom Whyte (bass) would be in the band – GT Moore and the Reggae Guitars – they put together in late 1973, joining TJ Robinson (from the *Firepoint* sampler, percussion), Tony Hannaford (also percussion) and Malcolm Mortimore (drums, ex-Gentle Giant and Roogalator). As suggested by their name, they played reggae, quite a change from Heron and *Bakhtiari Migration*, and a shift in style that is worth exploring.

Firstly, there was a specific link via keyboardist John Bundrick, who had played alongside them on Shusha's *This Is the Day*. Like Eggs Over Easy, Danny Adler, Joe Pasternak and the Archulettas, Bundrick was an American who pitched up in the UK in the early 70s. Originally in Texas late-psychedelic outfit Blackwell (one eponymous album, 1970) by 1971 he was in Sweden working with Bob Marley on the score of the film *Vill så gärna tro/Love is Not a Game*. This starred Johnny Nash, who had by that point been recording, sometimes with Marley, in the reggae idiom for some years. Bundrick subsequently played on Nash's big 1972 hit *I Can See Clearly Now* as well as managing to contribute to Uncle Dog's album. More importantly, after his return to London, he was brought in by Chris Blackwell to assist with the arrangements for *Catch a Fire*, Bob Marley's debut for Island.

Released in April 1973, this made little initial impression commercially, but led to Marley doing a session for John Peel and making an appearance on *The Old Grey Whistle Test*, both recorded on 1 May. His band then toured to promote the album, mixing traditional West Indian clubs with universities and colleges. Press reviews and interviews were favourable, tending to eulogise Marley (*Melody Maker* were asking whether he was a genius as early as February) with the general 'line' being taken that this would be the next big sound to emerge. By October, a follow-up album *Burnin'* had appeared, showcased like its first by a Peel session, and was notable for containing one of Marley's signature songs, *I*

Shot the Sheriff. It was another critical hit, much as Chris Blackwell would have wished.

In which context, it's important to remember that pre-1973 reggae had little appeal for the young white album-buying public. It was associated with rowdy scenes, gangs of skinheads, threatening moments in dance halls, the police wading in (or not) according to whom they judged the instigators to be, immense sound systems transported around ad hoc venues in furniture vans (or similar) and the heavy dub scene with its vast amounts of echo and strong drug use. It wasn't cool. What Marley offered – and Blackwell marketed – was reggae as an offshoot of rock, played on similar instruments, and available on albums rather than singles with some sort of overarching concept behind the songs. Many white musicians were inspired by its mixture of politically aware material, astute playing, commercial possibilities and the fact that it was black, as, of course, both jazz and rhythm and blues had been originally. By the spring of 1974, Eric Clapton had placed his imprimatur on the genre, recording a cover of *I Shot the Sheriff* for his album *461 Ocean Boulevard*. Released as a single, it reached No 1 in the US and No 9 in the UK that summer.

This, then, was the context around Moore and Hayward's shift from mainly acoustic progressive folk/blues to electric reggae. Signed by Charisma they played the Reading Festival in August 1974. This had Alex Harvey, Traffic and Focus as the main headliners, but amongst the array of other acts could be found Fumble, Chilli Willi and The Red Hot Peppers and The Winkies as the rock establishment gave a nod to the new bands emerging from the pub-circuit. *ZigZag* 46 (October 1974) carried a full-page advert for them, with the strapline, '*The Big Breakthrough in Rockin' Reggae! Move It! With the LIVE sound that's taken over '74!*' Live reviews were adulatory and much was expected of their initial releases.

For these, Charisma had selected Dave Bloxham as producer, presumably on the basis that he'd had a trio of pop-reggae hits with Greyhound on Trojan 1971-72.[6] Despite an imaginative debut single, a reggae cover of Diana Ross's 1971 hit *I'm Still Waiting*, and an album, *GT Moore and The Reggae Guitars*, that closed with an excellent extended version of Dylan's *Knockin' on Heaven's Door*, the sales were not sufficient to propel either into the charts. Both were admired, however, and Eric Clapton would notably release his own version of *Knockin' on Heaven's Door* in August 1975, with an arrangement similar to that used by Moore.[7]

By then the band had a new drummer, Steve Holley having taken over from Malcolm Mortimore, and had gone down to a 5-piece, losing both percussionists. This line-up appeared on the John Peel-hosted *In Concert* on 10 May 1975 and recorded another single, *Reggae Reggae*, and an album, *Reggae Blue*, but neither would sell even though the quality of their work, and of Moore's playing, continued to attract praise. In the spring of 1975 Moore and Bundrick were featured alongside Herbie Hancock, Bobby Womack and Betty Wright on the Johnny Nash hit *Tears on My Pillow*, a UK No 1. There were hopes that the band might do well in the US, and after a tour supporting Dr Feelgood, they recorded a third album in April 1976, but it wasn't released. The line-up for these sessions features 11 musicians and the band would in fact have over 20 different personnel down to their March 1977 demise, with Moore being the only constant. Later that year four of those who took part in the final sessions – Bundrick (keyboards), Ted Bunton (saxophone), Terry Wilson (bass) and Tony Braunagel (drums) – reached No 85 in the US charts with *Crawler*, by the band of the same name. So, who knows? Perhaps GT Moore and the Reggae Guitars would have cracked the US if they'd stayed together.[8]

For Moore himself it must have seemed a bit of an anti-climax. Despite playing on a UK No 1 single, and the soundtrack of an Oscar-nominated film (fertile ground here for a pub quiz question), he had little to show for his endeavours. He moved on to record with Lee 'Scratch' Perry and Poly Styrene, and it would be the esteem of his contemporaries that would reflect his true worth. Between 1970 and 1976 he played on ten albums, a prodigious output, and typical of many at that time. Listened to today his band sound as good as Clapton, and make for an interesting comparison with The Police. Perhaps their failing was that in 1974-75 they were just a bit ahead of the curve as regards the white reggae market.

Like Martin Stone and Alan King, Adler and Moore were both exemplary players. Both led bands that tried to map out new, exciting areas in guitar-led rock, drawing in different ways on black music for inspiration. There weren't too many other acts like them at the time. One such were The Sky Rockets, whose rhythm section, bass-player Andrew Bodnar and drummer Steve Goulding, would later feature in Bontemps Roulez. Neither band would release anything during their brief lifetimes, but both are important in this narrative, providing personnel who glue together the shifting membership of other outfits. And, both were reasonable value if you caught them live.

The Sky Rockets came together circa 1973, when Bodnar and Goulding placed an ad in *Melody Maker* offering themselves as *'rhythm section for hire'*. The band's key selling point then would have been that guitarist Steve Bonnett had previously been bass player with COB, aka Clive's Own Band, the Clive here being Clive Palmer, ex-Incredible String Band. Bonnett plays on their 1970 CBS album *Spirit of Love*, which was produced by Ralph McTell. This in turn led to him appearing on McTell's 1971 set *You Well-Meaning Brought Me Here*. The rest of The Sky Rockets were Will Stallibrass (harmonica/vocals) and Noel Brown (slide guitar). A slew of pub gigs followed, including a residency at the King's Head, Upper Street, where a folk club had operated since 1968 in a cavernous back room that was later fitted out as a theatre. Like so many such venues, the King's Head was an Irish pub with an Irish landlord. Rather idiosyncratically, the venue still charged customers in £sd (*'real money'*) after decimalisation, and would do so into the 80s when the practice lapsed.[9] Dave Robinson saw The Sky Rockets in 1974, decided they were worth a punt, but failed to get them any sort of deal, and the band drifted apart with Stallibrass going to Chilli Willi and the Red Hot Peppers and Noel Brown playing on some early Graham Parker demos and writing *Readers Wives* for Dave Edmunds.

A few months later Bonnett, Goulding and Bodnar put together Bontemps Roulez, with keyboardist Tony Downes and, after Chilli Willi finally bit the dust, Paul Bailey arriving on saxophone and guitar. Moving away from the country blues of The

Sky Rockets they played, not unlike Roogalator, funkier stuff with Goulding making it clear in later years how influential Charlie Gillett's show on Radio London had been in promoting awareness of this. Over approximately six months they too played pub gigs, including a residency at the Hope & Anchor, less than half a mile north of the King's Head, and cut demos both by themselves and supporting Frankie Miller. As with The Sky Rockets, there were no deals forthcoming and eventually, as Bodnar would confirm, 'Steve Goulding and I, plus various remnants of the Ducks, the Willies and Brinsley Schwarz – all of whom had broken up around the same time – were all hanging around Dave Robinson's studio at the Hope & Anchor. He asked us if we'd have a shot at backing Graham Parker on some demos he was doing.' As set out earlier in this account they enjoyed playing together and, after road-testing themselves at the Newlands Tavern, Peckham and a few other venues, commenced gigging and recording as Graham Parker and The Rumour.[10]

If guitar-driven bands like Roogalator and GT Moore and The Reggae Guitars had little to no success, a slightly more promising future awaited a number of jazz-funk outfits that emerged at around the same time. Usually, in terms of sales anything jazz tended to sell in limited amounts, whatever its quality, via a network of specialist record shops. This changed somewhat in the late 60s, when US jazz-rock outfits like Chicago and Blood Sweat and Tears appeared, both of whom were strikingly successful, particularly in the US. Some of this magic rubbed off in the UK, where locally the bestselling act to emerge were CCS. Fronted by Alexis Korner, their 1970 Led Zeppelin cover *Whole Lotta Love* was a big hit and served for many years as the main theme music for *Top of the Pops*. But they didn't sustain and most other bands exploring the same terrain made much less of an impact.

One that did, and stayed the course, were Gonzalez who came together in 1971. A couple of their founder members had been in The Gass (or just plain Gass) who appeared in Jack Good's rock musical *Catch My Soul*. After numerous personnel changes (like many jazz outfits they were often an extended clearing house of players) it was 1974 before they got a deal with EMI. There tended to be an awful lot of them. Their debut features no fewer than 13 musicians, and by the time of their second, 1975's *Our Only Weapon is our Music*, they were up to 18, including some of the key players from UK jazz-rock: Roy Davies (keyboards) and a brass section of Chris Mercer (alto and tenor saxophone), Bud Beadle (soprano and baritone saxophone and flute), Steve Gregory (soprano and tenor saxophone and flute), Mick Eve (tenor saxophone) and Ron Carthy (trumpet).[11]

Much of their output, such as *Clapham South* on their debut, is brilliantly played and sounds like a backing track for 70s crime thrillers or blaxploitation films that have somehow eluded the listener. John Peel was onside (they did three sessions, 1974-75) and they were a popular live draw, even if, apart from occasional shows at The Nashville, they didn't play too many pub gigs. How could they? They'd never have fitted on most of the stages. Eventually they veered into disco via funk and produced a hit single, *Haven't Stopped Dancing Yet* (No 15 UK/No 26 US), in 1979 – such a slick sound that it was featured on the score of the Joan Collins film *The Bitch*.

Their first couple of albums featured Glen LeFleur on drums. Like Ron Carthy, he'd played with Arrival before Gonzalez took off, and it would be from this template that the subsequent soul-funk bands evolved. Arrival's origins can be traced to The Excelles, a Liverpool soul covers band with 4 vocalists, Frank Collins, Paddy McHugh, Carroll Carter and Dyan Birch.[12] Of these Birch worked in Brian Epstein's NEMS record shop and had an elder sister (Pamela) who'd been guitarist in the all-girl Merseybeat outfit The Liverbirds a few years earlier. In late 1968 Collins and McHugh brought a demo tape to London and managed to get it to producer Tony Hall, backstage at an Aretha Franklin concert at the Hammersmith Odeon.

He signed them up the following day. It was fortuitous timing. A jazz buff and Decca A&R man, Hall had switched to producing dance music and had just overseen The Locomotive's *Rudi's in Love*, the UK's first ever white reggae hit. He was in the market for homegrown talent. All four singers were brought down to London, found accommodation and day jobs and the business started of building a band around them. Keyboards player Tony

O'Malley arrived via the Gunnell Agency, and the line-up was eventually completed by the additions of Don Hume (bass) and Lloyd Courtenay (drums).[13] A great deal of preparation followed at the end of which Decca released their debut single, *Friends*, in November 1969. Written by Terry Reid, whom Mickie Most produced, it reached No 8 in the UK.[14] Their May 1970 follow-up, *I Will Survive*, a band original, hit again, peaking at No 16. Both were carefully produced, expertly-played pop-soul songs, the soul here being very much end-of-the-decade/morning-after-the-party in style, rather like late-period Dusty Springfield.

Much was expected with the band appearing on *The World of Maynard Ferguson*, a London Weekend TV special that had them doing another number whilst careering around on roller skates.[15] There was more heavy promotion with an appearance at the Isle of Wight Festival on Friday 28 August, sharing the bill with Taste, Family and Chicago. Here they more than held their own, one account stating, '*Dressed in a bizarre variety of costumes, they managed to gain the audience's mass attention with 'Hard Road' and sustained it with Leonard Cohen's 'Hey, That's No Way to Say Goodbye', on which Dyan Birch sang lead. After 'Sit Down and Float' (which the crowd seemed to be doing anyway) they went into 'Not Right Now'. Frank Collins sat and played twelve-string acoustic guitar with Dyan sitting on the stage at his feet. It was an appealing sight. Unfortunately, an unruly mob decided to throw cans into the Press and VIP area during the number and rather spoiled the effect. They ended with the hot gospel song 'See the Lord', which though it went on rather too long was irresistible and many peace signs were noticeable throughout the congregation.*' Another merely recalls, '*The next act were called Arrival, they had a hit record that year and were more of a pop band. Nevertheless, they had a great vocal sound, and their music went down really well as we relaxed and soaked up the sun.*'[16]

Their debut album *Arrival* appeared the same month to good reviews. Dusty Springfield did the sleeve notes and most commentators praised Dyan Birch's singing. Sales didn't really happen but at that point you would have put money on Arrival being around, and successful, for quite some while. In early 1971 they switched to CBS, which was where things started to unravel.

Two follow-up singles failed to make the charts and personnel changes began to affect the band. LeFleur and Carthy arrived, Hume departed, replaced by Phil Chen, formerly of Jimmy James and the Vagabonds, one of the leading mod-soul bands of a few years earlier. George Lee and Raphael Pereira came in too, both ex-Ronnie Jones and the Q-Set, a mod-soul outfit that had also included Tony O'Malley. They toured with Thin Lizzy, did the title theme for the 1972 Neil Simon film *The Heartbreak Kid* and put out another album, which rather dumbly had the same title as the first. The reviews for this were less than great with *Melody Maker* being particularly acerbic, '*An album by a British group that somehow got stuck in a rut... the overall result is stuck at a generally dull level. Monotonous female voices have a lot to answer for. The songs are downers and naturally the LP is too*'. Like its predecessor it didn't sell and by the end of the year Carroll Carter had left, as had O'Malley, joining the Mick Cox Band. Arrival broke up in early 1973.[17]

Guitarist and songwriter Cox had been in Eire Apparent, and was joined in this outing by bassist Chris Stewart, also ex-Eire Apparent, and Andy Steele, formerly of The Herd, on drums. An eponymous album was recorded and released on Capitol and sold quite well in the US. Steele was replaced by Jim Stannard from Uncle Dog and plans were made to tour. But things were disorganised and Stannard soon suggested to O'Malley that they get their own band together. With Arrival gone, Collins, McHugh and Birch arrived as vocalists and they began holding auditions. Eventually a 10-piece band was assembled, the new recruits including saxophonist Mel Collins, formerly in King Crimson, guitarists Jim Mullen and Neil Hubbard from Vinegar Joe and Joe Cocker respectively, and bass player Alan Spenner, like Hubbard ex-Joe Cocker. The final addition was Jody Linscott, a percussionist who joined after performing with them at Dingwalls whilst working there as a waitress. This was a serious line-up with at least three established rock stars (Collins, Hubbard and Spenner) whose previous outfits had enjoyed significant success in the US.[18]

Naming themselves Kokomo they spent most of 1974 playing the gig circuit, doing a John Peel session in August and eventually landing Steve O'Rourke, who also handled Pink Floyd, as their manager. They signed to CBS and promoted their debut single *I'm Sorry Babe* by touring with Dr Feelgood and Chilli Willi and the Red Hot Peppers. Their debut album *Kokomo* appeared in June 1975. What was on offer was some remove from Arrival's *Dusty in Memphis* approach: this is much more in the mould of KC and the Sunshine Band, with funky rhythms, glittery costumes, multi-part vocals and lots of percussion. The reviews by the UK music media were positive: the *New Musical Express* rated it the best debut by a British band for several years. Either side of its release they did John Peel sessions, but neither the singles it yielded nor the album itself sold domestically. In the US, though, it dented the charts at No 159, which was by no means bad for an overseas act trying to break that market.

They subsequently spent a lot of time on the other side of the Atlantic, at one point taking part in the somewhat chaotic sessions for Bob Dylan's *Desire* LP. In Florida, Brad Shapiro, one of the great producers of four-beats-to-the-bar northern soul (he'd done Tami Lynn's *I'm Gonna Run Away from You*), took charge of *Rise and Shine*, their second album. For this, John Sussewell replaced Stannard as the band tried to capture the rhythmic sound of the Average White Band. They were only partially successful. A January 1976 single, *Use Your Imagination*, got to No 81 in the US Hot 100, and the album itself peaked at No 194 there. Critics were often less than kind, with one reviewer pointing out, '*If there's one thing we don't need, it's a group composed of exiles from second-line British boogie bands that has a tendency toward disco-oriented soul.*' [19]

With Steve O'Rourke increasingly preoccupied with Pink Floyd and *Animals*, the band ground to a halt. [20] At the end of 1976 they played some gigs with Joe Cocker after which they put their activities on hold. As with Arrival four years earlier they petered out. One is left wondering – with hindsight – if they couldn't have made more of an effort to keep going. They weren't doing badly commercially and there was still a market for their sound. Audiences in the UK had fond memories of their club gigs and in 1978 they duly spluttered back into life, released a third album in 1982, split in 1983, reformed in 1986 and ceased operating again in 1988. Since 2014 a version of the band, still with some of the original members, has continued to play live.

Via Tony O'Malley, Kokomo had a common ancestry with F.B.I., three of whose members, Raphael Pereira (guitar), Herschell Holder (trumpet) and Lloyd Smith (saxophone), had played with him in Ronnie Jones and the Q-Set. A 9-piece British funk band, from 1974 F.B.I. (which stood for Funky Bands Incorporated) trod the same path as Kokomo to much less acclaim, and were led by Root Jackson (congas and vocals) who had released 4 singles on the Beacon label 1968-70 as one half of Root and Jenny Jackson, a popular act on the northern soul circuit.

They came together when Jackson, Pereira, Holder, Smith and bass player Lennox Meade had a cabaret residency in Whitley Bay, backing acts like Jimmy Helms. This was ok financially, but less than satisfactory from an artistic point of view and as Holder said a little later, 'We all wanted to get something together that would be beautiful, and spend some time working on it without thinking too much about success.'[21] They held auditions and recruited guitarist Jamie Black, from Mac and Katie Kissoon, singer Bonnie Wilkinson, drummer Steve Dixon and Alan Fealdman, keyboards, previously one of Trifle, a 1970-71 jazz-rock outfit whose drummer Chico Greenwood went on to play with Ace. By January 1975 they were playing at Ronnie Scott's, after which, as Holder explained, 'I talked to Fred Granger at the Hope & Anchor, and we got to play a cancellation... After that, we had a regular gig there; and it just grew from that'.

A publishing contract with Alvin Lee's Space Songs followed a few months later. Not, on the face of it, an obvious choice. Except that Lee, after extensive touring with blues rockers Ten Years After, was actively looking for solo projects. Not long before he had produced an album for Mylon LeFevre, a US gospel-country-rock singer, and he clearly liked the idea of doing something with F.B.I. The band recorded in Lee's studio, with Chris Kimsey, who had been engineer on the 1971 Reg King and BB Blunder albums, co-producing and a deal was actively sought with a major label. In the meantime, they played every gig they could, though as Holder admitted, 'By the time you pay for petrol and hire a van and a minibus, *pay for roadies and so forth, you can't break even.'* It must have helped that Dave Robinson borrowed a couple of them (Holder and Smith) for Henry McCullough's 1975 solo outing *Mind Your Own Business.*[22]

Finally, a deal was reached with Tony Visconti's Good Earth label. After what must have seemed an age, a debut single, *The Time is Right to Leave the City*, appeared in December 1976, followed shortly afterwards by an album, *F.B.I.* Both were excellent. The playing is great, the songs strong and the arrangements benefit from being a bit less cluttered than their contemporaries. This is quality black British funk, great late-night music. They ought to have gone on to do more but seem to have broken up shortly afterwards, possibly because of difficulties experienced by their label. Despite announcing at the start of 1977 that Good Earth would expand its activities, with Tony Hall being recruited to oversee releases, by April *Billboard* were reporting that the offices had closed and the acts which it had managed had moved elsewhere. The final Good Earth release appeared in June, after which, in an echo of what had beset Brinsley Schwarz seven years earlier, *The Sunday Times* got on the case with a report that the label had been illegally hyping its releases into the charts. RCA denied any involvement and left the matter in the hands of the British Phonographic Industry.

It isn't clear if any action ensued from this, but the demise of F.B.I. occurred whilst all this played out. Sadly, they dispersed. Lennox Meade joined Local Heroes SW9, whose sole album appeared on Charlie Gillett's Oval Records. Raphael Pereira and Root Jackson were in the dub reggae act Jah Lion. Lloyd Smith played with Eddy Grant as did Herschell Holder, who was also involved with Black Slate, and Alan Fealdman resurfaced in Sniff 'n' the Tears. Here, he played alongside Loz Netto (guitar) and Luigi Salvoni (drums), both of whom had been in Moon, another of the UK's jazz-soul-funk outfits, a few years earlier.

Gigging from March 1975, Moon were a 7-piece led by singer Noel McCalla, backed by saxophonists Nick Payn and Doug Bainbridge, Graham Collyer (guitar) and Ron Lawrence (bass). Having fewer members than either Gonzalez, Kokomo or F.B.I.

certainly helped produce a sharper, more stripped-back sound and they quickly became a popular live act. As early as July 1975, Peel had them in for a session. A second followed in January 1976, after which they signed to CBS subsidiary Epic. Here they were produced by Stewart Levine, whose CV included an abundance of jazz-rock (and funk) releases by Hugh Masekela and The Crusaders. It was no surprise, therefore, that Moon's debut album, *Too Close for Comfort* (July 1976), was an immaculately put together set of originals that could easily have graced the US charts.

But, somehow, it didn't work for them. As with so many of the other bands that emerged from the pub circuit, however good they were, the record sales didn't materialise. Despite continued endorsement by Peel (two further sessions) and gravitating from venues like the Brecknock, where they played alongside Scarecrow, to the mainstream university/concert hall circuit, they were unable to progress. Luigi Salvoni left, replaced as drummer by John Shearer, and for their second album, *Turning the Tides*, CBS brought in Barry Blue as producer. Presumably an attempt to engineer a commercial breakthrough – Blue was producing Heatwave at the same time, and had written hits for himself and Lynsey de Paul – it was another extremely professional collection, well-played and sung and another commercial failure.

Two singles were lifted from it to no avail and, by the end of 1977, the band had gone. Fealdman and Netto then joined Salvoni in Sniff 'n' the Tears, a 6-piece rock outfit fronted by singer-songwriter Paul Roberts. Signed to Chiswick, their October 1978 debut single, *Driver's Seat*, stalled at No 42 in the UK due to a strike at the pressing plant (strikes were common in 1978). A classic piece of guitar-led driving music à la Dire Straits, a year later it reached No 15 in the US.[23] Their debut album, *Fickle Heart*, sold well there too, and both the single and album featured Noel McCalla on backing vocals. Further releases failed to replicate this and, by the time the band folded in 1983, none of the former Moon personnel remained in the line-up.

Notes

(1) Both of whom, prior to this, had been in Krayon Angels alongside keyboardist Lou Martin, bassist Stuart McDonald (both from heavy blues outfit Killing Floor) and drummer and actor Darryl Read. Read had previously been in Crushed Butler, considered by some to be a proto-punk outfit. Although Krayon Angels did not release anything commercially, it seems likely that they had a continuing involvement with Rosko on a couple of singles he released 1970-71.

(2) He also presented an annual year-end show in which he traced the evolution of rock and roll from its beginnings (which, from memory, he illustrated as being Louis Jordan's *Choo Choo Ch'Boogie* meets Hank Williams's *Move it on Over*) to the present.

(3) A single Smooth Loser track, from 1971, subsequently appeared on the 2020 Cherry Red compilation *Surrender to The Rhythm: The London Pub Rock Scene of The Seventies*.

(4) In fact, when the film was released as *People of the Wind* in October 1976 it was more than doubled in length and had her narration replaced by one from James Mason. This version was nominated for the Best Documentary Feature Oscar and also for a Golden Globe. In the light of this Guppy commented, '*What has saddened me, and frankly made me angry, is not the money – as I said I wanted to make the film and financial rewards were not my aim – but the fact that all the credits were taken from me on* People of the Wind *of which the idea, the production, and the text were mine.*' For more on this and the film itself see: https://archive.org/details/bakhtiarimigrationthesheepmustlive

(5) Guppy's *Guardian* obituary (24 March 2008, written by Roger Scruton) draws comparisons with Juliette Gréco. The daughter of Grand Ayatollah Mohammad Kazem Assar, she was also the mother of disgraced financier (and colleague of Boris Johnson) Darius Guppy. Her subsequent albums, all of which feature Gerald Moore, include *Shusha* (1974) *Before the Deluge* (1975) and the soundtrack for *People of the Wind* (1977).

(6) Bloxham produced four hit singles 1971-72: *Black and White*, *Moon River* and *I Am What I Am* on Trojan for Greyhound and *Brandy* on Horse for Scott English.

(7) Shusha, with Moore and his colleagues backing her, actually released a version of *Knockin' on Heaven's Door* that predates Clapton, on her album *This is the Day*.

(8)   Drummer Steve Holley did better than any of them, holding down the drum slot in Wings 1978-79.

(9)   On the King's Head see: https://www.mustrad.org.uk/articles/k_head.htm Clive Palmer had a residency there at one point. Much of the singing appears to have been unaccompanied. On The Sky Rockets and Bontemps Roulez see: https://thefatangelsings.com/tag/andrew-bodnar/

(10)   Bailey and Bonnett responded to these changes by forming Buster Crabbe with Neil Brockbank (bass) and Mike Gaffey (drums). They played about 40 gigs through to 1978. An early performance, at The Red Cow Hammersmith (27 October 1976), was taped and captures their set: ten numbers, closing with a cover of *Double Barrel*. Live work was plentiful but with punk the only game in town no record companies were interested. Down to a trio of Bonnett, Brockbank and Gaffey they finally signed to Logo and released a single, *Bontemps Roulez*, credited to Steve van Deller with Roulez-Roux in October 1979. It didn't sell and they broke up soon afterwards.

(11)   Between them the brass players had recorded with Georgie Fame and The Blue Flames, John Mayall's Blues Breakers, The Alan Price Set, Fleetwood Mac, Juicy Lucy, The Locomotive, Chicken Shack and Ginger Baker's Airforce as well as many sessions on pop and rock albums, including Ace's *Five a Side*.

(12)   An early sighting of them, as The Excelles with Carol and Diana, was at Quaintways, Chester in November 1967 as support act to The Freddy Mack Show.

(13)   Courtenay's previous bands included a spell with Honeybus.

(14)   Reid famously turned down the chance to join Led Zeppelin. His debut album, *Bang, Bang You're Terry Reid*, entered the US charts in December 1968, peaking at No 153. He followed it with *Terry Reid* in October 1969, from which *Friends* was lifted, which reached No 147. Both were Mickie Most productions... hence, again, the choice of Most as go-to producer for Brinsley Schwarz's early sessions.

(15)   The show can be viewed at https://www.youtube.com/watch?v=0DPy44UcxAw Arrival perform their opening number on roller skates.

(16)   See *Nights in White Satin: An Illustrated History of the Isle of Wight Festivals* Brian Hinton (1992) and https://monolithcocktail.com/a-z/archive-f-k/this-is-how-i-remember-it/

(17) Post-Arrival Glen LeFleur ended up in The Olympic Runners with Lisle Harper (ex-Gass) and George Chandler (ex-Gonzalez). The band released 7 albums 1974-79 and recorded the main title theme for the 1979 film *The Bitch*.

(18) It must have helped that just prior to these auditions Birch, Frank Collins, McHugh and Hubbard, together with the brass section from Gonzalez, appeared on an eponymous MAM LP by keyboardist Mike Storey. They are also featured, with Mel Collins and Spencer, on the Alvin Lee live double-album *In Flight*, recorded at the Rainbow in March 1974. This was a quite a successful venture, reaching No 65 in the US charts.

(19) See Mitchell Cohen *Phonograph Record* October 1975.

(20) At around this time McHugh with Frank and Mel Collins took part in the sessions for Cado Belle's debut album. Signed by Anchor in early 1976, Belle, who did a number of pub gigs without being primarily a 'pub-rock' band, were a 6-piece Scottish soul-funk outfit built around vocalist Maggie Reilly, releasing an LP, EP and 3 singles 1976-78. After their demise Reilly sang on Mike Oldfield's 1983 album *Crises* (No 6 UK) and accompanying single *Moonlight Shadow* (No 4 UK). Saxophonist Colin Tully scored the Bill Forsyth films *That Sinking Feeling* (1979), and, memorably, *Gregory's Girl* (1980).

(21) For this and subsequent quotes see *International Musician and Recording World* July 1975.

(22) Other session players on McCullough's album included Hubbard and Spenner from Kokomo, Frankie Miller and drummer Steve Chapman from The Mick Cox Band.

(23) The official video of *Driver's Seat* can be seen at: https://www.youtube.com/watch?v=9SCzVEUlqqA

DANNY ADLER

(ROOGALATOR)

I grew up in Cincinatti and later moved to the West Coast where I played a lot with R'n'B guys like Solomon Burke, Slim Harpo, Arthur Crudup and also did pick-up gigs backing Amos Milburn and John Lee Hooker. I went to New York in the fall of 1970 and joined Elephant's Memory (whose bass player I had taught). Their guitar player had quit and I took over. There was a lot of bullshit going on, drugs and even guns and the band were involved with The Yippies as well as John Lennon and Yoko Ono. We were under police surveillance, so, I got out of the States.

I arrived in the UK on 1 April 1971 and ended up in Earl's Court. I did sessions and joined a band in Bristol with Chris Gibbons and Jeff Pasternak called Smooth Loser, managed by Jeff's brother, the Emperor Rosko. He put us on a salary (£10 a week) and gave us a transit van with airline-style seats in it. We also got free amps from Orange through some deal Rosko had with them. We rehearsed and did demos in Denmark Street whilst living in a house in Easter Compton near Bristol and driving up to London to play places like The Greyhound, Fulham. We recorded a fair amount, including at Graham Gouldman's Strawberry Studios in Manchester, and one of Don Arden's team wanted to sign us, but nothing transpired.

I left for London and got a place to stay in Cremorne Road. Compared with most of the other bands on the circuit then, I was old school. Mad about The Beatles, The Kinks, The Rolling Stones, The Animals. I found many of the other bands, then, to be boring. There really wasn't that much going on I could get my teeth into. I used to go to Ronnie Scott's a lot, because if you were in the Musicians Union you could get in for £1. In 1972 I formed an early version of Roogalator with Malcolm Mortimore (ex-Gentle Giant) who was later in GT Moore and the Reggae Guitars. But it didn't last very long and I ended up in an Irish ceilidh band, Kevin Barry and The Echo's. I played guitar with them, alongside Cedric Thorose, and we did an album, *Real Home Grown Stuff Boys*. We played lots and lots of pubs; ballrooms too.

I left in 1974 when I had a stable line-up for Roogalator. I really rehearsed those guys... endlessly. I was so adamant about our sound. I was living in a squat in Stoke Newington and we were getting maybe £5-£10 per gig. But with us doing 4-5 gigs a week and me getting some sessions too I was a full-time musician. Some weeks we'd travel 1500 miles to and from wherever we were playing. Wilko really encouraged us in the early days (1975-76). He got us the opening slot on the big Dr Feelgood Theatre Tour and they also lent us some gear.

When we signed to Stiff and Virgin we got small advances. What both labels wanted was us to sign to 10-year publishing deals. I never wanted that, given how little money they were offering. A&R men would say things like, 'Gee Danny... *we really love the band but we can't figure out how to market you*'. The whole thing with Do It, run by our manager Robin Scott, started because we couldn't get a deal with anyone else. (Robin was a friend of Malcolm McLaren, whom I met... we had to borrow The Sex Pistols' PA on one occasion. The condition was we had to let them open for us. This was early 1976 some time. We did... and the audience walked out almost immediately!)

After Roogalator broke up, Charlie Gillett introduced me to Ian Stewart, and through him I met Charlie Watts. I played in Alexis Korner's Rocket 88 at one point, and later in the De Luxe Blues Band with Micky Waller, Bob Brunning and Bob Hall.

Out of all the stuff I recorded in the 70s, the things I liked best were *Cincinatti Fatback* and *All Aboard*. Looking back, I should have been a bit more accepting of what other people were doing... I was a perfectionist! I always dug Wilko Johnson as a guitarist and he definitely wrote some great tunes. Also, Ian Dury was kind of visionary and had great musicians in his band. Even though

The Clash wasn't my bag, Joe Strummer was a genuine good guy and was always evolving as an artist. He and Wilko were always very complimentary about Roogalator. XTC were also a very interesting original band. I've also got a lot of time for Robyn Hitchcock, who was later my labelmate on Armageddon Records (1980-81) and, of course, Nick Lowe, Dave Edmunds and Chilli Willi, a smokin' band.

GERALD MOORE

(GT MOORE and the REGGAE GUITARS)

I went to Maidenhead College of Art. I signed my first record deal with Peter Eden in Denmark Street when I was about twenty-one. For the next few years, we were constantly recording, including the film score for *People of the Wind*, which was nominated for an Oscar. Martin Scorsese said it was his favourite film and *The New York Times* called it *'pure genius'*.

In 1973, Peter suggested, *'why don't you make a reggae album?'* There was no sudden switch from folk-rock to reggae, as such. I've always been an encyclopaedic musician. On the 2nd Heron album, we did *Madman*, a ska tune. When I was 17 and playing in a soul band there was a lot of ska around... you'd go and see someone like Geno and they'd always open with a couple of instrumentals after which it'd be *Midnight Hour*, *Knock on Wood* and then *Al Capone's Guns Don't Argue* or *Guns of Navarone*. Most bands in the 70s did a reggae song in their set.

The majority of the people who played in the Reggae Guitars came from the commune where we lived. We played commune rock: good-time music. When we started, we had Malcolm Mortimore from Roogalator on drums. Malcolm was always trying to get George, his best mate, into the band. But I resisted it. They both ended up in Kilburn and the High Roads. We couldn't get a gig in typical rock clubs and pubs because we were playing reggae. And the Caribbean clubs wouldn't touch us because we were white. But we did get some. The rock world was very conservative, if not stale. I wanted to play something new and dynamic with an authentic sound. There was a feeling, *'let's make it real'* for white people and black people.

Island were interested saying, 'we'd just like to hear what you can do'. They offered us a small advance but, at the dinner to celebrate our signing, David Betteridge was there, not Chris Blackwell. I think Blackwell's view was he already had Bob Marley, the best reggae band in the world. I got really angry and wouldn't sign, which astonished the rest of the band. I think Island offered us an advance of £8000.

A little later we got a deal with Charisma and we played the 1974 Reading Festival shortly afterwards; wasn't a good gig for us. I got really pissed off. The crowd threw cans at the band, and there was all kinds of heckling. My Mum and Dad were there. At a time of high racial intolerance and violence we were a group of white men venerating black culture. But, it has to be said, those were dark days.

We toured with Jimmy Cliff and some of Greyhound gigged with us. Also, Angus from Aswad and the drummer of The Cimarons. After a while, though, more black people were digging us than white, and we were getting a lot of mixed-race couples at gigs. Things slowly started to change into where they are today. In terms of sales, I think more black people bought us than white. You have to remember there was a lot of prejudice against reggae as a music form, on top of which there was this view could white people play it?

We started playing with two drummers: Steve Holly, who later joined Wings and Tony Braunagel, who was with Johnny Nash's band. We could play bigger stages and in London the best gig we ever did was at the Roundhouse, with Betty Wright and Kokomo.

By 1975, Charisma thought we needed a US manager so I went over there to meet various business people. Our third album was never actually released and we carried on touring, especially in Holland, where we had a house in Den Haag. But the personnel turned over and the band eventually morphed into GT Moore and the Rhythm Tramps.

Ace were the best band on the pub circuit. They had a great singer. The venue I liked the most was The Rock Garden. And The Nashville Rooms too, we had the most fun there.

CHARLIE HART

(KILBURN and the HIGH ROADS)

I got involved with The People Band around 1969. At the end of a taxing evening rehearsing with Pete Brown and his Battered Ornaments, Lyn Dobson came over to me and said, *'Do you want to play some real music?'*. I ended up in Southgate playing full-on free jazz with Mel Davis and Terry Day and Lyn. It was a game changer for me. Mel played piano and was the central figure. The People Band recorded with Charlie Watts because Charlie's wife, Shirley, had been at the Royal College of Art and knew Terry, and also loved Mel's playing.

Ian Dury had been at the Royal College of Art too. He knew the remarkable pianist Russell Hardy and Terry Day, from their time at Walthamstow College of Art with Peter Blake. Because of this Ian was always hanging around our gigs, making a nuisance of himself. He was a bit of a ligger! We'd play somewhere like the 100 Club, and then someone would have to drive him home afterwards.

There was a much bigger audience for free music in Europe than there was in the UK. The People Band did a lot of gigs in the Netherlands and Belgium. We were more accepted there. We had a trio as well, OMMU, which was myself, Davey Payne and Terry. One day in 1970, I got a call from Ian saying he was forming a band and he wanted me in it. We rehearsed at George Khan's studio with Russell Hardy as Ian tried to be a rock star. At the beginning you wouldn't have thought it possible.

What actually happened to the line-up Ian started up in London with Russell, George Khan, myself, Ted Speight and Terry Day was that George ducked out, and Terry and I suggested bringing in Davey Payne, who had recently turned up at a People Band workshop in Wood Green. Of course, Davey fitted the bill brilliantly and was the only Kilburn to last through to the Blockheads. He was an extremely free player, and the combination of him and Charley Charles, Norman Watt-Roy et al was great... and very improbable! I don't know of many bands that incorporated improv to that extent.

Ian's relationship with musicians was difficult, because of the difficulty he had with playing an instrument himself. He'd get you in the band and then fall out with you. But it was brilliant of him to realise the possibilities... and yes... it was theatrical with an element of performance art.

The Kilburns started out in pubs as that's what you did. We played the venues: the first wave were places like The Tally Ho, The Kensington, the Hope & Anchor, Islington. Later there was a second wave: the Bull and Gate, The Pegasus, The Half Moon, Putney, the Hare & Hounds, Islington, The Dublin Castle. It was a different type of scene, more emphasis on the music and less on ambition, image and 'making it' in the music business.

The term pub-rock is bollocks. It's manufactured by the media. As Ian Dury said, 'You play pubs until you graduate somewhere else.'

THINGS MAY COME AND THINGS MAY GO, BUT THE ART SCHOOL DANCE GOES ON FOREVER

So said track one, side one of Pete Brown's 1970 album of the same name. Wrapped in a great cover by Brown's friend Mal Dean – a hand-drawn portrait of all the great art school alumni responsible, as Brown and Dean saw it, for the best of twentieth-century culture – those purchasing it also got a set of pop-art cartoons on an insert.[1] The song itself was decent enough, with rasping vocals and lyrics that faded out to a trad-jazz style chug played on banjo, trumpet and trombone. Which might seem incongruous now, but, as Peter Blake (Gravesend Technical College, School of Art) was happy to confirm some years later, *'all the dances were always Trad bands, it was George Melly and Chris Barber'.*[2]

Brown's benediction to art schools reflected how much they offered young people in the decades after 1945. After the academically gifted had been creamed off to Oxbridge and its equivalents, they provided an easy access to higher education for those with modest qualifications. Free accommodation in a hall of residence was provided as were generous maintenance grants. Apart from a steady stream of outstanding fine artists, it was a system that produced tens of thousands of designers, illustrators, theatre and TV technicians, advertising copywriters, garment cutters, couturiers, milliners, sculptors and engravers, all of whom were in demand as the UK economy expanded. Unofficially, as a side-product, they also produced a great many musicians and writers.[3] And, with their generous entertainment budgets, they held lots of dances. Given this, it was hardly surprising that, over time, particular bands developed whose appearance and sound matched, and appealed to, the character of art school audiences.

Early sightings of such acts, during the era of duffle coats and beards, included The Temperance Seven (Chelsea School of Art), an ensemble much given to droll send-ups of antique jazz and ragtime numbers.[4] Their natural successors were the Bonzo Dog Doo-Dah Band (Goldsmiths College), who, like them, initially dressed like everything had stopped circa 1912. Later, when denim, beards and men with an abundance of facial hair were all the rage, electric blues, led by John Mayall (Manchester College of Art), predominated. For some of those involved, it was about modern art embracing the music, usually via flash Americana. Lots of pop imagery: cartoons, modernity and glamour, all done with a provocative and ironic twist. Mentors like Blake and Richard Hamilton (Slade School of Fine Art) were keen on this, with Hamilton later endorsing his tuxedo-clad former pupil Bryan Ferry (Newcastle University, Fine Art) as, *'My finest creation!'*

Alongside this was a great deal of experimentation: improvised jazz, improvised theatre, 'happenings', light shows, poetry and much else. Kinetic structures and mixed media were pioneered by Bruce Lacey (Royal College of Art) and John Latham (Chelsea College of Art and Design). By the end of the 60s, the Drury Lane Arts Lab staged many such events, with The People Band, a free-jazz 10-piece who bang and blew everything available, being particularly prominent. In October 1968, Charlie Watts sponsored some recordings, on which one could find keyboardist Russell Hardy, saxophonists Lyn Dobson who played with The Locomotive and The Soft Machine and George Khan, then backing Pete Brown as one of The Battered Ornaments. Further sessions, from 1969, had Khan joined by fellow Ornaments Charlie Hart and Butch Potter together with Terry Day and Davey Payne; Payne formerly having worked with Bruce Lacey.[5] None of this was commercial, but there was an audience for it. John Peel played a demo tape by Hart and Albert Kovitz on 23 July 1969 and for a March 1970 gig at the prestigious Paradiso, Amsterdam, The People Band lined up as Paul Jolly and Davey Payne on alto saxophones, Albert Kovitz, clarinet, Charlie Hart, bass and Terry Day, drums.

Not long after this, Hart got a telephone call from Ian Dury (Walthamstow Art College). Dury, a friend of Russell Hardy, ticked most of the art school boxes: he'd marched to Aldermaston, had attended the International Poetry Incarnation (aka *Wholly Communion*) at the Albert Hall in June 1965, had been tutored by Peter Blake, been admitted as a mature postgraduate student to the Royal College of Art, and had done commercial illustrations for *London Life* and *The Sunday Times*. As he said himself, most of the time his musical tastes *'were towards modern free-form jazz'*.[6]

By the autumn of 1970, he was teaching at Canterbury College of Art and had decided he wanted to be a rock star. At 28, with no previous experience or musical aptitude, this was a big ask. Unsurprisingly, rather than launch himself into the unknown by replying to a *Melody Maker* ad from people he'd never met, he fell back on rehearsing with friends. In November 1970, whilst *I Hear You Knocking* was ascending to No 1, he got together with Hardy who brought along Khan, Hart, Day and jazz guitarist Ted Speight. For about six weeks they rehearsed at Khan's studio in Covent Garden, running through a set of rock and roll covers. More intriguingly, Dury also got them playing brutalised versions of weird 50s pre-rock and roll pop schlock like *Naughty Lady of Shady Lane* and *Twenty Tiny Fingers*, which does rather suggest some sort of manic performance art continuum from the People Band.

At this point no progress was made, though Dury and Hardy did settle on a name: Kilburn and the High Roads. The death of Gene Vincent on 12 October 1971, whom he idolised, spurred Dury into making a more concerted effort. With Hardy he drove down to Arles, Provence to visit Charlie Watts, to see if he would fund, and generally assist, their efforts. After all, he'd helped The People Band. Watts declined, bemused that Dury, whom he considered a good painter, would want to do such a thing. Despite this, by December a second version of the High Roads had been put together with Davey Payne, guitarist Keith Lucas (one of Dury's pupils) and a variety of bass players and drummers. They played a couple of art school gigs, recorded some demos with Mike Figgis, the film director and also ex-People Band, and by mid-1972, after Hart and Day rejoined, something substantial began to emerge. Dury and Hardy were writing decent original material and, although their set still included rock and roll covers, musically it was delivered with an energy almost unknown at that time.

Dave Robinson became their manager, and got them started on the business of slogging around the clubs and pubs with a couple of gigs at The Tally Ho. They became popular with the other bands on the scene. So much so that, when their van broke down, a benefit gig was played at Camden Town Hall (3 May 1973) by Brinsley Schwarz, Ducks Deluxe and Bees Make Honey to raise the funds to repair it. Charlie Gillett and Gordon Nelki took over as their managers, and they attracted their first rave review in the *New Musical Express* from Nick Kent who reckoned them, '*the most exciting performance I've yet witnessed; Ian Dury is simply the most charismatic figure I've seen on a British stage*'.

In October-November 1973, they toured as support to The Who and filmed a slot for *The Old Grey Whistle Test*, playing live in a pub.[7] This shows a capable band fronted by a somewhat unusual singer... Dury, rooted to the spot, sporting leather gauntlets (as styled by Gene Vincent) swivelling his head about and declaiming his lyrics in much the way a costermonger would boast about the value of his wares. Whatever it was, people liked it and, after nearly doing a deal with CBS, they were signed by Warner Brothers' UK subsidiary Raft, whose roster at that point included Family and Linda Lewis.

Here they were produced by Tony Ashton and began work in Apple studios on their debut album. Problems emerged even before they began with the departure of their rhythm section, replacements – Charlie Sinclair (bass) and Louis Larose (drums) – being found at short notice from pub-rock rivals Phoenix.[8] Despite this, the sessions went quite well, with a dozen original compositions being laid down even if, as would be so often the case with pub-rock acts, listening to them in the studio was never as exciting as seeing them live. For a couple of weeks things looked promising – they were profiled in *Penthouse* magazine – only for Warner Brothers to decide to close Raft. Initially the label's executives exercised their option for a second album, without agreeing a release date for the first one. Later they agreed to cancel their contract with the band keeping the PA and vans they had bought with their advance.

Dury then refused to consider a possible deal with Virgin that Gillett and Nelki had managed to put together.[9] He also tried to bring in Justin de Villeneuve as replacement manager. A revealing choice. De Villeneuve (real name Nigel Davies) had managed Twiggy through the 60s, turning her from a cockney fashion model, who couldn't sing or act, into an international star. They had split in 1973 and he was in the market seeking other clients. But he declined Dury's approaches, put off by the amount of commitment that was being demanded.[10] By this point Hardy and Larose left, replaced by David Rohoman on drums (returning to the position he had been ousted from a few months earlier) and Rod Melvin (Chelsea School of Art) on keyboards.

A new manager arrived too: Tommy Roberts (Goldsmiths College), friend of Peter Blake and proprietor at one point of the fashion establishment at 430 King's Road. Buying in to Dury's vision, Roberts dressed the band in retro 40s style outfits and had an elaborate stage set built for them. The band were relaunched on 29 September 1974 with a prestige gig at the King's Road Theatre. Amongst those present were Malcolm McLaren, Chris Spedding and Steve Jones, with McLaren recollecting, 'The show started at 11.30pm after the pubs had closed and the cinema finished programming for the night, Ian and Kilburn and The High Roads summed up the whole London arena of fashion, music and art at that time, and Tommy was expert in communicating that.' [11]

Roberts also got them a deal with Dawn, where Chris Thomas, noted for his success with Brian Ferry and Roxy Music, produced them. Their debut single *Rough Kids* appeared in November 1974, four years after Dury had started re-inventing himself as a rock singer. It didn't sell, but, significantly, was reckoned a fine release by McLaren's Sex Pistols, in particular Glen Matlock, 'It *was* Rough Kids *that swung it for me. I loved the staccato guitar at the beginning... A lot of bands around that time were very polite, but Ian was a stroppy bugger. I liked the fact that the Kilburns were confrontational'.*[12] A second single, *Crippled with Nerves*, followed in February 1975; a slow, romantic ballad it was easily Dury's least affected performance, and all the better for it. But it tanked too and, with nothing to show for their efforts, the band broke up at the end of May.

A projected European tour was cancelled. Dawn pressed ahead with the release of an album, *Handsome*, despite their disintegration. Containing rerecordings of 9 of the numbers shelved by Raft, and 3 further originals, Dury put together ad hoc line-ups for appearances on Janet Street-Porter's *The London Weekend Show* on 28 June (alongside Burlesque and Judge Dread) and 12 October. But with no sustained promotion, sales were again minimal.

With Dave Robinson now back managing him, Dury spent the next five months songwriting with Rod Melvin. It was time well spent. They produced two classics, *England's Glory* and *What a Waste*. The former was a brilliant verbal collage – a kind of oral equivalent of Blake's *Sgt Pepper* sleeve – that wouldn't have been out of place being performed by Olivier in *The Entertainer*. The latter gave Dury a No 9 hit in 1978. By the end of the year, Robinson had passed on the management baton to Peter Jenner and Andrew King, who put Dury on a retainer of £25 per week. A new band was assembled, now named Ian Dury and the Kilburns, with Ted Speight making a return on guitar, John Earle on saxophone, Giorgi Dionisiev, bass and Malcolm Mortimore, drums.[13] After a third and final appearance on *The London Weekend Show* on 7 January, performing *England's Glory*, they started out once again on the gig circuit.

The verdict from the music media was mixed at best, with *New Musical Express* reviewer Chas de Whalley opining, '*Dury isn't the guy for a slick back-up band, which means, ultimately, that he can't be groomed for stardom.*' By the spring of 1976, Melvin had left, Chas Jankel, formerly of Byzantium, taking over on keyboards. With reports that Dury's health was in some doubt, the Kilburns disbanded after a final gig at Walthamstow Town Hall on 17 June 1976, supported by The Stranglers and The Sex Pistols. Over 5 years the band had 5 changes of management and around 25 different members, something of a record. For the next ten months or so, Dury stayed out of sight as punk overwhelmed many of his contemporaries. He and Jankel wrote and demoed new songs, the first of which, *Sex and Drugs and Rock and Roll*, appeared on Stiff in August 1977. It didn't sell sufficiently to chart, but the album that followed a month later, *New Boots and Panties*, did. It reached No 5, and relaunched his career in some style. With yet another backing band, The Blockheads, he finally enjoyed success as a solo artist through to 1981.[14]

Dury was famous for living in Oval Mansions, a ruinous block of mansion flats, jammed up against a gasometer in Kennington. If he'd stayed in Wingrave, Buckinghamshire, where he'd been living with his wife and children when the band started, he'd have had neighbours like Pete Frame of *ZigZag* magazine and been close to key venues like Friars Aylesbury and The Nags Head, High Wycombe. With these connections, he might have built up just as much traction (and certainly no less) than another performer in that area, John Otway.[15]

Like Dury, Otway had an idiosyncratic approach, more akin to performance art than rock music. He'd been gigging locally for a few years, with an early 1971 sighting at High Wycombe Town Hall, supporting East of Eden, and had released a single on his own label in 1972. A little later, and now in a duo with Wild Willy Barrett, he signed to Track where Pete Townshend produced an April 1973 single, *Murder Man*. In a very contemporary gesture, potential buyers were told that profits would be donated to SWAPO and Shelter. If they were, they were minute as this pleasant enough piece of country-rock failed to sell. Undeterred they ploughed on, with Barrett having a couple of solo tracks on a folk sampler, *Guitar Workshop*, and (as Krazy Kong) putting out a reggae single, *Return of Kong*, on Transatlantic in 1975.

Otway developed an uninhibited stage show, and with his band, led by Barrett, and including *ZigZag* journalist Kris Needs on bass and Robyn Boult, drums, he gradually built up a reputation. With Track declining to release further recordings, they put out their next single, *Louisa on a Horse*, backed by *Beware of the Flowers*, on a local label in February 1976. Track rereleased it in November with a different flipside, and booked substantial ads in the music press to plug it. As with their debut, sales were low but, on the back of the punk explosion, the music media began taking an interest, often carrying interviews with Otway and frequently reviewing his gigs. They were on BBC Radio One *In Concert* on 21 May 1977, and after they'd recorded a live album at the Roundhouse that August, releasing the results via their fan club, Polydor took over their contract.

There was an advance of £250,000, much of which Otway blew on a house in Maida Vale and a Bentley. A debut single, *Racing Cars*, didn't do well, but the next, *Really Free*, backed with *Beware of the Flowers*, reached No 27 in the UK charts, after they'd appeared live on *The Old Grey Whistle Test*. Both songs were appealing, combining a wacky, humorous 'outsider' stance with rock. As memorable as Dury's best work, connecting the waywardness of 60s psychedelia with the angst of the 70s, they struck a chord with many people. In 1999, the lyrics of *Beware of the Flowers* would be voted in a BBC poll the 7th best ever written. (John Lennon's *Imagine* was top.) Back in 1977, though, by way of a follow-up, Otway hired a 100-piece orchestra for his next single, *Geneve*. An immense overwrought ballad teetering on the edge of collapse, it had no appeal to the younger audience who'd bought *Really Free* and his career promptly nosedived. Over the next decade, with and without Wild Willy, Otway released a further 15 singles and 3 more albums, none of which were significant hits. Like Dury, he peaked early, like Dury, he switched labels (including a spell at Stiff), and like Dury, he tried acting. And, like Dury, most of his commercial success came early on.

Which was not the case with Kevin Ayers after his 1968 departure from The Soft Machine. Nor was Ayers connected in anyway with pub rock. Most definitely not: almost all his gigs were at universities and concert halls where his highly original mixture of rock, blues, pop, deadpan humour and English whimsy went down well. Surprisingly though, after recording *Bananamour*, his final album for Harvest, he toured to promote this from May 1973 with 747 *'a pub-rock band put together by Archie Legget'*.[16] This included an appearance, accompanied by Them, on *The Old Grey Whistle Test* on 12 June, the footage of which is thus of some historical importance given how little we know about the band. [17] Separately from Ayers, they appeared at The Lord Nelson, Holloway Road on 9 July 1973 (Dr Feelgood played there two nights later) and were the subject of a massive write-up in *Melody*

Maker on 22 September, billed as *'a pub-rock band with jumbo sized talent'*.

Given a full-page spread, the type of coverage normally reserved for established stars, writer Steve Lake admitted that he had recently seen them in action at the Telegraph, Brixton. A photograph shows them relaxing at Island Studios and the piece ends with a firm promise, *'They'll make it. No sweat. Just watch.'* A 5-piece consisting of Henry Crallan (keyboards), Cal Batchelor and Sammy Mitchell (guitars), Archie Legget (bass and vocals) and Freddie Smith (drums), they could play in almost any style: Smith had even been in The Flirtations, whose 1968 single, *Nothing but a Heartache*, was one of the truly great northern soul releases.

The article clearly identifies Legget as the band leader, and lets him sketch in his background, *'I began by kicking cans around in the gutter with Maggie Bell and Alex Harvey, and right from the start we were always into black music, it's some sort of thread that seems to run through the slums of the world. Harlem, the Gorbals – all raunchy, funky music.'* A now forgotten figure, he had quite an exceptional career, one that makes for an interesting comparison with Barry Richardson's journey from Bluesville to Bees Make Honey. Beginning with the Bobby Patrick Big Six, who played Hamburg in the early 60s, backed Tony Sheridan and released a string of highly collectable singles, by 1965 he was in Paris working with Charles Aznavour, Francoise Hardy and Johnny Hallyday.[18] Returning to the UK in early 1971, he came into contact with Ayers, when the two of them were lodgers in June Campbell Cramer's Maida Vale flat.[19]

For much of 1972, he toured as one part of Kevin Ayers and Archibald. After which he led Ayers's band during the *Banana Follies* review, the results of which appeared on *Bananamour*. Ayers signed for Island after this, which may explain why Legget and his colleagues were recording at Island Studios when interviewed. Most of 747 subsequently backed Ayers on his debut Island album, *The Confessions of Dr Dream and other stories*, and various line-ups of the band gigged for the next year or so. But a deal never happened for them, despite being rated by Pete Frame as, *'the best of the third wave'* of pub-rock alongside Dr Feelgood, GT Moore and the Reggae Guitars and Kokomo. Like Martin Stone's Jive Bombers, they were destined to remain an act who bowled over audiences, got rave reviews and then receded from the collective memory. Legget was also in The Soporifics, who backed Ayers, Brian Eno, John Cale and Nico on the live album *June 1, 1974*. Like *Dr Dream*, this didn't sell sufficiently to chart and he continued to play mainly as a sideman, his own output during this period being limited to a single, *Jamaican Jockey*, released on Virgin in October 1975. A tough piece of soul-funk, if 747 were anything like this it remains a shame that their efforts remain somewhere in the vaults.

Although Kevin Ayers never directly involved himself with pub-rock, Brian Eno (Winchester School of Art) momentarily did, with a band that were already on that circuit. Remarkably, Eno both recorded and gigged with them as lead vocalist. The band in question were The Winkies, led by Canadian guitarist Philip Rambow, who arrived in London in 1973 after hearing that Island A&R man Muff Winwood liked one of his demo tapes.[20] In later years he would recollect, 'The pub-rock scene when I got into London was fantastic. It was friendly and you met musicians. You had opportunities to play on the night... I jammed with Ducks Deluxe in the early autumn of '73. And Paul Kennerley, who was the manager of The Winkies, came up and approached me to say, "That was pretty good. Would you like to be in a rock and roll band?" I said, "Yes, that's why I'm here!" My bass player Brian Turrington and I joined Guy Humphreys and Mick Desmarais and... Paul Kennerley... got us lots of gigs'.

One such outing early on was at The Lord Nelson, Holloway Road on 30 December 1973. Not long after this they came to the attention of Eno, who was looking for a backing band as he toured promoting his album *Here Come the Warm Jets*. Recorded in September 1973, this had seen him playing with quite an accumulation of people including Simon King (drums, Hawkwind) and Paul Rudolph (bass, Pink Fairies). But neither they, nor the others involved, were available for any sustained live work. When the album sold well, reaching No 26 in the UK charts after its January 1974 release, Eno actively sought out musicians for an extensive tour, with Rambow recollecting, 'So, he famously went looking for a band on the pub-rock circuit. We heard that he'd approached Dr Feelgood because they were happening at the time... and maybe a *couple of others, maybe Brinsley Schwarz. He saw all the bands that were around, and came to one of our gigs. And then he came backstage and we met him and we worked out a deal that was beneficial to both of us. Our manager, Paul, insisted that it would be called Eno and The Winkies; we do our own support set. We weren't giving up our career as The Winkies. And Brian, he's a fantastic person and had absolutely no problem with that. He understood that he was going to move on and do whatever he wanted to do. And so, we did a set as The Winkies, and then we changed our clothes and went on with him'.*

Starting at King's Hall, Derby on 13 February 1974, Eno and The Winkies were booked to play 20 dates over 27 days. It isn't clear how many of these they accomplished, but they were certainly well enough to do a John Peel Session on 26 February and *New Musical Express* reviewed their show at The Greyhound, Croydon two days earlier. A live album, recorded in Derby, emerged in 2021 and makes for interesting listening.[21] Eno is a capable and confident lead singer and the band are fine. They do 14 numbers, mostly around 3-4 minutes long, including covers of *Substitute* (The Who), *Fever* (Little Willie John) and *What Goes On* (The Velvet Underground), before rocking out with Neil Sedaka's *I Go Ape*. They might have been rated one of the better live bands of that time, a decisive step away from prog-rock towards something sharper and more accessible. It was not to be. Rambow again: *'The last time I saw him on that tour was when we dropped him off at his house that night in Maida Vale. Accompanied by three young women that he didn't know before the gig... the next time I saw him he was in the hospital'.*

As a result of his exertions, Eno had a collapsed lung. The remainder of his dates were cancelled. Fortunately, by virtue of their vicarious association with him, The Winkies signed with Chrysalis, where they began recording their debut album. After most of the early material, with Leo Lyons of Ten Years After at the mixing desk, had been scrapped, it finally appeared in February 1975. Produced by Guy Stevens, *The Winkies* has 10 tracks, with Rambow and Humphreys providing 4 songs apiece. It's an impressive set, neither glam nor heavy rock, and would have come across well live. Musically, this is a marriage of American pop and guitar-driven, sneering, energy. A bit like Cheap Trick or Tom Petty but, as with the comparisons between GT Moore and The Police, too early to catch that particular curve.

With fantastic timing, they broke up on the day their album was released. Brian Turrington (bass) and Mike Desmarais (drums) subsequently joined Sean Tyla in The Tyla Gang. Rambow hung around long enough to release a May 1975 solo single, *Dem Eyes*, and when that didn't sell, flew to New York. Here he featured in the burgeoning punk scene and was one of the acts included on the 1977 compilation *New York New Wave Max's Kansas City Vol II*. This gave him a certain cachet with discerning hipsters and duly brought him back across the Atlantic where he appeared with his new band on the *Hope & Anchor Front Row Festival* double album. He later co-wrote the 1981 Kirsty MacColl hit *There's a Guy Works Down the Chip Shop Swears He's Elvis*. All in all, quite an impressive CV, leaving one to wonder how much he might have achieved had the cards fallen differently for him a few years earlier.

The Fabulous Poodles, originally just The Poodles, were a 4-piece who came together in 1974 in the then desperately drab Inner London suburb of Deptford. Supplemented by keyboard players at the beginning and close of their careers, for the most part their line-up consisted of Bobby Valentino (violin/vocals), Tony De Meur (guitar/vocals), Ritchie Robertson (bass) and Bryn Burrows (drums).

Musically they were quirky: not many bands were led by a violinist in the mid-70s, and De Meur had previously worked in street theatre and mime with Lindsay Kemp. They also had a non-performing lyricist, John Parsons. What emerged from this combination was a lot of short, well played, clever and very English pop songs. Observational, tending to the absurd and not unlike late 60s Kinks. The band also worked on their appearance, piloting short hair and charity shop clothes somewhat before, and with much less fanfare than, several of their rivals.

By early 1975 they had signed with Private Stock, releasing a single, *Chicago Box Car*. A novelty number about a haircut, this was a capable piece of rock and roll pastiche that could easily have been lifted from the score of *The Rocky Horror Show* or the soundtrack of *Grease*. Private Stock were putting out stuff by Flash Cadillac and The Continental Kids and Rosko and The Roskettes at the same time, so it was a good fit with their catalogue, but The Poodles didn't sell and the label declined to commit to an album. Which seems with hindsight rather stupid as, on this evidence, the band were just as competent as the Kursaal Flyers.[22]

A great deal of gigging followed, during which their image sharpened with them resembling 40s/50s b-movie actors. Valentino, sporting a pencil thin moustache, could pass for an early Clark Gable and they began collecting admirers. John Peel had them in for a session in October 1976 with Paul Morley, who reviewed a Manchester gig favourably in the *New Musical Express* a few weeks later, stating, '*Pure, undisguised entertainment from a crackerjack fun quartet... who played like the Beatles never happened*'. Sadly, the punk tidal wave hit a few days later and it wasn't until mid-1977 that The Fabulous Poodles finally signed a deal, and then it was with Pye, arguably the second least fashionable label in the UK. (The least would have been Decca.) With critics increasingly seeing them as an anomaly from a bygone era, record sales at home were low.[23] But in the US their opening brace of albums, *Fabulous Poodles* (1977) and *Unsuitable* (1978), were amalgamated into *Mirror Stars*, which reached No 61 in the *Billboard* Hot 200 in early 1979.

They duly spent a great deal of time touring on the other side of the Atlantic, on one occasion headlining over The Flying Burrito Brothers and Johnny Winter. For their follow-up, *Think Pink*, Muff Winwood was brought in as producer but it only reached No 185 in the US and, after a final non-album single *Stompin' with the Cat* (a terrific rockabilly pastiche), they broke up at the end of 1980. De Meur, billed as Ronnie Golden, moved into comedy and Valentino, in some demand as a sideman, played on hits by Haysi Fantayzee, Billy Bragg, Bronski Beat, Mike Oldfield, The Christians and The Proclaimers. In the mid-90s he could be found fronting Los Pistoleros, a western swing band whose members included Martin Belmont, Bobby Irwin and BJ Cole, the latter the UK's most accomplished pedal steel guitarist. They were a fantastic live act. Encountering them in one of the surviving music pubs during the New Labour years was a strange experience and left one regretting that the world no longer had the easy informality and optimism that had been so prevalent two decades earlier.

The soil that produced De Meur, Valentino and their colleagues had more than its share of grit. A mile or two further into Kent, it was just as fertile. Bromley, venerated as the former residence of David Bowie, produced Burlesque, led from 1973 by the duo of Billy Jenkins and Ian Trimmer. Playing a mixture of jazz-rock and pastiches of various types they won a reputation as a hard-working 5-piece band, playing both the pub circuit as well as a significant number of college and university gigs.

In the summer of 1976, Arista signed them, the label at that point also being home to Max Merritt and the Meteors, Eric Carmen, Patti Smith and Slik. A live album, *Acupuncture*, was recorded at The Nashville that autumn and released with a single of the same name in February 1977. They appeared on *The Old Grey Whistle Test* in May (George Benson and Crawler were on the same show) but sales failed to develop. A second album, *Burlesque*, appeared at the end of the year to an equally restrained response and the band broke up soon afterwards. As with a number of other acts, they appeared on *Hope & Anchor Front Row Festival* (the recordings for which were done in November 1977) and that album would be their only official chart entry.

What happened? Well... Jenkins is clear that, at some point towards the end of 1976, his friend (and one-time band companion, pre-1973) Bill Broad/Billy Idol, together with others in the same social set, collectively moved away from pop-rock towards fast, Americanised garage-band music whilst increasingly decorating their appearance with the trappings of punk fashion. In a 2003 interview he would confirm, '*in the early seventies I heard Gary Glitter and thought, "Oh, this is the end of popular music?" Then punk was the same thing. This is pointless. This is competence swamping creativity. I[t] came out of all that Bromley Contingent; well, I didn't come out of it. There were people I knew that used to sit round while I'd be rehearsing when I was about fifteen, sixteen... At an adolescent age we were very close but then he (Broad) went to further education and I was on the road. And he got in with Siouxsie of*

Siouxsie and the Banshees and Steven Bailey aka Severin... When we were about eighteen, Billy supported my band when he was in Chelsea a couple of times, because we were doing quite good business with the rock thing. The last time we ever met... Billy said he was gonna make it in the pop world and I said "well I'm gonna be a musician". So, we shook hands and that was it'.[24]

Which is one way of saying that the impact of punk in the latter part of 1976 changed the way bands like Burlesque, and others tipped for success at that point, were seen within the fetid hothouse of the UK music media. In the space of a few months, they went from being serious prospects to unfashionable relics irrespective or even because of their musical abilities. The complex arrangements common to many Burlesque songs, and their use of parody, bring to mind Frank Zappa, who would enjoy a brief commercial renaissance a couple of years later with *Sheik Yerbouti*. If Burlesque had stayed together, maybe they could have done likewise. They chose not to. Instead, Jenkins and Trimmer carried on as a duo, performing satirical/comic political songs with a social observation bent, as can be heard on their 1981 album, *Live from London's Fabulous Comic Strip*.[25]

No overview of art-school based and 'arty' bands generally, or just bands that tended to play mainly to art school audiences during this period, would be complete without mentioning Ultravox! (The exclamation mark was optional, and would later be dropped.) Originally Dennis Leigh (vocals), Steve Shears (guitar) and Chris Allen (bass) they rehearsed and stored their gear in one of the halls at the Royal College of Art where Leigh had a postgraduate scholarship. Back in 1967, whilst at Preston Art College, he had been at the 14 Hour Technicolor Dream, an event he would later recollect as a *'distillation of magical things, all together in one place... You met a new generation, impatient to change the world and expand all horizons – imagination, intellect, artistic ambitions, sex, romance, poetry, noise as music... Everything seemed imminent somehow... I started making plans'.* The latest version of these was that he would be lead singer in a rock band. After recruiting a drummer, Warren Cann, via a *Melody Maker* ad, they gravitated to rehearsing in a warehouse behind Balfe Street, King's Cross, then an area noted for dingy housing, violent pubs, and sex work; Leigh noting, 'As *rehearsals finished at night in Albion Yard, we'd walk down the alleyway, past the familiar row of prostitutes entertaining clients – all busily on the job – and wish each other goodnight. Their voices were often a bit muffled.'* [26]

Via Cann, they also acquired a manager, Austin John Marshall (Slade School of Art, London College of Printing). Like Leigh, his roots went back to the 60s, and he was seriously well-connected: formerly married to Shirley Collins, he'd produced 3 of her albums, including the 1969 classic, *Anthems in Eden*, and had also produced Peter Neal's 1970 documentary drama with The Incredible String Band, *Be Glad for The Song Has No Ending*. Christened Tiger Lily, and suitably tightened by their Balfe Street sessions, the band landed a couple of gigs at the Marquee in August-September 1974 supporting the Heavy Metal Kids and Sharks, the latter an outfit led by Chris Spedding. After these they added a fifth member, Billy Currie, initially on violin, later on keyboards.

Some months later, via Marshall, they were handed the chance to record some music for a documentary film Neal and Anthony Stern had edited together from archive footage of 30s and 40s music and early blue movies.[27] This seems to have had a difficult genesis. Listed as being completed in February 1974, it wasn't reviewed by the BFI *Monthly Film Bulletin* until March 1975, which may explain why an unknown band were being entertained for such an opportunity. Marshall apparently told them it was about *'blues greats and vintage porn'*, and they assumed, wrongly, they would be recording their own material. Instead, they were charged with covering the 1929 Fats Waller-Louis Armstrong hit *Ain't Misbehavin'*, which was also the title of Neal's film.

But... it came with a recording contract, and their efforts were duly released as a single on the Gull label. Doing the song in the style of Roxy Music, *Melody Maker*, in a review published on 15 March, noted it was, *'One of those Temperance Seven-type things that crop up from time to time. The Fats Waller classic deserves more respectful treatment and doesn't lend itself easily to such juvenile behaviour, but fact is it's a compulsive song and this becomes more interesting with the addition of a fiddle and a more beaty approach as the song progresses. With the current interest in the film, I have a sneaking suspicion this might stand a chance.'*

As it happens, the film got middling reviews and wasn't the runaway success expected. Nor did Tiger Lily's version of *Ain't Misbehavin'* sell either. How could it? They hardly did any live work, preferring, as Cann said, to write and rehearse *'scores and scores of songs'* as they were *'determined to not get caught up in pub-rock, which we hated...'* But even diffident acts need to road test their material before an audience at some point, and Tiger Lily duly managed appearances at The Pied Bull, Islington (September 1975) and Dingwalls (January 1976) to do just that. Successfully putting their dalliance with vintage porn behind them, by the spring of 1976 they had fallen in with Steve Lillywhite, a 21-year-old tape engineer and would-be producer. Lillywhite worked on a lot of jazz-rock stuff by the likes of Nucleus and John Stevens' Away, and had access to a studio on Denmark Street. He got them the use of this during some downtime[28] and produced a demo that reached Island, who liked it and signed the band.

One of Lillywhite's demoed tracks, *The Wild, the Beautiful and the Damned*, was quickly included, track one, side one, on the Island sampler *Rock & Reggae & Derek & Clive*. Not perhaps the launch they were expecting, this was an odd mixture – side one also featured Eddie and the Hot Rods and Derek and Clive in one of their (rare) non-obscene moments; side two was all reggae. Released via *Melody Maker* in October 1976, it cost 65p, the paper commenting (wrongly) that it was, *'The first time the band have been heard on record. They are a brand-new British group whose debut album, from which this track has been taken, is currently being produced by Brian Eno. The band is as yet unnamed.'* (Actually, the album credits them as Ultravox!) Soon afterwards, they made their debut at The Nashville on 2 November 1976.

It was the first of several gigs there, almost a mini-residency. Despite some very average reviews (*Sounds*, 20 November commented, *'Maybe it was just the crowd, but nobody seemed able to generate much atmosphere and excitement on this Tuesday night at The Nashville'*) by mid-December they had started their first national tour, where pubs were avoided. They never looked back. After Leigh, who adopted the stage name John Foxx early on, and Shears left at the end of the 70s, the group continued with Midge Ure. They enjoyed 14 Top 30 singles and 7 Top 30 albums across the UK and Europe between 1980 and 1986, when, like Shakin' Stevens, they were one of the biggest-selling acts around.

The advance of Ultravox, with or without their exclamation mark, owed much to the social circumstances of the time. There was cheap, even free, housing to be had in London, warehouses, used and empty, to rehearse in, studio downtime available if you knew how to get it, and, in the case of Leigh, generous postgraduate grants that helped fund one's aspirations. In this context an immense number of bands, duos and singers were able to have a shot at success. Ultravox pushed an explicitly artistic agenda. Most of their contemporaries didn't... they mainly wanted to have a good time and/or develop their own contributions to the rock music canon. There were even some that put over a political point or two, and amongst these, in the dying days of the pub-rock period, could be found the Tom Robinson Band.

Their origins were in Café Society, who took shape circa 1970 when Robinson, a guitarist singer-songwriter, began rehearsing with Raphael Doyle. Both were attending Finchden Manor, a special school in Kent for troubled adolescents who didn't fit in with mainstream education. At this point their main influence seems to have been The Band and, by 1971, they had recorded some demos, 31 tracks in total, one of which was written by Hereward Kaye, an aspiring actor and singer from Middlesbrough.[29]

By 1973, all three were living in London and performing as the folk-rock trio Hereward and Friends. Playing places like Bunjies Folk Cellar, Litchfield Street, they eventually adopted the name Café Society and after appearing in similar venues, including the Troubadour in Earl's Court, came to the attention of The Kinks' Ray Davies. He signed them to his Konk label, and with his brother Dave and fellow bandmate John Gosling, produced their eponymous debut album. This, and a single, *(The) Whitby Two-Step*, appeared in September 1975. A tour as support to Barclay James Harvest followed, after which... not a great deal happened. Davies and his colleagues were preoccupied with rebooting The Kinks' career in the US, and, in any case, sales of the Café Society debut were minimal. (A figure of 600 is commonly mentioned.) Listened to today, *(The) Whitby Two-Step* is a whimsical music hall-style piece, not unlike some of The Kinks' own material, that sounds as if it could have been recorded pre-1914. It isn't surprising that it failed to sell, but Robinson expected more.

He had already put out two songs, *Good to be Gay* and *The Gay Switchboard Jingle*, on an EP funded by the Campaign for Homosexual Equality, who pressed up 300 for sale at their annual conference. Held in Sheffield over the 1975 August Bank Holiday, this actually appeared before the Konk album. The first track, intended as an anthem, was rewritten by him as *Glad to be Gay* and recorded by Café Society, only to be left in the can with Robinson claiming that Davies' view was, *'it's too bald a statement, it's always better to tease your audience and keep them guessing. It works much better if you keep it ambiguous'.* [30]

Increasingly estranged from their main benefactor, the band got a regular slot at The Golden Lion, Fulham whilst Robinson began preparing a solo career. By the summer of 1976 Café Society had broken up, and with Robinson switching to bass, the Tom Robinson Band emerged with Danny Kustow (another friend from Finchden Manor) on guitar, Mark Ambler, keyboards and Brian Taylor drums. They started gigging in November, almost exclusively in pubs and played just about all the key venues, many on several occasions: the Hope & Anchor, The Golden Lion, The Nashville, the Stapleton, the Brecknock, The Bridge House, The Greyhound, Fulham, The Rochester Castle, The Kensington and The Red Cow, Hammersmith.

It was within this 'pale', this geographically restricted network of venues put together by Dave Robinson, that music aficionados, rock company hangers-on, music media types and in-the-know activists could listen, normally without interruption and threats of violence, to Robinson's repertoire of 3-4 minute long rock songs with a political subtext. It's tempting, without resorting to generalisations or hindsight, to see this as a partially Irish phenomenon. Pubs and bars in Ireland put on a lot of music, much of it in an informal atmosphere. Dave Robinson's network wasn't necessarily informal, but it was less formal than, say, the concert hall and university network that was dominated by large agencies. And in Irish pubs and bars, politics were often an integral part of the music, as it also was here. Thus, for a brief period, there existed in the UK something akin to the cultural vibrancy of the political cabaret of Weimar Germany. Today a completely vanished world, and one that faded away rapidly post-1979, it was where Tom Robinson became famous.

Notes

(1)   Dean, who illustrated many of Michael Moorcock's early books, also played trumpet in The Amazing Band, a free jazz outfit, with Terry Day and Jim Mullen, who featured in Kokomo some years later.

(2)   Quoted in Martin Gayford *Modernists and Mavericks* (2018) p142-143.

(3)   Amongst whom we could count John Lennon (Liverpool College of Art), Keith Richards, Phil May and Dick Taylor (Sidcup Art College), Syd Barrett (Camberwell College of Arts), Ray Davies (Hornsey College of Art), Eric Clapton (Kingston College of Art), Jeff Beck (Wimbledon College of Art), Eric Burdon (Newcastle Art College) and Pete Townshend (Ealing Art College).

(4)   For evidence of this see their clip in Richard Lester's *It's Trad, Dad* (1962) at https://www.google.com/search?q=the+temperance+seven +its+trad+dad&oq=the+temperance+seven+its+trad+dad&aqs=chr ome..69i57j69i64.12639j1j15&sourceid=chrome&ie=UTF-8#fpsta-te=ive&vld=cid:8736b536,vid:Es_KvVGPovs

(5)   The People Band seem to have made their debut providing music for *No 3 Examination* by The People Show, performed at The Starting Gate, Wood Green (a jazz pub, with an upstairs room) in February 1967. Three of their number, George Khan, Frank Flowers and Terry Day, recorded the live album, *At the Hornsey Sit In*, at Hornsey College of Art in May 1968. See https://www. unfinishedhistories.com/history/companies/people-show/   and https://www.jazzmessengers.com/en/74862/george-khan/ah

(6)   For more on Dury see *Ian Dury: The Definitive Biography* Will Birch

(2010). For an example of Dury's magazine art see: http://www. magforum.com/glossies/harper.htm#lon

(7)   The footage of this can be seen at https://www.youtube.com/ watch?v=dhFaSuRP1uE

(8)   *The Encyclopaedia of Rock Vol 3 The Sounds of the Seventies* p222 lists Phoenix as a key band in the first wave of pub-rock bands alongside Ducks Deluxe, Clancy, Ace, Kilburn and the High Roads and Chilli Willi and the Red Hot Peppers. Information on them today is almost non-existent, but emails from Chris Birkin 19, 20 and 24 October 2022 confirm that Phoenix were formed in 1973 by Roy St John (a US draft dodger, living in a squat near Westbourne Grove) with Mick Paice (saxophone and harmonica), Adrian Pietryga (guitar, from John Dummer's Famous Music Band), Sinclair and Larose. The latter were replaced by Birkin and David Rohoman, with Rohoman eventually returning to Kilburn and the High Roads and a succession of other drummers taking his place. They played many gigs at The Kensington, usually due to the booked band cancelling and the landlord asking if they could step in at short notice. According to Birkin, '*...My wife insisted we go on holiday and we went to Tunisia for a fortnight. When I returned, Roy apologised and said he had recorded his songs using the band without me for Virgin, because he wanted a simpler country feel...*' Virgin released this as *Immigration Declaration*, a solo album by Roy St John in 1975, with Sinclair taking Birkin's place during the sessions. Phoenix carried on as before after Birkin's return, and recorded several songs Birkin co-wrote with St John, one of which Charlie Gillett played on his radio show. Dave Robinson also liked them, but advised Birkin to leave Phoenix which he did, joining Sniff 'n' the Tears. Birkin is clear the reason Phoenix fell by the wayside was, '*...down to not having a manager and a frontman who could not make up his mind if he wanted country or rock*'.

(9)   If they had signed, they'd have been a perfect PR match. Virgin already had Hatfield and the North, who were also originally from Canterbury as well as being named, like Kilburn and the High Roads, after a traffic sign. But Dury was having none of it, lambasting Gillett for even considering a '*hippie label*'.

(10)   Not long afterwards, de Villeneuve became manager of The Doctors of Madness, an arty band formed in Brixton in 1974. They would record 3 albums on Polydor 1976-78, but rarely played pubs.

(11)   For more on Roberts and the band, and a photograph of the

stage set, see: https://www.theguardian.com/fashion/2012/dec/18/tommy-roberts and https://paulgormanis.com/?p=8098

(12) See Birch p137

(13) Dionisiev and Mortimore were originally part of Danny Adler's Roogalator a few years earlier, after which Mortimore had been with GT Moore and the Reggae Guitars. Earle, from Dublin, would later be a frequently-used session player on various Stiff releases. The NME Book of Rock 2 (1976) described this version of the group as 'more adventurous than old, and may yet achieve the recognition they deserve'.

(14) The Blockheads were easily the most experienced of his various backing bands, and included Jankel, Davey Payne, John Turnbull and Mickey Gallagher (both of whom had been in Arc, Skip Bifferty and The Chosen Few, the latter a band led by Alan Hull 1964-65), Norman Watt-Roy (formerly in The Greatest Show on Earth and prior to that The Living Daylights) and Charley Charles (who'd played with Arthur Brown). In 1975-76, Turnbull, Gallagher, Watt-Roy and Charles were gigging and recording as The Loving Awareness Band for pirate radio entrepreneur Ronan O'Rahilly.

(15) Much of the text here follows information provided to the author by Pete Lockwood via email, 3 May 2022 and subsequently.

(16) See Soft Machinery in Pete Frame's Rock Family Trees (1980).

(17) This can be viewed at https://www.google.com/search?q=kevin+ayers+%2B+the+old+grey+whistle+test&oq=kevin+ayers+%2B+the+old+grey+whistle+test+&aqs=chrome..69i57j0i22i30.13216j1j15&sourceid=chrome&ie=UTF-8#fpstate=ive&vld=cid:92235357,vid:i2Y1sc6PR-0

(18) On Legget's career, and that of The Bobby Patrick Big Six, see https://thestrangebrew.co.uk/interviews/the-bobby-patrick-big-six/

(19) Cramer was a society model in the 40s and 50s who lived much of the year in Majorca. According to Ayers, she 'was an art groupie. She painted, she made things, and she never really got to where she wanted to be, but was very happy to be around people who were doing things in the biz, as it were, and she was happy to have us around. She gave us very good rates... the whole place, there was always something going on with musicians and painters and writers coming in... Even the fact of calling herself 'Lady June' is a fair indicator of her eccentricity, shall we say'.

(20) In connection with which note that Island signed Sparks, led by the Los Angeles-based Mael brothers, in October 1973. For more

on The Winkies and Philip Rambow see: https://thestrangebrew.
co.uk/interviews/philip-rambow/

(21) This can be heard at: https://pitchfork.com/thepitch/when-brian-eno-was-a-rock-star-live-highlights-from-his-early-days/ and https://aquariumdrunkard.com/2021/08/17/brian-eno-the-winkies-a-year-with-a-collapsed-lung-bbc-sessions-live-1974/

(22) The comparison with *The Rocky Horror Show* and retro kitsch is worth considering. It ran from June 1973 and was a huge influence on much of the pop culture of the period. Jonathan King (who also signed the Kursaal Flyers) recorded the original cast, releasing an album to accompany the show, as well as a tie-in single, *Sweet Transvestite*, on UK records. Neither charted, but the music on offer was unpretentious retro rock and roll, not unlike a lot of the material put out by the pub-rock bands.

(23) They were also the subject of snide reviews, particularly in *The NME Book of Music* (April 1978), '*A true dead-end... Hopelessly futureless, their act and records relying on notoriously impermanent humour and beat, with no socially redeeming factors...*'

(24) A detailed account of Jenkins's career is at https://www.billyjenkins.com/webzine/interview03.htm

(25) After which both embraced jazz-rock and toured as members of Ginger Baker's Nutters, live recordings of which appeared in 2010.

(26) See Interview with Warren Cann 30 October 1997 at http://www.discog.info/ultravox-interview.html and extensive comments by Leigh (John Foxx) 9 January 2020 at https://www.classicpopmag.com/2020/01/ultravox-interview-we-were-only-two-narcissists-down-but-we-still-had-three-left/

(27) The involvement of Marshall seems to be rather downplayed by the band, with Cann stating, '*We had a tentative some-time manager, a friend of mine named John Marshall, who seemed to be the only person about at the time who expressed any faith in us whatsoever and we were content to let him drum up any interest or work that he could. Through his contacts, he discovered the film and talked someone into letting us do something for the soundtrack.*' As can be seen, Marshall was actually a major figure, who, like Warhol, started out by designing album sleeves. See his *Guardian* obituary (14 November 2013) and also https://www.goldminemag.com/columns/austin-john-marshall-remembering-phil-spector-folk-rock

(28) Usually, time paid for by a previous booking, and not used

up. Occasionally, a period out of hours when the studio has no bookings at all and, as an engineer is on duty, might as well be put to productive use.

(29) On Doyle's recollections see https://www.bbc.co.uk/programmes/articles/SbFVK7NK75wjRV3c2S9m55/memory-tapes-february-2017 Robinson's are at http://www.finchden.com/mrlyward/times.htm The school had some interesting alumni, including Paul Kossoff and Alexis Korner who came back, at the peak of his fame, to give solo concerts in the head teacher's study.

(30) The backstory of how *Good to be Gay* morphed into *Glad to be Gay* can be found at https://gladtobegay.net/interview-tom-robinson/part-1/

BOBBY VALENTINO

(THE FABULOUS POODLES)

My father didn't really approve of the pop music of the early 60s, when my sister and I reached the age where we became interested in such things. It was a bit hypocritical as he enjoyed the pop music of his youth in the 1920s and 30s. So, we got to hear a lot of swing bands and, what I'd call, light classical, no Stockhausen, Schöenberg or anything challenging. As I grew older, I searched out almost anything including folk, country, blues, up to and including bubblegum pop. I could find musical worth in most things.

My mother used to play the violin and had a great mezzo-soprano voice (the female equivalent of my bass-baritone) and was pretty good, but all classical. She might have been a professional had World War 2 not broken out when she was 15 years old. She gave me a ¾ size violin for my 4th birthday and showed me a scale of D major. She pointed out that I could play most nursery rhymes with those 9 notes so I was walking round the house playing *Baa, Baa, Black Sheep* (no longer a PC title) and *Twinkle, Twinkle Little Star* very badly. I don't know how my parents could have stood it as I'm sure my intonation was all over the place at the time. I had violin lessons at primary school but didn't really improve much. I always thought I could do a better tune than the one I was supposed to read from the dots. I quit when I went to secondary school.

I was given a mandolin for my 13th birthday and became very good, so much so it was no longer a challenge. So, I went back to the violin but in a folky way. I ended up as part of the Blackheath Morris Men which was limiting, playing the same simple tunes all the time though it did teach me how to drink beer and play at 15.

A mate at school played guitar, we got together and I discovered improvisation. From then on, I really enjoyed it. I am influenced by all violin/fiddle players. For folk it was Dave Swarbrick from Fairport Convention, for jazz Stéphane Grappelli, Joe Venuti and Stuff Smith, for rock David LaFlamme of It's a Beautiful Day (check out their song *White Bird*), for blues, Papa John Creach from Jefferson Airplane and for prog-rock, Jean-Luc Ponty. I nick stuff from all of them and more but mostly I've been influenced by guitarists, saxophonists and to some extent synths. I can still remember some of the Steely Dan solos that I learned 50 years ago.

I always thought that nearly all the violinists I've heard couldn't really play pop and rock. So, I taught myself to be really positive and solid when playing so I could compete with the attack that guitarists achieve with a plectrum. I'm always advising other violinists to play rhythm as I feel it's important in a band. Also, if you believe the violin teachers, you'll end up doing the bowing in a classical, slightly polite way, which most rock violinists do. They are taught to do a down bow on beats 1 and 3 of a common time (4/4) bar, I do a down bow stroke on the off beats, 2 and 4, which are the strong beats in pop and rock.

I quit university after 2 terms. I hated the place and my fellow students (a bunch of creepy wimps). I ended up in Hastings where I got work as a musician. After that I tried going to Goldsmiths as a trainee teacher but, following my first school visit to a comprehensive in Newham, I immediately quit that as well: I was never going to be a schoolteacher. The Fabulous Poodles were formed in 1974. I was working in a temporary job at the Inland Revenue office in Catford and while there met a guy called Ken Simmons who had acted as crew to numerous local bands. He mentioned that his mate Bob Suffolk from Bickley was putting a band together. We met, and Bob said he was interested in doing 3-minute pop songs without the long boring solos that had become the fashion and wanted nothing to do with Prog Rock... in a way that was also the original punk approach. He invited Tony De Meur to be the singer and main songwriter and the whole thing seemed to work.

Tony De Meur and I lived in Speedwell House on Comet Street, Deptford which was an old council block. We were squatting there so had no rights at all. It was eventually demolished, and was a short distance away from the Crossfields Estate. This was run as a 'special lettings' scheme by Lewisham Council due to Deptford Church Street being turned into a dual carriageway, which was considered dangerous for children. Lewisham rehoused the original tenants and planned to demolish the place but, in the meantime, they let the flats out to single people and young couples with no kids, with the understanding it would only be temporary and because they weren't council tenants and wouldn't be rehoused at the end of the tenancy.

This led to the estate becoming inhabited by artists of all kinds: musicians, actors, writers, designers as well as students. As they were mostly middle-class, a lot of organising was done: the estate was cleaned up, people did up their flats and community functions were organised. The council were very pleasantly surprised and so the estate is still there. A Crossfields Festival was held in 1976 and continued for about 8 years. The line-up for the first festival included Dire Straits and The Fabulous Poodles, with the power coming from long extension leads from Mark Knopfler's ground floor flat. Members of both these bands had flats on Crossfields as well as a couple of guys from Squeeze. We used to meet up in The Oxford Arms (now The Birds Nest) on the evenings we weren't gigging.

In early 1975, we did a deal with Private Stock. There was an option for an album because they were hedging their bets. So, we released a single but it made no impact whatsoever so they dropped us. However, we had gained a reputation as a live band by then so kept going.

After a while, we got a deal with Pye. Brian Justice signed us. He worked for them as an A&R man, and had previously been our manager. We were paid an advance, I can't remember how much, and it was never recouped, but with it we rather stupidly bought a brand-new Mercedes 608D truck and a PA system. Pye got us on *The Old Grey Whistle Test* and Tony wore a badge saying, '*Please manage us*'. Somehow, we ended up being managed by Brian

Lane of Sun Productions who also managed Yes. He went to Epic Records in New York to try to sell us and was very surprised that they had heard of us, following a recommendation from Meatloaf after we were his support act in Manchester.

We did very well in the US with our first album and were playing in small 1,000-2,000 seat theatres. We received massive amounts of radio play there for both albums and were considered as part of the British New Wave of the late 70s along with Joe Jackson and Dire Straits. The US hated The Sex Pistols and the like. The Clash were the only UK punk band to eventually make a dent after touring constantly.

The pub-rock gigs I remember really enjoying were The Red Cow, Hammersmith and The Nashville. The Red Cow was quite awkward as it became so packed that the takings across the bar went down when we played there (the punters couldn't get to the bar), so the agent thought we weren't much good and weren't pulling an audience. The Nashville, where we moved after The Red Cow, was a great venue. I remember the time Viv Stanshall was our support act. He was certifiable. He came on bashing a tin tray on his head and just got madder, it was great. On the other hand, the Hope & Anchor was a bit of a problem because of the low ceiling above the stage. I couldn't stand up and play the violin; being 6' 3", my bow kept hitting the ceiling and they are quite fragile, it looked far too 'cabaret' sitting on a stool. We only did it once.

I always loved Kilburn and the High Roads, because of Ian Dury, and Brinsley Schwarz were great. The local pub-rock bands included Squeeze, Burlesque and Dire Straits, although I never saw Dire Straits do a pub gig. The first time I saw them they were support to a scratch band of firemen at a benefit gig during their strike in 1977, held in the old Albany Empire in Creek Road. Mark's playing astounded all but the firefighters who were more interested in the strike and their below-average band. The other bands I recall were Slack Alice, Bees Make Honey and Dr Feelgood, who I thought were great.

Our image was trashy Americana. A lot of this, as well as the artwork on our records and posters, was overseen by John Parsons, a graphic artist who also wrote many of the lyrics. Our look developed over time. When Tony De Meur joined, he had short hair and wore Oxfam suits. The rest of us were long-haired louts in faded blue jeans. When Richie joined, he had short hair so I got mine cut. When we needed a new drummer, he too cut his hair. We all ended up in second-hand demob suits or similar as they were really cheap and often of very good quality. When we got to America, we couldn't believe the thrift shops. Suits were about $1 and button-down collar shirts 10 cents. The Americans wouldn't wear second-hand clothes, especially those that might have been worn by black guys, but we absolutely loved them. We helped start the trend for what are now called vintage clothes which these days cost a fortune.

I think the punk scene helped us in its early days. The bands were interested in doing 3-minute pop songs with a crunchy feel. We were the same but had Tony as a front man and he was, and is, outrageously funny. It wasn't until punk became 'heavy metal on speed' that the nihilism, the anti-musicianship and the spitting started. After that, it ate itself. If you look back, punk was not successful, the sales were pitiful and the British punk bands had very little overseas profile. It was very parochial.

It's difficult remembering our best gig, as there were so many. When you're about a week into a tour, the gigs all blend together and the band becomes amazingly tight... so every night is like the best party ever. The best tour was the one we did with Tom Petty and the Heartbreakers. The gigs that didn't work stay more in the memory. The one at the 1930s Olympic Stadium in LA stands out. The headliners were Ted Nugent and Cheap Trick and we were the second band on. The audience hated us: we weren't 'heavy' enough for them. To show their approval they started throwing stuff; luckily, there was a big gap between the front row and the stage so we had plenty of time to dodge the missiles. Eventually, the stage became littered with cans and bags of earth. I knew there was a song coming up where I didn't play for the first 2 verses so I asked one of our crew to find me a large broom, which he did. So, I swept the stage in front of 50,000 people while wearing a light cream silk tuxedo, bow tie and a cummerbund my Granny had made for me. I got the only cheer we heard that day. A photo of me sweeping the stage was the only picture of the whole festival that made *Rolling Stone*, I still have a copy.

My greatest regret? Not saying 'Yes' when Tom Petty asked me to join the Heartbreakers.

BILLY JENKINS

(BURLESQUE)

I grew up at 91 Widmore Road, Bromley, started violin lessons aged 9 and sang in the church choir from about 9 to 12. Then, an older mate, Dave Stevenson, who had a guitar, he showed me a couple of chords and that was that... My big sister Caroline would go to the Three Tuns to see David Bowie. I recall seeing him do a free gig on Queensmead, Bromley. He had Tony Visconti on cello. Peter Green had just left Fleetwood Mac and did a set with his new band. I also recall a music festival in Norman Park, Hayes Lane where a young Carol Grimes performed.

A cocky John Lennon lookalike named Billy Broad came to my school when we were in the second or third year. He liked folk music and played a bit of guitar. He was into The Incredible String Band, Cat Stevens and Irish folk band Tír na nÓg. We became close buddies ('the two Bills') and in time he became Billy Idol. The four-storey family home in Widmore Road had 23 rooms and a great basement. We'd jam there for hours. Steve Bailey, who became Steve Severin with Siouxsie Sue, hung out there, but didn't yet play an instrument. Non-musicians as well, including the yet-to-be writer Hanif Kureishi. I was too busy making music. Folks would come and go through the basement front door. I was/am *very* focused.

I did my first gig aged about 14 in St Andrews Church Hall, Burnt Ash Lane, Bromley. Bill supported me on acoustic guitar. His dad ran a tool hire company and had a new employee, Jock McClean, just down from Glasgow who was also a keyboard player. He didn't consider his son, but suggested Jock contact me. So, aged fifteen, I started playing with Jock, a drummer pal and an American Paul McCartney lookalike. Doing 60s covers we had a weekly residency at The Ship and Billet, a long-gone pub in East Greenwich. At weekends, we started doing one-off gigs in USAF sites in Norfolk.

I left school aged just 16 in 1972, and my father was concerned that I should 'get a proper job', so I got a part-time cleaning job to pay some housekeeping and formed my own band. Placing an advert in *Melody Maker*, I met Ian Trimmer, a saxophonist from Sidcup. Our early influences were Chicago meets Miles Davis meets Albert King meets Charles Lloyd. Frank Zappa was also an influence but Sonny Rollins, Max Roach, Charlie Parker seemed much more anarchic. I was also into early twentieth-century classical: Erik Satie and Charles Ives.

The band became Burlesque. In the early days, and having to assure my father that I could earn a living as a musician, we moonlighted as The Jetset, playing standards in Working Men's Clubs. It not only brought in a few more pennies, but also gave us further experience in performing in different environments and to different age groups.

We played Bromley Technical College in March 1973 and, by the end of the year, had started a Sunday lunchtime residency at the Tramshed, Woolwich. Our first regular London pub-rock venue was the Brecknock, Camden in February 1975. We got £22.50. We would play 2 x 45-minute sets. My memory is of a stage in the backroom and never an amazing atmosphere, but the publican and us seemed to get on and we'd get rebooked quite often. We did pubs outside London too, like The Staging Post, Leeds (£30) and the Halfway Hotel in Goldthorpe, between Barnsley and Doncaster, for £25! Alex the publican there was a *wonderful* man. He'd book us in on a no music night, if we needed a stopover when travelling to the North-East or Scotland. When The Sex Pistols were booked into the Halfway Hotel, they got up on stage and Johnny Rotten started effing and blinding. Alex went up to them and said, *'I'll not have swearing in my pub. You can pack up and go home.'* And they did.

Of the main London gigs, The Greyhound, Fulham Palace Road was a grandiose venue, like an old music hall. But never that well attended. The Red Cow, Hammersmith paid about £35.

I think AC/DC used to play there too. The Rochester Castle, Stoke Newington was a long, long bar with the stage at the back. Always seemed that folks preferred staying at the other end, by the entrance. At The Golden Lion, Fulham, one always felt you had to raise the bar, as several rock musicians often hung around there. And, of course, the Hope & Anchor, Islington. We appeared on the double album *Hope & Anchor Front Row Festival* but it was the only time we played there!

For us, The Nashville Rooms in West Kensington was the best. We played there for the first time in September 1975, supporting Moonrider. You played in a separate room with a raised stage and good dressing room. Clive Davis came to see us there and signed us to Arista. Yes, we did get an advance (can't remember how much) and from my share (the biggest lump sum I'd ever received) I bought a guitar, a Quad amp and monitors. Still got 'em!

Burlesque spent all of January 1976 on tour in Holland. Every night, back at our Den Haag base, we'd listen to our recording of the night's gig. We concluded that we were rushing things and should slow the tempo down, putting more emphasis on the backbeat. When we returned to London, though, every band seemed to be playing at 1,000 mph! We did a gig at The Greyhound, Croydon with Billy Broad/Idol's new band (I can't remember if it was Chelsea or Generation X) where the crowd decided to swarm the stage. It was interesting that he didn't have the stagecraft to deal with it, we just let 'em swarm and got them singing and dancing alongside us.

At another gig, at The Nashville, we had The Stranglers as support. Hugh Cornwell and Jean-Jacques Burnel got the crowd riled up and a fight broke out, which really pissed us off, as the room was tainted by the violence for our set. I remember there was a letter printed in *Sounds* about the incident by someone in the audience that night. I recall a couple of gigs on the trot where the dressing rooms had been trashed and vandalised, Johnny Thunders and the Heartbreakers, I believe... and being stopped at the entrance to a B&B we'd prebooked by an apologetic owner who told us he couldn't let us stay as *'a punk band had caused a lot of damage and mayhem'*.

A couple of weeks before the last ever Burlesque gig in 1977, we did three sold-out nights at The Nashville. Supporting us was a youngish poet – John Cooper Clarke. Lovely chap. I note from my diaries that Bobby Valentino joined in on violin! I never saw or heard other bands though I'd read about them in the music press. We were so busy working and scratching a living playing music: 214 gigs in 76, 161 in 77. Plus, in a pub, we'd be the only band on. Only when playing colleges (which one would do a lot in those days) would one meet other bands.

We took 1978 as a sabbatical, living off meagre savings, after which Ian Trimmer and myself went out as a duo. We had to get back to earning a living; going out as a duo we were the perfect support act to bigger bands. But, once again, we'd moonlight as The Arnold Benjamin Quintet – only four of us, as 'Arnold *was always absent*'. We would do function work or jazz gigs. I recall Sunday lunchtime jazz gigs at South Hill Park Arts Centre in Bracknell. We spent a lot of 1981 working with Ginger Baker. Meanwhile, in 1981, I started The Voice of God Collective – which was a long way from the free jazz and jokes of Trimmer and Jenkins.

NEW ROSE

By the summer of 1975 something was stirring in UK music: a sharper sound, a more confrontational approach. Dr Feelgood had appeared on *The Old Grey Whistle Test*, and whilst their sales remained low(ish), on 23 August *Motorbikin'*, by Chris Spedding, entered the singles chart. Released on Mickie Most's RAK label, it eventually peaked at No 14. With simple lyrics and a danceable arrangement, it was a classic stripped-back rock song. Spedding himself – in black leathers on *Top of the Pops* – looked a very handsome and youthful 31. Although not widely known to the public, he was actually no stranger to the show or to hit singles. As far back as 1969, he'd been one of many session players on *Love at First Sight*, an instrumental cover by Sounds Nice of Serge Gainsbourg's *Je t'aime, moi non plus*. More recently, he had been involved with Typically Tropical, whose single *Barbados* reached No 1, and he was also a behind-the-scenes regular with Mike Batt's novelty act, The Wombles.[1]

One of the best guitarists in the country he had a clear, and accurate, opinion about what was lacking at that time, remarking some years later, '*In 1975 there wasn't that much exciting stuff so I thought why don't I write what I think is missing from the charts and that's how I came up with the retro rock'n'roll biker thing... I think the timing was wrong... I was too early for the Stray Cats' rockabilly revival, a year early for the punk thing.* Top of the Pops *had people like Roy Wood with his beard and platform shoes, the de rigueur uniform, and there was me with my straight-leg jeans, leather jacket and greasy hair... It came off for me, but only once – and a year later all the punks started looking like that.*' Another problem was he was so in demand for sessions that he hardly gigged at all. Like Dave Edmunds in 1970, you would have thought that, on the back of a hit single, he'd have dropped everything, put a band together, gone out on the road for the rest of the year and released a dynamic follow-up. Instead, it would be six months before his next single appeared, and when it did, he opted to cover an Australian No 1, Ted Mulry's *Jump in my Car*, which tanked. An album, *Chris Spedding*, appeared in early 1976 and did similarly little business, despite a cover on which he looked magnificent. (*NME* readers voted him best-dressed musician of 1975.)[2] What was left, though, was a feeling that if *Motorbikin'* could chart, then surely there was a gap in the market and other, similar, stuff could too.

It was a view shared by Ted Carroll and Roger Armstrong, the owners of *Rock On*. Carroll, from Dublin, had played in a showband in the early 60s before running rhythm and blues clubs in Monkstown and Killiney.[3] By 1967, he had moved into management, initially with Skid Row, later with Thin Lizzy. In this guise, he set up *Rock On*, operating originally out of a kiosk-cum-stall at the rear of an existing junk shop at 93 Golborne Road, Ladbroke Grove. With Elvis wallpaper and a priceless collection of retro 45s as his stock, not a few musicians beat a path to his door with Phil Lynott memorably singing on Thin Lizzy's November 1973 single *The Rocker*, '*Rock'n'Roll, I get my records at the Rock On stall, Rock'n'Roll, Teddy boy he's got them all.*'

By the summer of 1974, the band had shifted from Decca to Phonogram with Carroll being paid off as manager. Concentrating on his retail business, he opened a second branch of *Rock On* in Soho Market that September, bringing in Roger Armstrong to run it. Formerly Social Secretary at Queen's University, Belfast, Armstrong was also managing St James Gate, an outfit put together by Ruan O'Lochlainn, post-Bees Make Honey. After an album they recorded at Rockfield failed to get a release, most of the band went off to work with Ronnie Lane[4] and, by the end of 1974, Armstrong and Carroll were considering starting an independent label, initially to license and release the many long-extinct singles and albums that the major labels saw no point in reissuing, and then, possibly, to put out material by selected acts they saw on the London pub circuit.

It was broadly the same strategy that Marc Zermatti pursued with the French/Dutch label Skydog and Greg Shaw would follow in Los Angeles with Bomp! By the end of 1974, Skydog had released bootleg albums by Jimi Hendrix and The Velvet Underground, as well as a rare set from Kim Fowley (recorded in New Zealand) and a couple of live recordings by The Flamin' Groovies. Bomp! went for the Groovies too. Zermatti and Skydog would follow through with a single by Ducks Deluxe and an EP from Shakin' Stevens in 1975. Armstrong and Carroll sold imported copies of all of these, and knew they were popular releases. They duly set up Chiswick Records, but it turned out that licensing old material from UK majors was harder than anticipated. It took until March 1976 for EMI to agree a deal for Vince Taylor's *Brand New Cadillac*, which was constantly being requested at *Rock On* and almost impossible to obtain.[5] Signing a new band was easier.

The first they alighted on were Chrome, catching them at a gig in The Lord Nelson, Holloway Road with Armstrong judging them to be, '*a tough guitar/R&B band turning some fine boogie and rock and roll*'. Some demos followed at Dave Robinson's Hope & Anchor studio. After a couple of line-up changes, assisted via *Melody Maker* ads, the band were renamed The Count Bishops. By August 1975, the same month that Carroll opened a third branch of *Rock On* (the legendary one, adjoining Camden Town tube station), enough material had been recorded at Pathway Studios to produce the band's debut release, an EP *Speedball*, which appeared on 28 November 1975.

All 4 tracks on it were covers, including a breakneck-speed version of *Route 66* and a terrific reimagining of Big Joe Turner's *Teenage Letter*. It was a fine record, quite the equal in power and excitement of Dr Feelgood, despite, or even because of, the lack of original material. Both bands were in the tradition of the classic English guitar band circa 1965 – the early Stones, possibly a bit of the early Who. Image-wise, Feelgood were sharper, the Bishops looking at this stage like a biker band, rather similar to Mick Farren's Social Deviants. A 5-piece when the record was released, their singer Mike Spencer returned to the US in early 1976, leaving them with a line-up of Zenon Hierowski and John Crippen (guitars), Steve Lewins (bass) and Paul Balbi (drums). John Peel gave them a session in May 1976 and a second release, *Train, Train* (an original), followed in July. Sales were good for both their releases with costs being covered and a small profit made. It was a promising start for Chiswick.[6]

Their next project would be The Gorillas, a trio led by guitarist Jesse Hector, who had been fronting bands since the mid-60s without landing a deal. These included Crushed Butler with teenage actor Darryl Read on drums, who played a few gigs as a support act to Slade and Mott the Hoople. A little later there was Helter Skelter. Both recorded demos that were rejected by the record companies. Today, they sound very 1977, but were clearly far too early to ride the punk wave, which may account for their rejection in 1970-71. Another reason might have been that Hector looked quite aggressive and threatening, with cropped hair and immense sideburns, part-skinhead, part-teddy boy. The former image had never been marketable, as Slade found when they dallied with it in 1969-70.[7]

By 1973 they had changed their name, slightly jokingly, to The Hammersmith Gorillas, after the Third World War album track *Hammersmith Guerrilla*. It was the era of terrorist attacks, street demonstrations and leftist cells in squatted houses but, despite these associations, they managed to get signed by Penny Farthing, the label that had a huge hit with *Blue is the Colour* by the Chelsea Football Team. Here they were produced by Larry Page, and put out a tough cover version of The Kinks' *You Really Got Me* as their debut single in August 1974. There were further recordings, but no further releases, and Penny Farthing dropped them. Hector would later confirm, 'No one in the industry wanted to know, and then we met Ted at Rock On. He said he was going to start a little label... We were friends, then he started to realise that I was in a group, and heard You Really Got Me. He imported some French copies and they sold like mad, so he wanted us to make some records. So, we went in and done [sic] Shame, Shame, Shame and Moonshine, two songs I'd written. And that was in Dave Robinson's studio in the Hope & Anchor. So that was *supposed to be the first record out on Chiswick, but he put out another group, called the Count Bishops, first, I think'.*[8]

Dropping Hammersmith, and with Roger Armstrong producing, Chiswick released The Gorillas' *She's My Girl* in July 1976. It's a very good 2 minutes 45 seconds of guitar-bass-drums pop-rock, with strong, slightly idiosyncratic, vocals and an interesting chord sequence. For a 3-piece they make a lot of noise. Like The Count Bishops, The Gorillas were an extremely competent band, excellent value live and capable of wide appeal. Carroll and Armstrong's next signing (either their second or third depending on whether Hector's recollections are accurate) was The 101ers, a band formed in May 1974 after some of its members had seen Dr Feelgood play at their local pub.

They played their first gig at the Telegraph, Brixton Hill on 7 September 1974, supporting Dennis Bovell's Matumbi at a Chilean Solidarity Campaign fundraiser. Thereafter, they had a residency at The Chippenham Hotel, Shirland Road, in North Westminster, near the street where most of them lived. In their early stages, they had something of a fluid line-up, but John Mellor (guitar), Clive Timperley (guitar) and Richard Dudanski (drums) were a constant, augmented on occasion by Stephen Murray (aka Tymon Dogg, violin). Of these, Timperley and Murray were the most experienced. Both were ex-folkies. Timperley had been in Anaconda, a band that recorded two albums, neither of which were released despite one of them being produced by Shel Talmy.[9] Murray, as Tymon, arrived in London from Liverpool in the mid-60s, put out a single on Pye, and recorded abortively for Apple after which he toured with The Moody Blues, releasing a second single on their Threshold label. By 1972, he was busking and both were part of the London squatting scene which is where they met Mellor, who went by the musical pseudonym of Joe Strummer.

After bass player Dan Kelleher arrived from fellow squatting band The Derelicts, The 101ers coalesced into a stable 4-piece, and began playing a prodigious number of gigs: 145 in the year June 1975 to June 1976. These included benefits for fellow squatters at Tolmers Square and two festivals, at Stonehenge and Watchfield, alongside Hawkwind and Gong, reinforced by Arthur

Brown and East of Eden at the latter.[10] The remainder of their shows were virtually all in pubs around London, gradually shading into colleges. They were tight, exciting and in Strummer had an impressive front man. The press began taking notice, Allan Jones (*Melody Maker* 26 July 1975) noting Strummer's '*ragged charisma and sudden explosions of passion*', and Chas de Whalley (*New Musical Express* August 1975) commenting, '*They start out of time, finish out of time and play out of tune. They also churn out some very fine rock and roll with no pretence towards music, let alone art.*'

They recorded a set of demos in November 1975, the same month that Strummer saw Bruce Springsteen at the Hammersmith Odeon, a beneficial experience according to Timperley, '*Joe went from strength to strength as a front man, especially after he saw Bruce Springsteen at the Hammersmith Odeon in November. He was very impressed. After that he totally modelled himself on Springsteen. He thought Springsteen was where it was at.*'

By February 1976 they were playing at the Paradiso Amsterdam, and it was around this time that they signed to Chiswick. A debut single was recorded, at Pathway, in March and the band really were doing very well. But other forces were at work, and the tectonic plates of UK music were starting to shift. The Sex Pistols supported them at a couple of gigs at The Nashville in April, and at the second of these (23 April), Malcolm McLaren and Vivienne Westwood provoked a fight with audience members in order to generate publicity for the occasion, and their own band. It worked – McLaren et al were duly featured on the cover of the next *Melody Maker* – but Timperley would subsequently recollect, '*I remember standing with you (journalist Allan Jones) at the bar of The Nashville, the night of the so-called fight, at the second show, and we looked at each other as if to say, "What the fuck is this?" I liked the Pistols a lot as people, but the whole scene around them seemed totally fake.*'

Events now followed at a rapid pace. Unknown to the rest of the group, Strummer was subject to concerted approaches by Bernie Rhodes, a friend of McLaren's who was assembling a band of his own and had spotted Strummer's potential as a front man. At the same time, Strummer began complaining that Timperley, '*didn't move around enough on stage*' and wasn't suitable for a '*high-energy*' group. Timperley was duly cashiered and replaced by Martin Stone (who didn't move around much, either). The final denouement was not long in coming, and was conveyed to Dudanski: *'I was in bed at the squat in Orsett Terrace. I remember Joe shaking me awake, saying, "Wake up, Snakes. I've got something really important to tell you. This is the end. We've got to talk about it." I said, "In the morning, Joe. We'll talk about it then." I'd had this feeling something was up. He'd been very taciturn since The Golden Lion gig (30 May). Anyway, I went downstairs the next morning and there was Bernie, who I remembered from The Golden Lion. He started spewing out all this stuff about how crap The 101ers were and how punk was going to happen. It was a totally one-way conversation. Then he said he wanted me to be the drummer in the new band, to stick with Joe. Bernie was the main reason I didn't join The Clash. If there'd been a different manager, I might have thought about it. But there was no way I was going to have this guy telling me what to do.'* [11]

On 6 June, the day after The 101ers' final gig, Roger Armstrong was at The Windsor Castle, Harrow Road watching The Jam, a promising band from Surrey now making inroads into the London scene. Strummer, who lived a few streets away, saw him and conveyed the bad news. According to Armstrong, *'The place was half-empty, it was early evening. Joe stood next to me and said, "Have I done the right thing?" I said, "What the fuck are you talking about Joe?" He said, "I've started a band with this guy." And there was this skinny, long-haired kid standing in the background, Mick Jones. Joe said, "I've left The 101ers. We've split up." I just said, "What the fuck..." Of course, it was a shock, with the single just coming out. In the end, we just said, "Well, good luck to you, fair enough, off you go." It was disappointing, yes. But we didn't feel especially betrayed. You just moved on. At that time, people were forming and leaving bands all the time and there was always another band around the corner.'* Which was true, and one wonders if Armstrong thought that Strummer might not get much further anyway. Chiswick went ahead and released The 101ers' debut single, *Keys to your Heart*, on 27 June 1976, even though there was no band left to promote it. And then they pushed on, preparing a live EP by Rocky Sharpe and the Razors and recording The Count Bishops' second single.

Had Strummer not succumbed to temptation The 101ers would almost certainly have played at the European Punk Rock Festival, held at Mont-de-Marsan, 65 miles south of Bordeaux on 21 August 1976. Organised by Marc Zermatti, it was designed to showcase the best new bands of that type and, in particular, those recording for Chiswick and Stiff. The latter label had been started at the suggestion of Zermatti who recalls, *'we were with Nick Lowe and Jake* (Riviera) *in a pub in London. Jake was just out of a job as the road manager for Dr Feelgood. We decided that it was a good idea to help Jake to start a label in England on the same basis as Skydog. Then Nick offered to put £500 on the story and I offered to push the distribution in England through Bizarre Records with my friend Larry Debay. Actually, this company was a branch of Skydog and was also the first independent distributor in England at the time'.* Accordingly, as well as The Count Bishops and The Gorillas from Chiswick, Stiff acts that played at Mont-de-Marsan included Nick Lowe, Pink Fairies, The Tyla Gang and The Damned, whilst France was represented by Little Bob Story and Il Barritz. Eddie and the Hot Rods headlined.[12]

This was punk as defined by the music media in mid-1976, or as *The NME Book of Rock 2* would explain (after a preamble about The Kingsmen, The Seeds, The Troggs etc), *'punk rock revived as a term in the seventies, though in much more loosely defined context, to refer to US acts like Bruce Springsteen, Patti Smith and particularly, Nils Lofgren; in UK London bands like Eddie and the Hot Rods helped initiate* [sic] *new punk rock vogue'.* No mention here of The Sex Pistols, who, in some accounts, declined to attend Mont-de-Marsan despite Zermatti inviting them, or of The Clash, who stayed away *'in solidarity'.* But, although less than 2000 people saw the Festival, it was a hugely important event. Among those present was Caroline Coon who reviewed it enthusiastically in *Melody Maker* (4 September) stating that The Damned represented *'the authentic expression of a new lifestyle'.* The same edition of the paper covered that year's Reading Festival (held 27-29 August), and remarked how predictable it had become.[13]

Which was true. The foundations that had been put down by Robinson, Armstrong, Zermatti, Riviera, Debay and Carroll were starting to bear fruit. The Damned, playing only their fifth gig at Mont-de-Marsan, were one of a batch of groups now coming up fast as serious contenders. Musically, they were anchored by the fluid guitar playing of Brian James, who had started out in Bastard, a 4-piece rock band from Crawley. One account has Bastard playing the Harmony Farm Festival with Pink Fairies, Brinsley Schwarz and Stackridge as far back as September 1971.[14] It appears they gigged extensively and were popular with bikers. The most notable person in their line-up then seems to have been singer Alan Ward, whose day job was being a recording engineer at Morgan Studios in Willesden.

In 1973, Morgan opened a subsidiary studio in Brussels, and a year later Ward went to work there. The band went with him, did some demos, gigged around for a while and then split up. Ward, with drummer Nobby Goff, stayed in Belgium and became the nucleus of the band Elton Motello. James returned to the UK, where he rehearsed, but never gigged, with a collection of would-be Stooges/New York Dolls acolytes in Paddington known as The London SS. (The same personnel would include future members of The Clash and Generation X.) Via this connection, he met drummer Chris Miller, from Surrey rock band Rot, and shortly to be one of Nick Lowe's Tartan Horde/Bay City Rollers tribute project. Miller also worked at Fairfield Halls, Croydon alongside Ray Burns, at that point guitarist in Croydon band Johnny Moped.

In May 1976, James Burns (who had switched to bass) and Miller played two gigs at the Chapter Arts Centre, Cardiff as The Subterraneans, backing *New Musical Express* journalist (and guitarist) Nick Kent and his French girlfriend Hermine Demoriane. Demoriane was the star here: she'd written for *International Times* in the 60s, had done performance art with COUM Transmissions and generally hung out and intersected with people like Derek Jarman. (She would appear in his film *Jubilee*, as Chaos.)[15] This was quite a start for the trio and a little later they added the final piece of the jigsaw, a singer, and named themselves The Damned. The vocalist was David Lett, aka Dave Vanian (shortened from Transylvanian), whom James had seen at gigs and thought would make a good front man. He certainly looked phenomenal... like a character from a classic inter-war horror film, or possibly *The Rocky Horror Show*. In a 2019 interview Vanian would state, '*Long before I was in a band, I had black hair and was wearing black clothes and make-up. It's nothing today, but back then it would get you a whole barrage of insults. It wasn't really about looking like a vampire. I liked Victorian architecture and mourning rituals. Film noir was a big influence and rock'n'roll. I loved Gene Vincent, I liked Elvis but I always thought Roy Orbison had the best voice. Weirdly, they were all pallid with black hair. Also, the imagery in those silent German movies, where the men are made-up all over and have blacked out eyes.*' [16]

It also turned out (thankfully) that he could sing, and had a decent baritone voice. They played their first gig at the 100 Club in July 1976 and rapidly became known as an accomplished, exciting and funny band. Vanian had real stage presence, James was an excellent guitarist, Burns (now Captain Sensible) a multi-instrumentalist and fine on bass and Miller (aka Rat Scabies) a more than decent drummer. They signed to Stiff, releasing their debut single *New Rose* on 22 October 1976 and did a John Peel session in December. They also had a simple explanation about why they wanted to be in a band, with Scabies/Miller quoted early on as saying, '*We just want to entertain people... We want to have some fun and make a lot of money. I've been poor all my life... I want a big house, a big car, and a big colour TV... and so does everybody if they're honest*'.

Their rise had been meteoric, and owed nothing to the axis developing around McLaren and Rhodes. The abundance of venues, launch of independent record labels and the distribution network run by Skydog, Bizarre, Rock On and other local record shops was bringing into life quite a range of similar groups. A rough *tour d'horizon* at that point would have selected The Derelicts as the most political, The Stranglers the longest in the tooth, The Jam as the most conventional, Squeeze the most commercial and The Vibrators as the poppiest.

Cut from the same cloth as the 101ers, The Derelicts were formed in 1974 by Richard Williams (drums) with Sue and Barbara Gogan, sisters from Dublin. Barbara Gogan lived in a squat in Latimer Road, North Kensington and stressed that the ethos of the band developed very much from their surroundings, 'There were fundamental requirements for squatters – like organising against the police or the LEB trying to cut off your electricity – so you got to know each other and develop a friendliness born of trials against a common enemy. The whole street seemed to have this happy-go-lucky attitude to life – and one of the things that came out of it was The Derelicts, who were formed basically because a lot of people were tinkering around with instruments because of all the time on their hands'.

Despite shifting personnel, they managed to get residences at The Chippenham and The Elgin, both of which would later be taken over by the 101ers. By early 1976 they had evolved into a 5-piece, joined by Marion Fudger (bass) and John Studholme (guitar). Fudger, a former *Spare Rib* journalist, was a key ingredient with Gogan saying, 'she more or less took over for the period she was with us; rearranged the songs and the set, tightened us up considerably'. Signed to an agency deal by Albion, they moved out onto the pub and college circuit, supporting bands like Meal Ticket. Here they went down well, somewhat surprised that non-partisan crowds appreciated their political approach.

Sounds reviewed them as, 'a community band playing goodtime, dancing rock and roll in a straightforward bashing way'. The problem was, they had relatively few originals, tending to do quite a few covers in their set. For a moment, in the latter half of 1976, it looked as if they might break through, but, as Gogan admitted, 'by December we knew that there was no point in carrying on. Punk rock had arrived and the pub-rock scene as such was instantly dead'. There's little trace of them left, not even some unreleased demos but, like the Tom Robinson Band, they were quite a presence on the London music scene at one point. Barbara Gogan and Richard Williams were later in The Passions, with Clive Timperley, and had a 1981 hit with *I'm in Love with a German Film Star*, one of the truly iconic records of its time.[17]

In terms of experience, although much less well known then than either, The Stranglers were up there with Max Merritt and the Meteors and The John Dummer Blues Band. Guitarist and songwriter Hugh Cornwell had been in various groups with Richard Thompson circa 1965-66, and drummer Brian Duffy (aka Jet Black) had played in jazz outfits around London's suburbs as far back as the mid-50s. Neither had recorded or even come close to getting attention from the music press, and their musical fortunes only started to rise in 1972 when Cornwell was in Sweden studying for a PhD in biochemistry.

Here he became friends with Hans Wärmling, formerly guitarist in The Jackie Fountains, an R'n'B group that had released two singles in Sweden some years earlier. They formed a band, Johnny Sox, with Jan Knutsson (bass) and two US draft dodgers, Gyrth Godwin (vocals) and 'Chicago Mike' (drums). According to Cornwell, *'Johnny Sox were very, very Rockabilly, very fast. Two and a half minute songs about riding on freight trains and sweet little sisters... Very rock 'n' roll, very enjoyable... we had 50 songs – and no covers. It was all our own stuff'.*[18] In 1973 the band, minus Wärmling, left Sweden and moved to London where they squatted in a house in Maitland Park Road, Chalk Farm and started the business of grinding out gigs on the burgeoning pub circuit. They did this by approaching Paul Kennerley, manager of The Winkies, who also had responsibility for booking acts into pubs owned by the Fuller's brewery. They started to get gigs, Cornwell recollecting, *'We played the Brecknock a few times. The pub-rock scene was booming: Dr Feelgood, Eddie and the Hot Rods, Scarecrow, Kilburn and the High Roads, Ducks Deluxe, Brinsley Schwarz – these bands were packing houses.'* Perhaps inevitably, personnel changes kicked in. 'Chicago Mike' left and Brian Duffy joined as a replacement via *Melody Maker*. He was 36 years old, divorced, and a successful businessman in Guildford, Surrey, owning an off-licence and a small fleet of ice cream vans. Although his musical career had been in abeyance for about a decade, he wanted to join a gigging band and suggested Johnny Sox move out of the squat in Chalk Farm and into the spare rooms in his off-licence-cum-delivery depot, rehearse regularly in a space he had set up there and travel to and from their gigs in one of his vans. What band on the make wouldn't want this: somewhere to live and rehearse with transport laid on, provided by a fellow band member with a bit of money?[19]

They agreed and moved to Guildford, only for Godwin and Knutsson to return to Sweden in early 1974. Jean-Jacques Burnel, whom they had briefly met via Godwin, came in on bass and, at Cornwell's suggestion, Hans Wärmling was brought back as lead guitarist. Now renamed The Stranglers, they recorded a set of demos at TW Studios, located in a basement at 211 Fulham Palace Road, in December 1974. These included *Strange Little Girl* and *My Young Dreams* (both co-written by Wärmling). The second, in particular, is worth a listen, if only because it was nothing like the image the band would subsequently project and has zero to do with any punk sound. A really striking song, it sounds like a perfectly polished 1967-68 pop ballad.[20]

What happened next is slightly confusing. EMI duly rejected the demo, but a deal was forthcoming from Safari, a small mainly reggae and soul label whose owner Reg McLean briefly became the band's manager. By the time a release date for a debut single was being discussed, though, Wärmling had left, objecting to their continuing to play cover versions and accept bookings at functions. Safari never released the single. Wärmling's replacement was keyboardist Dave Greenfield who answered an advert placed in *Melody Maker* and auditioned. Like Duffy and Cornwell, he was no teenager. He'd spent the 60s in the Brighton-based Mark Adam Showband, before playing in The Blue Maxi, who released a single on Major Minor in 1970. This completed The Stranglers' classic line-up, and in the year that followed they would play 105 gigs, mainly in pubs. United Artists signed them in the autumn of 1976 with Kris Needs commenting in *ZigZag* 66 (November 1976), '*Among the hordes of bands currently playing London's pub and club circuit, The Stranglers are leading contenders to break out and hit unsuspecting mass audiences.*'

Not far from Guildford, 13 miles north to be precise, were The Jam, formed by various teenagers at Sheerwater Secondary School, Woking. Stabilising as a 4-piece of Bruce Foxton and Steven Brookes (guitars), Paul Weller (bass) and Rick Buckler (drums), they played almost exclusively 60s cover versions. Acetates were cut in 1973 and, by October 1974, they had appeared at The Greyhound, Croydon. March 1975 saw them recording demos at TW Studios after which their line-up was rejigged to a power trio of Paul Weller (guitar and vocals), Bruce Foxton (bass) and Rick

Buckler (drums). Weller, whose father managed the band, wrote almost all of their original material.

By July 1975, they were playing The Greyhound, Fulham and had adopted a retro mid-60s Mod image, very much like The Small Faces, who coincidentally reformed in that year after their 1968 hit, *Itchycoo Park*, was successfully rereleased. Weller and co wore tailored suits and had their hair styled à la 1966 but the overall impact was less like the real thing than an immaculate facsimile. The approach was rather similar to that taken a little later by The Flamin' Groovies, though in the Groovies' case there remained a druggy whiff about them... and The Jam were never druggy.

Like The 101ers and The Stranglers, they maintained a prodigious gigging schedule, gradually wrote more of their own material and began attracting attention: Armstrong was not alone when he took a look at them in June 1976. The music press began bracketing them with the punk bands, mainly, it would seem, due to their youth, and they eventually signed to Polydor in January 1977.

Most of Squeeze were pretty young too. The band started in 1973 when guitarist Chris Difford put a card in a corner-shop window advertising for another guitarist. Glenn Tilbrook responded and, after Julian 'Jools' Holland (keyboards), Harry Kakouli (bass) and Paul Gunn (drums) had been added, they made their debut at The Northover, a large pub on the edge of the sprawling LCC Downham Estate in November 1974.[21] Based in Deptford, like The Fabulous Poodles, they named themselves Squeeze as a facetious tribute to the Velvet Underground's oft-derided 1973 album *Squeeze*, on which none of the original members played.

Pictures of the band taken at this time have them looking very conventional, with long hair, bomber jackets and flares. On 30 June 1975, Tilbrook, Kakouli and Holland backed Peter Perrett at the Marquee. (Tilbrook lived in the same house as Perrett and Kakouli had been in his earlier project England's Glory, demoing an album in the style of Lou Reed.) Described as '*under-rehearsed and consequently a little untogether*' they moved on from this quickly and, by the autumn of 1975, they were playing a significant number of their gigs on the university and college circuit. In 1976, Gunn left and was replaced by Gilson Lavis, a solid pro who'd spent time in the pit band at The Talk of the Town as well as backing Chuck Berry, Jerry Lee Lewis and Dolly Parton on tour. Towards the end of that year, they signed to BTM, a label run by Miles Copeland whose roster was unashamedly prog: Renaissance, Caravan and Curved Air were all fellow artistes as were the Climax Blues Band who'd just hit No 10 in the UK charts with *Couldn't Get It Right*. Hopes would have been high and they selected *Take Me I'm Yours*, a disco song, for release as their debut single.

As with The Stranglers, it never appeared. BTM ran into serious financial problems, caused by the expense of an ambitious European tour for several of their acts, and ceased functioning, leaving Squeeze without a deal. Undeterred, they ploughed on and signed instead to Deptford Fun City, another Miles Copeland venture, where John Cale (ironically ex-Velvet Underground) produced their EP, *Packet of Three*, at Pathway Studios in April 1977. A new, and better, deal with A&M followed a few months later, and with it a rerecorded version of *Take Me I'm Yours*.

The Vibrators were led by Knox (aka Ian Carnochan), a 31-year-old guitarist who'd been playing in low-level groups that never made it on to vinyl since the 60s. Like Squeeze, and Perrett, there was a Velvet Underground connection here too. By the mid-70s he was part of a Lou Reed-style outfit called Lipstick, which, '*ran out of steam because I wasn't very good at booking gigs. That was at the end of 1975, I think, so I next started advertising in the back of Melody Maker as a singer/guitarist available for other bands. I actually got to play a lot of really funny gigs like that, just sitting-in with other bands, but it was also very disillusioning and I really didn't know what to do next*'. Lipstick might not have amounted to much, but their van driver, Jonathan Edwards, formerly drummer in Bazooka Joe, suggested Knox get together with John Ellis (guitar) and Pat Collier (bass), like Edwards also ex-Bazooka Joe.

He agreed, and after rehearsing for a month, and naming themselves The Vibrators, the quartet made their debut supporting The Stranglers at Hornsey Art School in March 1976. Further appearances quickly followed, not least because, '*Eddie and Pat just drove around London every evening, trying to book more gigs. They put an enormous amount of energy into it and we started getting more and more dates. We were still really just playing pub-covers at the time, because that's what you had to do if you started a band around then. Everyone knew* Johnny B Goode, *so that was what you played... we just wanted to get things going and we didn't want to spend ages rehearsing and getting all our own material together before we started playing live'.* As described here, The Vibrators clearly had the same funlike attitude of Bazooka Joe, a retro-band still on the scene at that point. Pictures of Knox and co, though, show them with a sharper appearance, and musically they were clearly tighter.[22]

A couple of gigs at the 100 Club were part of this slew, and led to them being put forward, by promoter Ron Watts, for use as Chris Spedding's backing band on 21 September 1976, the second day of the 100 Club Punk Special. This went well, with Spedding recommending them to producer Mickie Most. Most watched them at their next gig, and promptly booked them into the studio to back Chris Spedding on *Pogo Dancing*, released as a single by RAK on 19 November 1976. It was a 2-for-the-price-of-1 deal, with The Vibrators' own debut, *We Vibrate*, appearing on the same label on the same day. Both were bluesy pop/rock with *Pogo Dancing* almost a novelty tie-in, and very much the type of commercially-savvy productions to be expected from Most. By the time they appeared the band had also done a John Peel session (12 October 1976), the first by any of the bands deemed, later, to be part of the punk bandwagon. Most wanted a follow-up single, and although one was recorded, the band declined a long-term deal with RAK, feeling they would be marketed as teen fodder. They signed instead to CBS in early 1977.

This was where things stood on August Bank Holiday, 1976. In a country where unemployment had reached a post-1945 high of 1.44 million, the government had lost its Parliamentary majority and riots had wrecked the Notting Hill Carnival, those who took solace in the London music scene would have noted the presence of all these bands, and assumed that they would constitute the next wave of successful acts to appear from the pub circuit. Some of them might have even been classed as punk groups, part of a small but burgeoning scene, led at that point by Eddie and the Hot Rods.

Notes

(1) Spedding's other credits included Jack Bruce's *Songs for a Tailor*, Nilsson's *Schmilsson* and *Son of Schmilsson* and Eno's *Here Come the Warm Jets*, all successful albums. He was also on the soundtrack for the Apple film *Son of Dracula*. In 1968-69, he had been in The Battered Ornaments with Charlie Hart and George Khan, both later with Ian Dury.

(2) Interviews with Spedding, including his comments here, can be found at https://recordcollectormag.com/articles/man-turned-stones-said-yes-wombles and https://paulgormanis.com/?p=17381

(3) Carroll played bass in The Caravelles, 1960-62. See https://www.irishshowbands.net/bgcaravelles.htm

(4) To be precise, the second line-up of Ronnie Lane and Slim Chance, who released *Ronnie Lane* in February 1975. This included Steve Simpson, Charlie Hart (ex-Kilburn and the High Roads), Ruan O'Lochlainn (ex-Bees Make Honey) and Glen LeFleur (ex-Gonzalez). Simpson and Hart remained for the January 1976 follow-up *One for the Road*. Simpson was later in Meal Ticket; O'Lochlainn in Deke O'Brien's Nightbus. St James Gate (named after the location of the Guinness brewery in Dublin) were formed around singer Johnny Duhan, formerly of Granny's Intentions, who released 4 singles and an album on Deram 1967-70. Ed Deane, later of Bees Make Honey and Il Barritz, was a member in the latter stages.

(5) See *Music Week* 17 April 1976.

(6) *Speedball* sold 9175 copies through to 1980. The band were managed by Larry Debay, a Frenchman who co-ran Bizarre Records, an independent record distributor/mail order operation/wholesaler based in Praed Street, Paddington. Bizarre distributed The Flamin' Groovies' *Grease* EP, The Stooges' album *Metallic KO*, The Velvet Underground's *White Heat* EP and independent releases by Pere Ubu, Patti Smith and Television. For more on this see: https://www.britishrecordshoparchive.org/bizarre.html

(7) Darryl Read had formerly been in The Krayon Angels, the band that evolved into Smooth Loser with Danny Adler.

(8) See the interview with Hector at https://recordcollectormag.com/articles/hec-guy 26 January 2015.

(9) Anaconda were managed by Mike Noble, who went on to manage Joan Armatrading. They did demos with John Kongos in 1969 as

well as an album with Shel Talmy in 1971. Their main songwriter was Michalakis Sergides, whose prior band, Arcadium, put out an album, *Breathe Awhile*, on the Middle Earth label in 1969. See: http://pub4.bravenet.com/forum/static/show.php?usernum=313820429&frmid=6809&msgid=1416117&cmd=show

(10) On the August 1975 Watchfield Festival see https://www.ukrock festivals.com/watchfieldfestival-menu.html where the following is posted, *'There are various references... to a group referred to as '101'; these were in fact The 101ers, who were Joe Strummer's outfit prior to The Clash. For me, they were far and away the highlight of the whole do, standing out by dint of their appearance (besuited) and their music (high energy pop-R'n'B). They were so great that, the following year, I made the trek down to London (from Stoke) to see them again at the North East London Polytechnic. This was in May 1976, so must have been one of their last gigs before Joe joined The Clash. I chatted to Joe about the Watchfield show at this gig and he was very friendly'.*

(11) See *Uncut* 21 August 2015 at https://www.uncut.co.uk/features/joe-strummer-the-early-years-even-then-he-has-this-charisma-70350/3/ In this context note that Rhodes sacked Terry Chimes as Clash drummer early on. His comments here seem to suggest this was always his intention.

(12) See https://www.i94bar.com/interviews/vale-marc-zermati-champ ion-of-underground-rock. Lee Brilleaux of Dr Feelgood is also reputed to have provided start-up funding for Stiff. *ZigZag* 63 (August 1976) carries an advertisement for the label's first release, Nick Lowe's *So It Goes* (which retailed at 65p), with the strapline, *'this offer is not open to medallion purchasers or men who wear make-up'.* Other Stiff acts that were due to play Mont-de-Marsan, but didn't, included Roogalator, who pulled out because of the lack of a proper keyboard, and Richard Hell, who opted to stay in New York. The Damned were called in at short notice to replace him. Neither Plummet Airlines, who did a Peel session in September 1976 and released a Sean Tyla produced single in November, nor Motörhead, whose December single release was cancelled, appear to have been involved.

(13) Moon and Roy St John (formerly of Phoenix) were both at Reading in 1976 as were Eddie and the Hot Rods, who headed there immediately after appearing at Mont-de-Marsan.

(14) See https://www.ukrockfestivals.com/duddleswell-free-fest-1971.html

where the following is posted, '*The second was better organised music-wise – Brinsley Schwarz and the Fairies amongst others including a band called Bastard which later morphed into the Damned!!! I know – I booked them in '73 at a local free gig.*'

(15) See http://babylonwales.blogspot.com/2011/10/subterraneansin-cardiff.html

(16) See *GQ Magazine* 23 November 2019. Some accounts state that James also saw and considered John Ritchie/Sid Vicious for the lead singer role because of his striking appearance: which may explain that individual heaving a glass at Vanian and The Damned at the 100 Club in September 1976.

(17) Much of the information about The Derelicts is taken from *Pete Frame's Rock Family Trees Volume 2* 1983 p22. Gogan is also quoted as saying, '*The Derelicts had a much more political approach than The 101ers, and I think that The Clash picked up on that*' in *Let Fury Have the Hour: Joe Strummer, Punk, and the Movement that Shook the World* Antonino D'Ambrosio 2012.

(18) See comments by Cornwell in *Punk Rock: An Oral History* John Robb (2006) p53. The Swedish rockabilly scene was vibrant and produced Hank C Burnette (aka Sven-Åke Kenneth Högberg) who had a No 21 hit in the UK charts in October 1976 with *Spinning Rock Boogie*.

(19) An extremely detailed account of this period in the band's history can be found at https://thestranglers.co.uk/jet-black-the-early-years/

(20) *My Young Dreams* can be listened to at https://www.google.com/search?q=the+stranglers+my+young+dreams&oq=the+stranglers+my+young+dreams&aqs=chrome.0.69i59j69i64l2j69i60.8113j0j15&sourceid=chrome&ie=UTF-8#fpstate=ive&vld=cid:64d5f70e,vid:tCcuc88UTmM

(21) The Northover was used as a film set in *The Long Good Friday*.

(22) On the early years of The Vibrators see the interviews at https://vwmusicrocks.com/an-interview-with-ian-knox-carnochan-of-the-vibrators/ and http://www.fearandloathingfanzine.com/the-vibrators.html

GLEN MATLOCK

(THE SEX PISTOLS)

The first band I ever saw was Pentangle, at the Royal Albert Hall with my girlfriend. I would have been about 15? Pentangle were quite big then, and did the music for a TV series *Take Three Girls*. I thought they were quite good, actually. If you're asking about pub-rock... I saw all the major acts: Dr Feelgood, Bees Make Honey, Ducks Deluxe, Kilburn and The High Roads. Most of them at The Greyhound, Fulham, which was a step up from a traditional pub venue. More like a club. I remember seeing the Sensational Alex Harvey Band there, they came into Malcolm and Vivienne's shop the same weekend. Malcolm was a bit paranoid at that point, he didn't recognise them and thought they were tax collectors or something!

Often, I used to walk back home to Kensal Green after an evening out... all the way up Scrubs Lane, which is quite some distance. I also saw The Jam and The Stranglers in pubs as well as the 101ers at Acklam Hall. Originally, the 101ers did a fair number of covers in their set, stuff like *Gloria*. Towards the end of their time, though, they had more originals. Joe Strummer was working out what he was going to do. Out of all of them Dr Feelgood and Kilburn and The High Roads were the best, they had something different about them. Eddie and the Hot Rods were good as well.

Pub-rock was accessible. It wasn't expensive to see any of the bands and at that time you could get 4 pints of beer for £1. This was when I was earning £7 for doing a Saturday in *SEX*. I worked there in the school holidays too, getting £25 a week. One summer I was working in the Rolls-Royce accounts department on £35 a week and then topping this up with Saturdays in Malcolm and

Vivienne's shop. I was really flush with money! At *Let it Rock* (before it became *SEX*) we got our deliveries on a Friday from a Mr Green, a tailor in the East End that Malcolm knew. The Teds would be queuing around the block to buy their stuff. We were very busy. When Ian Dury first got a deal, he came into the shop. I measured him up. He wanted a big silk gown with his name across the back, like a boxer's, that he would wear when he came on stage.

There was a rock and roll scene too, though I didn't see most of the bands. I liked Fumble and Bazooka Joe, for instance, had a kind of rockabilly look. One I do remember seeing was Crazy Cavan and the Rhythm Rockers at Camden Town Hall in an enormous, almost empty hall with echo on the bass and lots of tremolo on the guitar. There couldn't have been more than seven people there.

With The Sex Pistols it was a deliberate decision: we didn't play pubs. And we neither entertained nor were offered deals by the labels that usually picked up the pub-rock acts. There was actually quite significant hostility between Malcolm McLaren and Jake Riviera. But we did overlap slightly with some of that scene. We did a gig at the 100 Club in 1976, supporting SALT, a blues rock band. I remember their harmonica player doing an incredibly long solo by himself whilst the rest of the group got drinks from the bar!

I wasn't really conscious how much of an Irish scene it was, though there was a slight country tinge to Brinsley Schwarz and Bees Make Honey. As for pub-rock, it was a necessary evil, but had its moments. The blokes you saw in the bands were all about 26 or older, which when you're about 17 seems a bit over the hill. But it did create an atmosphere where you felt you could get involved in music yourself.

NO FEELINGS

And had things been entirely logical that might just have happened. However, a dose of shock therapy was about to be administered.

By the mid-70s, Malcolm McLaren had been dealing with musicians for years. He'd sold them records and clothes. His shop had been hired to supply costumes for feature films and was well known on the London scene. But he wanted to manage a band. Particularly so after visiting New York and seeing the New York Dolls, Wayne County, Patti Smith, The Ramones, and Television in action. The latter in particular, with Richard Hell, a published poet, in their line-up pioneering spiky hair, torn t-shirts and tight jeans.

Whilst in New York in early 1975 he encountered a morose looking Sylvain Sylvain. Rhythm guitarist in the New York Dolls, Sylvain would later recollect, *'In 1975, I saw him at the Chelsea Hotel and I had a long face. He asked me what was going on and I said, "Things aren't going so good... We're about to break up." He was really sad and said, "I'd love to help you guys." He became our personal manager. He got us a loft on 23rd Street in Chelsea and we started practising and writing songs and came up with the red-patent-leather show. We all started wearing red – red shoes, red pants – and Malcolm said, "Why don't you put up a red flag?" Which was a brilliant idea. Of course, it was the final blow of the New York Dolls. A famous New Yorker said to me, "Now you're gonna do the Communist thing?" No one really got it. It was art for art's sake... It was a slap in the industry's face. He saw that in us. He saw that you didn't have to be a great singer or to be like Jeff Beck to call yourself a guitarist. It was the love of different and weird. And, if you're not weird, maybe you should be! Malcolm didn't follow the crowd – that wasn't him'.*[1]

McLaren took over as the band's manager, taking them on tour to South Carolina and Florida. The red outfits – presumably made by Vivienne Westwood – were done to match a new song they had, *Red Patent Leather*. A record of this time would survive as the album *Red Patent Leather*, recorded in New York in May 1975 and eventually released in France nine years later. Alas, the group split shortly afterwards, Sylvain remaining with singer David Johansen in a revised line-up that was soon dropped by their record label, whilst lead guitarist Johnny Thunders and drummer Jerry Nolan formed The Heartbreakers, initially with Richard Hell alongside them.[2]

Returning to London, and with no bands needing his services, McLaren eventually agreed to manage a quartet of teenagers who hadn't played a gig but were known to him through his shop at 430 Kings Road: bass player Glen Matlock who worked there and two others, guitarist Steve Jones and drummer Paul Cook, who mainly socialised on the premises. A fourth member, guitarist Wally Nightingale, didn't fit the New York punk image that McLaren wanted them to project and was quickly jettisoned. Whilst Jones, Matlock and Cook rehearsed, a search commenced for a suitable replacement guitarist and/or singer. McLaren named them The Sex Pistols.

Among those considered were *New Musical Express* journalist Nick Kent, who confirmed (ZigZag 59, April 1976) that, on his return from New York about a year earlier, *'I came back here and worked with a group called The Sex Pistols for a while... but there was no real empathy as far as I was concerned. They're young kids, about 18 or 19, Shepherd's Bush ex-mod types, and I'm 24 and a little more worldly, I suppose'*. There was also an approach made to Midge Ure, who encountered Bernie Rhodes at his place of work, McCormack's Musical Instruments, in Glasgow one day. Interviewed in 2012, he recollected Rhodes asked him to meet Malcom McLaren who was sitting outside the store in a car, *'I was in Slik at the time and our management owned the Glasgow Apollo. When bands had broken equipment, they used to come to me in McCormack's to see if I had something they could use... I thought that was what it was about. I spoke to this strange-looking character, Malcolm... He talked to me about the*

New York Dolls and his association with fashion and that he was putting this band together... Lo and behold, it was the Pistols'. It transpired that, *'They were selling knocked-off equipment. So, I turned down the Pistols but I bought an amp... It was a weird scenario to be asked to join the band without being asked if I was a musician or not. He asked me to join The Sex Pistols because of how I looked rather than what I could have brought to the band... I thought, "What kind of band is this?" It didn't make any sense until afterwards, when it became obvious the band had been created as a vehicle to sell the clothes... The Sex Pistols were the new wave Monkees. As it turns out, they were a brilliant band and the best Malcolm could have put together'.* [3]

The encounter in Glasgow wasn't quite as random as Ure suggests. According to Sex sales assistant Jordan, *'Malcolm and Bernie Rhodes had previously approached Midge Ure as a potential lead singer: in true Larry Parnes fashion, Malcolm started looking towards Scotland following the phenomenal success of the Bay City Rollers. Ure, whose band Slik had just been signed by the Rollers' label Bell, thankfully wasn't interested.'* Paul Cook also comments, *'I don't know what that was all about. Malcolm had gone up to Scotland to see him, but that was nothing to do with us.'* [4] It's easy to see why Ure;Slik, who signed to Polydor in July 1974, originally had an image that was all long hair and retro 30s suits, as can be seen in the promo-film for their debut single *The Boogiest Band in Town*, released that October. They look a bit Cockney Rebel, a bit Bay City Rollers but are musically tougher than the latter. They switched labels to Bell in March 1975 and released their second single, *Forever and Ever*, in November with a completely different image. As Ure said then: *'The change of image was entirely our own idea – the short hair, the James Dean look, the baseball outfits.'* It sounds like McLaren saw early publicity shots of the band looking like this, circa September/October 1975, just before the record was released and decided on the off chance to visit Ure and seek his services. Post-refusal, he must have pondered what-might-have-been when Slik, and Ure, hit No 1 in the UK with *Forever and Ever* in February 1976.

There was even a plan to bring over Sylvain Sylvain to front the band, with Sylvain remembering, *'He said The Sex Pistols were gonna be my band and he wrote me this seven-page letter that's now in* the Rock and Roll Hall of Fame. He said, "This is gonna be your band! It's going to be called The Sex Pistols!" He had some photos from a photo booth and on the back of them he would write things like, "We're thinking of calling this one Johnny Rotten. He can't sing, but he can definitely sing better than David Johansen!" I just never went, basically. I signed to RCA and had my own band.' In this scenario, Sylvain would have been lead guitarist, replacing Jones. Or possibly the plan was to have the band fronted by Sylvain and Ure, with Matlock as bass player and a drummer recruited via Melody Maker... whichever way these comments are weighed up now, they do suggest that McLaren had no loyalties to the actual band members from day one. In the event he settled with what he had, and with John Lydon (aka Rotten), a 19-year-old London Irish youth from Finsbury Park who, like Jones and Cook, had begun regularly hanging around SEX[5] confirmed as singer, the quartet began preparing to play live.

They made their debut at St Martin's College of Art, supporting Bazooka Joe, on 6 November 1975. They arranged to borrow Bazooka Joe's amps and drums, but 20 minutes into a set that consisted mainly of cover versions had begun trashing these. The power was immediately turned off and their performance ended abruptly. Thereafter McLaren, conscious that the band needed to maximise their live experience, offered to play for free, or more precisely, to play in a bar/common room area, with their own equipment, for reimbursement of expenses incurred in hiring a van, which 'should be no more than £8'. With over a hundred colleges, polytechnics, universities, art schools and drama schools around London at that time, all of whom booked bands weekly, or more often, this was a sensible way of approaching student union social secretaries.

A very polite and formal letter from McLaren, confirming these arrangements with Queen Elizabeth College, Kensington, survives.[6] This would be their fifth gig and took place on 28 November. Even better, it was reviewed in the New Musical Express on 27 December, the reviewer recording his dialogues with the Social Secretary thus: 'Were they good?' I asked brightly. 'They played for expenses', he countered. 'The Sex Pistols were huddled against a far

*wall of the dance floor. They are all about 12 years old. Or maybe about
19. They're managed by Malcolm who runs 'Sex' in the Kings Road, and
they're going to be the Next Big Thing. Or maybe the Next Big Thing
After That. Meanwhile we drank a lot.'* [7]

By the time this appeared they'd played Ravensbourne
Art College (9 December 1975), after which a small group of
supporters from Bromley began following them around. Early in
1976, two further opportunities presented themselves. The first of
these came when they were booked to support Eddie and the Hot
Rods at the Marquee on 12 February, and behaved outrageously.
As they had done on their debut, they trashed the other band's
gear and found themselves banned from the venue. As McLaren
would have calculated, the publicity they accrued outweighed any
inconvenience caused. Although *ZigZag* 60 (May 1976) eventually
had Paul Kendall stating, *'I'm firmly convinced too that the Rods are
a pointer to a whole bright new tomorrow for rock music… Unlike joke
bands like The Sex Pistols (who, when granted the privilege of supporting
the Rods at the Marquee recently, repaid the favour by smashing up their
gear, driving out their audience and pelting them with bottles)'*, this came
three months after Neil Spencer (*New Musical Express* 21 February)
had memorably reviewed the evening under the headline *Don't
Look Over Your Shoulder, but The Sex Pistols are Coming*. With far
more people reading *New Musical Express* than *ZigZag*, this was
quite a coup.[8]

The second event was their performance at Andrew Logan's
Valentine's Day party at Butler's Wharf. Logan, a performance
artist, sculptor and jewellery maker, was at the epicentre of a
cultural/bohemian circle named a few months later as *Them*.
Others involved with this included filmmaker Derek Jarman,
artist Duggie Fields, dancer Lindsay Kemp, various members
of the cast of the *Rocky Horror Show*, costume designer Luciana
Martinez, artist Kevin Whitney, fashion designer Zandra Rhodes
and broadcaster Janet Street-Porter. Apart from sightings at gallery
evenings and first nights, this was an extended social group that
could be seen in all its splendour at Logan's *Alternative Miss World*
show. McLaren and Westwood were known to them, but were not
central players. In terms of establishing the band's cachet, it was

important to gatecrash this scene, which they duly did. One eye witness recording that McLaren, 'got them to play at Andrew Logan's party, and then invited everyone... Logan was freaking out because he had this nice space and there were all these people'.[9] Spotting the music press present, McLaren got Jordan, the sales assistant from SEX, to jump on stage and take her clothes off whilst Lydon started smashing the equipment. As with the Marquee, photographs of this were widely distributed and the gossip value was immense.

More followed. Ron Watts caught them at High Wycombe College (20 February) and gave them a series of bookings at Oxford Street's 100 Club venue. They were also booked as support act a couple of times at The Nashville, and on the second of these, 23 April 1976, Westwood and McLaren instigated the brawl that led to another ban, and further publicity. The getting-banned-to-get-publicity strategy was actually a bit unfortunate in some ways as The Sex Pistols were now quite proficient. They played 73 gigs through 1976 and developed into a tight guitar band with several excellent, sharp songs that matched Lydon's rasping vocals.

On 15 May, McLaren felt sufficiently confident to put them in the studio with Chris Spedding producing their demos. Spedding would later recall, 'It was clear that, in 1976, people wanted something new, but I could never understand why the people in the music business couldn't immediately see it. They were very resistant to the Pistols, they thought they were terrible. They were frightened and intimidated by them. I took the songs to Mickie Most first of all... but he couldn't figure out the Pistols at all, though his teenage son loved them. I thought the Pistols were just what we needed. They played me all their tunes and I chose the best three that they had, Problems, Pretty Vacant and No Feelings. I thought they were the ones to get a deal with. Which they did, with EMI. And all that stuff about them not being able to play their instruments was rubbish'.[10]

This was the best of the group. Some of what followed would be the worst as McLaren and the group's followers waged war against possible contenders, knocking them aside on their way to the top. At the 100 Club on 12 June, a friend of Lydon's, John Ritchie (aka Sid Vicious), attacked Nick Kent with a bicycle chain, possibly at McLaren's instigation. The band opted not to play Zermatti's

European Punk Rock Festival on 21 August, preferring instead to appear on Granada TV's *So it Goes*. Presented by Tony Wilson on 4 September, they performed *Anarchy in the UK* in brilliantly chaotic fashion, with Jordan boogying away at the side of the stage dressed like a concentration camp guard. It was their TV debut and got them seen by far, far more people than made the trip to Mont-de-Marsan. After this McLaren organised the 100 Club Punk Festival, held 20-21 September. Eddie and the Hot Rods were not involved. The first evening, with The Sex Pistols, The Clash and The Subway Sect (another Rhodes band) passed off without any major incidents. The second, with Chris Spedding, The Vibrators, The Damned and The Buzzcocks (a Manchester outfit formed after its members had seen the Pistols play locally), ended in chaos. Ritchie/Vicious threw a glass at The Damned, a band perceived as rivals, which shattered on a pillar, the flying shards injuring several of the crowd and permanently blinding a teenage girl in one eye. McLaren's comments about this were callous, but also designed to impress and linger in the memory, *'The violence was magnificent; it was something that gave all those kids a terrific identity, made them proud of their future. So, someone got blinded? Well, there are far worse things that happen for far worse causes. One person blinded, a couple people badly hurt – the achievement outweighed it completely.'* [11]

The 100 Club banned (for the moment) all punk acts. But the event made The Sex Pistols, and nobody else, the leaders of that scene and despite/because of the press coverage, EMI signed The Sex Pistols on 8 October 1976, with an advance of £40,000, equivalent to about £350,000 in current (2022) values. In less than a year, McLaren had persuaded the music press, and the UK major record labels, that a small niche movement involving probably less than a couple of thousand people at that point was a major event waiting to happen. It was a triumph, and the moment the dam burst, either sweeping aside many of the conventional bands that dominated the scene, or obliging them to update their images. The music media quickly followed too. *ZigZag* 65 (October 1976) had Hugh Cornwell and Jean-Jacques Burnel of The Stranglers doing the month's album reviews. The following month the magazine provided conflicting views about The Sex Pistols from observers who were incredulous that a band that seemed so limited could be exerting so much influence. Pete Frame commented, 'The Sex Pistols (who drew the magnificent total of 95 people to the Civic Hall in Dunstable this week) have the same kind of attraction as a nasty road accident, and they seem to be aiming at an audience of remarkably low brain power.' John Walters, John Peel's producer, was slightly kinder, 'The Sex Pistols do have some sort of awful charisma.' [12]

The band had selected Anarchy in the UK as their debut single, John Peel playing an advance copy on 19 November, the week prior to its release. It was actually the 6th punk record to reach the shops, coming after two from The Count Bishops, one from The Damned and two featuring The Vibrators. Unlike the others, it charted, entering the UK on 11 December, eventually reaching No 38. With Lydon/Rotten reeling off the names of terrorist organisations, at a time when the political consensus in the UK was fracturing, and McLaren proclaiming the song, 'a call to arms to the kids who believe that rock and roll was taken away from them. It's a statement of self-rule, of ultimate independence' it was clearly the battle standard of a new genre, and one that owed little to the bands that had slogged their way through the pub circuit in search of fame.

Battalions of similar acts began appearing. By the end of 1976, the list included The Boys, The Subway Sect, Chelsea, The Lurkers and Generation X, all of whom emerged from the small London punk scene. Importantly, this wasn't just a London thing. Others arrived from elsewhere: The Suburban Studs from Birmingham, The Buzzcocks and Slaughter and the Dogs from Manchester, Penetration from Durham and The Rezillos from Edinburgh, many as a result of seeing the Pistols live or catching them on TV. All would receive extensive publicity through 1977 as punk rock, with The Sex Pistols as its dominant act, officially became the music industry's latest sound.

Just as important as the sudden predilection for 2-minute songs about frustration and urban blight was the change in look. Long hair, bomber jackets, flared trousers, plaid shirts and all the other accoutrements of the 70s would-be rock star were abruptly discarded. Some wannabes opted for en bloc replacement by whatever clothing McLaren and Westwood were offering. On grounds of cost, this wasn't an option for most and a thrift shop look emerged... old suit jackets, bedecked with a few badges and simple t-shirts predominating. But hair had to be short and trousers had to be straight to the point of stricture.

Thus repackaged, but not necessarily musically different from how they would have sounded in the absence of The Sex Pistols, a whole range of bands took the stage. The Boomtown Rats arrived from Dublin. In Deptford, Dire Straits provided a clear continuum of the classic American guitar-rock pub-rock sound. Both Wire and Dead Fingers Talk would have wended their way through the art school dances anyway. Others featured a number of music business veterans starting afresh and not volunteering details about their past: The Only Ones with guitarist Alan Mair, formerly of The Beatstalkers (once Scotland's Beatles) and drummer Mike Kellie, ex-Spooky Tooth; The Radio Stars, with lead vocalist Andy Ellison, once of John's Children; and The Police, with drummer Stewart Copeland from Curved Air and guitarist Andy Summers whose distinguished CV included spells with Zoot Money's Big Roll Band, Dantalian's Chariot, The Soft Machine and Eric Burdon and the Animals.

Of these, The Boomtown Rats, Dire Straits and The Police were hugely successful. So much so that it's worth considering a counter-factual. Suppose Malcolm McLaren had been hit by a bus crossing the King's Road one day in 1973, or sidelined by a street robbery in New York in 1975? What would have been different?

Well, Vivienne Westwood would still have made her clothes, and would have become a presence on the fashion scene. Dave Edmunds, Dr Feelgood, the Kursaal Flyers, Eddie and the Hot Rods and Graham Parker and the Rumour were already established and would have remained on that trajectory. Selecting others solely by the admittedly narrow standard of commercial success, achieved then or later, Shakin' Stevens, Darts, Elvis Costello, Nick Lowe, Ian Gomm, Gonzalez, Sniff 'n' the Tears, Ian Dury, John Otway and Wild Willy Barrett, Philip Rambow, The Fabulous Poodles, Ultravox, The Tom Robinson Band, Squeeze, The Stranglers, The Damned and The Jam were all sufficiently well known by late 1976 to have gone on and achieved something, perhaps on different record labels, and over a slightly different timescale, but undoubtedly something. As would have been the case with Dire Straits, too.

On the other hand, it seems undeniable that no Malcolm McLaren would have meant no Sex Pistols, and by extension no Lydon and no Public Image Limited either. Would The Clash have happened? Probably not. Strummer would have done more stuff with The 101ers; even if he made a pitch for superstardom, it would have come later. What of the bands that followed? Generation X, The Buzzcocks, The Rezillos and The Boomtown Rats were all marketed as punk in early 1977, as were any number of others. Would this have happened in the absence of The Sex Pistols? It's tempting to think not, and certainly never as quickly. But surely the live shows being done by The Count Bishops, Dr Feelgood and The Damned in 1976-77 would have inspired them anyway, rather than their first encounter with Lydon and co. It's possible, though less likely, that Siouxsie and the Banshees might, in time, have emerged too on that basis.

Advocates of the great man theory of history might well counter at this point that this is just a conceit and none of the above happened. McLaren wasn't hit by a bus in 1973. He lived, and by force of personality and shrewd judgement, engineered a distinct swing in the music and fashion world a few years later, meaning that certain things were different from that point. This is true. But, it's also worth remembering that McLaren made a lot of pseudo-political and cultural noise too. His proclamations about anarchy, freedom, revolution and liberation did not come to pass, except insofar as the Thatcherite agenda, of which he might be considered a willing accomplice, desired. Politically, the UK moved sharply to the right at the end of the 70s. The UK of 2023 is much harder for young people to live in than the UK of 1976, even if they can stream whatever music they wish 24 hours of the day and wear more or less whatever they like. Musicians and creative people generally also have much less money.

As for the musical changes that occurred in 1976-77, surely these were short-lived and largely illusory? By the early 80s, with the UK economy imploding under the weight of a major recession, venues, including much of the pub circuit, were closing and student unions no longer had entertainment budgets. The music industry responded by switching to clean, safe and very commercial acts. The days of being signed to make an album of whatever you liked were gone. Nobody got famous anymore by throwing glasses at gigs, or attacking journalists or smashing up venues. Looking at who sold records post-1976, it was the bands and singers who navigated their way through the pub circuit, most of whom had evolved organically from earlier outfits, who generally did better and lasted longer than the punk acts.[13]

Half a century later, they may be unfashionable, but they produced a lot of good music, and an appreciation of their legacy is long overdue.

Notes

(1)   See *Rolling Stone* 12 April 2010 at https://www.rollingstone.com/music/music-news/new-york-dolls-sylvain-sylvain-remembers-malcolm-mclaren-78305/ David Johansen is also on record as saying that McLaren *'helped us out a lot – without asking for any particular monetary compensation.'*

(2)   Jake Riviera saw this version of The Heartbreakers whilst touring the US with Dr Feelgood and thought them the best rock and roll band he'd ever seen. Hence the move by Stiff to sign Richard Hell in 1976.

(3)   See https://www.dailyrecord.co.uk/entertainment/celebrity/midge-ure-turned-down-offer-1129894

(4)   Quoted in *Defying Gravity: Jordan's Story* Jordan Mooney with Cathi Unsworth (2019) p124.

(5)   No anarchist, up until late 1976 Lydon was still attending mass and confession every week with his mother. See *London Calling: A Counter Cultural History of London Since 1945* Barry Miles p353.

(6)   This can be seen at http://www.philjens.plus.com/pistols/pistols/28Nov75_Malcolm.html

(7)   See https://flashbak.com/sex-pistols-the-first-time-the-media-mentioned-them-1975-47764/

(8)   For a full version of the review see https://paulgormanis.com/?p=17084

(9)   Quoted in *England's Dreaming: The Sex Pistols and Punk Rock* Jon Savage
        (1991) p148. The Sex Pistols performed on a stage put together from
        materials that were used in the shooting of Jarman's film, *Sebastiane*
        (1976) in which Jordan and many members of *Them* had minor acting
        roles. A retrospective exhibition *THEM: Duggie Fields, Derek Jarman,
        Andrew Logan, Luciana Martinez, Kevin Whitney* was held at The
        Redfern Gallery, Cork Street W1 22 January-15 February 2020. The
        catalogue reprints an October 1976 *Harpers & Queen* article, which
        notes, 'A group *who take a dim view of much Themness are the people who
        run the Sex clothing store... The Sex shop people, untypically, have political
        views, of a kind which they describe as anarchic... Their associated pop-group
        The Sex Pistols are alleged to cause trouble wherever they go. The Sex people
        hate retro, and seem perfectly sincere about it...'*

(10)   Quoted at https://www.loudersound.com/features/chris-spedding-
        on-the-rolling-stones-the-sex-pistols-and-the-womble Spedding later
        came in for some criticism for appearing with The Vibrators at the
        100 Club punk festival, to which he responded: '*I wasn't in any way
        jumping on the bandwagon – the bandwagon had rather jumped on me.*'

(11)   Quoted at https://pleasekillme.com/malcolm-mcclaren/?fbclid=
        IwAR05hFuKeOnnGTtTkCSmhAB7SbxhcYg7_faLfAYsfnk
        2d8a3Uh1MVFSPqt0

(12)   Note as well the comments by Tom Robinson in *Pete Frame's Rock
        Family Trees Volume 2* 1983 p16, '*I saw The Pistols at the 100 Club...
        Their attitude was totally different from any band I'd ever seen. At the
        time I really resented it, and left after about 20 minutes... I was disturbed,
        turned off, but simultaneously intrigued*' and https://louderthanwar.
        com/punks-40th-may-11th-1976-sex-pistols-start-residency-100-club/
        where Vic Godard, later of The Subway Sect recollects, '*We were in
        the West End looking for gigs to go to. We walked up Wardour Street and
        we heard a big kerfuffle going. We thought, "What's going on in there?" We
        went in. The Sex Pistols had already done a few numbers, so we saw the tail
        end of it. It looked like they were getting thrown out of the place!*' Initially
        an admirer, he would later modify his views about the band, being
        quoted in Jon Savage's *England's Dreaming: Sex Pistols and Punk Rock*
        1991 p419, '*I thought The Sex Pistols were the end of Rock 'n' Roll... But
        as it turned out, they weren't. Nor were The Clash... we wanted to sound
        like The Velvet Underground or The Seeds, nothing remotely heavy... Our
        guitarist refused to allow any macho, Rock 'n' Roll attitudes on stage*'.

(13)   Looking at the decade from 1977 to 1986, and counting only Top

30 UK entries and Top 100 US entries, the pre-punk (or non-punk) acts outsold the punk acts by a factor of three. Shakin' Stevens, Elvis Costello, Ultravox, The Stranglers, The Jam (and later The Style Council) together with The Boomtown Rats, The Police and Dire Straits were all particularly successful. On the punk side so were The Clash and Siouxsie and the Banshees. The Clash also managed to go big in the US, but were outsold there by Elvis Costello. Much was made of the political agenda of Strummer and co... but Costello had one too, as did Annie Lennox of The Tourists and The Eurythmics who outsold everyone and could hardly be considered a punk act.

DISCOGRAPHY

Single, EP and LP releases by pub-rock and associated acts from *Spirit of Woodstock* to *Anarchy in the UK*

AUGUST 1970
Shakin' Stevens and the Sunsets *Spirit of Woodstock*

OCTOBER 1970
Shakin' Stevens and the Sunsets *A Legend* (LP)
Dave Edmunds *I Hear You Knocking*
Brett Marvin and the Thunderbolts *Thoughts on You*
Brinsley Schwarz *Country Girl*

NOVEMBER 1970
Legend *Life*
Brinsley Schwarz *Despite it All* (LP)

DECEMBER 1970
Legend *Legend* (LP)

JANUARY 1971
The Wild Angels *Red Hot 'n' Rockin'* (LP)

MARCH 1971
Dave Edmunds and Rockpile *I'm Comin' Home*
Legend *Don't You Never*

APRIL 1971
The Wild Angels *Three Nights a Week*

The Famous Music Band *Nine by Nine*
Legend *Moonshine* (LP)
Ernie Graham *Ernie Graham* (LP)
Third World *Miracles*

MAY 1971
Rock and Roll Allstars *Baby Can You Feel It*

JUNE 1971
Brett Marvin and the Thunderbolts *12 Inches of Brett Marvin and the Thunderbolts* (LP)
Colin Scot *Hey Sandy!*

JULY 1971
Shakin' Stevens and the Sunsets *I'm No JD* (LP)
Dave Edmunds *Blue Monday*
Brett Marvin and the Thunderbolts *Little Red Caboose*
Colin Scot *Colin Scot* (LP)

AUGUST 1971
Terry Dactyl and the Dinosaurs *Seaside Shuffle*
Steve Ellis *Have You Seen My Baby*

DECEMBER 1971
Rock and Roll Allstars *Rock and Roll Allstars Play Party Rock* (EP)
The John Dummer Band featuring Nick Pickett *Medicine Weasel*

JANUARY 1972
Rock and Roll Allstars *Red China Rocks* (LP)

FEBRAURY 1972
Brinsley Schwarz *Silver Pistol* (LP)

MARCH 1972
Shakin' Stevens and the Sunsets *Sweet Little Rock and Roller*
Shakin' Stevens and the Sunsets *Rockin' and Shakin'* (LP)

APRIL 1972
The Wild Angels *Jo Jo Ann*
The John Dummer Band featuring Nick Pickett *Blue* (LP)
Max Merritt with The Meteors *Let it Slide*

MAY 1972
Brewers Droop *Sweet Thing* (EP)

JUNE 1972
Dave Edmunds *Rockpile* (LP)
The Houseshakers *Demolition Rock* (LP)
The Flamin' Groovies *Slow Death*

JULY 1972
Dave Edmunds *Down, Down, Down*

SEPTEMBER 1972
The Wild Angels *Out at Last* (LP)
Fumble *Hello Mary Lou*
Uncle Dog *River Road*
Brinsley Schwarz *Nervous on the Road* (LP)

OCTOBER 1972
Brewers Droop *Opening Time* (LP)
Uncle Dog *Old Hat* (LP)
Gerald Thomas Moore *Song of America*

NOVEMBER 1972
The Wild Angels *Beauty School Dropout*
Fumble *Fumble* (LP)
Terry Dactyl and the Dinosaurs *On A Saturday Night*
Chilli Willi and the Red Hot Peppers *Kings of the Robot Rhythm* (LP)

DECEMBER 1972
Dave Edmunds *Baby I Love You*
The Flamin' Groovies *Married Woman*

JANUARY 1973
The Wild Angels *Running Bear*

MARCH 1973
John Dummer Oobleedooblee Band *Oobleedooblee Jubilee*

APRIL 1973
Crazy Cavan and the Rhythm Rockers *Teddy Boy Boogie*
John Dummer Ooobleedooblee Band *Oobleedooblee Jubilee* (LP)
The Hitters *Hypocrite*
John Otway and Wild Willy Barrett *Murder Man*

MAY 1973
Dave Edmunds *Born to be with You*
Fumble *Million Seller*
Terry Dactyl and the Dinosaurs featuring Jona Lewie *She Left I Died*

JUNE 1973
The Wild Angels *Greased Lightning*
Brett Marvin and the Thunderbolts *Ten Legged Friend* (LP)

JULY 1973
Fumble *Alexandra Park*

AUGUST 1973
Crazy Cavan and the Rhythm Rockers *The Original Sound of Crazy Cavan and the Rhythm Rockers* (EP)
Brinsley Schwarz *Speedoo*

SEPTEMBER 1973
The Droop *Louise*

OCTOBER 1973
The Wild Angels *Clap Your Hands and Stamp Your Feet*
Bees Make Honey *Knee Trembler*
Brinsley Schwarz *Please Don't Ever Change* (LP)

NOVEMBER 1973
Bees Make Honey *Music Every Night* (LP)
Ducks Deluxe *Coast to Coast*

JANUARY 1974
Curtis Knight Zeus *The Devil Made Me Do It*
Curtis Knight Zeus *The Second Coming* (LP)

FEBRUARY 1974
Ducks Deluxe *Ducks Deluxe* (LP)

MARCH 1974
Brett Marvin and the Thunderbolts *Thunderbolt Rag*
Brinsley Schwarz *I've Cried My Last Tear*
Brinsley Schwarz *Brinsley Schwarz's Original Golden Greats* (LP)

APRIL 1974
Ducks Deluxe *Fireball*

MAY 1974
Curtis Knight Zeus *People, Places and Feelings*

JUNE 1974
The Hellraisers *Remember When?* (LP)
Brinsley Schwarz *(What's So Funny 'bout) Peace, Love and Understanding?*

JULY 1974
Slack Alice *Motorcycle Dream*
Brinsley Schwarz *The New Favourites Of...* (LP)

AUGUST 1974
Shakin' Stevens and the Sunsets *Honey Honey*
Shakin' Stevens and the Sunsets *Shakin' Stevens and the Sunsets* (LP)
Gonzalez *Pack it Up*

SEPTEMBER 1974
Dave Edmunds *Need a Shot of Rhythm and Blues*

Ace *How Long*
Gonzalez *Gonzalez* (LP)
The Hammersmith Gorillas *You Really Got Me*

OCTOBER 1974
Starry Eyed and Laughing *Money is no Friend of Mine*
Ducks Deluxe *Love's Melody*
GT Moore and the Reggae Guitars *GT Moore and the Reggae Guitars*
(LP)

NOVEMBER 1974
Fumble *Not Fade Away*
Jona Lewie and the Chris Barber Band *Piggy Back Sue*
Dr Feelgood *Roxette*
Starry Eyed and Laughing *Starry Eyed and Laughing* (LP)
Chilli Willi and the Red Hot Peppers *Bongos over Balham* (LP)
Ducks Deluxe *Taxi to the Terminal Zone* (LP)
Clancy *Back on Love*
GT Moore and the Reggae Guitars *I'm Still Waiting*
Kilburn and the High Roads *Rough Kids*

DECEMBER 1974
Fumble *Poetry in Lotion* (LP)
Charlie and the Wide Boys *Gilly I Do* (EP)
Ace *Five A Side* (LP)

JANUARY 1975
Dr Feelgood *Down by the Jetty* (LP)
Brinsley Schwarz *Everybody*
The Limelight *I Should Have Known Better*

FEBRUARY 1975
Dave Edmunds *I Ain't Never*
Fumble *Don't Take Love*
Starry Eyed and Laughing *Nobody Home*
The Knees *Day Tripper*
Chilli Willi and the Red Hot Peppers *Breathe a Little*

Ducks Deluxe *I Fought the Law*
Kilburn and the High Roads *Crippled with Nerves*
The Winkies *The Winkies* (LP)
Poodles *Chicago Box Car (Boston Back)*
Matchbox *Rock and Roll Band*

MARCH 1975
Dr Feelgood *She Does it Right*
The Brinsleys *There's a Cloud in My Heart*
Ace *I Ain't Gonna Stand for This No More*
Kokomo *I'm Sorry Babe*
Tiger Lily *Ain't Misbehavin'*

APRIL 1975
Dave Edmunds *Subtle as a Flying Mallet* (LP)
Blue Goose *Loretta*

MAY 1975
Brett Marvin and the Thunderbolts *Blow Me Down*
Blue Goose *Blue Goose* (LP)
Gonzalez *Hole in My Soul*
Philip Rambow *Dem Eyes*

JUNE 1975
Clancy *Baby Don't You Do It*
Clancy *Seriously Speaking* (LP)
Kokomo *Kokomo* (LP)
Kilburn and the High Roads *Handsome* (LP)

JULY 1975
Dr Feelgood *Back in the Night*
The Kursaal Flyers *Chocs Away* (LP)
The Kursaal Flyers *Speedway*
Tartan Horde *Bay City Rollers We Love You*
Kokomo *I Can Understand It*
Chris Spedding *Motorbikin'*

AUGUST 1975
Max Merritt *A Little Easier*
Starry Eyed and Laughing *Good Love*
GT Moore and the Reggae Guitars *Reggae Reggae*
Tom, Rose and Annie *Glad To Be Gay*

SEPTEMBER 1975
Max Merritt and The Meteors *A Little Easier* (LP)
Starry Eyed and Laughing *Thought Talk* (LP)
GT Moore and the Reggae Guitars *Reggae Blue* (LP)
Roy St John *Immigration Declaration* (LP)
Café Society *The Whitby Two-Step*
Café Society *Café Society* (LP)

OCTOBER 1975
Jona Lewie *The Swan*
Dr Feelgood *Malpractice* (LP)
Max Merritt and The Meteors *Slipping Away*
Archie Legget *Jamaican Jockey*

NOVEMBER 1975
Fumble *One Last Dance*
Brett Marvin and the Thunderbolts *Hawaiian Honeymoon*
The Kursaal Flyers *Hit Records*
Ace *No Future in Your Eyes*
Clancy *Good Judgement*
Kokomo *Anytime*
The Count Bishops *Speedball* (EP)

DECEMBER 1975
Ace *Time For Another* (LP)
Gonzalez *Our Only Weapon Is Our Music* (LP)

JANUARY 1976
Clancy *Everyday* (LP)
Gonzalez *Got My Eye On You*
Kokomo *Use Your Imagination*

Chris Spedding *Jump In My Car*

FEBRUARY 1976
The Kursaal Flyers *The Great Artiste* (LP)
Eddie and the Hot Rods *Writing on the Wall*
Kokomo *Rise and Shine* (LP)

MARCH 1976
Graham Parker and the Rumour *Silly Thing*
Chris Spedding *New Girl In The Neighbourhood*

APRIL 1976
Shakin' Stevens and the Sunsets *Jungle Rock*
The Kursaal Flyers *Cruisin' for Love*
Graham Parker and the Rumour *Howlin Wind* (LP)
Chris Spedding *Chris Spedding* (LP)
Nightbus *Face Down in the Meadow*
The Snakes *Teenage Head*

MAY 1976
Shucks *Two Days – Two Tracks* (LP)
Roy St John *The Way You Look Tonight*
Chris Spedding *Guitar Jamboree*

JUNE 1976
The Flamin' Groovies *Shake Some Action* (LP)
Eddie and the Hot Rods *Wooly Bully*
Charlie and the Wide Boys *Great Country Rockers* (LP)
Clancy *You Have Made My Life So Sweet*
The 101ers *Keys To Your Heart*
Deke O'Brien *Nightbus* (LP)

JULY 1976
Dave Edmunds *Here Comes the Weekend*
The Flamin' Groovies *Don't You Lie to Me* (EP)
Crazy Cavan and the Rhythm Rockers *Knock! Knock!*
Jona Lewie *Hallelujah Europa*

Eddie and the Hot Rods *Live at the Marquee* (EP)
Max Merritt *Out of the Blue* (LP)
Graham Parker and the Rumour *Soul Shoes*
Moon *Lone Ranger*
Moon *Too Close for Comfort* (LP)
The Gorillas *She's My Gal*

AUGUST 1976
Crazy Cavan and the Rhythm Rockers *Rockability* (LP)
Nick Lowe *So It Goes*
The Count Bishops *Train Train*
Nightbus *Sing Harmony*

SEPTEMBER 1976
Fumble *Rock 'n' Roll School*
Dr Feelgood *Stupidity* (LP)
Max Merritt *Whisper in my Ear*
Starry Eyed *Song on the Radio*
Pink Fairies *Between the Lines*
Tyla Gang *Styrofoam*
Roogalator *All Aboard With the Roogalator*
Gonzalez *Brandy You're A Fine Girl*
Cado Belle *Cado Belle* (LP)

OCTOBER 1976
Dave Edmunds *Where or When*
Rocky Sharpe and the Razors *Drip Drop* (EP)
Dr Feelgood *Roxette* (live)
The Kursaal Flyers *Little Does She Know*
Eddie and the Hot Rods *Teenage Depression*
Lew Lewis and his Band *Boogie on the Street*
Graham Parker and the Rumour *Hotel Chambermaid*
Moon *Day Dreamin'*
The Damned *New Rose*
Cado Belle *Got to Love*

NOVEMBER 1976
The Flamin' Groovies *Shake Some Action*
Eddie and the Hot Rods *Teenage Depression* (LP)
Graham Parker and the Rumour *Heat Treatment* (LP)
John Otway and Wild Willy Barrett *Louisa On a Horse*
Chris Spedding and The Vibrators *Pogo Dancing*
The Vibrators *We Vibrate*
Plummet Airlines *Silver Shirt*
Richard Hell *I Could Live With You In Another World* (EP)
The Sex Pistols *Anarchy In The UK*

BIBLIOGRAPHY

Nik Cohn *A Wop Bop A Loo Bop A Lop Bam Boom* (1969)

The Encyclopaedia of Rock Volumes 1-3 (1975-76)

The NME Book of Rock 2 (1976)

Julie Davis *Punk* (1977)

The NME Book of Music (1978)

Julie Burchill and Tony Parsons *The Boy Looked at Johnny: The obituary of rock and roll* (1978)

Pete Frame's Rock Family Trees (1980)

Terry Hounsome *New Rock Record* (1981)

Pete Frame's Rock Family Trees Vol 2 (1983)

Jon Savage *England's Dreaming: Sex Pistols and Punk Rock* (1991)

Brian Hinton *An Illustrated History of the Isle of Wight Festivals* (1992)

Vernon Joynson *The Tapestry of Delights* (1995)

The International Who's Who in Popular Music (2002)

Martin Strong *The Great Rock Discography* (2002)

Nick Kent *The Dark Stuff* (2004)

Graeme Thompson *Complicated Shadows: The Life and Music of Elvis Costello* (2005)

John Robb *Punk Rock: An Oral History* (2006)

Terry Murphy *The Bridge House: Memories of a Legendary Rock and Roll Hangout* (2007)

Barry Miles *London Calling: A Countercultural History of London since 1945* (2010)

Will Birch *Ian Dury: The Definitive Biography* (2010)

Antonino D'Ambrosio *Let Fury Have the Hour: Joe Strummer, Punk, and the Movement that Shook the World* (2012)

Mike Wade *Hole in My Pocket: The True Legend of Mickey Jupp: The Rock and Roll Genius who Refused to be a Star* (2015)

James Birch and Barry Miles *The British Underground Press of the Sixties* (2017)

Martin Gayford *Modernists & Mavericks* (2018)

Will Birch *Cruel to be Kind: The Life and Music of Nick Lowe* (2019)

Jordan with Cathi Unsworth *Defying Gravity: Jordan's Story* (2019)

Richard Morton Jack *Galactic Ramble: The fullest ever study of the 60s and 70s UK music scene* (2020)

David Curtis *London's Arts Labs and the 60s Avant-Garde* (2020)

Various back editions, as noted, of *Disc and Music Echo*, *Melody Maker*, *New Musical Express*, *Record Collector*, *Record Mirror*, *Rolling Stone*, *Sounds* and *ZigZag*.

INDEX

Bloxham, Dave, 228, 239
Blue Goose, 71, 78, 85-6, 88, 91, 149
Blue Maxi, The, 295
Blue Set, The, 70
Blue, Barry, 238
Blues Band, The, 93-4, 200, 225
Blues Healers, The, 218
Bluesville, 23, 124-5, 136, 139
Bluesville, Seven Sisters Road, 257
Blunder, BB, 197-8, 211, 236
Bobby Patrick Big Six, 257, 270
Bobin, John, 103
Bodnar, Andrew, 145, 187, 207,
    230-1
Bolan, Mark, 103-4
Bomp! Records, 61, 285
Bond, Graham, 25, 47, 57, 65, 76,
    94, 205
Bonnett, Steve, 230, 240
Bontemps Roulez, 187, 207, 230,
    240
Bonzo Dog Doo-Dah Band, 20, 250
Boomtown Rats, The, 126, 312-3,
    316
Booth, James, 57
Bopper, Big, 46
Boult, Robyn, 255
Bourne Hall, 26
Bovell, Dennis, 287
Bowie, David, 19, 35, 40, 44, 50, 56,
    94, 103, 113, 121, 140, 172, 262,
    279
Boyle, Peter, 130
Boyles, Dennis, 132
Boys, Jerry, 226
Boys, The, 87, 92, 189, 311
Bragg, Billy, 261
Bragg, Melvyn, 113-4
Brainbox, 59
Bramall, Peter, 204
Branson, Richard, 222
Braunagel, Tony, 229, 246
Brecknock, Camden, 14, 25, 89,
    238, 267, 280, 294
Brel, Jacques, 226
Brendell, Steve, 216
Brett Marvin and the Thunderbolts,
    76, 80, 91

Brewers Droop, 17, 25, 28, 58, 80-1,
    83, 87
Bridge House, The, Canning Town,
    26, 29-30, 89, 92, 120, 267
Bright, Bette, 67
Brilleaux, Lee, 93, 105-6, 107, 110-1,
    115, 300
Brinsley Schwarz, 33, 36, 38, 42-3,
    58, 61, 71, 76, 83, 94, 101, 107,
    109, 114, 120, 134, 138, 149, 153,
    156, 161-6, 168-75, 177-9, 181-3,
    185-6, 189, 192, 197, 201, 203,
    205-7, 212-6, 221, 231, 237, 240,
    252, 259, 276, 291, 294, 301, 303
Britton, Geoff, 52
Bromley Technical College, 280
Bronski Beat, 261
Brood, Herman, 88
Brooker, Gary, 97, 101, 105
Brookes, Steven, 295
Brooks, Elkie, 101
Broonzy, Big Bill, 95
Brown, Arthur, 144, 172, 270, 288
Brown, James, 70, 160
Brown, Joe, 54
Brown, Nick, 146-7
Brown, Noel, 207, 230
Brown, Pete (and his Battered
    Ornaments), 247, 249-50, 299
Brown, Roger, 75
Bruce, Jack, 57
Brunning, Bob, 93, 225, 243
Buck, Peter, 9, 119
Buckle, Rod, 76-7
Buckler, Rick, 295-6
Bull and Gate, The, Kentish Town,
    128, 248
Bull, Richie, 111, 151
Bunch, The, 149, 156
Bundrick, John, 227, 229
Bunjies Folk Cellar, 266
Bunton, Ted, 229
Burchill, Julie, 36-7, 153
Burke, Kevin, 9, 33
Burke, Pat, 215
Burke, Solomon, 110, 242
Burlesque, 114, 254, 262-3, 276,
    280-2

●LDCASTLE BOOKS

POSSIBLY THE UK'S SMALLEST
INDEPENDENT PUBLISHING GROUP

Oldcastle Books is an independent publishing company formed in 1985 dedicated to providing an eclectic range of titles with a nod to the popular culture of the day.

Imprints vary from the award winning crime fiction list, NO EXIT PRESS (now part of Bedford Square Publishers), to lists about the film industry, KAMERA BOOKS & CREATIVE ESSENTIALS. We have dabbled in the classics, with PULP! THE CLASSICS, taken a punt on gambling books with HIGH STAKES, provided in-depth overviews with POCKET ESSENTIALS and covered a wide range in the eponymous OLDCASTLE BOOKS list. Most recently we have welcomed two new sister imprints with THE CRIME & MYSTERY CLUB and VERVE, home to great, original, page-turning fiction.

oldcastlebooks.com

   kamera BOOKS creative ESSENTIALS | Pulp! THE CLASSICS | HIGH STAKES |

| OLDCASTLE BOOKS | KAMERA BOOKS | HIGHSTAKES PUBLISHING
| POCKET ESSENTIALS | CREATIVE ESSENTIALS | THE CRIME & MYSTERY CLUB
| NO EXIT PRESS | PULP! THE CLASSICS | VERVE BOOKS